# Measuring Poverty and Wellbeing in Developing Countries

United Nations University World Institute for Development Economics Research (UNU-WIDER) was established by the United Nations University as its first research and training centre and started work in Helsinki, Finland, in 1985. The mandate of the institute is to undertake applied research and policy analysis on structural changes affecting developing and transitional economies, to provide a forum for the advocacy of policies leading to robust, equitable, and environmentally sustainable growth, and to promote capacity strengthening and training in the field of economic and social policy-making. Its work is carried out by staff researchers and visiting scholars in Helsinki and via networks of collaborating scholars and institutions around the world.

*United Nations University World Institute for Development*
*Economics Research (UNU-WIDER)*
*Katajanokanlaituri 6B, 00160 Helsinki, Finland*
*www.wider.unu.edu*

'This book makes accessible the recent advances in consumption and multidimensional poverty measurement. The combination of literature review, computer code, and worked examples fill a major gap, making it possible for researchers in developing countries to estimate and analyse these metrics.'

*John F. Hoddinott, H.E. Babcock Professor of Food and*
*Nutrition Economics and Policy, Cornell University*

'This excellent volume combines theoretical discussion of the utility-consistent cost of basic needs poverty approach and first-order dominance multidimensional poverty analysis, empirical application, and practical tools in the form of user guides for estimation software . . . essential reading for applied poverty researchers.'

*Paul Shaffer, Department of International*
*Development Studies, Trent University*

# Measuring Poverty and Wellbeing in Developing Countries

*Edited by*
Channing Arndt and Finn Tarp

A study prepared by the United Nations University World Institute
for Development Economics Research (UNU-WIDER)

OXFORD
UNIVERSITY PRESS

# OXFORD
UNIVERSITY PRESS

Great Clarendon Street, Oxford, OX2 6DP,
United Kingdom

Oxford University Press is a department of the University of Oxford.
It furthers the University's objective of excellence in research, scholarship,
and education by publishing worldwide. Oxford is a registered trade mark of
Oxford University Press in the UK and in certain other countries



Published in the United States of America by Oxford University Press
198 Madison Avenue, New York, NY 10016, United States of America

British Library Cataloguing in Publication Data

Data available

Library of Congress Control Number: 2016939850

ISBN 978–0–19–874480–1 (hbk.)
        978–0–19–874481–8 (pbk.)

Printed in Great Britain by
Clays Ltd, St Ives plc

# Foreword

Despite decades of research and advances in data and methodologies, measuring poverty and reconciling this with patterns of economic growth is a complex issue. This contentiousness, and the fact that poverty remains widespread and persistent in sub-Saharan Africa (SSA) and in other parts of the globe, charged UNU-WIDER to launch in 2011 a major research project—Reconciling Africa's Growth, Poverty, and Inequality Trends: Growth and Poverty Project (GAPP)—to re-examine growth, poverty, and inequality trends in SSA and in other developing regions.

Another key motivation for the GAPP project was that poverty analysis in developing countries remains, to a surprisingly high degree, an activity undertaken by technical assistance personnel and consultants based in developed countries. This book was designed to enhance the transparency, replicability, and comparability of existing practice; and in so doing, it also aims to significantly lower the barriers to entry to the conduct of rigorous poverty measurement and increase the participation of analysts from developing countries in their own poverty assessment.

The book focuses on the measurement of absolute consumption poverty as well as a specific approach to multidimensional analysis of binary poverty indicators. The intent is not to give the impression that these two domains alone are sufficient for rigorous poverty assessment. On the contrary, the editors highlight that this book is designed to serve as a companion to the recently published volume entitled *Growth and Poverty in Sub-Saharan Africa* (Arndt, McKay, and Tarp 2016). That volume emphasizes repeatedly the desirability of the application of multiple approaches across multiple datasets combined with a concerted effort to triangulate results in order to develop a reasonably complete and coherent picture of living standards and their evolution as one moves across space or through time.

I hereby sincerely express my appreciation and admiration of the academic and analytical skills of the entire project team that made this volume possible and the detailed methodological expertise and knowledge of the case countries brought out so clearly. It is my hope that the tools developed in this volume will be adopted by scholars and analysts in Africa, other developing regions, and beyond, in taking charge of the poverty analyses of developments in their respective countries.

The research project—Reconciling Africa's Growth, Poverty, and Inequality Trends—was generously supported by the governments of Denmark, Finland, Sweden, and the United Kingdom, with a special project contribution additionally provided by the Finnish government. UNU-WIDER gratefully acknowledges this vital research funding.

*Finn Tarp*
*Helsinki, October 2016*

# Acknowledgements

UNU-WIDER's Growth and Poverty Project (GAPP) brought together a highly qualified team of more than forty researchers from Africa and beyond. Without their dedication and professional competence, this book and its less technical sibling would not have been possible. We wish to express our sincere appreciation of all of the high-level academic input, together with the copious goodwill and patience—which were much needed when doing the original groundwork followed by numerous revisions and updates of the individual chapters.

A series of intensive planning meetings, involving many of the authors, helped shape the project, with the results presented at several UNU-WIDER development conferences and on many other occasions across African countries. We are grateful to all of those who offered critique and most helpful comments. They include Oxford University Press's economics commissioning editor, Adam Swallow, and his team as well as three anonymous referees. Their efforts were essential in helping to sharpen our research questions and approaches to analysing one of the most intricate challenges facing the development profession, the growth renaissance in developing countries and its impact on poverty reduction.

UNU-WIDER and its dedicated staff provided steady support, including research assistance, which goes far beyond the normal call of duty. Particular thanks go to Dominik Etienne for excellent programming; Anne Ruohonen for consistent project assistance; Lorraine Telfer-Taivainen for all of the careful editorial and publication support on finalizing the book manuscript, including the many contacts with Oxford University Press; and the group of copy editors for helping to put out the numerous UNU-WIDER working papers produced during the course of the project.

*Channing Arndt and Finn Tarp*
*Helsinki, October 2016*

# Contents

## Part III. Summing-Up and Lessons Learnt

# List of Figures

# List of Tables

# List of Boxes

# List of Abbreviations

| | |
|---|---|
| CBN | cost of basic needs |
| CDF | cumulative distribution function |
| CSA | Central Statistics Agency (Ethiopia) |
| CSO | Central Statistical Office (Zambia) |
| DHS | Demographic and Health Survey |
| EA | enumeration area |
| EFOD | executing first-order dominance |
| EPM | Enquête Périodique auprès des Ménages (Madagascar) |
| FCT | Federal Capital Territory (Nigeria) |
| FEI | food energy intake |
| FGT | Foster, Greer, and Thorbecke |
| FISP | Farm Input Subsidy Programme (Malawi) |
| FISP | Farmer Input Support Programme (Zambia) |
| FOD | first-order dominance |
| FRA | Food Reserve Agency (Zambia) |
| GAMS | General Algebraic Modelling System |
| GAPP | Growth and Poverty Project |
| GDHS | Ghana Demography Health Survey |
| GLSS | Ghana Living Standards Survey |
| GSS | Ghana Statistical Service |
| HICES | Household Income, Consumption and Expenditure Survey (Ethiopia) |
| HIES | Household Integrated Economic Survey, formerly Household Income and Expenditure Survey (Pakistan) |
| IFPRI | International Food Policy Research Institute |
| IHS | Integrated Household Survey (Malawi) |
| INSTAT | Institut National de la Statistique (Madagascar) |
| LCMS | Living Conditions Monitoring Survey (Zambia) |
| LSMS | Living Standards Measurement Survey |

| | |
|---|---|
| MDG | Millennium Development Goal |
| MICS | Multiple Indicator Cluster Survey |
| MODA | Multiple Overlapping Deprivation Analysis |
| MPI | Multidimensional Poverty Index |
| NBS | National Bureau of Statistics (Nigeria) |
| ND | net dominance |
| PBS | Pakistan Bureau of Statistics |
| PIHS | Pakistan Integrated Household Survey |
| PLEASe | Poverty Line Estimation Analytical Software |
| PRSP | Poverty Reduction Strategy Paper |
| RDA | required daily allowance (calories) |
| TDHS | Tanzania Demographic and Health Survey |
| TPI | temporal price indices |
| UBOS | Uganda Bureau of Statistics |
| UCA | Uganda Census of Agriculture |
| UNHS | Uganda National Household Survey |
| UNPS | Uganda National Panel Survey |
| WHO | World Health Organization |

# Notes on Contributors

**Olu Ajakaiye**, a Research Professor of Economics at the Nigerian Institute of Social and Economic Research, is currently Executive Chairman of the African Centre for Shared Development Capacity Building, Ibadan, Nigeria. Previously, he was Director-General of NISER and Director of Research at the African Economic Research Consortium, Nairobi, Kenya. He has a PhD in economics from Boston University.

**Olufunke A. Alaba** is a researcher and lecturer at the Health Economics Division, University of Cape Town, South Africa. She holds a PhD in economics, and her major research focuses on applied microeconomics related to poverty, inequality, and health.

**Samuel Kobina Annim** is an Associate Professor at the Department of Economics, University of Cape Coast, Ghana. His areas of research concentration are microfinance/access to finance, poverty and inequality, and health outcomes. His publications can be found in academic journals such as *World Development, Journal of Development Studies*, and *Journal of International Development*. In addition, he consults for development partners and governments, both in Africa and South East Asia.

**Channing Arndt** is a Senior Research Fellow at the United Nations University World Institute for Development Economics Research—UNU-WIDER. He has substantial research management experience including leadership of interdisciplinary teams. His programme of research has focused on poverty alleviation and growth, agricultural development, market integration, gender and discrimination, the implications of the HIV/AIDS pandemic, technological change, trade policy, aid effectiveness, infrastructure investment, energy and biofuels, climate variability, and the economic implications of climate change.

**Ulrik Beck** is a PhD student of economics at the University of Copenhagen, Denmark. He holds BA and MA degrees in economics from the University of Copenhagen and has been a visiting graduate student at Cornell University and UC-Berkeley. His research interests are development economics using applied microeconomics with a focus on agricultural issues and poverty measurement.

**M. Azhar Hussain** is currently an Associate Professor of Economics at the Department of Social Sciences and Business, Roskilde University, Denmark. His research and contributions to the literature have focused on statistical analysis of societal welfare measurement issues in both developed and developing countries.

**Afeikhena T. Jerome** is currently engaged by the Food and Agriculture Organization of the United Nations at the Sub-Regional Office of Eastern Africa, Addis Ababa, Ethiopia. He is also a Visiting Professor at Igbinedion University, Okada, Nigeria.

As an accomplished development expert and practitioner, he has published widely on African development issues.

**Sam Jones** is an Associate Professor of Development Economics at the University of Copenhagen. He has published widely on issues such as foreign aid, economic growth, contract farming, education quality, and tourism. A primary focus of his research is on sub-Saharan Africa. He worked for over seven years as an advisor to the Mozambican government in the Ministry of Planning and Finance and the Ministry of Planning and Development.

**Raymond Elikplim Kofinti** is a graduate student at the Department of Economics, University of Cape Coast, Ghana. His research interests are in household welfare, economics of education, and microeconometric analysis of economic phenomena.

**Vincent Leyaro** is a Senior Lecturer in the Department of Economics, University of Dar es Salaam, Tanzania. He was previously Associate Economics Affairs Officer at the United Nations Economic Commission for Africa (UNECA) in Addis Abba, Ethiopia. He completed a PhD in economics at the University of Nottingham, UK, in 2010. Leyaro has specialist research interests in trade, trade policy reforms, and regional integration; economic development and poverty analysis; labour markets analysis; household analysis and migration issues; and political economy, with a focus on governance issues and implications for natural resources.

**Kristi Mahrt** is a consultant for the United Nations University World Institute for Development Economics Research (UNU-WIDER). Her research focuses on multidimensional and consumption poverty estimation.

**Gibson Masumbu** is a Research Fellow at the Zambia Institute for Policy Analysis and Research, where he heads the Human Development Unit. He holds an MA in economic policy management from the University of Zambia. His research interests lie in the area of human development—particularly poverty analysis, employment and unemployment, rural development, and rural finance. His recent research work has been on topics such as youth labour-demand constraints, multidimensional poverty analysis, first-order dominance analysis of welfare, self-employment, energy poverty, and employment projection models.

**Richard Mussa** is a Senior Lecturer in economics at Chancellor College, University of Malawi. He holds a PhD in economics from the University of Cape Town. He has undertaken research on the Malawian economy with a particular focus on poverty and inequality, nutrition, technical efficiency of agricultural production, non-linear pricing in food markets, equity of healthcare finance, and youth unemployment and child labour.

**Malokele Nanivazo** is a Visiting Scholar at the University of Kansas in the Department of Economics and consults for the United Nations Economic Commission for Africa. Prior to joining the University of Kansas, she worked as a Research Fellow at UNU-WIDER in Helsinki. Her research focuses on gender, poverty, conflicts, growth, rural transformation, trade, and foreign aid.

**Fiona Nattembo**, a Uganda national, has a Bachelor's degree in statistics and Master's degree in population and reproductive health, both from Makerere University, Uganda.

She has worked at the Uganda Bureau of Statistics and is currently a research assistant at the International Food Policy Research Institute in the Kampala office. Her research interests are migration, poverty, and wellbeing.

**Hina Nazli** is a Research Fellow at the International Food Policy Research Institute's Pakistan Strategy Support Program. Her research focuses on poverty estimation, food and nutrition security, technology adoption in agriculture, and gender analysis. She has vast experience in conducting, managing, and analysing large-scale household surveys. She has presented her research at national and international conferences and has published widely in refereed journals.

**Olanrewaju Olaniyan** is a Senior Lecturer in the Department of Economics, University of Ibadan, Nigeria. He has experience in social policy work in developing countries. His areas of research focus on health economics, economics of education, welfare analysis, and social protection. He holds a PhD in economics from University of Ibadan.

**Lars Peter Østerdal** is a Professor in the Department of Economics, Copenhagen Business School. His research is in health economics, fair allocation, game theory, and analysis of welfare, inequality, and poverty.

**Karl Pauw** is a Research Fellow and Country Program Leader of the Malawi Strategy Support Program of the International Food Policy Research Institute (IFPRI) in Lilongwe, Malawi. He holds a PhD from the University of Cape Town in South Africa. His broad area of interest is development and agricultural policy impact analysis, with a specific focus on better understanding the micro–macro interactions between policies and outcomes using economy-wide and micro-simulation modelling techniques.

**Faly Rakotomanana** is Director of the Household Survey Unit at the National Statistical Institute (INSTAT) of Madagascar. His primary research interests are related to poverty and labour markets.

**Tiaray Razafimanantena** is a Lead Economist at the Centre de Recherches, d'Etudes et d'Appui l'Analyse Economique Madagascar (CREAM), and a lecturer at the University of Antananarivo. He was previously Director of the Household Survey Unit at the National Statistical Institute (INSTAT) of Madagascar. His primary research interests are related to poverty, labour markets, and inflation.

**Vincenzo Salvucci** is a UNU-WIDER Research Fellow (since March 2016), currently working as resident adviser at the Directorate of Economic and Financial Studies (DEEF) of the Ministry of Economics and Finance in Maputo, Mozambique. His research interests focus on poverty analysis in developing countries. He has explored issues related to poverty, inequality, and child malnutrition, mainly using micro data for Mozambique.

**Haruna Sekabira** has a Master's degree in agricultural and applied economics from Makerere University in Uganda, and is currently a research assistant and PhD student at the University Goettingen. A Ugandan national, his main research is on smallholder participation in modern supply chains and impacts on income, poverty, and development.

**Nikolaj Siersbæk** is a PhD student in the Department of Business and Economics and the Centre of Health Economics Research (COHERE), University of Southern Denmark.

His research is in applied econometrics, welfare analyses, health economics, and housing economics.

**Kenneth Simler** is currently Senior Economist at the World Bank and based in Kuala Lumpur, Malaysia. He received his PhD degree from Cornell University. He has published widely in the analysis of poverty and wellbeing in developing countries.

**David Stifel** is a Professor of Economics at Lafayette College and Chair of the Lafayette International Affairs Program. His primary research interests are poverty measurement and analysis, rural infrastructure and markets, and agriculture and rural livelihoods.

**Finn Tarp** is Director of UNU-WIDER and Coordinator of the Development Economics Research Group (DERG) at the University of Copenhagen. He is a leading international expert on issues of development strategy and foreign aid, with a sustained interest in poverty, income distribution, and growth. He has published widely in international academic journals alongside various books. He is a member of the World Bank Chief Economist's Council of Eminent Persons and is a resource person of the African Economic Research Consortium (AERC).

**Bjorn Van Campenhout**, a Belgian national, is a Research Fellow at the International Food Policy Research Institute based in Kampala, Uganda. He holds a PhD in economics from the University of Leuven, Belgium. Bjorn's main areas of interest are smallholder market participation, commodity market integration, and poverty dynamics.

**Edward Whitney** is a former research analyst at IFPRI and a current PhD student in the Agriculture and Resource Economics programme at the University of California, Davis. He received his Master of Arts in International Development from the American University in 2012. His previous work includes extensive analysis of poverty in Pakistan, a targeting evaluation of a programme in Malawi, and a replication of a previous impact evaluation study.

**Tassew Woldehanna** is an Associate Professor of Economics at Addis Ababa University. He is a development economist whose primary research interests are food security, employment, child welfare and poverty, education, and health.

Part I
# Principles and Choices

# 1

# Measuring Poverty and Wellbeing in Developing Countries

## Motivation and Overview

*Channing Arndt and Finn Tarp*

## 1.1 Introduction

Detailed analyses of poverty and wellbeing in developing countries, based on large-scale, nationally representative household surveys, have been ongoing for more than three decades. The large majority of developing countries now conduct on a regular basis a variety of household surveys—income, consumption, health, demographics, labour force, household enterprise, and others. And the information base in developing countries with respect to poverty and wellbeing has improved dramatically. Nevertheless, appropriate measurement of poverty remains complex and controversial (Ravallion 2016). This is particularly true in developing countries where (i) the stakes with respect to poverty reduction are high; (ii) the determinants of living standards are often volatile; and (iii) related information bases, while much improved, are often characterized by significant non-sample error.

It also remains, to a surprisingly high degree, an activity undertaken by technical assistance personnel and consultants based in developed countries. This book seeks to enhance the transparency, replicability, and comparability of existing practice. In so doing, it also aims to significantly lower the barriers to entry to the conduct of rigorous poverty measurement and increase the participation of analysts from developing countries in their own poverty assessment.

The book focuses on two domains: the measurement of absolute consumption poverty and a specific approach to multidimensional analysis of binary poverty indicators. In choosing these two areas of focus, the intent is not to give the impression that these two domains alone are sufficient for rigorous poverty assessment. On the contrary, we highlight that this book is designed to serve as a companion to the recently published volume entitled *Growth and Poverty in Sub-Saharan Africa* (Arndt, McKay, and Tarp 2016). That volume emphasizes repeatedly the desirability of the application of multiple approaches across multiple datasets, combined with a concerted effort to triangulate results, in order to develop a reasonably complete and coherent picture of living standards and their evolution as one moves across space or through time.

## 1.2 Facilitating Rigorous Measurement

While a comprehensive assessment of living conditions requires a multi-pronged approach, solid work within each prong encounters a multiplicity of challenges and choices. This is particularly true with respect to estimating absolute poverty lines for the measurement of consumption poverty. The mechanics of estimating multidimensional measures are often somewhat more straightforward. However, the first-order dominance (FOD) approach in focus here is not immediately straightforward to code and requires a considerable amount of data management. In both cases, there is substantial advantage to beginning the analytical process with a series of computer codes that reliably accomplish specific tasks within the overall analytical process.

The editors, in collaboration with many others, have for the last fifteen years gradually developed a unique toolkit (i.e. an analytical code stream referred to as Poverty Line Estimation Analytical Software–PLEASe) for consumption poverty analysis in developing countries based on our experience as advisors, researchers, teachers, and practitioners in a wide variety of contexts (see, for example, Arndt et al. 2016). More recently, we have developed analogous software for estimating multidimensional poverty measures based on FOD. The associated code stream is labelled EFOD.

The existence of these software packages served as an important motivation for the Growth and African Poverty Project (GAPP) initiated in 2011 by UNU-WIDER. GAPP has already resulted in the companion volume mentioned above (Arndt et al. 2016), which sought to analyse trends in poverty and wellbeing in as many as possible of the twenty-four largest countries in sub-Saharan Africa (SSA). These studies were conducted by leading international researchers with expert knowledge of the countries in question, working alongside leading local researchers. The analytical teams returned to the primary datasets used for poverty analysis in each country, with an insistence on applying best techniques to at least two comparable surveys over the period studied. GAPP completed studies in sixteen of the twenty-four most populous countries in Africa and nine of the top ten.

With respect to consumption poverty measurement, GAPP successfully applied the PLEASe code stream, appropriately modified for country circumstances, to Ethiopia, Madagascar, Malawi, Mozambique, and Uganda. More recently, PLEASe has been successfully applied to Pakistan. With respect to multidimensional poverty measurement, the FOD approach was applied to the Democratic Republic of the Congo (DRC), Mozambique, Nigeria, Tanzania, and Zambia (all using versions of EFOD). While the companion volume sought to illuminate the story of growth and poverty in SSA since about 1995, the present book enters more into the nitty gritty of how specific estimations were performed. The eleven countries featured in this volume provide a diverse set of examples of the challenges and issues confronted in practical poverty assessment, including both differences in data availability and quality as well as variance in country circumstances.

As noted, a salient observation from GAPP is the extraordinarily high level of dependence of many developing countries on external assistance for the conduct of poverty analysis, particularly the analysis of consumption poverty. Nearly all of the countries included in the GAPP project have relied on substantial technical assistance for extended periods in order to produce official consumption poverty rates. Even in the cases where local analysts are strongly engaged, capacity building leaves much to be desired. Two critical factors appear to be at work: (i) the occasional nature of detailed household consumption surveys; and (ii) the complexity of the analysis. This challenging combination generates a situation whereby, once data from a new survey is available for analysis, the personnel who had worked on the previous survey have often either moved on to new areas of activity or have substantial needs for retraining in order to effectively conduct the analysis.

This book seeks to step into this breach for the analysis of consumption poverty and for multidimensional analysis using the FOD approach. Part I of this volume briefly reviews the conceptual issues involved in estimating absolute poverty lines and determining multidimensional first-order dominance. These conceptual issues are then supplemented by a series of practical country applications in Part II, where emphasis is given to the particular challenges and specificities of each case. The country applications illustrate the imperative of adjusting approaches to reflect country-specific circumstances in order for the analysis to be meaningful. It is our hope that such a scaffolding of the issues and practicalities should enable significant numbers of analysts in developing countries to engage in this type of analysis and more rapidly assimilate the concepts and approaches involved.

With respect to estimation of absolute poverty, the case studies illustrate that, in practical terms, there often exists vast swathes of agreement across competing methodologies (see also Arndt et al. 2015). For example, within PLEASe, it is relatively straightforward to implement a large array of approaches to absolute poverty line estimation including (but not limited to):

(i) a single national consumption basket with national average prices;

(ii) a single national basket priced at regional levels;

(iii) rural, urban, or more refined regional baskets with associated price differences;

(iv) different approaches to defining the consumption bundles, such as the iterative procedure by Ravallion and Bidani (1994), or simpler alternatives;

(v) fixed or flexible bundles through time; and

(vi) in the case of multiple flexible bundles, imposition (or not) of the utility consistency requirement of Arndt and Simler (2010).

Turning to multidimensional, often non-monetary, indicators, these are now broadly recognized as important (e.g. Alkire et al. 2015; Alkire and Foster 2011; Foster et al. 2013). Non-monetary measures frequently have the advantage of directly relating to policy agendas and are readily available from censuses and household surveys (e.g. is a child attending school, or does a health post exist within 30 minutes travel time from the household?) (Sonne-Schmidt, Østerdal, and Tarp 2008, 2015). While consensus has emerged on the need to consider the multidimensionality of poverty, methods for incorporating multiple indicators into welfare analysis remain contentious with debate centred on the implications of imposing strong assumptions in terms of weighting schemes, the actual extent of new information provided by generating combined indicators, and the nature of welfare functions.

This book furthers this discussion in its use of the FOD approach. This straightforward method allows multidimensional welfare comparisons across populations over time and space while requiring no more restrictive assumptions than a preference to be non-deprived as opposed to deprived in any dimension. Data requirements—which come in the form of binary indicators—are normally less demanding than detailed consumption surveys. Thus, even while addressing multidimensional poverty, the method is frequently less data-intensive in implementation (as demonstrated in the country applications).

Via this book volume, readers have access to the PLEASe and EFOD code streams. We seek to provide these code streams in a manner that is clearly documented, modularized, and transparent. In providing and documenting standard sets of computer codes that can be used as an initial basis for poverty analysis, we take motivation from deep involvement in the initial design and dissemination of the standard computable general equilibrium model made available by the International Food Policy Research Institute (Löfgren et al. 2002); the standard global general equilibrium model developed by the Global Trade Analysis Project (GTAP) at Purdue University (Hertel 1997); as well as contributions to the analysis of stabilization and structural adjustment in Africa (Tarp 1993) relying on a coded merger of widely used models for macroeconomic analysis (Brixen and Tarp 1996a, 1996b).

These standard sets of computer codes are of fairly obvious value to students and analysts seeking to gain skills in economy-wide modelling. They have also proven to be a boon to expert modellers as the standard code sets permit initiation of activities from a *known*, flexible, and advanced baseline. While any tool can be misused, there are large numbers of examples of imaginative analyses, adapted to specific country circumstances, which were greatly facilitated by the existence of a known and flexible base. We have over the years contributed to this academic literature (e.g. Arndt et al. 2012; Tarp et al. 2002), and believe it is critically important that it is widely disseminated and understood in applied work.

Demand for such products has been notably high. For example, the book volume on the GTAP model, which is the reference to the underlying code, records more than 3,000 citations on Google Scholar. The corresponding publication for IFPRI, a technical paper, was the number one download, by a considerable margin, from the IFPRI website for years; and the Brixen and Tarp volumes have been standard references in both teaching and analysis in Africa and beyond. We hope that the PLEASe and EFOD codes can prove similarly valuable to the community engaged in consumption poverty analysis and in multidimensional measures.


## 1.3 Structure of the Volume

The remainder of Part I of this volume is dedicated to presenting the theory underlying the PLEASe and EFOD code streams. Chapter 4 provides an overview of the practical application of these code streams.

In Part II, a chapter is allocated to each country application; and they present the data issues encountered, the chosen solution to resolving those issues, the modifications to the code stream necessary to accommodate local conditions, and the implications of alternative decisions for the spatial and temporal distribution of measured welfare/poverty. The overall objectives of the applications are to highlight the formidable advantages to beginning from a standardized and known code stream that has been well documented and modularized and to provide concrete examples of the issues encountered in practical poverty estimation and the steps taken to address those issues.

We stress that the intent of making code streams available and understood is not to channel poverty analysis into any one particular approach. Rather, the intent is to lower the barriers to entry to conducting detailed, thoughtful, and locally appropriate poverty analyses by providing analysts with functional tools with a known and reliable starting point.

Part III sums up and highlights lessons learned. Part III also contains an additional chapter addressing estimation of inequality. Because poverty lines are employed to compute real consumption across the full income distribution, alternative poverty line estimates imply differences in measured inequality. This chapter explores these differences, building on the country cases. The last chapter concludes and looks forward.

Finally, two appendices provide documentation of the PLEASe and EFOD code streams. These are intended to be living documents available for download alongside the associated code.

# References


Alkire, S. and J. Foster (2011). 'Counting and Multidimensional Poverty Measurement', *Journal of Public Economics*, 99(7): 476–87.

Alkire, S., J. Foster, S. Seth, M. E. Santos, J. M. Roche, and P. Ballon (2015). *Multidimensional Poverty Measurement and Analysis*. Oxford: Oxford University Press.

Arndt, C., R. Distante, M. A. Hussain, L. P. Østerdal, Pham L. Huong, and M. Ibraimo (2012). 'Ordinal Welfare Comparisons with Multiple Discrete Indicators: A First-Order Dominance Approach and Application to Child Poverty', *World Development*, 40(11): 2290–301.

Arndt, C., A. M. Hussain, V. Salvucci, F. Tarp, and L. P. Østerdal (2015). 'Poverty Mapping Based on First-Order Dominance with an Example from Mozambique', *Journal of International Development*, 28(1): 3–21.

Arndt, C., A. McKay, and F. Tarp (eds) (2016). *Growth and Poverty in Sub-Saharan Africa*. Oxford: Oxford University Press.

Arndt, C. and K. Simler (2010). 'Estimating Utility Consistent Poverty Lines', *Economic Development and Cultural Change*, 58: 449–74.

Brixen, P. and F. Tarp (1996a). *The South African Economy: Macroeconomic Prospects for the Medium Term*. London and New York: Routledge.

Brixen, P. and F. Tarp (1996b). 'South Africa: Macroeconomic Perspectives for the Medium Term', *World Development*, 24(6): 989–1001.

Foster, J., S. Seth, M. Lokshin, and Z. Sajaia (2013). *A Unified Approach to Measuring Poverty and Inequality: Theory and Practice*. Washington, DC: World Bank.

Hertel, T. W. (1997). *Global Trade Analysis*. Cambridge: Cambridge University Press.

Löfgren, H., R. L. Harris, and S. Robinson (2002). *A Standard Computable General Equilibrium (CGE) Model in GAMS*. Washington, DC: International Food Policy Research Institute.

Ravallion, M. (2016). *The Economics of Poverty: History, Measurement, and Policy*. Oxford: Oxford University Press.

Ravallion, M. and B. Bidani (1994). 'How Robust Is a Poverty Profile?', *World Bank Economic Review*, 8: 75–102.

Sonne-Schmidt, C., L. P. Østerdal, and F. Tarp (2008). 'Ordinal Comparison of Multidimensional Deprivation: Theory and Application', Discussion Paper 08-33, Department of Economics, University of Copenhagen.

Sonne-Schmidt, C., L. P. Østerdal, and F. Tarp (2015). 'Ordinal Bivariate Inequality: Concepts and Application to Child Deprivation in Mozambique', *Review of Income and Wealth*. Available online: DOI: 10.1111/roiw.12183.

Tarp, F. (1993). *Stabilization and Structural Adjustment: Macroeconomic Frameworks for Analysing the Crisis in Sub-Saharan Africa*. London and New York: Routledge.

Tarp, F., K. Simler, C. Matusse, R. Heltberg, and G. Dava (2002). 'The Robustness of Poverty Profiles Reconsidered', *Economic Development and Cultural Change*, 51(1): 77–108.

# 2

# Absolute Poverty Lines

*Channing Arndt, Kristi Mahrt, and Finn Tarp*

## 2.1 Introduction

A voluminous literature exists on the estimation of absolute poverty lines. In summing up this literature, one cannot do better than Martin Ravallion's recent book *The Economics of Poverty: History, Measurement, and Policy* (Ravallion 2016). This book devotes nearly 150 pages to the issues associated with measuring welfare in general and the estimation of poverty lines in particular. It provides a succinct and accessible overview of what is known and what is not known in these broad domains, often with particular focus on measuring welfare in developing countries. There is little point in attempting to summarize or further condense this work. Instead, the focus in this chapter is to place the methods described in the present volume, as well as their practical application, within the broad canvas painted by Ravallion.

A first fundamental choice is whether to estimate an absolute poverty line at all. Ravallion (2016) goes to considerable lengths to emphasize that measuring welfare on the basis of consumption of private goods represents only one facet of welfare. As such, consumption-based poverty metrics provide only a partial view into the welfare of individuals or households, which may or may not accord with other important facets of welfare. For example, a population may uniformly prefer to sacrifice substantial private consumption to live in zones with better public services. Hence, on a broad-based metric of welfare that includes both public and private goods, subpopulations living in zones with poor public services should be considered worse off than those living in zones with better public services for identical levels of private consumption.

Serious difficulties in estimating the value of public services to individual households have largely precluded their inclusion in household consumption. These and other limitations are fully recognized and discussed in more detail in section 2.3. Concomitantly, Ravallion's (2016: 76) admonition 'best current practice is sensibly eclectic, often using a combination of methods' is fully endorsed.

While a focus on private consumption has limitations, any 'sensibly eclectic' approach almost surely includes consideration of private consumption. Private consumption is a very important facet of welfare, particularly in cases where levels are exceedingly low. There is a vast difference between choosing between going to the movies or not and choosing between adequately feeding yourself or your children. It is perfectly clear that substantial shares of the population in all of the case countries considered in Part II face the latter choice on a disturbingly regular basis. In these circumstances, the ability to rigorously document progress/stagnation/regress in expansion of consumption possibilities is highly desirable. And the conclusions so derived can have profound implications, not least for public policies.

Hence, there is, on the one hand, little doubt that private consumption capabilities form only one facet of a comprehensive assessment of living standards for a population. On the other hand, it is also clear that private consumption is an important facet whose measurement should be done well. Experience in this domain also strongly indicates that measuring private consumption possibilities is challenging. It involves a multitude of methodological choices and trade-offs. These choices often interact with imperfect data and a desire to maintain consistency with previous choices in order to generate comparable results through time. The remainder of this chapter outlines the ideas that underpin the choices made for the analysis of consumption poverty in the case studies in Part II of this book.

## 2.2 Absolute Poverty Lines and Utility

Poverty lines can be described as either absolute or relative thresholds for distinguishing the poor from the non-poor. Relative poverty lines measure poverty in relation to the wellbeing of the society. A well-known example of a relative poverty line is the European Union's threshold of 60 per cent of median income. Absolute poverty lines identify those living below an arbitrarily fixed level of wellbeing. Absolute poverty lines are especially appealing in the context of developing countries where the focus remains on attaining minimum standards of living for large portions of the population.

Ravallion (1998) describes two steps in the process of defining absolute poverty lines. The first step involves specifying a reference level of utility representing a minimum standard of living. The second step involves identifying a money metric threshold between the poor and non-poor that is associated with the reference utility level. As utility is unobservable, the threshold is associated with actual consumption, which is observable. Consumption of a bundle of goods generates, for given preferences, a set level of utility. If the goods comprising the bundle are freely available at given prices, then the cost of the bundle is easily established. An individual or household with the capability to spend the cost of the bundle can thus attain at least the reference level of utility.

Note that, while poverty lines are derived on the basis of consumption bundles and the associated opportunity cost to the household of acquiring the bundle (normally approximated by prevailing prices), poverty lines are, in this conception, fundamentally rooted to a reference level of utility. The associated bundles should therefore adhere to two desirable properties: consistency and specificity. Consistency demands that consumption bundles reflect a reference utility level that is fixed across spatial and temporal domains. The easiest way to ensure consistency of the bundles across space and time is to select the same bundle across all spatial and temporal domains. Specificity relates to the relevance of the bundles and associated poverty lines to local conditions.[1]

Almost invariably, there is tension between these two desirable properties even if one restricts attention uniquely to food consumption, which often represents half to three quarters of total private consumption of poor people in developing countries. A common tension arises purely from differences in relative prices. In developing countries, relative prices for basic foods frequently vary substantially across space and through time; and consumption patterns often vary accordingly with relatively inexpensive goods appearing more prominently in consumption patterns. A fixed bundle is consistent, in that it delivers the same utility level, but fails to account for substitution effects, thus violating specificity. As Ravallion (2016: 8) states, 'as long as there is substitutability, the poverty bundles must vary with prices'.

The issues can be seen more formally with respect to an expenditure function derived from standard utility theory.

$$z_{ij}^u = e(p_i, x_{ij}, u_z) \quad \forall i, j \tag{2.1}$$

$$z_{ij}^u = p_i q_{ij}(p_i, x_{ij}, u_z) \tag{2.2}$$

In equation (2.1), the reference utility level ($u_z$) can be obtained at cost $z_{ij}^u$ given a vector of prices ($p_i$) faced by household $j$ in region $i$. Households may have varying characteristics, $x_{ij}$, such as the number and demographic composition of members, which influence the cost of attaining the reference

---

[1] A careful reading of Ravallion and Bidani (1994) and Thorbecke (2004) leaves open some ambiguity on the exact interpretation of the consistency and specificity properties between the two definitions provided. We will throughout employ the terms in the sense defined in this paragraph.

utility level. Equation (2.2) simply defines an associated least cost consumption bundle, $q_{ij}$, for reference utility level ($u_z$), prices ($p_i$), and household characteristics ($x_{ij}$). Because the bundle is least cost, any other bundle that provides reference utility level $u_z$ must cost at least as much as $z_{ij}^u$ for given prices and characteristics.

When substitution possibilities are present, the optimal consumption bundle ($q_{ij}$) varies with prices ($p_i$) and so does the cost of attaining the reference utility level ($u_z$). This cost is the appropriate poverty line, and the associated bundle is both consistent (constant utility level) and specific (adapted to the conditions of the region). As noted, large variations in relative prices are frequently observed across space and through time; and consumption patterns are generally responsive to these relative price differentials. Ignoring these differentials by selecting a single bundle either across space or through time is potentially highly problematic (Tarp et al. 2002). At the same time, the reference utility level ($u_z$) is never observed and the fundamental preference parameters that underlie the expenditure function are extraordinarily difficult to estimate. Hence, alternative (more specific) bundles that reflect differential relative prices may also provide different levels of utility, violating consistency.

## 2.3 Cost of Basic Needs

At the outset of attempts to estimate consumption poverty, two principal approaches to deriving poverty lines were advanced: the food energy intake (FEI) approach (Dandekar and Rath 1971; Greer and Thorbecke 1985), and the cost of basic needs (CBN) approach (Ravallion 1994, 1998; Ravallion and Bidani 1994; Ravallion and Sen 1996; Wodon 1997). With time, the CBN approach has gradually predominated. CBN is in focus here.[2]

The CBN approach follows logically from the discussion in section 2.2. It estimates poverty lines based on the cost of attaining a reference utility level as represented by a bundle of goods. In the CBN approach as applied to the country cases considered here, the reference utility level is low, reflecting, as the name suggests, basic needs. In practice, the explicit goods bundle frequently contains only foods. This is so because prices of non-foods vary drastically with quality and/or are represented by broad categories in household surveys (e.g. clothing), rendering estimation of meaningful quantities impossible. Of course, foods vary in quality as well, but the variation in the quality of basic foods purchased by poor people is not as profound.

---

[2] The Pakistan case study contains an application of the FEI approach including comparisons to CBN results developed using a modified version of PLEASe.

The food bundle is ideally based on the consumption patterns of the poor (specificity) and is normally required to meet a pre-set minimum caloric requirement that may vary with demographics or other factors. Consistent with the discussion in section 2.2, food poverty lines measure the cost of acquiring the food bundle(s). Even if the bundles do not vary across space or time, their cost is generally obtained by evaluating the bundle at specific regional and temporal prices.

The food poverty line so obtained is then supplemented by a non-food poverty line, which can be viewed as a single aggregate non-food good. An attractive approach to estimating the non-food poverty line is to use the average non-food expenditure of those households with consumption at or near the food poverty line (Ravallion 1998). This approach follows from the observation that even very poor people allocate non-trivial resources to non-foods, such as housing, clothing, and transport. The non-food purchases of households whose total consumption is 'near' the food poverty line are defined as basic because these items are perforce displacing consumption on food and thus forcing the household to consume a basket of foods that is inferior to the CBN poverty line basket in quantity, quality, or both.

The poor are then identified as those with consumption levels below the total poverty line (the sum of the food and non-food poverty lines). From this point, the Foster, Greer, and Thorbecke (FGT) class of decomposable poverty measures (Foster et al. 1984) are typically calculated. The most famous and frequently deployed FGT measure is the poverty headcount, which simply states the percentage of the population that lives below the poverty line.

We have already discussed the tension between consistency and specificity; however, even if this tension is resolved entirely, the CBN methodology has features of which the analyst, as well as the consumer of poverty analysis, should be aware.

First, the CBN approach, as described in this section, seeks to measure the cost of attaining minimum basic needs, which is distinct from identifying whether households actually satisfy these basic needs. A caloric standard applied to the food bundle provides an anchor for setting the reference welfare level. It is not an indication that a given household in fact attains that nutritional standard (or other standards for that matter). A household with total private consumption greater than the CBN poverty line may choose to allocate resources such that it does not meet its nutritional needs, yet this household would still be deemed non-poor because it has the *capability* to meet basic needs through purchase of the CBN basket.

Second, largely due to data limitations, the standard CBN methodology makes no attempt to measure the allocation of resources within households. In a non-poor household, it is possible that the basic needs of only some household members, but not others, are met. Combined, these two features raise the spectrum of households with children wherein the adults heavily consume alcohol, entertainment, and tobacco while providing completely inadequately for their children. Yet, these children would be considered non-poor as long as the total value of consumption (including the value of consumption on adult goods) is greater than the poverty line threshold.

At the same time, these two aspects of the CBN approach avoid paternalism. It may be considered paternalistic if a household is categorized as poor because the consumption allocations of the household do not conform to some externally imposed norms. The CBN approach avoids paternalism at the cost of potentially violating some widely held norms, such as that a member of a non-poor household whose basic needs are not being met due to unequal allocation of resources within the household should be categorized as poor.

Third, important classes of goods are excluded. As noted earlier, the focus is on private goods, ignoring publicly provided goods and services. If, for example, public services are better in urban than in rural areas, then the focus on private goods understates rural poverty relative to urban poverty, *ceteris paribus*. Some private goods are also ignored. Specifically, services generated within the household are generally not counted, largely because they are so difficult to value. If one member of a household spends considerable time providing services such as cooking, the whole household may be able to eat much better than their neighbour, who has the same level of private expenditure but allocates less time to home-produced services such as cooking.

Finally, and referencing equations (2.1) and (2.2) more generally, varying the poverty line as a function of household characteristics is possible in principle but forces difficult choices in practice. For example, are basic needs in terms of private consumption for children less than the basic needs of private consumption for adults? If each person counts the same, then the total consumption of the household can be divided by the number of people living in the household, irrespective of age, to arrive at a per capita measure. If not, an adult equivalent scale, which is a specific estimate of how much less children (and sometimes women) need to consume to meet basic needs as opposed to (male) adults, is required. This choice can substantially influence the estimated prevalence of child poverty, defined as children who live in households categorized as poor.

A second example relates to household economies of scale. A two-person household might attain a higher living standard than a one-person household with the same level of per capita expenditure. Most obviously, sharing a dwelling can provide better housing services for the same cost. Durable goods, such as a radio or cooking equipment, are (in principle) easily shared at low cost. And larger households might be able to buy food and other items in bulk at lower prices. As household size increases, these economies of scale almost surely decline. Diseconomies of scale may appear at some point. However, rigorously estimating household economies of scale is exceedingly difficult.

In sum, while the CBN method is widely applied and broadly accepted as a guidepost to best practice in estimating absolute poverty lines, the methodology is not without its challenges. In many cases, the best solution is to adopt multiple approaches as noted earlier and as highlighted in Ravallion (2016). Answers to questions such as:

- What do the anthropometric data say about the nutritional status of children?

- Are public services available and of reasonable quality?

- How sensitive are consumption poverty measures to the choice of adult equivalence scales and/or estimates of household economies of scale?

provide a more complete and nuanced picture and maintains the focus of the consumption poverty measure on the facet of welfare it is designed to measure—household-level private consumption. Given this focus, the key is to measure household-level private consumption correctly. To this end, we look at approaches for enhancing specificity while maintaining minimum consistency requirements in section 2.4.

## 2.4 Consistency and Specificity

Figure 2.1 illustrates the advantages and drawbacks of attaining consistency via fixed bundles. The example focuses on changes in relative prices through time; however, the conclusions drawn from this example fully extend to the case when bundles are fixed across spatial domains. Consider a representative household in two time periods that consumes two goods $c_1$ and $c_2$ where preferences are fixed over time. The utility curve $U^z$ represents the minimum welfare associated with the poverty line. Estimating the poverty line amounts to estimating the minimum cost of attaining the reference welfare level and therefore is represented by the budget line tangent to $U^z$ at prevailing prices. As period one prices are reflected in the slope of the budget line $M^1$, $(c_1^1, c_2^1)$ is the optimal bundle that yields minimum welfare and therefore expenditure level $M^1$ represents the period one poverty line.

Suppose relative prices change in period two, as reflected in the slopes of $M^2$ and $M^{2'}$. If the poverty analyst follows the practice of maintaining consistency by holding the period one consumption bundle fixed and evaluates it at period two prices, the cost of acquiring $(c_1^1, c_2^1)$ is $M^{2'}$, i.e. the fixed poverty line. Clearly, this is not an optimal solution and violates the property of

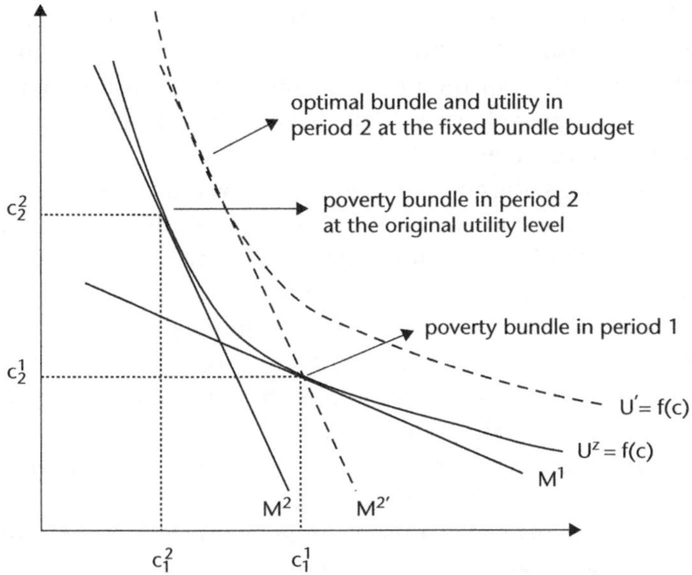


**Figure 2.1.** Illustration of the implications of substitution effects

*Source*: Authors' illustration

specificity in that it fails to allow for a response to the prices prevailing in period two. At the fixed poverty line, a utility-maximizing household would choose a consumption bundle associated with the higher utility curve, $U'$. Therefore, with fixed bundles, the period one and period two poverty lines are associated with different utility levels. If in period two the reference household's expenditure exceeds $M^2$ but is equal to or less than the fixed poverty line, $M^{2'}$, the household would be deemed poor. However, at expenditure levels in this range, the household would attain a utility level greater than the utility associated with the period one poverty line. At the constant welfare level, $U^z$, the reference household would opt to consume the flexible bundle $(c_1^2, c_2^2)$ at a lower cost resulting in a lower utility-consistent poverty line, $M^2$. In short, imposing the fixed bundle $(c_1^1, c_2^1)$ in period two violates the property of specificity and in so doing overestimates the cost of acquiring the minimum welfare level.

It is important to highlight that this overestimation of the period two poverty line when holding the bundle from period one constant through time is a function of starting at a cost-minimizing consumption point in period one. However, if specificity is violated in estimating period one bundles and results in a non-optimal bundle, the impact of the bundle carried forward to period two is uncertain. To see this, let us think conceptually of a country with six relatively distinct spatial domains with differing price vectors for basic foods and corresponding differences in consumption patterns. If we (for example) define a single national consumption bundle as the average consumption of households in the lower third of the nominal consumption distribution across all spatial domains, then we have a single (average) bundle that may not reflect consumption patterns in any of the domains. Assuming constant preferences across spatial domains, the chosen single bundle would provide some reference level of utility (e.g. it is consistent). If preferences permit substitution between goods, then, by standard cost minimization, households in region $i$ could obtain the reference level of utility at a cost that is less than or equal to the cost of the chosen single bundle evaluated at region $i$ prices.

However, the extent of this overestimation is unknown for any of the six regions. Because the single consumption bundle applied to each spatial domain may be substantially untethered from actual consumption behaviour in any domain, it is impossible to know, without further information, the implications of these overestimations for the regional poverty profile. Furthermore, if one moves forward in time to analyse a new household survey and one simply applies updated prices to the single chosen bundle from the previous survey, the biases due to the failure of specificity in the estimation of the change in poverty are entirely unknown at the national level or at any of the regional levels. This is so because the chosen single bundle potentially does not correspond with actual consumption patterns in any region in any period. As the extent of error may become smaller or larger when one moves across space or through time, the implications for poverty evolution are also unknown. This contrasts with Figure 2.1 which shows that maintaining a previously optimal bundle through time only has the potential to bias upward the estimated poverty rate.

As has been noted, a potential solution to the shortcomings of a single, fixed consumption bundle is to estimate multiple (flexible) bundles across time and space. This approach has been applied in many recent studies (see Tarp et al. 2002; Gibson and Rozelle 2003; Mukherjee and Benson 2003; MPF/IFPRI/PU 2004; Datt and Jolliffe 2005; Ravallion and Lokshin 2006). The use of flexible bundles increases specificity in ensuring that bundles reflect the consumption patterns of poor households in each domain. As seen in Figure 2.1, flexible bundles have the advantage of allowing consumers to respond to variations in relative prices by consuming relatively cheaper foods. If utility were observable, flexible bundles would also resolve the issue of utility inconsistency, as each poverty line would be anchored to $U^z$. However, in practice, utility is not observable. Without utility consistency, differences in poverty rates between domains could merely reflect differences in utility levels across poverty lines for each domain rather than differences in standards of living within domains. This potential loss of consistency underpins the choice of sticking with a single bundle.

To come to grips with this issue, analysts have turned to revealed preference theory to test whether regional poverty lines are utility-consistent (Gibson and Rozelle 2003; Ravallion and Lokshin 2006). Spatial revealed preference conditions can be written:

$$\sum_i p_{ir} * q_{is} \geq \sum_i p_{ir} * q_{ir} \quad \forall r, s \quad r \neq s \tag{2.3}$$

where preferences are defined on $I$ [i $\in$ I] commodities; $r$, $s$ represent indices for the set of spatial domains considered, R [r, s $\in$ R]; and the variables $p$ and $q$ represent prices and quantities, respectively. The conditions compare the cost of a consumption bundle in a given domain, $r$, to the cost of a bundle from another domain, $s$, evaluated at prices observed in $r$. If the bundles represent the same level of utility and preferences are constant, a rational consumer would choose the least cost bundle. A failure of this condition indicates consumers opted to buy a more expensive bundle even though a cheaper combination was available. The chosen bundle is therefore revealed preferred. A rational consumer only chooses a higher cost bundle if it provides greater utility. Thus, a failure of revealed preference conditions indicates the consumption bundles do not provide a consistent level of utility.

Revealed preference conditions impose very mild conditions on the nature of the welfare function. All that is required is that consumers prefer more to less. For people living near absolute poverty, this is a banal assumption. In addition, the prices used must be a reasonable estimation of the opportunity costs *to the consumer* of the goods in the bundles that are being compared (societal opportunity costs are different). If a good is subsidized and freely available at the subsidized price, then the subsidized price is a very good approximation of the opportunity cost to the consumer. If the subsidized good is only available one day a week and requires waiting in line for hours in order to purchase it, then the subsidized price understates the opportunity cost to the consumer of purchasing the good. This latter situation pertains with some frequency in developing countries and requires that attention be paid to whether prices represent opportunity costs to the consumer in empirical analyses.

The use of revealed preferences to check for utility consistency also imposes assumptions about consumer preferences. Specifically, satisfaction of all revealed preference conditions implies that there exists a coherent preference set (assuming the representative consumer prefers more to less) that corresponds with the observed consumption behaviour. This coherent preference set becomes the reference against which all comparisons are made.

The fundamental assertion made when one applies revealed preference conditions to making welfare comparisons is that this reference preference set is reasonable. Indeed, in imposing revealed preference conditions, one is seeking to arrive at the best possible comparator for evaluating the welfare derived from private consumption expenditure, particularly for households living 'near' the absolute poverty line. It is worth highlighting that, in comparing the welfare of household A to the welfare of household B, some observable reference is required. Bundles that reflect consumption patterns (specificity) and satisfy revealed preference conditions (consistency) would appear to be prime candidates to serve as the reference.

There are cases where preferences rather than prices clearly influence consumption patterns. For example, rather than prices, religious dietary restrictions may significantly influence the consumption patterns in a subset of regions. Box 2.1 considers the impact of regional climate variations on caloric needs as well as food preferences. In these and other cases, the question is not whether preferences are the same everywhere. Clearly, they are not. Nevertheless, the question remains: what reference comparator should be chosen in order to make welfare comparisons? Even when preferences clearly differ, there is still a good argument that bundles that reflect the specificities of distinct regions and satisfy revealed preferences are reasonable choices for the reference. These bundles essentially posit that there exists a preference set for a representative consumer whose consumption is unconstrained by dietary restrictions; who is equally content to consume any of the bundles; and who would choose to consume the bundle from region $r$ at time $t$ when faced with prevailing prices and having a budget set at the poverty line. In other words, arguments must be advanced that a better reference comparator is available.

---

**Box 2.1.** REVEALED PREFERENCES, BUNDLES, AND CLIMATE

---

Ravallion and Lokshin (2006) point out that energy requirements plausibly vary across climates with inhabitants of colder climates requiring greater calorie intake as compared with warmer climates. Their case, Russia, is an extreme example. Differing climates also create different growing conditions strongly affecting the food production mix within regions. Given the strong tendency for food to be produced and consumed locally, particularly in developing countries, differing agro-climatic zones will also tend to have strong impacts on the relative prices of foods and hence the composition of the food bundle.

Once again, if one wishes to make comparisons of welfare levels across agro-climatic zones, one requires a reference comparator. One potential approach would be to develop bundles that satisfy revealed preference conditions across spatial domains that comprehend very different agro-climatic zones and that yield a constant quantity of calories across space and/or through time. These bundles could then be scaled to provide more calories in colder climates and fewer calories in warmer climates in order to reflect the differentials in basic needs for calorie consumption. The key question is whether a reference comparator developed in this manner is inferior to a feasible alternative.

## 2.5 Estimating Specific Utility-Consistent Poverty Lines

Revealed preference conditions are straightforward to apply to actual consumption bundles derived in poverty line estimation analysis. The conditions themselves are exacting and failures are frequently widespread. For instance, Ravallion and Lokshin (2006) apply revealed preference conditions to bundles from twenty-three spatial domains in Russia. The comparison matrix is thus $23 \times 23$. The diagonal of the matrix compares regions to themselves and can be ignored. There are thus 253 = 23*22/2 matched pairs defined as spatial domain A compared with spatial domain B and vice versa. Of these 253 possibilities, only six matched pairs satisfied revealed preference conditions. Similar results are found in Papua New Guinea by Gibson and Rozelle (2003) and in Mozambique and Egypt by Arndt and Simler (2010).

Arndt and Simler (2005, 2007, 2010) introduce a methodology based on information theory for resolving revealed preference violations. Using the cross-entropy criterion, they minimize the directed distance between the original consumption shares and estimated shares satisfying revealed preference conditions. The mathematical programme typically also ensures that the caloric content of the original consumption bundle is maintained. To satisfy revealed preferences, quantities likely need to be modified, thus altering composition of the food baskets.

$$\min \sum_r \sum_i s_{ir}^{ent} \ln \left( \frac{s_{ir}^{ent}}{s_{ir}^{orig}} \right) \tag{2.4}$$

Where:

$q_{ir}$ are variables representing quantities consumed;

$s_{ir}^{ent}$ are variables representing food shares of the reference bundle;

$s_{ir}^{orig}$ are parameters representing initial food shares of the reference bundle;

$i, i'$ are indices of goods in the consumption bundles; and

$r, s$ are indices of domains across space.

Subject to:

$$\sum_i p_{ir} {}^* q_{is} \geq \sum_i p_{ir} {}^* q_{ir} \qquad \forall r, s \quad r \neq s \tag{2.4a}$$

$$s_{ir}^{ent} \sum_{i'} p_{i'r} q_{i'r} = p_{ir} q_{ir} \qquad \forall i, r \tag{2.4b}$$

$$\sum_i calpg_i q_{ir} = cal \qquad \forall r \tag{2.4c}$$

$$0 \leq s_{ir}^{ent} \leq 1, \; q_{ir} \geq 0 \qquad \forall i, r \tag{2.4d}$$

The first constraint ensures that revealed preference conditions are satisfied across regions given prices, $p_{ir}$. The second constraint defines entropy budget shares, $s_{ir}^{ent}$, as a function of the modified quantities, $q_{ir}$. The third condition constrains the basket to attain caloric requirements (parameter $cal$), which are held constant across regions, by multiplying quantities by calories per unit (e.g., grams) of each good (parameter $calpg_i$). Temporal constraints are also possible to impose (Arndt and Simler 2010 and Chapter 4, section 4.2.4).

Arndt and Simler (2010) apply the maximum-entropy method to poverty lines in Mozambique and Egypt and discuss the philosophy of estimation under an information-theoretic approach. Briefly, the information-theoretic approach seeks to preserve, to the greatest degree possible, the information content inherent in the original budget shares (specificity) while ensuring that revealed preference conditions are satisfied (consistency). The procedure also ensures that the bundle provides a targeted level of calories in keeping with standard CBN practice.

## 2.6 Conclusion

Like it or not, there is no single set procedure for estimating absolute poverty lines. The CBN approach provides a series of valuable guideposts that are well rooted within consumer theory. But in actual practice, numerous choices must be made. This chapter has sought to explore the broad contours of some of the more fundamental choices with an extra dose of attention devoted to the long-running debate on reconciling consistency and specificity. Differing country circumstances will almost surely lead to different choices with respect to the overall approach. In addition, past choices often strongly influence current choices due to the desire to make relevant comparisons with earlier analyses. Chapter 4, the case studies in Part II, and the provided codes are meant to facilitate focus on the actual key choices and their implications.

This chapter began by emphasizing that private consumption represents only one facet of welfare, albeit an important one. We also highlighted in section 2.3 a series of limitations that are almost invariably associated with CBN-type approaches to welfare measures. And we reaffirmed the idea that the best mode for addressing these limitations is to employ multiple methods, particularly those better suited to providing insight where the typical CBN approach falls short. As a contribution to this end, Chapter 3 focuses on drawing conclusions from a series of indicators, each representing a facet of welfare, in a multidimensional framework. Hence, we now turn to broadening our conception of welfare.

## References

Arndt, C. and K. R. Simler (2005). 'Estimating Utility-Consistent Poverty Lines', Food Consumption and Nutrition Division Discussion Paper No. 189. Washington, DC: International Food Policy Research Institute (IFPRI).

Arndt, C. and K. R. Simler (2007). 'Consistent Poverty Comparisons and Inference', *Agricultural Economics*, 37: 133–9.

Arndt, C. and K. R. Simler (2010). 'Estimating Utility-Consistent Poverty Lines with Applications to Egypt and Mozambique', *Economic Development and Cultural Change*, 58(3): 449–74.

Dandekar, V. M. and N. Rath (1971). *Poverty in India*. Pune: Indian School of Political Economy.

Datt, G. and D. Jolliffe (2005). 'Poverty in Egypt: Modeling and Policy Simulations', *Economic Development and Cultural Change*, 53: 327–46.

Foster, J., J. Greer, and E. Thorbecke (1984). 'A Class of Decomposable Poverty Measures', *Econometrica*, 52(3): 761–65.

Gibson, J. and S. Rozelle (2003). 'Poverty and Access to Roads in Papua New Guinea', *Economic Development and Cultural Change*, 52(1): 159–85.

Greer, J. and E. Thorbecke (1985). 'Food Poverty Profile Applied to Kenyan Smallholders', *Economic Development and Cultural Change*, 35: 115–41.

MPF/IFPRI/PU (Mozambique Ministry of Planning and Finance/International Food Policy Research Institute/Purdue University) (2004). 'Poverty and Well-Being in Mozambique: The Second National Assessment', Report, Ministry of Planning and Finance, Maputo.

Mukherjee, S. and T. Benson (2003). 'The Determinants of Poverty in Malawi', *World Development*, 31: 339–58.

Ravallion, M. (1994). *Poverty Comparisons*. Geneva: Harwood Academic Publishers.

Ravallion, M. (1998). 'Poverty Lines in Theory and Practice', Living Standards Measurement Study Working Paper No. 133. Washington, DC: World Bank.

Ravallion, M. (2016). *The Economics of Poverty: History, Measurement, and Policy*. Oxford: Oxford University Press.

Ravallion, M. and B. Bidani (1994). 'How Robust Is a Poverty Profile?', *World Bank Economic Review*, 8: 75–102.

Ravallion, M. and M. Lokshin (2006). 'Testing Poverty Lines', *Review of Income and Wealth*, 52(3): 399–421.

Ravallion, M. and B. Sen (1996). 'When Method Matters: Monitoring Poverty in Bangladesh', *Economic Development and Cultural Change*, 44: 761–92.

Tarp, F., K. R. Simler, C. Matusse, R. Heltberg, and G. Dava (2002). 'The Robustness of Poverty Profiles Reconsidered', *Economic Development and Cultural Change*, 51: 77–108.

Thorbecke, E. (2004). 'Conceptual and Measurement Issues in Poverty Analysis', UNU-WIDER Discussion Paper 2004/04. Helsinki: UNU-WIDER.

Wodon, Q. (1997). 'Food Energy Intake and Cost of Basic Needs: Measuring Poverty in Bangladesh', *Journal of Development Studies*, 34: 66–101.

# 3

# Multidimensional First-Order Dominance Comparisons of Population Wellbeing

*Nikolaj Siersbæk, Lars Peter Østerdal, and Channing Arndt*

## 3.1 Introduction

A central question in applied welfare economics is how to make comparisons of population wellbeing across groups or over time. Appropriate comparison concepts have many potential uses. For example, if a study is able to detect that one population group is clearly worse off than another (i.e. is overall poorer or has less social welfare), society might wish to undertake policies aimed at narrowing this gap. Also, since reducing poverty or improving social welfare over time is often a key objective for public policies and reforms, the ability to make relevant comparisons over time is crucial for the formulation of meaningful goals and for policy evaluation.

The traditional approach to comparing population wellbeing is the use of a social welfare (or poverty) measure based on a one-dimensional individual wellbeing indicator, typically a monetary variable such as income or wealth. However, it has long been recognized that poverty and wellbeing are multidimensional phenomena, which are not adequately represented by a single income variable. As Sen (1976) points out, there is good reason to think that sometimes a richer person may have lower wellbeing than a poorer person; e.g. if he is disabled. This has given rise to numerous proposals of appropriate dimensions to include in multidimensional welfare analyses, including (but not restricted to) health and education (World Bank 1990) as well as standards of living (Sen 1988) to name a few.

Multidimensional welfare is often measured by aggregating multiple dimensions and weighting each dimension (see e.g. Alkire and Foster 2011; Roelen and Gassmann 2008; Rippin 2010). The method is covered in-depth in Alkire et al. (2015) in a comprehensive representation of multidimensional poverty measurement and analysis, which the reader is encouraged to consult. The weighting is primarily made in order to reflect societal judgements about different dimensions as well as to be able to obtain a single measure of the welfare for a given population. This aggregation procedure enables the analyst to rank the populations. Furthermore, the approach is very convenient and can easily be justified when there exists a reasonably high degree of consensus about which weights should be applied. There is, however, no natural and generally agreed methodology to obtaining these weights. Often, it is not easy to say if one dimension is more important than another, and even when it is, quantifying by how much is often very difficult and perhaps not even meaningful to people.

The challenges described above have motivated the development of methods for comparing population wellbeing, poverty, or inequality with multidimensional indicators that are methodologically 'robust' in the sense that the conclusions obtained do not rely on predetermined weights on each dimension. In the context of applied welfare economics, such methods were popularized by Atkinson and Bourguignon (1982) who showed how stochastic dominance techniques for comparisons of probability distributions can be used to make comparisons of populations across broad classes of underlying social welfare functions. Such techniques have been further refined and applied by, e.g., Atkinson and Bourguignon (1987), Bourguignon (1989), Atkinson (1992), Bourguignon and Chakravarty (2003), Duclos et al. (2006, 2007), Gravel et al. (2009), Gravel and Mukhopadhyay (2010), Muller and Trannoy (2011), Gravel and Moyes (2012), and many others.

These contributions apply dominance concepts, which rely on assumptions that are typically formulated in terms of a specified sign on the second- (and higher-)order partial- or cross-derivatives of the underlying individual utility function considered by a utilitarian planner. This leads to so-called lower- or upper-orthant dominance (or even more demanding concepts). For example, Duclos and Échevin (2011) assume substitutability between health and income, i.e. an underlying utility function with a negative cross-partial derivative between health and income.

These concepts, while considerably more robust than methods relying on given weights, do not apply to ordinal data, where only the ranking of outcomes along each dimension is known to the analyst (based on a more-is-better assumption) but no information is available regarding, for example, the complementarity/substitutability relationship across the dimensions. However, welfare indicators are often ordinal in nature. For example, a higher educational attainment (e.g. a university degree) is considered to be better than a lower (e.g. primary school), but quantifying by how much is not easily done and perhaps not even meaningful.

A natural concept for making comparisons of population distributions with multidimensional ordinal data is *first-order dominance* (FOD), also known as the *usual (stochastic) order* in the probability theory literature (see e.g. Shaked and Shanthikumar 2007). A finite (population, probability) distribution A first-order dominates distribution B if one can obtain distribution B from A by shifting (population, probability) mass within A from preferred to less preferred outcomes (where a less preferred outcome is not better in any dimension and is strictly worse in at least one dimension). Hence, if one distribution first-order dominates another, it is unambiguously better than the other. Thus, under the assumption that outcomes within each distribution can be ranked—e.g. we prefer the child attending school as opposed to not— the FOD approach provides a maximally robust way of making comparisons of multidimensional welfare. Technically, it does so without making any assumptions on utility functions and/or social welfare functions other than a more-is-better assumption. No additional assumptions are required about the strength of preferences for each dimension, nor about the relative desirability of changes between levels within or between dimensions (Arndt et al. 2012).

The absence of restrictive assumptions in the FOD approach makes the concept not only robust but also intuitively appealing. However, robustness comes at a cost. First, the result of comparing two distributions may be indeterminate. In other words, it may happen that distribution A does not dominate B and B does not dominate A. This makes the analyst unable to distinguish groups A and B according to wellbeing based on the selected indicators. Second, the FOD approach provides no information about whether a dominating distribution is slightly or substantially better than a dominated distribution. This chapter will discuss a way of mitigating these costs by applying a bootstrapping approach that provides a measure for the probability of observing dominances under resampling. This can serve both as a robustness check for the magnitude of the dominances observed and for the probability of observing dominance. Furthermore, if one is willing to accept the likelihood of performing well in head-to-head comparisons with other groups as an indicator of the relative wellbeing of a group, a full ranking of the groups can be calculated (Arndt et al. 2016).

The remainder of this paper is structured as follows: section 3.2 provides an overview of the theory of FOD with definitions and intuitive explanations using examples. Section 3.3 discusses faster checking algorithms and an alternative dominance criterion than FOD; and lastly, section 3.4 sums up and concludes.

## 3.2 Theory and Examples

This section provides the basic definitions and theory of the FOD approach, illustrated with some simple examples. Furthermore, a practical linear programming method for detecting dominances is described and the bootstrapping procedure is explained.

### 3.2.1 One-Dimensional FOD

Suppose first that the outcome of interest is one-dimensional. The outcome could, for example, be individual income (or wealth). In this case, there is a natural ordering of outcomes (assuming that a higher income is better), but only this single dimension is taken into account.

#### 3.2.1.1 NOTATIONS AND DEFINITIONS

Let $X$ denote a finite set of real-valued outcomes. Let the distribution of wellbeing of population A be described by a probability mass function[1] $f$ over $X$, i.e. $\sum f(x) = 1$ and $\sum f(x) \geq 0$ for all $x \in X$. Similarly, let the distributions of populations B and C be described by the probability mass functions $g$ and $h$ respectively.

As a very simple example, suppose that there are only two possible outcomes, $X = \{0, 1\}$. We will always assume that higher numbers are better, so 0 is the bad outcome ('income-deprived'), and 1 is the good outcome ('not income-deprived'). In this situation, a population distribution is completely described by its share of individuals being income-deprived. Table 3.1 shows distributions for three hypothetical populations.

In the one-dimensional case, $f$ first-order dominates $g$ if and only if any of the following (equivalent) conditions hold:[2]

(a) $g$ can be obtained from $f$ by a finite number of shifts of probability mass in $f$ from one outcome to another that is *worse*.

(b) Social welfare is at least as high for $f$ as for $g$ for any non-decreasing additively separable social welfare function, i.e. $\sum_{x \in X} f(x)w(x) \geq \sum_{x \in X} g(x)w(x)$ for any weakly increasing real function $w(\cdot)$.

(c) $F(x) \leq G(x)$ for all $x \in X$, where $F(\cdot)$ and $G(\cdot)$ are the cumulative distribution functions (CDFs)[3] corresponding to $f$ and $g$.

---

[1] A probability mass function is a function that to each outcome assigns the probability of that outcome. In the context of population comparisons, it assigns the share of the population in that outcome.

[2] Note that FOD is conventionally defined in the weak sense, i.e. a distribution always dominates itself.

[3] CDFs express the probability that the real-valued outcomes $X$ will have a value less than or equal to $x$.

Condition (a) provides perhaps the most intuitive definition of FOD. It provides a natural criterion for the case where one distribution is *unambiguously* better than another. Condition (b) is a robustness property in relation to social welfare comparisons and thus provides a link to welfare economics (and to expected utility theory in the case of a probability distribution). If there is FOD, social welfare will be at least as high for the dominating population *no matter the functional form of the social welfare function* as long as $w(\cdot)$ is weakly increasing. For ordinal data, this condition on $w(\cdot)$ simply means that outcomes can be ranked from worse to better. As noted in the Introduction, no additional assumptions are required. Condition (c) turns out to be equivalent to the first two conditions and is useful for checking FOD.

### 3.2.1.2 CHECKING ONE-DIMENSIONAL FOD

In the one-dimensional case, FOD can be checked in a simple and effective way with direct application of condition (c). To illustrate, consider the CDFs $F(\cdot)$, $G(\cdot)$, and $H(\cdot)$ corresponding to the three probability mass functions, $f$, $g$, and $h$, respectively; cf. Table 3.1. We have $F(0) = 0.35$, $G(0) = 0.50$, $H(0) = 0.40$, and of course $F(1) = G(1) = H(1) = 1$. These are shown in Figure 3.1 (the black line illustrates $F(x)$, the gray line illustrates $G(x)$, and the dotted line illustrates $H(x)$).

**Table 3.1.** Distributions $f$, $g$, and $h$ (per cent), one-dimensional

| Population A | | |
|---|---|---|
| $f$ | | Total |
| Income | 0 (deprived) | 35 |
| | 1 (not deprived) | 65 |
| Total | | 100 |
| | Population B | |
| $g$ | | Total |
| Income | 0 (deprived) | 50 |
| | 1 (not deprived) | 50 |
| Total | | 100 |
| | Population C | |
| $h$ | | Total |
| Income | 0 (deprived) | 40 |
| | 1 (not deprived) | 60 |
| Total | | 100 |

*Source*: Authors' hypothetical example

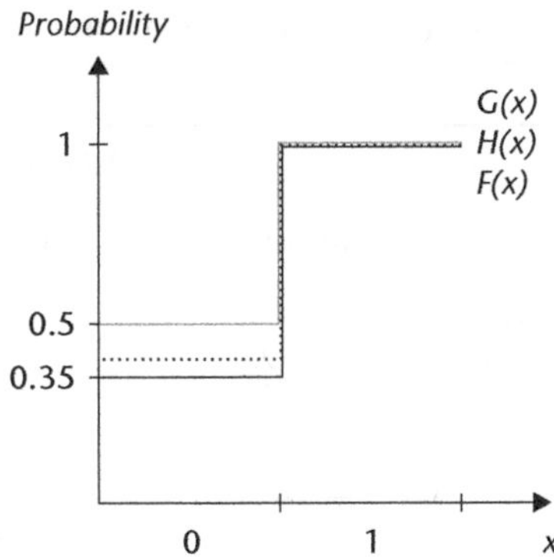


**Figure 3.1.** Multidimensional first-order dominance comparisons of population wellbeing

*Note*: The black line illustrates $F(x)$, the gray line illustrates $G(x)$, and the dotted line illustrates $H(x)$.

As can be seen from the graph, $F(x) \leq H(x) \leq G(x)$ for all $x \in X$. More precisely, $F(0) < H(0) < G(0)$ whereas $F(1) = G(1) = H(1) = 1$. Hence $f$ dominates both $g$ and $h$. Since $H(x) \leq G(x)$ for all $x \in X$, $h$ dominates $g$.

Condition (a) also provides an intuitive way of explaining dominances. For example, it can be seen from Table 3.1 that $f$ dominates $g$ since $g$ can be obtained from $f$ by shifting probability mass from one outcome to another that is *worse*. More precisely, shifting fifteen percentage points from (1) to (0) in $f$ yields exactly $g$.

### 3.2.2 Multidimensional FOD

Now suppose that the outcome is multidimensional. In the case of two dimensions, these could, for example, be income and health. In the case of three dimensions, one may wish to add educational attainment, and so on.

#### 3.2.2.1 NOTATIONS AND DEFINITIONS

Let $Y$ be a finite set of (multidimensional) outcomes. A distribution of wellbeing of population A is described by a probability mass function $f$ over $Y$, i.e. $\sum f(y) = 1$ and $f(y) \geq 0$ for all $y \in Y$. Similarly, let the distributions of populations B and C be described by the probability mass functions $g$ and $h$ respectively.

To illustrate, suppose that the two dimensions each have two possible outcomes, 0 or 1. Thus, $Y = \{(0,0), (0,1), (1,0), (1,1)\}$. One dimension could be *income* (dimension I) and the other dimension could be *health* (dimension II). Then the outcome (0,0) for a person means that she is deprived in both dimensions, while the outcome (1,0) means that she is not deprived in the first dimension (I) but deprived in the second dimension (II), and so on.

**Table 3.2.** Distributions *f*, *g*, and *h* (per cent), two-dimensional

Population A

| *f* | | II (health) | | Total |
|---|---|---|---|---|
| | | 0 (deprived: bad) | 1 (not deprived: good) | |
| I (income) | 0 (deprived: poor) | 10 | 25 | 35 |
| | 1 (not deprived: rich) | 25 | 40 | 65 |
| Total | | **35** | **65** | **100** |

Population B

| *g* | | II (health) | | Total |
|---|---|---|---|---|
| | | 0 (deprived: bad) | 1 (not deprived: good) | |
| I (income) | 0 (deprived: poor) | 25 | 25 | 50 |
| | 1 (not deprived: rich) | 25 | 25 | 50 |
| Total | | **50** | **50** | **100** |

Population C

| *h* | | II (health) | | Total |
|---|---|---|---|---|
| | | 0 (deprived: bad) | 1 (not deprived: good) | |
| I (income) | 0 (deprived: poor) | 30 | 10 | 40 |
| | 1 (not deprived: rich) | 10 | 50 | 60 |
| Total | | **40** | **60** | **100** |

*Source*: Authors' hypothetical example

Suppose that three probability mass functions *f*, *g*, and *h* are distributed as shown in Table 3.2. Note that distributions over dimension I (*income*) in the rightmost column are identical to those in Table 3.1 representing a situation where the same populations are considered but now an additional dimension is taken into consideration.

In the case of multidimensional outcomes, *f* first-order dominates *g* if and only if any of the following (equivalent) conditions hold:[4]

(A) *g* can be obtained from *f* by a finite number of shifts of probability mass from one outcome to another that is *worse*.

(B) Social welfare is at least as high for *f* as for *g* for any non-decreasing additively separable social welfare function, i.e. $\sum_{y \in Y} f(y)w(y) \geq \sum_{y \in Y} g(y)w(y)$ for any weakly increasing real function $w(\cdot)$.

(C) $\sum_{y \in Z} g(y) \geq \sum_{y \in Z} f(y)$ for any lower comprehensive set $Z \subseteq Y$.[5]

---

[4] The equivalence between (B) and (C) was shown by Lehmann (1955). It was also proved independently by Levhari et al. (1975). Kamae et al. (1977) observed that the equivalence between (A) and (C) is a consequence of Strassen's Theorem (Strassen 1965). See also Østerdal (2010).

[5] A set $Z \subseteq Y$ is lower comprehensive if $y \in Z$, $z \in Y$, and $z \leq y$ implies $z \in Z$.

Each condition is the natural multidimensional extension of its counterpart for the one-dimensional case. Again, note that condition (A) provides an intuitive criterion for one distribution being unambiguously better than another, (B) provides a foundation in welfare economics but one that is not conveniently amenable to testing, while (C) provides a directly testable condition that may not be particularly intuitive.

### 3.2.2.2 CHECKING MULTIDIMENSIONAL FOD

First, due to the intuitive nature, we appeal to condition (A). It can be seen from Table 3.2 that $f$ dominates $g$, since it is possible to obtain $g$ from $f$ by shifting probability mass in $f$ from better to worse outcomes. More precisely, shifting fifteen percentage points of probability mass from $(1,1)$ to $(0,0)$ in $f$ yields exactly $g$, which implies that $f$ dominates $g$. The distribution $f$ is thus unambiguously preferred to the distribution $g$.

However, consider $f$ and $h$. Neither $f$ dominates $h$, nor does $h$ dominate $f$. Intuitively, this is the case since $f$ would be better if what matters most is minimization of the share of the population who are deprived in dimensions II (health) since $f(0,0) + f(1,0) = 35 < h(0,0) + h(1,0) = 40$. On the contrary, $h$ would be better if what matters most is maximization of the share of the population not deprived in neither dimension since $h(1,1) = 50 > f(1,1) = 40$. Consequently, no dominances are detected since no assumptions are made about the relative importance of the different dimensions. Note that the conclusion that $f$ does not dominate $h$ is in contrast to the one-dimensional case. This illustrates that the conclusions might change when more dimensions are added to the analysis. It is therefore important to bear in mind that an analysis applying few welfare indicators may conclude that one population dominates another whereas a multidimensional FOD analysis of the same populations with more indicators may be indeterminate. Attention should therefore be given to include important dimensions that cover overall wellbeing reasonably well.

As mentioned, condition (C) provides a direct method for checking multidimensional FOD. In our example, $f$ dominates $g$ if and only if the following four inequalities are jointly satisfied:[6]

    *(i)* $g(0,0) \geq f(0,0)$
    *(ii)* $g(0,0) + g(0,1) \geq f(0,0) + f(0,1)$
    *(iii)* $g(0,0) + g(1,0) \geq f(0,0) + f(1,0)$
    *(iv)* $g(0,0) + g(1,0) + g(0,1) \geq f(0,0) + f(1,0) + f(0,1).$

---

[6] Note that the fifth inequality $g(0,0)+g(1,0)+g(0,1)+g(1,1) \geq f(0,0)+f(1,0)+f(0,1)+f(1,1)$ is always satisfied with equality by the definition of the probability mass functions since $\sum f(y) = \sum g(y) = 1$.

Considering the distributions in Table 3.2 in relation to the four inequalities above, it can be seen that, when comparing $f$ and $g$, each of the four inequalities $(i)$–$(iv)$ are (strictly) satisfied; $(i)$ $g(0,0) \geq f(0,0)$ since $0.25 > 0.10$, $(ii)$ $g(0,0) + g(0,1) \geq f(0,0) + f(0,1)$ since $0.25 + 0.25 > 0.10 + 0.25$, $(iii)$ $g(0,0) + g(1,0) \geq f(0,0) + f(1,0)$ since $0.25 + 0.25 > 0.10 + 0.25$, and $(iv)$ $g(0,0) + g(1,0) + g(0,1) \geq f(0,0) + f(1,0) + f(0,1)$ since $0.25 + 0.25 + 0.25 > 0.10 + 0.25 + 0.25$. Hence, $f$ dominates $g$, as already observed. When comparing each of the other distribution pairs, it can easily be seen that at least one of the inequalities is violated. For example, when comparing $f$ and $h$, inequalities $(i)$–$(iii)$ are satisfied whereas inequality $(iv)$ is not.

### 3.2.2.3 DETECTING FOD IN PRACTICE

Criterion (C) provides a simple method for detecting dominance, which can be visually perceived in cases with few outcomes such as in the example with two binary indicators giving four different outcomes in total. However, the number of inequalities to be checked increases drastically when more dimensions and levels are added. For real-world applications, computationally efficient algorithms for checking dominance are required (Range and Østerdal 2013). Mosler and Scarsini (1991) and Dyckerhoff and Mosler (1997) show that, appealing to definition (A), checking FOD corresponds to determining if a certain linear program has a feasible solution. FOD can thus be determined using a linear programming package. The first empirical implementation of this approach was provided by Arndt et al. (2012) in a study of child poverty in Mozambique and Vietnam.

Let A and B be two populations characterized by probability mass functions $f$ and $g$ respectively. For outcomes $y$ and $y'$ with $y' \leq y$, let $t_{y,y'}$ be the amount of probability mass transferred from outcome $y$ to $y'$. Note that the first subscript denotes the source of the transfer whereas the second denotes the destination.

Given the conditions outlined above, population A dominates population B if and only if there exists a feasible solution to the following linear program:[7]

$$f(y) + \sum_{y' \geq y} t_{y',y} - \sum_{y' \leq y} t_{y,y'} = g(y) \, \forall y \in Y, t_{y,y'} \geq 0, t_{y,y} = 0. \tag{3.1}$$

To provide an example, let us return to Table 3.2. There, $f$ dominates $g$ since it is possible to obtain $g$ from $f$ by shifting fifteen percentage points of probability mass from outcome $(1,1)$ to $(0,0)$; cf. condition (A). In terms of the linear program in equation (3.1), this implies that for $y = (0,0)$ and $y' = (1,1)$, $t_{y',y} = 0.15$ in

---

[7] The approach differs slightly from that outlined by Mosler and Scarsini (1991) and Dyckerhoff and Mosler (1997). In particular, the transfers here are absolute and not relative. Note furthermore that most linear programming packages require the specification of an objective function. This can be defined as an arbitrary constant function.

order for the equality to be fulfilled for $y = (0, 0)$. Furthermore, for $y = (1, 1)$ and $y' = (0, 0)$, $t_{y,y'} = 0.15$ in order for the equality to be fulfilled for $y = (1, 1)$. It is thus possible to fulfil all the constraints for all $y \in Y$ whereby $f$ dominates $g$. An implementation of the FOD approach using linear programming in GAMS is reviewed in Chapter 4.

### 3.2.3 *Mitigating the Limitations of FOD*

As mentioned previously, due to the absence of strong assumptions such as predetermined weights, there are some inherent limitations to the FOD approach. First, when comparing two groups, it may be the case that no dominations are found and hence the FOD approach might yield an indeterminate result. This provides little information about the populations' relative wellbeing, as was the case when considering $f$ and $h$ with multiple dimensions in section 3.2.2.2. Second, the FOD approach provides no information about the strength of dominance. For example, if population A dominates population B, the FOD check itself provides no information as to whether A is marginally or substantially better than B. Both of these limitations can be mitigated using a bootstrapping approach as described below.

#### 3.2.3.1 BOOTSTRAPPING

To mitigate the limitations mentioned in section 3.2.3, a bootstrapping procedure can be applied (Arndt et al. 2012). In general, bootstrapping is a procedure that relies on random sampling with replacement from the original dataset. When comparing populations A and B, $J$ samples of size $K$ are drawn with replacement for each population group where $K \leq N$, $N$ being the number of individuals in that population in the original sample. In the bootstrap procedure shown in Chapter 4, the samples are drawn in clusters from each stratum with $K = N$. When a cluster is drawn, all households in that cluster are drawn. Due to the drawing with replacement, each cluster (and thus household) may appear more than once. The FOD approach is then applied to each of the $J$ bootstrap samples. When these repeated bootstrap samples are compared using the FOD approach, the final output can be interpreted as an empirical probability that population A dominates population B since the original sample is a subsample from a larger population. These probabilities yield significantly more information than only applying FOD to the original data where, for example, an indeterminate result will make it impossible to draw further conclusions about the comparative wellbeing of the two populations. The bootstrapping procedure thus enables the analyst to extract some information about the strength of conclusions based on the probability of dominance under resampling.

For example, with bootstrapping, we may find that occasionally A dominates B and occasionally the inverse is true, but most of the time the results are indeterminate, i.e. *rough equality* of A and B. Alternatively, we may find that the probability that A dominates B is fairly high, the probability that B dominates A is very low or zero, and the probability of an indeterminate result is somewhat low, i.e. *likely dominance* of A over B, or we might find that A dominates B almost always, i.e. *solid dominance* of A over B.

As a concrete example, say that population A dominates B in 995 of the $J = 1,000$ bootstrap samples and that A dominates C in 870 of the bootstrap samples. This corresponds to a 99.5 per cent chance of A dominating B and an 87 per cent change of A dominating C. In this example, A is thus better than C (*likely dominance* of A over C) and considerably better than B (*solid dominance* of A over B). If no dominations between B and C are obtained in the original sample, the ranking of these is ambiguous. However, if, for example, C dominates B in four (0.4 per cent) of the bootstrap samples whereas B dominates C in eighty (8 per cent) of the bootstrap samples, B is seemingly better than C (though *rough equality* of B and C).

Furthermore, if one is willing to accept the tendency to outperform other groups as an overall relative indicator of population wellbeing, it is possible to provide an intuitive ranking of all population groups via the Copeland (1951) method, which is analogous to the way in which teams are ranked by assigning points to wins, draws, and losses from matchups in a sports tournament. For instance, for each population group ($n$ population groups in total), one can count how many of the $(n-1)$ other population groups it dominates and from that subtract the number of times it is dominated by these other groups. This yields a score in the interval $[-(n-1), n-1]$ which can then be normalized to the interval $[-1, 1]$ (see e.g. Arndt et al. 2016).

## 3.3 Further Considerations

### 3.3.1 *Faster Solution Algorithms*

The linear programming approach presented provides a practical method for checking FOD for many applied problems. For most applications, the method is computationally fast enough to allow for a great number of pairwise comparisons as well as, if desired, hundreds of bootstrap repetitions for each pair of distributions compared. In applications with multiple binary indicators, the linear programming method is particularly suitable.[8]

---

[8] Even with binary indicators, the linear programming approach might actually be computationally challenged, but that is only so if the number of dimensions is large (Hussain et al. 2016).

However, the linear programming approach is not the fastest possible way to make FOD comparisons. Using a network flow formulation of the problem, as outlined in Preston (1974) or Hansel and Troallic (1978), it is possible to check FOD via computation of the maximum flow. As discussed in Range and Østerdal (2013), the problem of checking FOD for multidimensional distributions can also be formulated as a special bipartite network problem related to the classical transportation problem. Generally, these formulations are computationally faster than the linear programming method. In particular, for the bivariate case, Range and Østerdal (2013) provide an algorithm for checking FOD where the worst-case computational complexity grows linearly in the size of the problem (determined by the total number of outcomes).

### 3.3.2 *Alternative Dominance Criterion*

There are many other dominance criteria in the literature than FOD. In general, the alternative dominance criteria all impose stronger underlying assumptions on the underlying utility/social welfare functions. A comprehensive overview of alternative dominance criteria is outside the scope of this chapter—see e.g. Shaked and Shanthikumar (2007) for an extensive review. However, we will compare FOD with the lower-orthant dominance ordering, which is one of the most frequently used alternative dominance criteria in welfare economics.

As mentioned in the Introduction, the FOD approach differs from the criteria for robust welfare comparisons of the Atkinson–Bourguignon type (see Atkinson and Bourguignon 1982; Atkinson and Bourguignon 1987; Bourguignon 1989; Atkinson 1992). These are variations of *orthant stochastic orderings* (see Dyckerhoff and Mosler 1997) even though the name first-order dominance has sometimes been used synonymously with orthant stochastic orderings in the welfare economics literature (e.g. Atkinson and Bourguignon 1982). Orthant dominance is not suitable to ordinal data. However, if one assumes substitutability between dimensions (as e.g. Duclos and Échevin 2011, where substitutability between health and income is assumed, i.e. an underlying utility function with a negative cross-partial derivative), a criterion less restrictive than FOD can be used. In particular, $f$ orthant dominates $g$ if and only if:

$$(C_0) \quad \sum_{z \leq y} g(z) \geq \sum_{z \leq y} f(z) \text{ for all } y \in Y.$$

The label $(C_0)$ is used to indicate that this condition relates to condition (C) in the case of multidimensional FOD in section 3.2.2.1. However, condition $(C_0)$ is less restrictive than (C). This implies that condition $(C_0)$ may be satisfied even though conditions (A), (B), and (C) are not. For a two-dimensional comparison with binary indicators (as in Table 3.2), $f$ orthant dominates $g$ if and only if each of the following three conditions are satisfied:

($i_0$) $g(0,0) \geq f(0,0)$
($ii_0$) $g(0,0) + g(0,1) \geq f(0,0) + f(0,1)$
($iii_0$) $g(0,0) + g(1,0) \geq f(0,0) + f(1,0)$.

The labels ($i_0$)–($iii_0$) are used to indicate that these conditions relate to conditions ($i$)–($iii$) in section 3.2.2.2. Note that the fourth inequality ($iv$) need not be satisfied for orthant dominance. Returning to $f$ and $h$ in Table 3.2, recall that neither $f$ first-order dominates $h$, nor does $h$ first-order dominate $f$. However, in the case of orthant dominance, it can be seen that: ($i_0$) $h(0,0) \geq f(0,0)$ since $0.30 > 0.10$, ($ii_0$) $h(0,0) + h(0,1) \geq f(0,0) + f(0,1)$ since $0.30 + 0.10 > 0.10 + 0.25$, and ($iii_0$) $h(0,0) + h(1,0) \geq f(0,0) + f(1,0)$ since $0.30 + 0.10 > 0.10 + 0.25$. Hence $f$ orthant dominates $h$ even though $f$ does *not* first-order dominate $h$.

## 3.4 Conclusion

Population wellbeing is increasingly recognized as a multidimensional phenomenon that is not adequately described by a single dimension (e.g. by income only). Several methods of measuring and comparing welfare have been proposed where application of a weighting or counting scheme to different dimensions is used. It is often, however, difficult to determine these weights. Due to the sensitivity of the outcome to the weights applied, different conclusions about welfare rankings are likely to occur if the weighting scheme differs from one analysis to another. While comparisons using, for example, lower orthant (stochastic) orderings following Atkinson and Bourguignon (1982) are considerably more 'robust' than applying weighting schemes, they typically apply conditions formulated in terms of the second- (or higher-)order cross-partial derivative and do not apply to ordinal data.

The first-order (stochastic) dominance (FOD) approach requires only that the outcomes in each dimension can be ranked from worse to better. The FOD approach can be applied to ordinal multidimensional data, enabling the analyst to perform wellbeing comparisons across population groups with a minimum of assumptions imposed. FOD is thus robust across all possible weighting schemes. This advantage is accompanied by limitations in that the FOD approach can yield indeterminate outcomes and does not directly provide information with respect to degree of dominance. A bootstrapping approach can be used to obtain more information, thus mitigating these limitations. Moreover, a Copeland approach can be used to obtain a ranking (i.e. a complete and transitive ordering) of all groups being compared.

Finally, it is worth mentioning that even though the FOD approach and bootstrapping procedure enable the analyst to rank population welfare without assumptions about weights, the analysis should ideally be performed together with alternative welfare measurements, which provide cardinal information about the relative size of wellbeing differences under fixed weights assumptions. As Ferreira (2011) puts it, looking at a few core, truly irreducible, dimensions and applying dominance analysis (as well as a number of indices) is likely to contribute to the design and targeting of policy actions. Thus, FOD comparisons should form part of a broader population wellbeing analysis strategy.

# References


Alkire, S. and J. Foster (2011). 'Counting and Multidimensional Poverty Measurement', *Journal of Public Economics*, 95(7–8): 476–87.

Alkire, S., J. Foster, S. Seth, M. E. Santos, J. M. Roche, and P. Ballon (2015). Multidimensional Poverty Measurement and Analysis. Oxford: Oxford University Press.

Arndt, C., R. Distante, M. A. Hussain, L. P. Østerdal, P. L. Huong, and M. Ibraimo (2012). 'Ordinal Welfare Comparisons with Multiple Discrete Indicators: A First Order Dominance Approach and Application to Child Poverty', *World Development*, 40(11): 2290–301.

Arndt, C., M. A. Hussain, S. Vincenzo, F. Tarp, and L. P. Østerdal (2016). 'Poverty Mapping Based on First-Order Dominance with an Example from Mozambique', *Journal of International Development*, 28(1): 3–21.

Atkinson, A. B. (1992). 'Measuring Poverty and Differences in Family Composition', *Economica*, 59(233): 1–16.

Atkinson, A. B. and F. Bourguignon (1982). 'The Comparison of Multi-Dimensioned Distributions of Economic Status', *Review of Economic Studies*, 42(2): 183–201.

Atkinson, A. B. and F. Bourguignon (1987). 'Income Distribution and Differences in Need', in G. R. Feiwek (ed.), *Arrow and the Foundations of the Theory of Economic Policy*. New York: New York University Press, 350–70.

Bourguignon, F. (1989). 'Family Size and Social Utility: Income Distribution Dominance Criteria', *Journal of Econometrics*, 42(1): 67–80.

Bourguignon, F. and S. R. Chakravarty (2003). 'The Measurement of Multidimensional Poverty', *Journal of Economic Inequality*, 1(1): 25–49.

Copeland, A. H. (1951). 'A "Reasonable" Social Welfare Function', University of Michigan Seminar on Applications of Mathematics to the Social Sciences.

Duclos, J.-Y. and D. Échevin (2011). 'Health and Income: A Robust Comparison of Canada and the US', *Journal of Health Economics*, 30(2): 293–302.

Duclos, J.-Y., D. E. Sahn, and S. D. Younger (2006). 'Robust Multidimensional Poverty Comparisons', *Economic Journal*, 116(514): 943–68.

Duclos, J.-Y., D. E. Sahn, and S. D. Younger (2007). 'Robust Multidimensional Poverty Comparisons with Discrete Indicators of Well-Being', in S. P. Jenkins and J. Micklewright (eds), *Inequality and Poverty Re-Examined*. Oxford: Oxford University Press, 185–206.

Dyckerhoff, R. and K. Mosler (1997). 'Orthant Orderings of Discrete Random Vectors', *Journal of Statistical Planning and Inference*, 62(2): 193–205.

Ferreira, F. H. G. (2011). 'Poverty Is Multidimensional. But What Are We Going to Do About It?', *Journal of Economic Inequality*, 9(3): 493–5.

Gravel, N. and P. Moyes (2012). 'Ethically Robust Comparisons of Bidimensional Distributions with an Ordinal Attribute', *Journal of Economic Theory*, 147(4): 1384–1426.

Gravel, N., P. Moyes, and B. Tarroux (2009). 'Robust International Comparisons of Distributions of Disposable Income and Regional Public Goods', *Economica*, 76(303): 432–61.

Gravel, N. and A. Mukhopadhyay (2010). 'Is India Better Off Today than 15 Years Ago? A Robust Multidimensional Answer', *Journal of Economic Inequality*, 8(2): 173–95.

Hansel, G. and J. Troallic (1978). 'Measures marginales et théorème de Ford-Fulkerson', *Zeitschrift für Wahrsheinlichkeitstheorie und verwandte Gebiete*, 43(3): 245–51.

Hussain, M. A. (2016). 'EU Country Rankings' Sensitivity to the Choice of Welfare Indicators', *Social Indicators Research*, 125(1): 1–17.

Kamae, T., U. Krengel, and G. L. O'Brien (1977). 'Stochastic Inequalities on Partially Ordered Spaces', *Annals of Probability*, 5(6): 899–912.

Lehmann, E. L. (1955). 'Ordered Families of Distributions', *Annals of Mathematical Statistics*, 26(3): 399–419.

Levhari, D., J. Paroush, and B. Peleg (1975). 'Efficiency Analysis for Multivariate Distributions', *Review of Economic Studies*, 42(1): 87–91.

Mosler, K. C. and M. R. Scarsini (1991). Stochastic Orders and Decision under Risk. Heyward, CA: Institute of Mathematical Statistics.

Muller, C. and A. Trannoy (2011). 'A Dominance Approach to the Appraisal of the Distribution of Well-Being across Countries', *Journal of Public Economics*, 95(3–4): 239–46.

Preston, C. (1974). 'A Generalization of the FKG Inequalities', *Communications in Mathematical Physics*, 36(3): 233–41.

Range, T. M. and L. P. Østerdal (2013). 'Checking Bivariate First Order Dominance', Discussion Papers on Business and Economics No. 9/2013. Odense: Department of Business and Economics, University of Southern Denmark.

Rippin, N. (2010). 'Poverty Severity in a Multidimensional Framework: The Issue of Inequality between Dimensions', Courant Research Centre, Poverty, Equity and Growth Discussion Paper 47. Göttingen: University of Göttingen.

Roelen, K. and F. Gassmann (2008). 'Measuring Child Poverty and Wellbeing: A Literature Review', Maastricht Graduate School of Governance Working Paper Series 2008/WP001. Maastricht: Maastricht University.

Sen, A. K. (1976). 'Poverty: An Ordinal Approach to Measurement', *Econometrica*, 44(2): 219–31.

Sen, A. K. (1988). The Standard of Living. Cambridge: Cambridge University Press.

Shaked, M. and J. G. Shanthikumar (2007). Stochastic Orders. New York: Springer Science and Business Media.

Strassen, V. (1965). 'The Existence of Probability Measures with Given Marginals', *Annals of Mathematical Statistics*, 36(2): 423–39.

World Bank (1990). World Development Report 1990: Poverty. New York: Oxford University Press for the World Bank.

Østerdal, L. P. (2010). 'The Mass Transfer Approach to Multivariate Discrete First Order Stochastic Dominance: Direct Proof and Implications', *Journal of Mathematical Economics*, 46(6): 1222–8.

# 4

# Estimation in Practice

*Channing Arndt and Kristi Mahrt*

## 4.1 Introduction

Chapters 2 and 3 in this book present the theoretical foundations to the cost of basic needs (CBN) and the first-order dominance (FOD) approaches. This chapter furthers the discussion by outlining how each approach translates from theory to the practical estimation of poverty/wellbeing. In this chapter, we provide an overview of the specific steps involved in estimation and highlight the analyst's role in customizing procedures to individual country contexts.

The procedures in focus here are implemented via sets of Stata and GAMS code. The code whose default stream is associated with the utility-consistent CBN approach is referred to as the Poverty Line Estimation Analytical Software (PLEASe). The procedure for FOD analysis is called Estimating FOD (EFOD). The PLEASe and EFOD user guides contain more detailed descriptions of the technical aspects of implementation such as data requirements and particulars of the code.

The remainder of this chapter provides an overview of the steps taken in the PLEASe and EFOD code streams. Within this overview, references are made to the country-specific applications of PLEASe and EFOD presented in Part II. These references highlight a few of the methodological challenges encountered in implementation, incorporation of country-specific factors, and considerations in interpreting results, including making comparisons with other poverty analyses.

## 4.2 PLEASe

The default PLEASe approach, which follows the basic CBN methodology, has four notable features. First, the typical consumption pattern of the reference population, poor households, is estimated using an iterative procedure to identify which households are deemed poor. Second, the approach allows for the definition of multiple spatial domains. Within these domains, poverty lines are estimated allowing for flexible consumption bundles that vary over time and space, thus accounting for differences in regional and temporal consumption patterns. Third, revealed preference tests are employed to ensure that regional and temporal consumption bundles represent a consistent level of utility. Finally, if these revealed preference conditions fail, a minimum cross-entropy methodology is employed to adjust consumption bundles to satisfy constraints. When calculating poverty lines in multiple periods, data is carried forward to enable both spatial and temporal revealed preference comparisons and for the imposition of both spatial and temporal revealed preference constraints on estimated bundles.

It is important to emphasize that the PLEASe approach and the associated Stata and GAMS code are meant to provide a framework for *initiating* analysis from an advanced base rather than to prescribe an exact set of methodological choices. The analyst must consider the country environment and perhaps the legacy of existing poverty estimation procedures to tailor the methodology as appropriate. The PLEASe methodology can accommodate a wide range of methodological variation, such as whether to use a single national consumption bundle or regional bundles, whether to impose spatial and/or temporal utility consistency, and a multitude of other choices as well.

### 4.2.1 *Consumption*

Poverty estimation begins with the choice of a welfare indicator. Consumption is normally the preferred metric in monetary poverty estimation for a number of reasons. Most importantly, consumption is smoother with fewer fluctuations than income. Additionally, consumption is likely to more effectively capture the welfare derived from self-employment, which is particularly relevant in developing countries where large portions of the population engage in self-employed activities, notably in agriculture.

To account for household composition, the default welfare measure in the PLEASe approach is per capita household consumption. An alternative normalization, using some form of adult equivalent scale, can be implemented with relatively little recoding. For instance, to maintain consistency with official methodologies in Pakistan, Whitney et al. (Chapter 9) employ an adult-equivalent scale rather than per capita consumption.

Deaton and Zaidi (2002) and Deaton and Grosh (2000) detail the assembly of consumption data from household surveys. Consumption provides a measure of the total value of food and non-food consumed, which includes purchases, home-produced items, and gifts received, as well as the use values of household durable goods and the imputed rent of owner-occupied housing. As stated in Chapter 2, section 2.3, the consumption measure excludes the value of home-produced services and public goods and services. In the default PLEASe code, household consumption provides the basis for estimating food prices, food consumption bundles, and a non-food allowance. Therefore, the value and quantity of food consumed are required at the household and product level whereas non-food consumption values can be aggregated at the household level.[1]

Seasonal food price fluctuations imply that purchasing power is not constant throughout the year. Without accounting for seasonality, welfare would appear to be higher during relatively expensive periods when the quantity of food consumed remains constant. When appropriate, the PLEASe methodology incorporates an intra-temporal price index to adjust nominal food consumption values within the survey period.

### 4.2.2 Poverty Lines

#### 4.2.2.1 FOOD POVERTY LINES

Flexible spatial and temporal food poverty lines are determined by the consumption patterns of poor households in a given domain. The methodology allows consumption bundles and the corresponding poverty lines to be estimated regionally in each time period to allow for variations in prices, preferences, and household composition. When relevant, both flexible and fixed (i.e. previous-period bundles with current-period prices) poverty lines are generated.

As discussed in Chapter 2, estimating regional food consumption improves the specificity of the poverty lines, allowing the poverty lines to reflect regional consumption patterns (Thorbecke 2004). These regional bundles capture the substitution between goods that occurs as prices vary by region. Selecting spatial domains merits careful consideration of factors such as rural and urban distinctions and regional homogeneity in pricing and preferences.

When selecting spatial domains, one must be careful not to *overlook sample size in each spatial domain.* Note that, in the default implementation of PLEASe, consumption bundles are defined based on the consumption patterns of the poor. Thus, in areas with relatively few poor households, the size of the domain may need to be larger in order to generate a sufficiently large sample of poor households.

---

[1] When quantities of food consumed are not available, food prices from other sources may be substituted in analysis provided that they are collected for a sufficiently wide variety of foods and at a sufficiently detailed regional level to adequately capture price variation.

The analyst is encouraged to err initially on the side of defining too few spatial domains rather than too many. Experience in, for example, Ethiopia (Stifel and Woldehanna, Chapter 5) indicates that division into an excessive number of spatial domains can cause computational difficulties and may, as a consequence, generate nonsensical results. The PLEASe framework allows the analyst to easily change the number of spatial domains in order to conduct sensitivity analysis. Analysis of robust price and consumption differentials, along with sample size, should guide the choice of spatial domain.

Regional food poverty lines are based on four factors: average regional caloric needs; the typical composition of the diet consumed in poor households; the caloric content of this diet relative to regional caloric needs; and the cost of obtaining this diet at prevailing domain-specific prices. For the first factor, the default PLEASe approach estimates an average daily regional caloric requirement based on regional demographics. Specifically, target caloric needs within each spatial domain are adjusted not only according to the gender and age composition of each region, but also according to local fertility rates and the probability of breastfeeding.

For the second factor, identifying the typical food choices and prices relevant to poor households requires a method for determining reference households. For instance, the reference households could be all households with consumption below median consumption or below the previous period's poverty line. The default PLEASe approach aims to define reference households as those who are deemed poor. However, which households are actually poor is not known a priori. To ensure that the subset of poor households selected is actually poor in terms of the poverty lines drawn by the CBN methodology, an iterative procedure is adopted following Ravallion (1994). Initially, households within each spatial domain are ranked by total per capita daily consumption and an arbitrarily specified bottom percentile of households is selected. This initial bottom percentile should be a best prior estimate of the poverty rate.

Preliminary estimates of regional poverty lines are obtained based on the consumption patterns of this initial set of poor households. A series of steps, described in more detail below in this section, are then performed in order to derive a preliminary estimate of poverty rates. The new bottom percentile is then defined by these poverty rates with the reference set of households becoming those who are defined as poor. This process is repeated until estimated poverty rates converge with the rate determining the reference set of households, which generally occurs within only a few iterations.

Though the default PLEASe method identifies reference households via the iterative procedure, the code is flexible, allowing the analyst to choose alternative approaches. For instance, in their analysis of consumption poverty in Ethiopia, Stifel and Woldehanna (Chapter 5) encounter a failure to converge in several regions and thus eliminate the iterative procedure. Whitney et al. (Chapter 9) strive to maintain procedural consistency with official poverty estimates for Pakistan by omitting the iterative procedure and instead identifying reference households as those with consumption in the bottom sixtieth percentile. Note that this approach also has the advantage of setting the sample on which calculations are performed to a fixed value. Beck et al. (Chapter 7) also maintain consistency with the official Malawian methodology by selecting reference households as the bottom sixtieth percentile of consumption on a national basis; however, this is accomplished without eliminating the iterative procedure. Rather, consumption is deflated after each iteration using spatial price indices derived from regional poverty lines, thus altering the regional composition of the bottom sixtieth percentile of households on a national basis.

In each iteration, we determine the set of unit prices (i.e. seasonally adjusted consumption value divided by quantity) prevailing among poor households in each spatial domain. After tossing out the top and bottom 5 per cent of household-level prices, food prices in each spatial domain are calculated as the value share weighted mean price per gram. Specifically, in each spatial domain, household weighted aggregate expenditure is divided by household weighted aggregate quantity. As an alternative, mean and median household unit prices are computed and can be substituted for value share weighted prices. These pricing choices frequently have material impacts on calculated poverty rates and should be held constant both across space and through time.

We also trim the bundles in order to focus on the most commonly consumed food items among the poor. Specifically, the top 90 per cent of food items are selected according to their share of the total food expenditure among all poor households. Eliminating this bottom 10 per cent drops a normally long list of foods consumed by a relatively few households. As the bottom echelon of food expenditures tends to contain expensive calories, we assume that 90 per cent of food consumption represents 95 per cent of caloric intake. In line with the third and fourth of the four factors mentioned above, food quantities are scaled such that bundles attain 95 per cent of regional caloric needs while maintaining food share compositions. Finally, the total cost of purchasing food bundles at local prices is divided by 0.9 to reflect 100 per cent of food expenditures, which yields food poverty lines.

### 4.2.2.2 NON-FOOD POVERTY LINES

Non-food poverty lines estimate the cost of acquiring non-food items essential to achieving minimum welfare. Attaining a minimum welfare level requires certain basic non-food expenditures necessary for both survival and participation in essential aspects of society such as school and employment

(Ravallion 1998). Therefore, even what is deemed as essential food consumption may be forgone in order to acquire items such as basic shelter, clothing, and healthcare.

Households with total consumption at or below the food poverty line then, by definition, do not meet their basic food needs as long as some consumption expenditure is allocated to non-food. In other words, these households must sacrifice a basic caloric diet in order to acquire non-food items. Therefore, expenditures on non-food items by these households are considered as required for meeting essential non-food needs. In the default PLEASe methodology, regional non-food poverty lines are estimated to be the average non-food consumption of households with total consumption within 20 per cent of the food poverty line. In calculating this average, a triangular weighting scheme is used to give greater weight to households with total consumption closer to the food poverty line.

This is only one of many methods for setting non-food poverty lines. For example, it may be useful to consider households with food consumption rather than total consumption in the neighbourhood of the food poverty line. In this case, the household meets basic food needs and therefore any non-food spending is at or in excess of what is necessary to achieve minimum welfare. Ravallion (1998) refers to this approach as an upper bound on the non-food poverty line. Beck et al. (Chapter 7) maintain consistency with official estimates by following this upper-bound approach in Malawi. Alternatively, rather than calculate the average non-food consumption of households near the poverty line, one could calculate average food shares of total consumption for those with either total consumption or food consumption near the food poverty line. Food shares would then be used to scale the food poverty line to obtain the total poverty line. Each of these approaches may be preferred in a given country context and can relatively easily be implemented with a few lines of recoding.

### 4.2.3 *Poverty Measurement*

The total poverty line is the sum of the food poverty line and the non-food poverty line and serves as a threshold for separating poor and non-poor households. From these regional poverty lines, regional poverty rates are derived using the Foster Greer Thorbecke (FGT) class of poverty measures (Foster et al. 1984).

In the iterative procedure for estimating poverty lines, the regional poverty headcount rates calculated as discussed in section 4.2.2 provide an updated estimate of the percentile of per capita consumption that identifies a household as poor. It is now possible to redefine the reference set of poor households and to identify new consumption bundles, prices, and corresponding poverty lines. This iterative procedure is repeated a default of five times. After five iterations, it is normally the case that the poverty rates calculated in iteration four are very close to the poverty rates calculated in iteration five. This convergence implies that the estimated food and non-food bundles are based on the consumption patterns of the poor. However, convergence is not guaranteed even with a very large number of iterations. Graphs are produced to provide a visual check of convergence. Analysts are strongly encouraged to verify convergence. If convergence fails, the analyst would then be forced to choose an arbitrary share of the population as the reference population.

### 4.2.4 *Utility Consistency*

Having identified a set of regional poverty lines based on the consumption patterns of the poor, the PLEASe methodology addresses the possibility that, while the poverty lines provide a measure of welfare in each region, they may not provide a consistent measure of welfare levels across regions or through time. Utility consistency is assessed by testing revealed preference conditions on the food consumption bundles and prices obtained in the final iteration. Prior to conducting these tests, the bundles are rescaled to provide a constant level of calories across regions (and through time). Should the bundles fail revealed preference tests, the first step is to consider why this may be the case. This is particularly true if failures are widespread and/or of very large magnitude. An error may have entered into the calculations or data. Errors in units are particularly common. If a quantity in a bundle is in grams and its associated price is in currency units per kilogram, then this error has the potential to severely bias estimates.

Aside from checking for errors, the analyst should also consider whether any additional information can be brought to bear in order to arrive at improved estimates. This hunt for additional information is highly consistent with the philosophy of estimation that underlies the minimum cross-entropy procedure presented in Chapter 2, section 2.5. The philosophy of estimation is to impose all available information and nothing more.[2] Once all available information has been exploited, the minimum cross-entropy estimation approach can be justifiably applied to adjust consumption bundles to satisfy revealed preference conditions as well as calorie requirements.

Within the minimum cross-entropy procedure, spatial revealed preference conditions are as in equation (2.4a) in Chapter 2 and reproduced in equation (4.1). Temporal conditions are illustrated in equations (4.2) and (4.3). In the

---

[2] See Robinson, Cattaneo, and El-Said (2001) for a discussion and further references.

case where temporal conditions are applied, they are simply added to the constraint set of the optimization problem depicted in Chapter 2, equation 2.4.

$$\sum_i p_{ir}^2 * q_{is}^2 \geq \sum_i p_{ir}^2 * q_{ir}^2 \qquad \forall r,s \ \ r \neq s \tag{4.1}$$

$$\sum_i p_{ir}^2 * q_{ir}^1 \geq \sum_i p_{ir}^2 * q_{ir}^2 \qquad \forall r \tag{4.2}$$

$$\sum_i p_{ir}^1 * q_{ir}^2 \geq \sum_i p_{ir}^1 * q_{ir}^1 \qquad \forall r \tag{4.3}$$

In these equations, $i$ indexes food products; $r$ and its alias, $s$, represent the set of spatial domains; and, $p^1, p^2, q^1, q^2$ represent prices and quantities in the first and second time period. The logic of the temporal constraints is the same as the logic of the spatial bundle. Consider equation (4.3), for example: this condition states that the bundle chosen in period 2 in region $r$ when evaluated at period 1 prices must, by minimization, cost at least as much as the bundle that was actually chosen when period 1 prices prevailed, assuming the bundles provide the same level of utility. The analyst can choose to impose spatial constraints, spatial and temporal constraints, or bypass utility consistency and impose no constraints.[3]

After entropy-adjusting quantities to obtain utility-consistent food bundles, the bundles are evaluated at the regional food prices obtained in the final iteration. New non-food poverty lines are estimated using the same approach as applied in the iterative procedure. The utility-consistent total poverty line in each domain is the sum of the utility-consistent food poverty line and the updated non-food poverty line. From here, final FGT poverty measures and spatial price indices are computed.

Note that the default PLEASe approach sequentially ensures temporal constraints are met. Consider an analysis of three surveys undertaken in different time periods. First-period poverty lines are estimated imposing only the regional revealed preferences constraint (equation 4.1) because there are no pre-existing bundles. Second-period poverty lines should be utility-consistent between regions (equation 4.1) as well as the first and second periods (equations 4.2 and 4.3), which is achieved by leaving first-period food bundles intact and adjusting second-period bundles to satisfy all three constraints. Finally, third-period utility consistency involves testing revealed preferences spatially as well as between the second and third periods (not the first) and adjusting only third-period food bundles. As emphasized, these are the default settings, not a prescription for how things should be done in every case.

---

[3] The existence of viable prices to operationalize revealed preference tests is sometimes an issue. For example, region A may consume a particular type of dried fish, but region B does not consume that particular type at all or only very rarely. The price of dried fish in region B is thus not known. The default PLEASe solution is to apply the maximum price observed in any spatial domain to region B. This default may or may not be appropriate, depending on country and region circumstances.

## 4.3 EFOD

This section considers the estimation of multidimensional poverty and presents the implementation of FOD and its associated package of Stata and GAMS code, EFOD. Compared to poverty line estimation with the complexities of assembling consumption data and the array of choices possible throughout the PLEASe approach, EFOD is relatively easy to implement. In contrast, EFOD requires significant effort in determining which indicators to use and somewhat more effort in interpreting results. Briefly, the procedure involves three key stages: creating indicators, operationalizing FOD, and interpreting results.

### 4.3.1 *Indicators*

The heart of FOD analysis involves carefully assembling a set of binary welfare indicators. This process involves several key steps. First, one requires data. This can come in the form of Demographic and Health Surveys, census data, or data from living standards measurement (LSMS-type) surveys, among other possibilities.

Second, one must organize the data into populations and then into groups whose welfare levels one would like to compare. There are enormous possibilities for populations and division into groups. An example of a population to study might be children aged 0–5. This population could be grouped by gender, province, and time period. One would then be setting up to examine whether, for example, girls aged 0–5 in province $A$ at time $T$ are better off than boys aged 0–5 in province $A$ at time $T$ alongside many other possible permutations. A second population example could be households and subsequent groups determined by the ethnicity of the household head. One would then be setting up to examine whether households headed by ethnic group $A$ are better off than households headed by ethnic group $B$ and so forth.

Third, one must define welfare indicators. As noted, proper definition of indicators is critical. The indicators must apply to the population in question. If the population is children aged 0–5, then an indicator like school attendance is not relevant because children that young typically do not attend school. School attendance would more properly apply to the population of children aged 7–17. For children aged 0–5, relevant indicators often include anthropometric data, education level of the mother or primary caretaker, proximity and/or use of health services, and other similar indicators.

Note that FOD analysis requires each observation to have non-missing values in all indicators, which could eliminate particular indicators from consideration. For example, immunization histories are often collected only for children under two, thus prohibiting the use of an immunization indicator when analysing children aged 0–5. In a discussion of child and woman indicators in Tanzania, Arndt et al. (Chapter 14) further explore indicator choices for subpopulations.

Mahrt and Nanivaso (Chapter 11) address an additional consideration in selecting indicators—the potential for different patterns of deprivation across indicators to result in indeterminate outcomes. FOD dominance requires superior welfare outcomes to be manifested throughout the population and across indicators. While this property generates robust results, in some cases it may lead to high levels of indeterminacy. For example, if rural and urban deprivation in a given indicator is significantly different from of the deprivation pattern in all other indicators, FOD comparisons are likely to result in a high degree of indeterminate outcomes. This is seen in the inclusion of a bed net indicator in FOD analysis in the Democratic Republic of Congo (Chapter 11) and a shared sanitation facility indicator in Zambia (Mahrt and Masumbu, Chapter 15). In such cases the contribution of the indicator must be weighed against the resulting inability to clarify differences.

Setting thresholds within each indicator to separate the poor from the non-poor requires a careful balance of policy goals, data availability, and consistency between time periods. It is important to highlight that, while the FOD procedure admits in principle ordinal data, in practice, EFOD is coded to consider only binary data. Hence, one might classify children aged 0–5 who are any one of stunted, underweight, or wasted as deprived (0) in the anthropometrics dimension and all others as not deprived (1). Similarly, one might consider children whose primary caretaker has completed at least primary school as not deprived and all others as deprived. As will be discussed in subsequent chapters, these thresholds (e.g. completed primary school) are often important determinants of results and should be considered carefully.[4] The end result should be a dataset where each member of the population is an observation. Variables identify the group to which this population member belongs and the welfare status (deprived or not deprived) of the population member for each chosen welfare indicator.

Finally, one must consider the number of binary indicators to employ for the analysis. Note that the number of permutations of welfare states increases by a factor of two with the addition of each indicator. Specifically, there are $2^N$ permutations where $N$ is the number of indicators chosen. There are trade-offs here. More indicators imply a broader analysis. At the same time, more indictors lead to many more permutations, eventually resulting in a very small

---

[4] Survey data may not allow indicator thresholds to align with policy goals or perceptions of deprivation. Chapters 13 and 15 explore the impact of indicator thresholds, in analyses of household welfare in Nigeria and Zambia, respectively.

number of observations occupying certain permutations even for very large datasets. For example, if one chooses to make comparisons on the basis of seven indicators, there are then $2^7$=128 possible permutations. Example permutations include those deprived in all indicators {0,0,0,0,0,0,0}, those not deprived in all indicators {1,1,1,1,1,1,1}, those not deprived in indicator one and deprived in all other indicators {1,0,0,0,0,0,0}, and so forth (125 additional permutations). Because of this 'curse of dimensionality', the available code handles only up to seven indicators. Further, because we are often making comparisons between specific subgroups (e.g. children aged 0–5 in region $A$ at time $T$ versus children aged 0–5 in region $B$ at time $T$), the number of observations for these groups may be insufficient to adequately populate 128 permutations. In practice, five dimensions are often chosen, resulting in $2^5$=32 permutations.[5]

### 4.3.2 *Implementing EFOD*

Once a dataset specifying populations, groups, and indicators is assembled, it is straightforward to collapse the data to show means as well as the shares of each group by permutation. For example, with five welfare indicators, mean values of .10, .52, .31, .29, .33 respectively for girls in region $A$ and time $T$ would indicate that 10 per cent of girls in that region and time period are not deprived in indicator one, 52 per cent are not deprived in indicator two, and so forth.

Each permutation also has a corresponding share. If 1 per cent of girls aged 0–5 in region $A$ and at time $T$ are not deprived in any dimensions, then the permutation (1,1,1,1,1) has the corresponding value or share 0.01. Note that each permutation thus corresponds to a particular welfare state. Within each subpopulation, the sum of shares across the thirty-two welfare states (permutations) should be equal to one. This procedure generates the distributions for each subpopulation.

To conduct the FOD analysis, these distributions for all subpopulations to be compared are fed into a GAMS program that implements the linear programming approach to determining FOD presented in Chapter 3. This generates one set of comparisons using the original data. The option exists to draw bootstrap samples from the original data in order to run a much larger number of comparisons, producing an estimated probability of domination.

---

[5] If the dimensions can be naturally grouped, one may initially collapse related dimensions into a single dimension and then (sequentially) refine dimensions. For more details and an illustration of such an approach, see Hussain et al. (2015).

### 4.3.3 *Output and Interpretation*

A series of outputs are automatically generated and presented in three sets of tables consisting of means, shares, and FOD results. Spatial FOD results make comparisons across groups (e.g. girls in region $A$ compared with region $B$) within a single time period. Temporal results compare each group to itself across time periods. Both spatial and temporal results are presented for the original data (static) and the bootstraps. In static results, 1 indicates dominance and 0 indicates indeterminacy. Bootstrap results indicate the probability of domination over all bootstrap samples. The probability that $A$ dominates $B$ is defined as the number of times $A$ dominates $B$ divided by the number of samples. Recognizing that $A$ can dominate $B$ as well as $B$ dominate $A$, the probability of net domination measures the probability that $A$ dominates $B$ less the probability that $B$ dominates $A$. The probability of net domination falls in the interval $[-1,1]$. Spatial rankings are generated based on a Copeland approach, which is described in Chapter 3. In effect, the Copeland approach calculates the average probability that a given area net dominates all other areas. Care must be taken in interpreting the subset of ranking results where differences in probabilities of domination are very small. In these cases, results are highly sensitive to small perturbations introduced through bootstrap sampling.

Interpreting FOD results may require more investigation than simply glancing over tables. Indeterminate results generally occur when two groups are either very different or very similar. For example, if few areas show signs of advancement or regression over time, it is worth the effort to determine the source of stagnation. Examination of indicator means may shed light on the source of stagnation. A given area may not rigorously progress for dynamic reasons, such as good progress in some indicators and regress in others. Alternatively, very little may have happened over time in any indicator and the FOD analysis is simply reflecting this lack of progress. Finally, recall that FOD results depend on the full distribution of indicator outcomes. Thus, it is possible for a region to progress on average through time but for FOD to result in an indeterminate outcome. Such a result would suggest that the region's seemingly superior performance did not extend to all segments of the population. In sum, dominant outcomes are strong indicators of broad-based progression throughout the population.

We turn now to a series of practical applications in Part II.

## References

Deaton, A. and M. Grosh (2000). 'Consumption', in M. Grosh and P. Glewwe (eds), *Designing Household Survey Questionnaires for Developing Countries: Lessons from Ten Years of LSMS Experience*. Washington, DC: World Bank, 91–133.

Deaton, A. and S. Zaidi (2002). 'Guidelines for Constructing Consumption Aggregates for Welfare Analysis', Living Standards Measurement Study Working Paper No. 135. Washington, DC: World Bank.

Foster, J., J. Greer, and E. Thorbecke (1984). 'A Class of Decomposable Poverty Measures', *Econometrica*, 52(3): 761–5.

Hussain, M. A., M. M. Jørgensen, and L. P. Østerdal (2015). 'Refining Population Health Comparisons: A Multidimensional First Order Dominance Approach', *Social Indicators Research*. Available online: DOI: 10.1007/s11205-015-1115-2

Ravallion, M. (1994). *Poverty Comparisons*. Geneva: Harwood Academic Publishers.

Ravallion, M. (1998). 'Poverty Lines in Theory and Practice', Living Standards Measurement Study Working Paper No. 133. Washington DC: World Bank.

Robinson, S., A. Cattaneo, and M. El-Said (2001). 'Updating and Estimating a Social Accounting Matrix Using Cross Entropy Methods', *Economic Systems Research*, 13(1): 47–64.

Thorbecke, E. (2004). 'Conceptual and Measurement Issues in Poverty Analysis', WIDER Discussion Paper 04. Helsinki: UNU-WIDER.

# Part II
# Country Applications

# 5

# Estimating Utility-Consistent Poverty in Ethiopia, 2000–11

*David Stifel and Tassew Woldehanna*

## 5.1 Introduction

Since the turn of the century, the Ethiopian economy has experienced strong economic growth and structural improvements. Rapid infrastructure growth, increased agricultural production and commercialization, better-functioning food markets, and a strong social safety net programme are all part of the changing economic landscape (Dorosh and Schmidt 2010) that is likely to have paid dividends in terms of poverty reduction. Yet measuring these dividends in Ethiopia is complicated by conceptual and practical data-related issues. This is not surprising given the complexity of measuring poverty in a manner that is consistent over time and space, yet is also sensitive to local conditions.

There are two important measurement issues related to the consistency and specificity of poverty estimates over time and space. First, evidence that differing commodity lists (Pradhan 2000) and recall periods (Scott and Amenuvegbe 1990) affect the levels of reported consumption from household surveys highlights the importance of the comparability of the data used to construct nominal household consumption aggregates. Second, the appropriate estimation of poverty lines is also essential not only as a poverty threshold, but also as a cost-of-living index that allows interpersonal welfare comparisons when the costs of consuming basic needs vary over time and space (Ravallion 1998). The challenge is to estimate poverty lines that are consistent over time and space (i.e. the reference standard of living is fixed), and yet are also characterized by specificity in which the poverty lines reflect local consumption patterns and norms (Ravallion and Bidani 1994).

The purpose of this chapter is to describe how the standardized PLEASe computer code stream based on Arndt and Simler's (2010) utility-consistent approach to measuring consumption poverty can be adapted in order to analyse poverty in Ethiopia in 2000, 2005, and 2011. We document how the utility-consistent approach to spatial deflation differs from the approach undertaken by the national statistical office to produce the official poverty estimates (i.e. using consumer price indices), and how the trends in these estimates differ. Further, we highlight the importance of accounting for changes in the duration and time of year for data collection, and how this can be especially problematic for consistency in the presence of annual inflation of over 30 per cent. In addition, the Ethiopia case provides an example of the challenge of conducting revealed preference tests of the utility consistency of regionally estimated poverty lines (i.e. do the consumption patterns in other spatial domains cost no less than the own-domain consumption patterns when both are evaluated at own-domain prices) when spatial consumption patterns differ substantially.

The structure of this chapter is as follows. In section 5.2, we elaborate on the methodology and describe the primary data sources. Section 5.3 describes how the data were prepared for the exercise and how the PLEASe code was adapted for these data. In section 5.4, we present the estimates of poverty based on the utility-consistent approach to calculating poverty lines, and explore the differences between these estimates and the original estimates made by the Ethiopian Central Statistics Agency (CSA) (MoFED 2008 and MoFED 2012). Section 5.5 provides concluding remarks.

## 5.2 Methodology and Data

In this section, we briefly describe the methodology and primary data sources used to measure poverty and inequality in a manner that is consistent over time and space, and which is specific to local consumption patterns and norms.

### 5.2.1 *Methodology*

As with any analysis of poverty, choices need to be made regarding (i) the welfare indicator, (ii) the threshold between the poor and the non-poor, and (iii) the measure of poverty. First, in this particular analysis, we concentrate on a money measure of welfare—per capita household consumption. The household consumption aggregate that we use as our welfare indicator is constructed in a standard manner by aggregating food and non-food expenditures, the estimated value of own-produced food and non-food items and of in-kind payments, gifts received, and the estimated use value of durable goods and housing (Deaton and Zaidi 2002).

Second, with regard to the poverty threshold, we estimate poverty lines[1] for twenty spatial domains in Ethiopia (Addis Ababa, Harari, and urban and rural areas for the Afar, Amhara, Benishangul-Gumuz, Dire Dawa, Gambella, Oromiya, SNNP, Somali, and Tigray regions). Food poverty lines are estimated first, and are anchored to calorie requirements that are calculated for purposes of specificity separately for each domain based on the demographic structure and fertility patterns in the domain. This is a departure from the common practice for poverty analysis in Ethiopia of using a standard requirement of 2200 calories per person per day, with the poverty line calculated in 1995/6 and adjusted for inflation for analysis in later years. An iterative approach is used to find the least-cost consumption bundle that meets domain-specific calorie requirements and that reflects consumption patterns of the poor in the spatial domain. This provides specific initial estimates of the food poverty lines. Revealed preference tests are then conducted to test the utility consistency of these poverty lines (i.e. do the consumption patterns in other spatial domains cost no less than the own-domain consumption patterns when both are evaluated at own-domain prices). When the tests are violated, maximum-entropy methods are used to reconcile the differences so that domain specificity is maintained in the new poverty lines, while utility consistency is not violated.[2] Once the region-specific food poverty lines are determined, they are scaled up by the share of non-food consumption representative of the households around the food poverty lines, to get the region-specific poverty lines.

With the welfare indicators and poverty lines in hand, we primarily employ the Foster–Greer–Thorbecke (1984) class of poverty indices to measure levels and changes in poverty. We also move beyond the use of poverty indices to analyse changes in poverty by employing standard tests of stochastic dominance. In order to do this, we note that poverty lines are more than poverty thresholds, they also serve as cost-of-living indexes that allow interpersonal welfare comparisons. As such, we use the poverty lines to map nominal household consumption to real household consumption using indexes constructed from these poverty lines (Blackorby and Donaldson 1987). Once mapped into comparable real values, the distributions of household consumption are then used to conduct dominance tests and to measure inequality.

---

[1] See Chapter 2 of this book for more details about the general procedure. The household consumption aggregates and poverty lines were calculated using the PLEASe software.

[2] We note that revealed preference conditions should also hold over time (i.e. do the consumption patterns in the same spatial domain but in different time periods cost no less than the own-domain consumption patterns at a specific time when both are evaluated at own-domain prices for that specific time). When these conditions are violated over time, similar maximum-entropy methods can be used to reconcile the differences (Arndt and Simler 2010).

### 5.2.2 Data

The primary data sources used in this analysis are the 1999/2000 (hereafter 2000), 2004/5 (hereafter 2005) and 2010/11 (hereafter 2011) Ethiopia Household Income, Consumption and Expenditure Surveys (HICES). The HICES, conducted by the Central Statistical Agency (CSA), are nationally representative stratified and clustered surveys that contain information on household characteristics, expenditure, activities, and infrastructure. The main objective of the HICES was to provide data on levels, distributions, and patterns of household income, consumption, and expenditures.

Given that the HICES are used to construct the household consumption aggregates for the analysis of monetary poverty, it is important to be aware of comparability issues related to them. Coverage of the three surveys is similar (major urban areas, rural regions, and other urban areas), and although the sample sizes grew from 17,332, to 21,274, to 27,830, for the 2000, 2005, and 2011 surveys, respectively, this is unlikely to affect the comparability of the welfare measures over time. There are, however, other differences in the data collection method that may be problematic. First, although the questionnaires are nearly identical, the item codes used for the expenditure/consumption recall differed for each of the three years. For example, the numbers of food codes used in the data collection process were 252, 872, and 653 in the 2000, 2005, and 2011 surveys respectively. Evidence that more detailed lists of commodity items are associated with higher levels of reported consumption from household surveys (Pradhan 2000) warrants care in interpreting changes in poverty given that the household consumption aggregates may not be entirely comparable.

Second, the change in the data collection period complicates comparability due to issues of seasonality and inflation. The 2000 and 2005 surveys were conducted in two relatively short and similarly timed rounds (July–August and January–February) during low inflation periods, whereas the 2011 survey was conducted over the course of a year (8 July 2010 to 7 July 2011) that was characterized by inflation of over 30 per cent.[3] Further, it is difficult to gauge the consequences that seasonal variation in consumption patterns may have on the comparability of the 2011 consumption aggregate relative to the aggregates from the earlier surveys. As a form of sensitivity analysis, we estimated poverty lines on the subset of the sample of households in the 2011 survey who were interviewed in the same quarters as those in the 2000 and 2005 surveys. Although the poverty estimates from this subsample do not

---

[3] Headey et al. (2012) document a rapid rise in urban food prices for the poor during the 2011 survey period that outpaced the growth of urban nominal wages.

differ substantively from those of the full sample, we remain cautious about interpreting changes in poverty between these surveys.

## 5.3 Application of PLEASe

### 5.3.1 *Data Preparation*

The bulk of the work in applying PLEASe to the Ethiopia household survey data was related to preparing the data themselves. The PLEASe manual (Arndt et al. 2013) provides guidance for creating standard data files with common variable names. We therefore do not elaborate on this here. But it is worth emphasizing that in following the manual it is important to pay close attention to the units (e.g. daily and metric) and to item codes when preparing the data as these have the potential to be an unnecessary source of error. In addition, certain country-specific decisions need to be made in the process of preparing the data.

For Ethiopia, the choice of the spatial domains ('spdomain' in 'hhdata.dta') and the number of iterations used to calculate initial poverty lines were complicated by convergence problems encountered when running the PLEASe code on the 2011 data. Initially, the domains were defined over the urban and rural areas in the chartered city of Dire Dawa and the nine ethnically-based and politically autonomous regional states, as well as the chartered city of Addis Ababa (only urban). But when the PLEASe code was run on the 2011 data, the program encountered problems while iterating over the poverty lines that would then be used to prepare the data for the revealed preference tests. As noted in Arndt et al. (2013), the program estimates initial poverty lines by valuing the minimum cost of consuming domain-specific calorie requirements based on the consumption patterns of the poorest $X$ per cent households in each domain, where $X$ is defined by the user. This process is repeated over five iterations using the poverty lines from the previous iteration as the thresholds for determining the consumption patterns of the poor households. Five iterations generally result in poverty lines and consumption patterns that converge to steady values. In some spatial domains (e.g. rural and urban Benshangul, rural Gambella, and rural and urban Harari), however, poverty dropped so low after the second iteration that there were too few poor households to calculate poverty lines. In particular, when price observations for valuing the consumption patterns of the poor households are based on only a few observations, they are dropped. Consequently, the price files for these domains were empty and food poverty lines could not be calculated. It is not clear why the data led to this problem, but two adjustments proved sufficient to resolve it. First, the convergence process was limited to one iteration. We discuss the implications of this in section 5.3.2

in the description of the PLEASe code preparation. Second, the rural and urban areas of Harari were merged into one spatial domain. Given the relatively small spatial area that makes up Harari, this is defensible. As a consequence of the latter adjustment, we ended up with twenty spatial domains (except for the 2005 data in which there were eighteen spatial domains because there was no data for urban and rural areas of Gambella).

### 5.3.2 *PLEASe Code Preparation*

Once the data were appropriately formatted and were sufficiently cleaned, the next step was to adjust the PLEASe code for the Ethiopia case. This involved adjusting two Stata do-files located in the PLEASe directory for each survey year entitled 'new'. Each of these files is addressed in turn.

1. '000_boom.do':

Aside from setting the path so that Stata recognized the locations of the various files on the analysts' computers, the 'year' needed to be set for each of the three years of the analysis. For example, when PLEASe was run on the 2005 HICES, the appropriate line of code was

```
global year '2005'
```

It is worth noting here that intertemporal (between survey years) revealed preference tests cannot be conducted with these data since the number of food codes changed each year (see section 5.2.2). As such, the numerical value for the variable in the PLEASe code that indicates the previous year ('prevyear') was left blank:

```
global prevyear
```

2. '010_initial.do':

This is an important file that defines the parameters and code options used in the remainder of the PLEASe code. The instructions in this file are self-explanatory, but it is worth noting that 'spdom_n' was set to 20 to reflect the number of spatial domains and to correspond to the numbers in the 'spdomain' variable.

As noted previously, one of the adjustments made in order to address the convergence problems in the 2011 data was to limit convergence process to one iteration. This is done in the '010_initial.do' file by setting 'it_n' to 1. As a consequence of this, care must be taken in setting the initial quantile that defines the poor for purposes of estimating the minimum cost of consuming domain-specific calorie requirements for the food poverty line. Poverty line

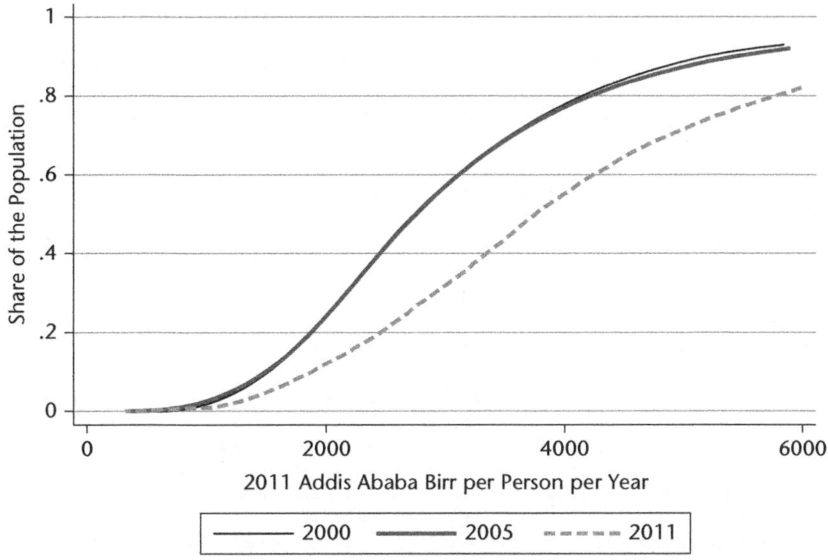


**Figure 5.1.** Cumulative distributions of household per capita consumption, Ethiopia 2000–11

*Source*: Authors' calculations from HICES data

estimates can be sensitive to this initial threshold. Thus for the 2011 data, we cautiously set this threshold equal to the fortieth percentile . . .

global bottom '40'

The rationale for using this particular threshold was the combination of a national poverty estimate of 46.0 per cent poor in 2005 using the PLEASe code combined with indications of considerable growth between 2005 and 2011 (see Figure 5.1). Using 46.0 per cent from 2005 appeared to be too high, while using the CSA estimate for 2011 of 29.6 was likely to result in low estimates of poverty that would be open to criticism. A conservative threshold of 40 per cent is a reasonable compromise.

## 5.4 Poverty Estimates

Based on utility-consistent poverty lines derived from application of the PLEASe code to the HICES data, we find that poverty rates in Ethiopia at the turn of the century were high, but that they fell substantially by 2011 (Table 5.1). In 2000, 46.8 per cent of the population was poor, compared to 23.8 per cent in 2011. Most of the decline, however, occurred between 2005 and 2011 as the poverty rate only fell by just under one percentage point

**Table 5.1.** Utility-consistent and original CSA poverty estimates, Ethiopia 2000–11

| | UC Estimates | | | CSA Estimates | | | Difference | | |
|---|---|---|---|---|---|---|---|---|---|
| | 2000 | 2005 | 2011 | 2000 | 2005 | 2011 | 2000 | 2005 | 2011 |
| *National* | | | | | | | | | |
| Headcount Ratio ($P_0$) | **46.8** | **46.0** | **23.8** | **44.2** | **38.7** | **29.6** | **−2.6** | **−7.3** | **5.8** |
| Depth of Poverty ($P_1$) | 12.6 | 12.3 | 6.3 | 11.9 | 8.3 | 7.8 | −0.7 | −4.0 | 1.5 |
| Severity of Poverty ($P_2$) | 4.8 | 4.5 | 2.4 | 4.5 | 2.7 | 3.1 | −0.3 | −1.8 | 0.7 |
| *Urban* | | | | | | | | | |
| Headcount Ratio ($P_0$) | **39.0** | **22.7** | **13.3** | **45.4** | **39.3** | **30.4** | **6.4** | **16.6** | **17.1** |
| Depth of Poverty ($P_1$) | 10.8 | 4.7 | 3.2 | 12.2 | 8.5 | 8.0 | 1.4 | 3.8 | 4.8 |
| Severity of Poverty ($P_2$) | 4.1 | 1.5 | 1.2 | 4.6 | 2.7 | 3.2 | 0.5 | 1.2 | 2.0 |
| *Rural* | | | | | | | | | |
| Headcount Ratio ($P_0$) | **48.0** | **50.0** | **25.9** | **36.9** | **35.1** | **25.7** | **−11.1** | **−14.9** | **−0.2** |
| Depth of Poverty ($P_1$) | 12.9 | 13.5 | 6.9 | 10.1 | 7.7 | 6.9 | −2.8 | −5.8 | 0.0 |
| Severity of Poverty ($P_2$) | 4.9 | 5.0 | 2.7 | 3.9 | 2.6 | 2.7 | −1.0 | −2.4 | 0.0 |

*Notes*: 'UC' indicates Arndt and Simler (2010) utility-consistent poverty lines estimated with PLEASe. 'CSA' indicates original poverty lines calculated by CSA. The rates are all multiplied by 100.

*Source*: Authors' elaboration based on data from CSA and authors' calculations based on data from HICES

between 2000 and 2005. The more distribution-sensitive poverty measures (i.e. the depth ($P_1$) and severity ($P_2$) of poverty) indicate similar patterns of decline over time. That is, marginal declines in the depth and severity of poverty between 2000 and 2005 were followed by substantial improvements between 2005 and 2011. Figure 5.1 illustrates this more completely as the nearly overlapping distributions of per capita consumption for 2000 and 2005 (spatially and regionally deflated by the utility-consistent poverty lines) are first-order dominated by the 2011 distribution.

Poverty is largely a rural phenomenon, with 48.0 per cent of the rural population below the poverty line in 2000, compared to 39.0 per cent in urban areas. Although the rural headcount ratio fell by a remarkable 22.1 percentage points, urban areas as a whole saw even greater declines in poverty, as the urban poverty rate fell to under 14 per cent by 2011. Most of the decline in urban poverty took place in the first half of the decade, falling by just over sixteen percentage points. Conversely, rural poverty rose marginally during this period, with all of the gains occurring after 2005.

These utility-consistent poverty estimates differ considerably from CSA's original estimates (MoFED 2008 and MoFED 2012). As illustrated in Table 5.1, the original national headcount ratio estimates are lower than the utility-consistent estimates by 2.6 percentage points for 2000 and by 7.3 percentage points in 2005, and they are higher by 5.8 percentage points for 2011. The urban utility-consistent poverty estimates are all lower than the CSA estimates, while the rural utility-consistent estimates are higher for 2000 and 2005 and are nearly identical for 2011. Although the patterns are the same for the depth and severity of poverty, the differences are less stark.

Both approaches indicate that poverty fell substantially in Ethiopia over the course of the 2000s. But the utility-consistent poverty estimates suggest that poverty fell by even more than the original CSA estimates did despite using a higher initial cutoff of 40 per cent for 2011 (see section 5.3). It is worth noting, however, that the differences in the estimated declines are greater for the headcount ratios than for the distribution-sensitive poverty measures, suggesting that the two approaches estimate spatially price-adjusted real household consumption aggregates that are more similar at the lower end of the distribution than around the poverty line.

What accounts for these differences? Both approaches use similar methods to construct the nominal household consumption aggregate (Deaton and Zaidi 2002), and indeed the nominal household consumption aggregates are themselves similar. The source of the differences thus follows from the handling of the poverty lines and deflation. As shown in Table 5.2, the CSA and utility-consistent poverty lines differ for each of the spatial domains, and those differences are larger in 2005 and 2011 than in 2000. While the utility-consistent poverty lines on average are 5.6 per cent lower on average in 2000, they are 10.5 per cent lower in 2005 and 26.6 per cent lower in 2011. However, the utility-consistent poverty lines are only uniformly lower across all spatial domains in 2011. In both 2000 and 2006, they are lower than the CSA poverty lines in roughly 60 per cent of the cases. Even in 2011, the differences were not uniformly even. Indeed, they ranged from 13 per cent in urban Amhara to 45 per cent in Addis Ababa.

To understand why the poverty lines differ for the two approaches, we must understand how the CSA poverty lines were derived. The original CSA approach to maintaining consistency was to use the 1995 poverty line as the benchmark. More specifically, the national poverty line was calculated for 1995/6 in Addis Ababa values. In subsequent years this poverty line was scaled up to 2000, 2005, and 2011 prices using the CPI. The inflated 1995/6 poverty line was then applied to the 2000, 2005, and 2011 regionally deflated household consumption aggregates to calculate poverty. The consumption aggregates were regionally deflated using price indices calculated in each stratum relative to the consumption basket for the capital (Addis Ababa) using the maximum number of common items (i.e. items consumed in all of the strata). This differs from the utility-consistent approach in that the latter estimates poverty lines for each region for each year and relies on revealed preference tests and maximum-entropy methods to maintain consistency.

Further, the original 1995/6 national food poverty line, which forms the basis of the national poverty line, was estimated as the cost of consuming 2200 calories per adult per day based on the consumption patterns of poor

**Table 5.2.** Original CSA and utility-consistent poverty lines, Ethiopia 2000–11

|  | 2000 | | | 2005 | | | 2011 | | |
|---|---|---|---|---|---|---|---|---|---|
|  | Orig | UC | % Diff | Orig | UC | % Diff | Orig | UC | % Diff |
| Addis Ababa | 4.58 | 3.22 | −29.8 | 5.13 | 2.27 | −55.8 | 16.10 | 8.86 | −45.0 |
| Afar—rural | 3.05 | 3.07 | 0.5 | 3.59 | 3.09 | −13.9 | 10.58 | 8.89 | −16.0 |
| Afar—urban | 3.05 | 3.27 | 7.3 | 3.59 | 2.68 | −25.3 | 10.58 | 8.00 | −24.3 |
| Amhara—rural | 2.68 | 2.52 | −5.8 | 3.47 | 3.84 | 10.5 | 9.83 | 7.77 | −21.0 |
| Amhara—urban | 2.68 | 2.78 | 3.8 | 3.47 | 3.31 | −4.5 | 9.83 | 8.52 | −13.3 |
| Benshangul—rural | 2.65 | 2.66 | 0.3 | 3.71 | 4.54 | 22.3 | 9.92 | 6.77 | −31.7 |
| Benshangul—urban | 2.65 | 2.83 | 6.7 | 3.71 | 3.99 | 7.7 | 9.92 | 7.41 | −25.3 |
| Dire Dawa—rural | 3.45 | 3.58 | 3.9 | 3.90 | 4.07 | 4.5 | 12.90 | 8.68 | −32.7 |
| Dire Dawa—urban | 3.45 | 3.42 | −0.9 | 3.90 | 2.69 | −31.1 | 12.90 | 9.19 | −28.8 |
| Gambela—rural | 3.01 | 2.79 | −7.3 |  |  |  | 11.03 | 7.76 | −29.7 |
| Gambela—urban | 3.01 | 2.80 | −6.8 |  |  |  | 11.03 | 7.22 | −34.6 |
| Harari | 3.76 | 3.48 | −7.3 | 4.54 | 2.87 | −36.7 | 12.71 | 9.10 | −28.4 |
| Oromiya—rural | 2.66 | 2.26 | −15.0 | 3.52 | 3.94 | 11.9 | 10.16 | 7.52 | −26.0 |
| Oromiya—urban | 2.66 | 2.43 | −8.7 | 3.52 | 3.20 | −9.2 | 10.16 | 8.00 | −21.3 |
| SNNP—rural | 2.52 | 2.36 | −6.3 | 2.93 | 3.73 | 27.3 | 9.39 | 5.57 | −40.7 |
| SNNP—urban | 2.52 | 2.62 | 4.0 | 2.93 | 3.31 | 12.9 | 9.39 | 6.93 | −26.2 |
| Somali—rural | 3.25 | 2.90 | −10.8 | 3.82 | 3.05 | −20.1 | 11.73 | 8.31 | −29.1 |
| Somali—urban | 3.25 | 3.43 | 5.5 | 3.82 | 2.83 | −26.0 | 11.73 | 8.69 | −25.9 |
| Tigray—rural | 3.82 | 2.84 | −25.7 | 4.67 | 3.44 | −26.3 | 10.71 | 9.17 | −14.4 |
| Tigray—urban | 3.82 | 3.10 | −18.7 | 4.67 | 2.94 | −37.0 | 10.71 | 8.86 | −17.3 |

*Notes*: 'Orig' indicates original poverty lines calculated by CSA. 'UC' indicates Arndt and Simler (2010) utility-consistent poverty lines estimated with PLEASe. '% Diff' indicates the percentage difference.

*Source*: CSA and authors' calculations from HICES

households ranked by the consumption aggregate. This also differs from the utility-consistent approach, which does not fix the calorie requirements to be the same across all regions. Rather it allows the demographic characteristics of the particular region to dictate the differing calorie requirements. In particular, it calculates the average calorie requirements in a spatial domain for people of all ages, not just adults. As illustrated in Table 5.3, the utility-consistent minimum calorie requirements differ across regions and range from 114 calories higher than the CSA-standard 2200, to 82 calories lower. One would thus expect, *ceteris paribus*, that the utility-consistent poverty lines would be higher than the original when the minimum calorie requirement of the former is greater than 2200, given that the former is based on the estimated cost of acquiring more calories than the latter. Conversely, one would expect the utility-consistent poverty lines to be lower when the utility-consistent minimum calorie requirement is less than 2200. This, however, is only the case for half of the comparisons.

The source of the differences in the utility-consistent and CSA poverty lines thus must also follow from the composition of the basket used to value the region-specific calorie requirements. Unfortunately, the original code used to construct the 1995/6 poverty line and regional deflators is not available.

**Table 5.3.** Region- and time-specific minimum calorie requirements

| | | | | Difference from CSA standard (2200) | | |
| --- | --- | --- | --- | --- | --- | --- |
| | 2000 | 2005 | 2011 | 2000 | 2005 | 2011 |
| Addis Ababa | 2289 | 2314 | 2305 | 89 | 114 | 105 |
| Afar—rural | 2172 | 2177 | 2226 | −28 | −23 | 26 |
| Afar—urban | 2276 | 2253 | 2232 | 76 | 53 | 32 |
| Amhara—rural | 2157 | 2164 | 2186 | −43 | −36 | −14 |
| Amhara—urban | 2191 | 2224 | 2259 | −9 | 24 | 59 |
| Benishangul—rural | 2141 | 2179 | 2146 | −59 | −21 | −54 |
| Benishangul—urban | 2179 | 2210 | 2217 | −21 | 10 | 17 |
| Dire Dawa—rural | 2168 | 2138 | 2146 | −32 | −62 | −54 |
| Dire Dawa—urban | 2212 | 2285 | 2249 | 12 | 85 | 49 |
| Gambella—rural | 2201 | | 2172 | 1 | | −28 |
| Gambella—urban | 2193 | | 2,205 | −7 | | 5 |
| Harari | 2202 | 2190 | 2175 | 2 | −10 | −25 |
| Oromiya—rural | 2132 | 2127 | 2142 | −68 | −73 | −58 |
| Oromiya—urban | 2192 | 2213 | 2246 | −8 | 13 | 46 |
| SNNP—rural | 2151 | 2134 | 2141 | −49 | −66 | −59 |
| SNNP—urban | 2219 | 2196 | 2263 | 19 | −4 | 63 |
| Somali—rural | 2171 | 2151 | 2131 | −29 | −49 | −69 |
| Somali—urban | 2186 | 2170 | 2142 | −14 | −30 | −58 |
| Tigray—rural | 2118 | 2151 | 2173 | −82 | −49 | −27 |
| Tigray—urban | 2144 | 2176 | 2192 | −56 | −24 | −8 |

*Source:* Authors' calculations from *HICES* data

Thus we cannot compare the consumption baskets used to create the utility-consistent poverty lines with the original from 1995/6. But the food consumption baskets derived from the utility-consistent approach shown in Table 5.4 give an indication of how the baskets differ substantially over the spatial domains in 2011, including urban and rural areas within regions. Given that the CSA poverty lines are defined over the regions (urban and rural combined), not over these more disaggregated spatial domains, differences in food consumption baskets are likely to be an important contributor to the different poverty line estimates.

## 5.5 Concluding Remarks

This chapter describes the application to Ethopia of the standardized PLEASe computer code stream based on Arndt and Simler's (2010) utility-consistent approach to measuring consumption poverty. In doing so, we highlight the importance of adapting the code stream to address changes in data collection periods and strata for the respective surveys over time. Indeed, changes in the

**Table 5.4.** Household food consumption baskets by spatial domain, Ethiopia HICES 2011

| | Addis | Afar | | Amhara | | Benishangul | | Dire Dawa | | |
|---|---|---|---|---|---|---|---|---|---|---|
| | Ababa | Rural | Urban | Rural | Urban | Rural | Urban | Rural | Urban | Harari |
| Teff—unmilled | 0.035 | 0.004 | 0.004 | | | | | | | |
| Teff—milled | 0.198 | 0.025 | 0.108 | 0.080 | 0.168 | 0.024 | 0.034 | | 0.072 | 0.061 |
| Wheat—unmilled | 0.004 | 0.005 | | 0.003 | 0.003 | | | 0.009 | 0.004 | 0.004 |
| Wheat—milled | 0.026 | 0.042 | 0.047 | 0.060 | 0.040 | 0.008 | 0.014 | 0.190 | 0.061 | 0.094 |
| Barley—unmilled | | | 0.008 | 0.005 | | | | | | |
| Barley—milled | | | | 0.034 | 0.005 | | | | 0.017 | |
| Maize—unmilled | | | | 0.020 | 0.003 | 0.030 | 0.027 | 0.015 | | |
| Maize—milled | 0.009 | 0.284 | 0.062 | 0.054 | 0.034 | 0.064 | 0.032 | 0.060 | 0.016 | 0.092 |
| Sorghum—unmilled | | | 0.004 | | | | | 0.008 | 0.006 | |
| Sorghum—milled | | 0.026 | 0.089 | 0.136 | 0.125 | 0.162 | 0.126 | 0.293 | 0.093 | 0.150 |
| Millet—milled | | | | 0.024 | 0.005 | 0.057 | 0.058 | | | |
| Rice | 0.006 | | | | | | | | 0.025 | 0.010 |
| Mixed cereals—milled | | | 0.004 | | | | | | | |
| Other cereals—unmilled | | | | 0.025 | 0.011 | 0.011 | 0.015 | | | |
| Other cereals—milled | 0.003 | 0.003 | 0.044 | 0.006 | | | 0.003 | | 0.020 | 0.004 |
| Horse beans—unmilled | | | | 0.006 | | | | | | |
| Horse beans—milled | 0.004 | 0.004 | 0.009 | 0.053 | 0.056 | 0.014 | 0.020 | | 0.006 | |
| Chick peas—unmilled | | | 0.003 | 0.004 | 0.006 | | | | | |
| Chick peas—milled | 0.003 | | | 0.008 | 0.005 | | | | | |
| Peas—unmilled | | | | | | | | | | |
| Peas—milled | 0.048 | 0.006 | 0.022 | 0.027 | 0.029 | 0.013 | 0.025 | 0.012 | 0.028 | 0.008 |
| Lentils—unmilled | 0.003 | | 0.011 | 0.002 | | | | | | |
| Lentils—milled | 0.021 | 0.004 | 0.008 | | 0.009 | | 0.009 | | | |
| Haricot beans—unmilled | | | | | 0.002 | 0.012 | 0.015 | | 0.010 | |
| Haricot beans—milled | | | | 0.002 | | 0.058 | 0.033 | | | |
| Vetch—milled | 0.013 | 0.004 | 0.055 | 0.043 | 0.036 | 0.010 | 0.018 | | | |
| Fenugreek—unmilled | | | | | | 0.004 | | | | |
| Fenugreek—milled | | | | | | | | 0.031 | 0.014 | 0.039 |
| Soya beans—unmilled | | | | 0.004 | | 0.042 | 0.022 | 0.003 | | |
| Mixed pulses—milled | 0.042 | 0.013 | 0.005 | 0.009 | 0.026 | 0.004 | 0.013 | | | 0.012 |
| Other pulses—unmilled | | | 0.003 | | | | | | | |

| | | | | | | | | | | |
|---|---|---|---|---|---|---|---|---|---|---|
| Other pulses—milled | | | | | | 0.002 | | | | |
| Linseed—oilseed | | | | 0.002 | | 0.006 | | | | 0.004 |
| Other oilseeds | | | | | | 0.003 | 0.003 | | | |
| Spaghetti | 0.003 | 0.009 | 0.007 | | | | | | 0.010 | 0.013 |
| Macaroni | 0.005 | 0.008 | 0.012 | | | 0.006 | 0.005 | 0.015 | 0.024 | 0.009 |
| Injera | 0.077 | | 0.031 | 0.005 | 0.019 | | 0.010 | 0.006 | 0.075 | 0.065 |
| Wheat bread | 0.092 | 0.010 | 0.043 | 0.005 | 0.039 | 0.006 | 0.011 | 0.016 | 0.110 | 0.073 |
| Biscuit | 0.002 | | 0.004 | | | 0.007 | 0.005 | | 0.004 | 0.003 |
| Other prepared foods | | | 0.019 | 0.002 | 0.004 | | 0.003 | | 0.011 | 0.007 |
| Beef | 0.015 | 0.003 | | 0.009 | 0.009 | 0.015 | 0.021 | | | 0.022 |
| Mutton–Goat | 0.003 | | | 0.003 | 0.003 | | 0.020 | | | |
| Chicken | | | | 0.006 | | 0.005 | | | | |
| Other meat | | | | | | 0.003 | | | | |
| Fresh fish | | | | | | | | | | |
| Dried fish | | | 0.012 | | | 0.008 | 0.006 | | | |
| Milk | 0.004 | 0.322 | 0.014 | 0.005 | | 0.002 | | 0.086 | 0.011 | 0.049 |
| Cottage cheese | | | | 0.003 | | 0.004 | 0.004 | | | |
| Yogurt | | | | | | 0.003 | 0.005 | | | |
| Butter (milk) | | 0.006 | | | | | | | | |
| Other dairy | | 0.005 | | | | | | | | |
| Butter (oil) | | | | 0.002 | | 0.006 | 0.013 | | | |
| Edible oils | 0.096 | 0.037 | 0.082 | 0.029 | 0.061 | 0.073 | 0.085 | 0.073 | 0.072 | 0.066 |
| Ethiopian kale | 0.005 | | | 0.005 | 0.004 | 0.007 | 0.017 | | | |
| Cabbage/Lettuce/Spinach | 0.004 | | | | 0.003 | | | | | |
| Tomato | 0.007 | 0.006 | 0.024 | | 0.005 | 0.005 | 0.007 | 0.012 | 0.041 | 0.032 |
| Onion | 0.041 | 0.018 | 0.052 | 0.014 | 0.032 | 0.048 | 0.047 | 0.016 | 0.041 | 0.041 |
| Garlic | 0.003 | | 0.003 | | 0.002 | 0.011 | 0.011 | | 0.003 | |
| Green pepper | 0.004 | | | 0.003 | 0.006 | 0.011 | 0.007 | | | |
| Pumpkin | | | | 0.004 | | 0.005 | | | | |
| Canned tomato | | | | | | | | | | |
| Other vegetables | | | | | | 0.038 | 0.005 | | | |
| Banana | | | | | | 0.003 | 0.006 | | 0.003 | |
| Mango | | | | | | 0.003 | 0.005 | | | |
| Other fruit | | | | | | | | 0.003 | 0.003 | |
| Potato | 0.013 | | 0.004 | 0.030 | 0.020 | 0.008 | 0.029 | 0.010 | 0.018 | 0.017 |

(continued)

**Table 5.4.** Continued

| | Addis Ababa | Afar | | Amhara | | Benishangul | | Dire Dawa | | Harari |
|---|---|---|---|---|---|---|---|---|---|---|
| | | Rural | Urban | Rural | Urban | Rural | Urban | Rural | Urban | |
| Sweet potato | | | | | | | 0.005 | 0.026 | | |
| Kocho (from enset) | | | | | | | | | | |
| Amicho (from enset) | | | | | | | | | | |
| Godere | | | | | | | | | | |
| Other tubers | | | | | | | | | | |
| Salt | 0.004 | 0.015 | 0.012 | 0.007 | 0.006 | 0.021 | 0.017 | 0.009 | 0.004 | 0.007 |
| Sugar | 0.045 | 0.057 | 0.065 | 0.003 | 0.014 | 0.017 | 0.022 | 0.023 | 0.056 | 0.039 |
| Sugar cane | | | | | | 0.002 | 0.003 | | | |
| Candy | | | | | | 0.003 | | | | |
| Other refined food | | | | 0.020 | 0.019 | 0.004 | | | | |
| Outside meals | 0.055 | 0.032 | 0.024 | 0.071 | 0.060 | 0.045 | 0.027 | 0.046 | 0.092 | 0.025 |
| Spices | 0.080 | 0.026 | 0.084 | 0.144 | 0.109 | 0.088 | 0.110 | 0.015 | 0.028 | 0.030 |
| Number of food items | 34 | 26 | 34 | 42 | 35 | 46 | 45 | 23 | 31 | 27 |

**Table 5.4.** Continued

| | Gambela | | Oromiya | | SNNP | | Somali | | Tigray | |
| --- | --- | --- | --- | --- | --- | --- | --- | --- | --- | --- |
| | Rural | Urban | Rural | Urban | Rural | Urban | Rural | Urban | Rural | Urban |
| Teff—unmilled | | | 0.002 | 0.010 | | | | | | |
| Teff—milled | 0.006 | 0.018 | 0.045 | 0.108 | 0.016 | 0.079 | | | 0.045 | 0.139 |
| Wheat—unmilled | | 0.009 | 0.009 | 0.008 | 0.008 | 0.007 | | 0.018 | 0.007 | |
| Wheat—milled | 0.009 | 0.056 | 0.051 | 0.057 | 0.013 | 0.018 | 0.133 | 0.070 | 0.147 | 0.127 |
| Barley—unmilled | 0.004 | | 0.006 | 0.005 | 0.015 | 0.005 | | | | |
| Barley—milled | | | 0.021 | 0.012 | 0.006 | | | 0.005 | 0.067 | 0.027 |
| Maize—unmilled | 0.016 | 0.020 | 0.045 | 0.021 | 0.059 | 0.035 | 0.052 | 0.022 | 0.005 | 0.006 |
| Maize—milled | 0.295 | 0.221 | 0.135 | 0.078 | 0.127 | 0.124 | 0.062 | 0.033 | 0.061 | 0.019 |
| Sorghum—unmilled | | | 0.005 | | | | 0.046 | 0.019 | | |
| Sorghum—milled | 0.041 | 0.006 | 0.068 | 0.056 | 0.017 | | 0.035 | 0.029 | 0.175 | 0.103 |
| Millet—milled | 0.004 | | 0.013 | 0.011 | | | | | 0.003 | 0.002 |
| Rice | | | | 0.005 | | | 0.044 | 0.073 | | |
| Mixed cereals—milled | | | | 0.003 | 0.004 | | | | 0.009 | 0.011 |
| Other cereals—unmilled | 0.013 | | 0.033 | 0.008 | 0.028 | 0.009 | | | 0.023 | 0.008 |
| Other cereals—milled | | 0.028 | | 0.006 | | 0.004 | 0.021 | 0.087 | | 0.004 |
| Horse beans—unmilled | | | 0.006 | 0.003 | 0.013 | 0.009 | | | | |
| Horse beans—milled | 0.022 | | 0.021 | 0.026 | 0.010 | 0.004 | | | 0.055 | 0.038 |
| Chick peas—unmilled | | | 0.002 | | | 0.002 | | | | |
| Chick peas—milled | | | | | | | | | 0.008 | 0.006 |
| Peas—unmilled | | | | | 0.004 | | | | | |
| Peas—milled | 0.030 | 0.025 | 0.012 | 0.033 | 0.005 | 0.018 | | 0.005 | 0.040 | 0.020 |
| Lentils—unmilled | | | | | | | | | | |
| Lentils—milled | | 0.006 | 0.003 | 0.008 | | 0.007 | | | 0.003 | 0.002 |
| Haricot beans—unmilled | | 0.005 | 0.007 | 0.008 | 0.006 | | 0.004 | 0.019 | | |
| Haricot beans—milled | 0.015 | | 0.008 | | | | | | | |
| Vetch—milled | 0.009 | 0.008 | 0.006 | 0.012 | | | | | 0.018 | 0.057 |
| Fenugreek—unmilled | | | | | 0.002 | | | | | |
| Fenugreek—milled | | | 0.005 | 0.005 | | | 0.006 | 0.004 | | |
| Soya beans—unmilled | | | 0.013 | 0.002 | 0.016 | 0.008 | 0.003 | | | |

(continued)

**Table 5.4.** Continued

| | Gambela | | Oromiya | | SNNP | | Somali | | Tigray | |
|---|---|---|---|---|---|---|---|---|---|---|
| | Rural | Urban | Rural | Urban | Rural | Urban | Rural | Urban | Rural | Urban |
| Mixed pulses—milled | | | 0.006 | 0.004 | | 0.008 | | | | 0.006 |
| Other pulses—unmilled | | | | | | | | | | |
| Other pulses—milled | | | | | | | | | | |
| Linseed—oilseed | | | | | | | | | | |
| Other oilseeds | | | | | | | | | | |
| Spaghetti | | | | | | | 0.011 | 0.020 | | |
| Macaroni | | | | 0.006 | | 0.003 | 0.010 | 0.010 | | |
| Injera | 0.005 | 0.009 | | 0.039 | 0.008 | 0.056 | | 0.021 | | 0.010 |
| Wheat bread | | 0.019 | 0.005 | 0.043 | 0.006 | 0.063 | | 0.021 | 0.004 | 0.017 |
| Biscuit | | 0.006 | 0.002 | 0.005 | | | | 0.003 | | |
| Other prepared foods | | 0.007 | 0.003 | | 0.005 | 0.009 | | 0.003 | | |
| Beef | 0.004 | 0.029 | 0.007 | 0.014 | 0.025 | 0.015 | | | 0.012 | 0.034 |
| Mutton–Goat | | | | 0.003 | | 0.006 | | | | |
| Chicken | 0.010 | | 0.002 | | | | | | 0.007 | |
| Other meat | 0.007 | 0.005 | | | | | | | | 0.008 |
| Fresh fish | 0.079 | 0.059 | | | | | | | | 0.003 |
| Dried fish | 0.004 | 0.016 | | | | | | 0.012 | 0.006 | |
| Milk | 0.079 | 0.131 | 0.060 | 0.021 | 0.019 | 0.005 | 0.114 | 0.060 | 0.002 | |
| Cottage cheese | | | 0.008 | 0.004 | 0.009 | | | | | |
| Yogurt | | | | | 0.005 | 0.003 | | | | |
| Butter (milk) | | | 0.007 | | 0.011 | 0.003 | | | 0.010 | |
| Other dairy | | | | | | | 0.004 | 0.009 | | |
| Butter (oil) | | | 0.019 | 0.006 | 0.019 | 0.009 | | | | |
| Edible oils | 0.043 | 0.058 | 0.056 | 0.085 | 0.033 | 0.059 | 0.111 | 0.090 | 0.047 | 0.067 |
| Ethiopian kale | 0.007 | 0.019 | 0.022 | 0.014 | 0.064 | 0.058 | | | 0.004 | |
| Cabbage/Lettuce/Spinach | | | | | | 0.003 | | | 0.002 | 0.010 |
| Tomato | | 0.012 | 0.004 | 0.010 | | 0.003 | 0.010 | 0.020 | 0.010 | 0.020 |
| Onion | 0.024 | 0.022 | 0.025 | 0.036 | 0.015 | 0.025 | 0.010 | 0.018 | 0.017 | 0.030 |
| Garlic | 0.009 | | 0.006 | 0.006 | 0.016 | 0.013 | | | 0.003 | |
| Green pepper | | | 0.007 | 0.008 | 0.009 | 0.009 | | | | 0.002 |
| Pumpkin | 0.005 | | 0.005 | 0.002 | | 0.002 | | | 0.003 | |

| | | | | | | | | | | |
|---|---|---|---|---|---|---|---|---|---|---|
| Canned tomato | | | | | | | 0.003 | 0.004 | | |
| Other vegetables | 0.100 | 0.106 | 0.014 | 0.010 | 0.016 | 0.013 | | | | |
| Banana | 0.003 | | | | 0.002 | 0.005 | | | | |
| Mango | 0.007 | | | | | | | | | |
| Other fruit | | | | | 0.002 | 0.004 | | | 0.007 | 0.002 |
| Potato | 0.008 | | 0.009 | 0.019 | 0.006 | 0.016 | | 0.008 | 0.003 | 0.011 |
| Sweet potato | 0.009 | | 0.011 | 0.002 | 0.034 | 0.035 | | | | |
| Kocho (from enset) | 0.009 | | 0.045 | 0.003 | 0.162 | 0.052 | | | | |
| Amicho (from enset) | | | | | 0.030 | 0.007 | | | | |
| Godere | 0.006 | | | | 0.036 | 0.022 | | | | |
| Other tubers | 0.004 | | 0.002 | | 0.015 | 0.007 | | | | |
| Salt | 0.015 | 0.017 | 0.018 | 0.009 | 0.014 | 0.010 | 0.011 | 0.007 | 0.008 | 0.009 |
| Sugar | 0.025 | 0.021 | 0.012 | 0.031 | | 0.014 | 0.220 | 0.216 | 0.012 | 0.026 |
| Sugar cane | | | 0.002 | 0.003 | | | | | | |
| Candy | | | | | | | | | | |
| Other refined food | | | | | | | | | 0.007 | 0.009 |
| Outside meals | 0.018 | 0.030 | 0.040 | 0.037 | 0.021 | 0.059 | 0.007 | 0.062 | 0.066 | 0.058 |
| Spices | 0.033 | 0.007 | 0.061 | 0.070 | 0.044 | 0.052 | 0.006 | 0.008 | 0.083 | 0.081 |
| Number of food items | 36 | 29 | 49 | 48 | 43 | 46 | 22 | 30 | 35 | 33 |

duration and time of year for data collection can be especially problematic for consistency in the presence of annual inflation of over 30 per cent. In addition, the Ethiopia case provides an example of how to address convergence problems encountered when running the PLEASe code. Careful consolidation of spatial domains and limiting the number of iterations in the estimation of poverty lines are potential solutions.

According to our estimates using utility-consistent poverty lines from the application of the PLEASe code stream, national poverty fell from 46.8 per cent in 2000, to 46.0 per cent in 2005, and finally to 23.8 per cent in 2011. Poverty is considerably higher in rural areas (48.0 per cent) where more than 80 per cent of the population lives, compared to urban areas (39.0 per cent). Although the rural headcount ratio fell by 11.2 percentage points, urban areas as a whole saw even greater declines in poverty, as the urban poverty rate fell to 13.3 per cent by 2011.

Although the patterns of decline in poverty as estimated using utility-consistent poverty lines are similar to those from the original CSA estimates, the utility-consistent poverty estimates fell by even more than the CSA estimates did. These differences stem from the handling of the poverty lines and deflation. Unlike the CSA approach that maintains consistency over time by using the 1995 poverty line as a benchmark and scales it up to 2000, 2005, and 2011 prices using the CPI, the utility-consistent approach estimates poverty lines for each region for each year and relies on revealed preference tests and maximum-entropy methods to maintain consistency. Although differing region-specific calorie requirements contribute partly to the disparity among the poverty lines of the two approaches, the differing compositions of the baskets used to value these calorie requirements likely played a more important role. The specificity of these utility-consistent weights, based on consumption patterns of the poor in the spatial domains, is a strength of this approach compared to the previous approach taken by the CSA.

# References


Arndt, Channing, Ulrik Richardt Beck, M. Azhar Hussain, Kenneth Simler, and Finn Tarp (2013). 'User Guide to Poverty Line Construction Toolkit: Version 2.0', Development Economics Research Group, University of Copenhagen, Denmark.

Arndt, Channing and Kenneth Simler (2010). 'Estimating Utility-Consistent Poverty Lines with Applications to Egypt and Mozambique', *Economic Development and Cultural Change*, 58(3): 449–74.

Blackorby, Charles and David Donaldson (1987). 'Welfare Ratios and Distributionally Sensitive Cost-Benefit Analysis', *Journal of Public Economics*, 34: 265–90.

Deaton, Angus and Salman Zaidi (2002). 'Guidelines for Constructing Consumption Aggregates for Welfare Analysis', Living Standards Measurement Study Working Paper 135. Washington, DC: World Bank.

Dorosh, Paul and Emily Schmidt (2010). 'The Urban–Rural Transformation in Ethiopia', ESSP II Working Paper 13, International Food Policy Research Institute/Ethiopia Strategy Support Program II, Addis Ababa, Ethiopia.

Foster, James, Joel Greer, and Erik Thorbecke (1984). 'A Class of Decomposable Poverty Measures', *Econometrica*, 52: 761–6.

Headey, Derek, Fantu Nisrane, Ibrahim Worku, Mekdim Dereje, and Alemayehu Seyoum Taffesse (2012). 'Urban Wage and Food Price Inflation: The Case of Ethiopia', ESSP II Working Paper 41, International Food Policy Research Institute/Ethiopia Strategy Support Program II, Addis Ababa, Ethiopia.

MoFED (2008). 'Dynamics of Growth and Poverty in Ethiopia (1995/96–2004/05)', Development Planning and Research Department, Ministry of Finance and Economic Development, Addis Ababa, Ethiopia.

MoFED (2012). 'Ethiopia's Progress towards Eradicating Poverty: An Interim Report on Poverty Analysis Study (20010/11)', Development Planning and Research Department, Ministry of Finance and Economic Development, Addis Ababa, Ethiopia.

Pradhan, Menno (2000). 'How Many Questions Should Be in a Consumption Questionnaire? Evidence from a Repeated Experiment in Indonesia', Working Paper 112, Cornell Food and Nutrition Policy Program, Cornell University, Ithaca, NY.

Ravallion, Martin (1998). 'Poverty Lines in Theory and Practice', Living Standards Measurement Study Working Paper No. 133. Washington, DC: World Bank.

Ravallion, Martin and Benu Bidani (1994). 'How Robust Is a Poverty Profile?', *World Bank Economic Review*, 8: 75–102.

Scott, Christopher and Ben Amenuvegbe (1990). 'Effect of Recall Duration on Reporting of Household Expenditures: An Experimental Study in Ghana', Social Dimensions of Adjustment in Sub-Saharan Africa Working Paper No. 6. Washington, DC: World Bank.

# 6

# Estimating Utility-Consistent Poverty in Madagascar, 2001–10

*David Stifel, Tiaray Razafimanantena, and Faly Rakotomanana*

## 6.1 Introduction

Madagascar is one of the poorest countries in the world, with macroeconomic indicators suggesting that the nation is poorer today than it was over forty years ago. Average real per capita income in 2010 was approximately one third of what it was in 1960. Yet our understanding of poverty in Madagascar is incomplete because it is hampered by issues with data and methodology. This is not surprising given the complexity of measuring poverty in a manner that is consistent over time and space, yet is also sensitive to local conditions. The contemporary literature on poverty in Madagascar has stressed consistency over time by focusing on the comparability of the survey instruments used to estimate nominal household consumption aggregates, the key welfare measure used in calculating poverty (Paternostro et al. 2001; Amendola and Vecchi 2007). Evidence that differing commodity lists (Pradhan 2000) and recall periods (Scott and Amenuvegbe 1990) affect the levels of reported consumption from household surveys led Malagasy statisticians to make every effort to ensure that the survey instruments used to measure poverty were comparable from 2001 onward.

The nominal household consumption aggregate, however, is but one admittedly important component of poverty measurement. Another is the poverty line. The appropriate estimation of poverty lines is essential not only to gauge a poverty threshold, but also as a cost-of-living index that allows interpersonal welfare comparisons when the costs of consuming basic needs vary over time and space (Ravallion 1998). The challenge is to estimate poverty lines that are consistent over time and space (i.e. the reference standard of living is fixed), and yet are also characterized by specificity in which the poverty lines reflect local consumption patterns and norms (Ravallion and Bidani 1994).

The purpose of this chapter is to adapt the standardized PLEASe computer code stream based on Arndt and Simler's (2010) utility-consistent approach to measuring consumption poverty in order to analyse poverty in Madagascar in 2001, 2005, and 2010. We document how the utility-consistent approach to intertemporal and spatial deflation differs from the approach undertaken by the national statistical office (INSTAT) to produce the official poverty estimates (i.e. using urban consumer price indices), and how the trends in these estimates differ substantially. Further, we highlight the importance of addressing extreme values for calculating unit prices, and how to handle redistricting when conducting revealed preference tests of the utility consistency of not only regionally estimated poverty lines (i.e. do the consumption patterns in other spatial domains cost no less than the own-domain consumption patterns when both are evaluated at own-domain prices), but of these poverty lines over time.

The structure of this chapter is as follows. In section 6.2, we elaborate on the methodology used to calculate poverty and describe the primary data sources. Section 6.3 describes how the Madagascar data was prepared for the exercise and how the PLEASe code was adapted for these data. In section 6.4, we present the estimates of poverty based on the utility-consistent approach to calculating poverty lines, and explore the differences between these estimates and the original estimates made by INSTAT (2002, 2006, and 2011). Section 6.5 provides concluding remarks.

## 6.2 Methodology and Data

In this section, we briefly describe the methodology and household survey data sources used to measure poverty in a manner that is consistent over time and space, and which is specific to local consumption patterns and norms.

### 6.2.1 *Methodology*

As with any analysis of poverty, choices need to be made regarding (i) the welfare indicator, (ii) the threshold between the poor and the non-poor, and (iii) the measure of poverty. The household consumption aggregate is constructed in a standard manner by aggregating food and non-food expenditures, the estimated value of own-produced food and non-food items and of in-kind payments, gifts received, and the estimated use value of durable goods and housing (Deaton and Zaidi 2002).

We briefly outline the procedure used to estimate poverty lines[1] for twelve spatial domains in Madagascar (urban and rural for each of the six provinces). Food poverty lines are estimated first, and are anchored to calorie requirements that are calculated separately for each domain, for purposes of specificity, based on the demographic structure and fertility patterns in the domain. This is a departure from the common practice, for poverty analysis in Madagascar, of using a standard requirement of 2133 calories per person per day. An iterative approach is used to find the consumption bundle that meets the domain-specific calorie requirements and that reflects consumption patterns of relatively poor households in the spatial domain. This provides specific initial estimates of the food poverty lines. Revealed preference tests are then conducted to test the utility consistency of these poverty lines (i.e. do the consumption patterns in other spatial domains cost no less than the own-domain consumption patterns when both are evaluated at own-domain prices). When these tests are violated, maximum-entropy methods are used to reconcile the differences so that domain specificity is maintained in the new poverty lines, while utility consistency is not violated. Once the region-specific food poverty lines are determined, the weighted averages of non-food consumption of households around the poverty line are added to the food poverty lines, to get the region-specific poverty lines.

With the welfare indicators and poverty lines in hand, we employ the Foster–Greer–Thorbecke (1984) class of poverty indices to measure levels and changes in poverty.

### 6.2.2 Data

The primary data sources used in this analysis are the 2001, 2005, and 2010 Madagascar Enquête Périodique auprès des Ménages (EPM). The EPM are general-purpose LSMS-type cross-section surveys conducted by the Institut National de la Statistique (INSTAT). They are nationally representative, stratified, and clustered surveys conducted over three-month periods at the end of the calendar year, and contain information on household characteristics, expenditure, activities, and infrastructure. Detailed consumption information is collected for the purpose of constructing welfare measures.

Over the course of the three surveys, the sample size grew from 5080 in 2001 to 11,781 in 2005, and to 12,460 in 2010. This reflects the need for the latter two surveys to be representative, at the urban and rural levels, of each of the twenty-two administrative regions created in 2004 as part of the government's decentralization programme. Fortunately, the forty-four strata in these 2005 and 2010

---

[1] See Chapter 2 of this book for more details about the general procedure. The household consumption aggregates and poverty lines were calculated using the PLEASe software.

surveys can be grouped to represent the same twelve strata in the 2001 survey (urban and rural for six provinces). Further, while slight changes were made to the questionnaire in response to demands from the government and from donors who financed the surveys, INSTAT's efforts over the years to maintain comparability for welfare measurement—reflected in the nearly identical questionnaire modules for food and non-food expenditures, education and health expenditures, housing values and characteristics, ownership of durable goods, gifts and remittances, and in-kind payments—bode well for consistent poverty and inequality measurement. Nonetheless, some issues arose with regard to estimating poverty with the PLEASe software. These are discussed in section 6.3.

## 6.3 Application of PLEASe

### 6.3.1 *Data Preparation*

The bulk of the work in applying PLEASe to the Madagascar household survey data was related to preparing the data themselves. The PLEASe manual (Arndt et al. 2013) provides guidance for creating standard data files with common variable names. We therefore do not elaborate on this here. But it is worth emphasizing that in following the manual it is important to pay close attention to the units (e.g. daily and metric) and to item codes when preparing the data as these can be an easily avoided source of error. In addition, certain country-specific decisions need to be made in the process of preparing the data. We review the three most important ones for Madagascar here.

First, the choice of the spatial domains ('spdomain' in 'hhdata.dta') was complicated by the fact noted in section 6.2.2 that administrative decentralization in Madagascar led to the creation of twenty-two administrative regions from the original six provinces between the 2001 and 2005 surveys. For two reasons, we proceeded with twelve spatial domains for the analysis of all three survey years rather than twelve for 2001 and forty-four for 2005 and 2010. First, the common spatial domains allow for intertemporal revealed preference tests over the survey years. Revealed preference conditions should hold not only over space, but also over time. When these conditions are violated over time, similar maximum-entropy methods can be used to reconcile the differences as described in the methodology section (Arndt and Simler 2010). These tests, however, require comparisons over the same geographic spaces (i.e. do the consumption patterns in the same spatial domain but in different time periods cost no less than the own-domain consumption patterns at a specific time when both are evaluated at own-domain prices for that specific time). Fortunately, the food items listed in the EPM questionnaires did not change over time, allowing for such intertemporal tests to be conducted provided that the spatial domains remained the same over all three surveys.

As such, they were defined to be the same. A second reason for using twelve spatial domains in the analysis for 2005 and 2010 despite having forty-four strata is that fewer domains help to reduce the impact of extreme values for unit prices calculated in these data. We will go on to elaborate on this.

Second, before running PLEASe on country-specific data, it is important to check that the 'quantity' and 'value' variables in the constructed 'cons_nom_in. dta' data file result in reasonable unit prices at the household item level. Since unit prices (the values per unit backed out of information on total quantities and values spent on particular items) are used to value home consumption and to calculate poverty lines, extreme values of these prices can distort poverty estimates. Such extreme values, along with unrealistic initial poverty estimates, were found in the 2005 and 2010 EPM data. This was not the case, however, for the 2001 EPM. Since unit prices are the ratio of the amount spent on an item divided by the quantity purchased, there are two potential sources of error when unit prices take on extreme values. In the Madagascar case, as in the cases of many developing countries where local measurement units are prevalent, the measurements of quantities were problematic. The same care that was taken in checking and verifying both values and quantities of food items purchased in the 2001 EPM was difficult to achieve in 2005 and 2010 because of the logistical challenges associated with the more than doubling of the sample sizes. The pragmatic approach taken by the INSTAT survey team was to focus the enumerators' and supervisors' attention on the accuracy of reported expenditure values for the latter two surveys. As such, the expenditure values are reliable for these two years, while the expenditure quantities are less so.

To minimize the likelihood that extreme values would unduly influence the poverty estimates using PLEASe, household item quantities reported in the 2005 and 2010 EPM data were replaced with imputed quantities when the reported quantities resulted in unit prices that were outside of the 95 per cent confidence interval around the median for the particular item in the spatial domain. In such cases, during the data preparation stage, item-specific unit prices were replaced by the spatial-domain median, and the imputed quantity was calculated as the reported total value divided by the median unit price. These adjustments primarily affected important food items such as local rice, imported rice, paddy, maize, cassava, and sweet potatoes, and constituted roughly 6 per cent of reported food items. In addition to data cleaning, defining spatial domains to represent larger areas (i.e. urban and rural areas in the original six provinces rather than urban and rural areas in the twenty-two regions) allowed for average unit prices to be calculated in a manner that was less susceptible to the effects of extreme values. Admittedly, the cost of this sample aggregation is less regional specificity. But, combined with the benefits of allowing intertemporal revealed preference testing, this was considered to be a reasonable cost worth incurring.

Finally, adjustments needed to be made to the input data in the 'hhdata.dta' to recognize that the EPM surveys were conducted over a relatively short time period (three months). PLEASe allows for adjustments to be made to household consumption to take into account temporal price variation over the year using temporal price indices (TPI). Since this was not the case with the EPM data, these within-survey temporal adjustments did not need to be made. Consequently, two TPI variables were not relevant to the Madagascar case but are required in the PLEASe code. These variables were created in 'hhdata. dta' and set equal to one for all households. The first is the 'survquar' variable, which in standard applications is the sequential interview quarter (i.e. four survey quarters over the course of the year). Secondly, 'reg_tpi', is the identifier for the regions used in TPI calculations. Finally, in the initialization file '010_initial_$year', the global macros 'tpi_reg_n', which specifies the number of TPI regions, and 'temp_n', which specifies the number of time periods used in TPI calculations, are each set to one. With these settings, the TPI equals one in all cases and therefore no TPI adjustments are made.

### 6.3.2 *PLEASe Code Preparation*

Once the data were appropriately formatted and were sufficiently cleaned, the next step was to adjust the PLEASe code for the Madagascar case. This involved adjusting two Stata do-files located in the PLEASe directory for each survey year entitled 'new'. Each of these files is addressed in turn.

1. '000_boom.do':

Aside from setting the path so that Stata recognized the locations of the various files on the analysts' computers, the 'year' needed to be set for each of the three years of the analysis. For example, when PLEASe was run on the 2005 EPM, the appropriate line of code was:

```
global year '2005'
```

Additionally, the year of the previous survey needed to be defined in order for the intertemporal (between survey years) revealed preference tests to be conducted. When applied to the 2005 EPM data, the previous survey year was 2001. Hence the appropriate PLEASe code is:

```
global prevyear '2001'
```

When applied to the 2001 EPM, however, there was no previous survey year for such comparisons to be made. As such, the numerical value for the year was left blank:

```
global prevyear
```

2. '010_initial.do':

This is an important file that defines the parameters and code options used in the remainder of the PLEASe code. The instructions in this file are self-explanatory. In addition to the TPI-related globals mentioned in section 6.3.1, 'spdom_n' was set to 12 to reflect the number of spatial domains and to correspond to the numbers in the 'spdomain' variable.

## 6.4 Poverty Estimates

Poverty rates in Madagascar, as measured using PLEASe,[2] are high and rose over the course of the three survey periods (Table 6.1). In 2001, 57.8 per cent of the population was poor, compared to 59.1 per cent in 2005, and 61.7 per cent in 2010. Although poverty is largely a rural phenomenon, with over 63 per cent of the rural population below the poverty line, it is also becoming increasingly urban. The urban headcount ratio rose by nearly ten percentage points, from 34.2 per cent in 2001 to 43.8 per cent in 2010.

These poverty estimates based on utility-consistent poverty lines differ considerably from INSTAT's original estimates. The original estimates are uniformly higher than the utility-consistent estimates. For example, the original national headcount ratios are 9.7 to 14.8 percentage points higher than the utility-consistent poverty rates. The differences are less stark with the poverty severity estimates, ranging from 1.2 to 9.1. Moreover, the estimated changes in poverty over the three survey periods are different in nature. The original estimates indicated that the national poverty level fell by one percentage point between 2001 and 2005, compared to the 3.3 percentage point rise using the utility-consistent estimate. Although both approaches estimate a rise in the headcount ratio between 2005 and 2010, the magnitude from the original estimates (7.8 percentage points) is markedly higher than from the utility-consistent estimates (2.6 percentage points). Further, while the original estimates found large increases in the depth and severity of poverty (8.1 and 6.2 percentage points, respectively), the utility-consistent approach found little change (0.1 and −0.4 percentage points, respectively).

In urban areas, while the INSTAT poverty estimates are uniformly higher than the utility-consistent poverty estimates, the changes over time are similar. Both show large increases in the urban headcount ratio between 2001 and 2005 of roughly eight percentage points, followed by smaller increases (between one and two percentage points) in the latter half of the decade. In

---

[2] The poverty rates are reported in the comma-delimited povmeas_ent.csv file in the PLEASe 'out' directory. Poverty lines can also be found in the povlines_ent.csv file in the same directory.

**Table 6.1.** Original INSTAT and utility-consistent poverty estimates, Madagascar 2001–10

| | INSTAT Estimates | | | UC Estimates | | | Difference | | |
|---|---|---|---|---|---|---|---|---|---|
| | 2001 | 2005 | 2010 | 2001 | 2005 | 2010 | 2001 | 2005 | 2010 |
| *National* | | | | | | | | | |
| Headcount Ratio ($P_0$) | **69.7** | **68.8** | **76.5** | **57.8** | **59.1** | **61.7** | **11.9** | **9.7** | **14.8** |
| Depth of Poverty ($P_1$) | 34.9 | 26.8 | 34.9 | 24.8 | 23.3 | 23.4 | 10.2 | 3.5 | 11.5 |
| Severity of Poverty ($P_2$) | 20.9 | 13.4 | 19.6 | 13.4 | 12.0 | 11.6 | 7.5 | 1.3 | 7.9 |
| *Urban* | | | | | | | | | |
| Headcount Ratio ($P_0$) | **43.9** | **52.0** | **54.2** | **34.2** | **42.7** | **43.8** | **9.7** | **9.3** | **10.4** |
| Depth of Poverty ($P_1$) | 18.1 | 19.3 | 21.3 | 12.8 | 15.4 | 16.0 | 5.3 | 4.0 | 5.3 |
| Severity of Poverty ($P_2$) | 9.7 | 9.4 | 11.0 | 6.5 | 7.6 | 7.8 | 3.2 | 1.8 | 3.2 |
| *Rural* | | | | | | | | | |
| Headcount Ratio ($P_0$) | **77.2** | **73.5** | **82.2** | **64.6** | **63.7** | **66.2** | **12.6** | **9.8** | **16.0** |
| Depth of Poverty ($P_1$) | 39.8 | 28.9 | 38.3 | 28.2 | 25.5 | 25.3 | 11.6 | 3.4 | 13.1 |
| Severity of Poverty ($P_2$) | 24.2 | 14.5 | 21.7 | 15.4 | 13.3 | 12.6 | 8.8 | 1.2 | 9.1 |

*Notes*: 'INSTAT' indicates original poverty lines calculated by INSTAT. 'UC' indicates Arndt and Simler (2010) utility-consistent poverty lines estimated with PLEASe. The rates are all multiplied by 100.

*Source*: Authors' elaboration based on data from INSTAT and authors' calculations based on data from EPM

terms of the depth and severity of urban poverty, both approaches found similarly sized increases over the decade. But the INSTAT estimates attribute this more to the changes in the latter half of the decade, while the utility-consistent estimates attribute it more to the changes in the first half.

The differences stemming from the two approaches are more dramatic for rural areas than for urban areas both in terms of levels and changes. As with the national estimates, the INSTAT rural poverty estimates are uniformly and substantially higher than the utility-consistent estimates (e.g. between 9.8 and 16.0 percentage point differences for the headcount ratios). Further, the large swings in rural poverty that the INSTAT estimates show are either muted or non-existent for the utility-consistent estimates, depending on the poverty measure considered. For example, while the INSTAT headcount ratio falls by 3.7 percentage points between 2001 and 2005 and then rises by 8.7 percentage points between 2005 and 2010 (for a total rise of 5.0 percentage points over the decade), the utility-consistent estimates suggest a smaller initial decline (0.9 percentage points) and subsequent rise (2.5 percentage points). For the more distribution-sensitive poverty measures, both approaches indicate declines in the depth and severity of rural poverty over the entire decade. But this is where the similarity ends. The INSTAT estimates suggest substantial swings in the interval (large declines in the first half of the decade mostly offset by large increases in the latter half), whereas the utility-consistent estimates indicate smaller and persistent decreases.

The estimates of and changes in poverty levels for spatial domains (urban and rural areas within the pre-2004 provinces) show considerable variation

**Table 6.2.** Original INSTAT and utility-consistent poverty estimates by spatial domain, Madagascar 2001–10

| | INSTAT Estimates | | | UC Estimates | | | Differences | | |
|---|---|---|---|---|---|---|---|---|---|
| | 2001 | 2005 | 2010 | 2001 | 2005 | 2010 | 2001 | 2005 | 2010 |
| Antananarivo—urban | 29.2 | 41.6 | 49.8 | 21.1 | 37.3 | 35.1 | 8.1 | 4.3 | 14.7 |
| Antananarivo—rural | 56.6 | 64.7 | 73.4 | 45.3 | 64.2 | 53.1 | 11.3 | 0.4 | 20.3 |
| Fianarantsoa—urban | 59.1 | 71.6 | 63.1 | 42.5 | 59.7 | 54.7 | 16.7 | 11.9 | 8.4 |
| Fianarantsoa—rural | 87.8 | 78.7 | 92.1 | 74.3 | 65.9 | 77.4 | 13.5 | 12.9 | 14.7 |
| Toamasina—urban | 60.6 | 55.8 | 56.9 | 46.8 | 44.3 | 45.8 | 13.8 | 11.5 | 11.1 |
| Toamasina—rural | 88.2 | 75.6 | 83.6 | 74.2 | 62.4 | 65.1 | 14.0 | 13.1 | 18.5 |
| Mahajanga—urban | 50.1 | 47.0 | 51.9 | 36.5 | 37.8 | 45.9 | 13.7 | 9.2 | 6.0 |
| Mahajanga—rural | 78.3 | 76.6 | 75.9 | 71.8 | 62.4 | 60.5 | 6.5 | 14.2 | 15.4 |
| Toliara—urban | 51.5 | 64.3 | 64.5 | 50.2 | 43.7 | 57.1 | 1.2 | 20.6 | 7.4 |
| Toliara—rural | 83.4 | 77.4 | 86.6 | 70.5 | 65.0 | 72.9 | 13.0 | 12.5 | 13.7 |
| Antsiranana—urban | 27.2 | 33.8 | 34.1 | 21.9 | 27.8 | 27.8 | 5.3 | 6.0 | 6.2 |
| Antsiranana—rural | 79.0 | 69.8 | 76.3 | 60.0 | 54.1 | 68.1 | 19.1 | 15.7 | 8.2 |
| Urban | 43.9 | 52.0 | 54.2 | 34.2 | 42.7 | 43.8 | 9.7 | 9.3 | 10.4 |
| Rural | 77.2 | 73.5 | 82.2 | 64.6 | 63.7 | 66.2 | 12.6 | 9.8 | 16.0 |
| National | 69.7 | 68.8 | 76.5 | 57.8 | 59.1 | 61.7 | 11.9 | 9.7 | 14.8 |

*Notes:* 'INSTAT' indicates original poverty lines calculated by INSTAT. 'UC' indicates Arndt and Simler (2010) utility-consistent poverty lines estimated with PLEASe. The rates are all multiplied by 100.

*Source:* Authors' calculations from EPM data

between the original INSTAT and the utility-consistent estimates (Table 6.2). In some cases, the two methods produce remarkably similar headcount ratios (e.g. roughly 64 per cent in rural Antananarivo in 2005). Whereas in others, the differences are marked (e.g. 79 per cent poor in rural Antsiranana in 2001 according to the INSTAT estimates, and 60 per cent poor according to the utility-consistent estimates). While in most cases the patterns of change are similar, there are instances where they differ substantively. For example, the INSTAT estimates show large rises in both urban and rural poverty in Antananarivo in both the first and second halves of the decade, whereas the utility-consistent estimates suggest that the large rises in poverty there between 2001 and 2005 are offset by declines (large for rural areas) between 2005 and 2010.

What accounts for these differences? Both approaches use similar methods to construct the nominal household consumption aggregate (Deaton and Zaidi 2002), and indeed the nominal household consumption aggregates are similar. The source of the differences thus follows from the handling of the poverty lines and deflation. As shown in Table 6.3, the INSTAT and utility-consistent poverty lines differ substantially for each of the spatial domains. On average, the utility-consistent poverty lines are 33 per cent lower than the INSTAT poverty lines. But this is not uniform as the differences range from 21 per cent in urban Antsiranana in 2005 to 45 per cent in rural Fianarantsao in 2005. Given the importance of specificity in constructing poverty lines, it is

**Table 6.3.** Original and utility-consistent poverty lines, Madagascar, 2001–10

| | 2001 | | | 2005 | | | 2010 | | |
| --- | --- | --- | --- | --- | --- | --- | --- | --- | --- |
| | Orig | UC | % Diff | Orig | UC | % Diff | Orig | UC | % Diff |
| *Ariary per person per day* | | | | | | | | | |
| Antananrivo—urban | 542 | 358 | −33.9 | 836 | 646 | −22.7 | 1284 | 866 | −32.6 |
| Antananrivo—rural | 522 | 340 | −35.0 | 821 | 536 | −34.7 | 1200 | 770 | −35.8 |
| Fianarantsoa—urban | 502 | 326 | −35.0 | 818 | 521 | −36.3 | 1197 | 851 | −28.9 |
| Fianarantsoa—rural | 513 | 301 | −41.3 | 823 | 451 | −45.2 | 1287 | 762 | −40.8 |
| Toamasina—urban | 550 | 362 | −34.2 | 835 | 572 | −31.5 | 1361 | 937 | −31.1 |
| Toamasina—rural | 523 | 333 | −36.4 | 822 | 501 | −39.1 | 1311 | 789 | −39.8 |
| Mahajanga—urban | 498 | 338 | −32.1 | 824 | 574 | −30.3 | 1209 | 922 | −23.7 |
| Mahajanga—rural | 468 | 347 | −25.8 | 791 | 514 | −35.0 | 1176 | 748 | −36.4 |
| Toliara—urban | 515 | 406 | −21.2 | 884 | 502 | −43.2 | 1289 | 940 | −27.1 |
| Toliara—rural | 523 | 338 | −35.4 | 794 | 498 | −37.2 | 1355 | 819 | −39.5 |
| Antsiranana—urban | 612 | 473 | −22.8 | 909 | 718 | −21.0 | 1388 | 1,080 | −22.2 |
| Antsiranana—rural | 607 | 420 | −30.7 | 902 | 593 | −34.2 | 1366 | 920 | −32.7 |
| *Relative to Urban Antananarivo* | | | | | | | | | |
| Antananrivo—urban | 100.0 | 100.0 | — | 100.0 | 100.0 | — | 100.0 | 100.0 | — |
| Antananrivo—rural | 96.4 | 94.9 | −1.6 | 98.1 | 82.9 | −15.5 | 93.4 | 89.0 | −4.7 |
| Fianarantsoa—urban | 92.7 | 91.2 | −1.6 | 97.8 | 80.6 | −17.6 | 93.2 | 98.3 | 5.5 |
| Fianarantsoa—rural | 94.7 | 84.0 | −11.2 | 98.4 | 69.8 | −29.0 | 100.2 | 88.0 | −12.2 |
| Toamasina—urban | 101.5 | 101.0 | −0.4 | 99.8 | 88.4 | −11.3 | 106.0 | 108.3 | 2.2 |
| Toamasina—rural | 96.6 | 93.0 | −3.7 | 98.3 | 77.5 | −21.2 | 102.1 | 91.1 | −10.7 |
| Mahajanga—urban | 91.9 | 94.4 | 2.7 | 98.5 | 88.8 | −9.8 | 94.1 | 106.5 | 13.1 |
| Mahajanga—rural | 86.3 | 96.9 | 12.3 | 94.5 | 79.5 | −15.9 | 91.6 | 86.4 | −5.7 |
| Toliara—urban | 95.1 | 113.4 | 19.2 | 105.7 | 77.6 | −26.6 | 100.3 | 108.6 | 8.2 |
| Toliara—rural | 96.5 | 94.4 | −2.2 | 94.9 | 77.1 | −18.8 | 105.5 | 94.6 | −10.3 |
| Antsiranana—urban | 113.1 | 132.1 | 16.8 | 108.7 | 111.1 | 2.2 | 108.1 | 124.8 | 15.4 |
| Antsiranana—rural | 112.0 | 117.4 | 4.9 | 107.8 | 91.8 | −14.9 | 106.4 | 106.3 | −0.1 |

*Notes*: 'Orig' indicates original poverty lines calculated by INSTAT. 'UC' indicates Arndt and Simler (2010) utility-consistent poverty lines estimated with PLEASe. '% Diff' indicates the percentage difference.

*Source*: Authors' calculations from EPM data

informative to consider the regional poverty lines relative to the poverty line in the capital, urban Antananarivo. When doing so, an interesting pattern emerges when the two methods give different costs of living compared to the capital. In the four instances where the INSTAT rural poverty lines indicate higher costs of living compared to urban Antananarivo (2005 Anstiranana, 2010 Fianarantsoa, 2010 Toamasina, and 2010 Toliara) the utility-consistent rural poverty lines suggest that relative costs of living are lower, which is more consistent with our intuition about differences in urban and rural price levels.

To understand why the poverty lines differ for the two approaches, we must understand how the INSTAT poverty lines were derived. The original INSTAT approach to maintaining consistency with regard to the poverty lines was to use 2001 as the benchmark. The national poverty line was calculated for 2001, and in subsequent years this poverty line was scaled up to 2005 and 2010 prices using the Antananarivo CPI. This inflated 2001 poverty line was then applied to the 2005 and 2010 regionally deflated household consumption aggregates to calculate poverty. The consumption aggregates were regionally deflated using Paasche indices calculated in each stratum relative to the consumption basket for the capital (Antananarivo) using the maximum number of common items (i.e. items consumed in all of the strata). For 2001, the spatial deflators were calculated from EPM data. This differs from the utility-consistent approach in that the latter estimates poverty lines for each region for each year and relies on revealed preference tests and maximum-entropy methods to maintain consistency.

Further, the original 2001 national food poverty line, which forms the basis of the national poverty line, was estimated as the cost of consuming 2133 calories per person per day based on the consumption patterns of the poorest 30 per cent of households ranked by the consumption aggregate. This also differs from the utility-consistent approach, which does not fix the calorie requirements to be the same across all regions. Rather it allows the demographic characteristics of the particular region to dictate the differing calorie requirements. In addition, the PLEASe code estimates initial poverty lines by valuing the minimum cost of consuming domain-specific calorie requirements based on the consumption patterns of the poorest 60 per cent of households in each domain.[3] This process is repeated over five iterations using the poverty lines from the previous iteration as the thresholds for determining the consumption patterns of the poor households. As illustrated in Table 6.4, the utility-consistent minimum calorie requirements differ across regions and are on average 43 to 62 calories higher than the INSTAT-standard 2133. One would thus expect, *ceteris paribus*, that the utility-consistent poverty lines would be higher than the original, given that the former is based on the estimated cost of acquiring more calories than the latter, and given that the initial consumption patterns reflect those of the poorest 60 per cent of households rather than the poorest 30 per cent. But this is not the case. Indeed, as illustrated in Table 6.2, the utility-consistent poverty lines range from 21 to 46 per cent *lower* than the de facto original regional poverty lines (calculated by deflating the national poverty line to region-specific prices).

The source of the lower utility-consistent poverty lines thus must follow from the composition of the basket used to value the region-specific calorie requirements. Unfortunately, the original Stata code used to construct the 2001 poverty line and regional deflators cannot be located. Thus we cannot compare the consumption baskets used to create the utility-consistent poverty

---

[3] Note that 60 per cent poor is a conservative estimate given INSTAT's national poverty estimates (see Table 6.1).

**Table 6.4.** Region- and time-specific minimum calorie requirements

| | 2001 | 2005 | 2010 | Difference from INSTAT standard (2133 calories/day) | | |
| --- | --- | --- | --- | --- | --- | --- |
| | | | | 2001 | 2005 | 2010 |
| Antananrivo—urban | 2221 | 2224 | 2212 | 88 | 91 | 79 |
| Antananrivo—rural | 2182 | 2178 | 2177 | 49 | 45 | 44 |
| Fianarantsoa—urban | 2176 | 2197 | 2185 | 43 | 64 | 52 |
| Fianarantsoa—rural | 2171 | 2169 | 2146 | 38 | 36 | 13 |
| Toamasina—urban | 2189 | 2230 | 2224 | 56 | 97 | 91 |
| Toamasina—rural | 2165 | 2187 | 2175 | 32 | 54 | 42 |
| Mahajanga—urban | 2189 | 2218 | 2189 | 56 | 85 | 56 |
| Mahajanga—rural | 2181 | 2167 | 2132 | 48 | 34 | −1 |
| Toliara—urban | 2185 | 2180 | 2170 | 52 | 47 | 37 |
| Toliara—rural | 2167 | 2169 | 2130 | 34 | 36 | −3 |
| Antsiranana—urban | 2202 | 2212 | 2216 | 69 | 79 | 83 |
| Antsiranana—rural | 2144 | 2207 | 2152 | 11 | 74 | 19 |
| Minimum | 2144 | 2167 | 2130 | 11 | 34 | −3 |
| Maximum | 2221 | 2230 | 2224 | 88 | 97 | 91 |
| Mean | 2181 | 2195 | 2176 | 48 | 62 | 43 |

*Source*: Authors' calculations from EPM data

lines with the original basket from 2001. Nonetheless, we can compare the province-level urban CPI weights (these are only calculated at the urban level) to the utility-consistent consumption basket weights aggregated to the same level. As illustrated in Table 6.5 for 2010, the utility-consistent consumption baskets place more weight on non-food items compared to the CPI baskets, offsetting the higher calorie requirements of the former.

## 6.5 Concluding Remarks

This chapter provides an application to Madagascar of the standardized PLEASe computer code stream based on Arndt and Simler's (2010) utility-consistent approach to measuring consumption poverty. In applying the code, we highlight the importance of addressing extreme values for calculating unit prices, and how to handle redistricting when conducting revealed preference tests of the utility consistency of not only regionally estimated poverty lines (i.e. do the consumption patterns in other spatial domains cost no less than the own-domain consumption patterns when both are evaluated at own-domain prices), but of these poverty lines over time.

We document how the utility-consistent approach to intertemporal and spatial deflation differs from the approach undertaken by INSTAT to produce the official poverty estimates (i.e. using urban consumer price indices), and

**Table 6.5.** Comparison of consumption weights in CPI and EPM 2010 poverty lines

| | Antananarivo | Fianarantsoa | Toamasina | Mahajanga | Toliara | Antsiranana | Total |
|---|---|---|---|---|---|---|---|
| **CPI weight structure in 2010** | | | | | | | |
| Food and beverages | 48.7 | 50.7 | 55.0 | 57.9 | 60.1 | 50.1 | 50.6 |
| Clothing and footwear | 6.2 | 10.7 | 8.9 | 10.1 | 4.4 | 7.3 | 6.8 |
| Housing, water, electricity, gas, and other fuels | 19.5 | 16.3 | 12.5 | 13.1 | 14.0 | 19.4 | 18.0 |
| Furnishings, household equipment, and routine house items | 4.5 | 4.8 | 4.6 | 5.0 | 4.0 | 5.1 | 4.5 |
| Health | 2.4 | 3.1 | 2.8 | 4.8 | 2.4 | 1.6 | 2.6 |
| Transport | 9.4 | 3.9 | 4.3 | 2.5 | 5.5 | 6.6 | 7.9 |
| Recreation and culture | 2.5 | 2.5 | 4.3 | 2.6 | 1.6 | 1.1 | 2.5 |
| Education | 3.5 | 5.3 | 4.0 | 2.5 | 3.3 | 6.1 | 3.7 |
| Restaurants and hotels | 2.0 | 0.2 | 0.6 | 0.2 | 2.6 | 0.0 | 1.6 |
| Miscellaneous goods and services | 1.4 | 2.4 | 3.0 | 1.4 | 2.0 | 2.7 | 1.7 |
| Total | 100 | 100 | 100 | 100 | 100 | 100 | 100 |
| **Difference relative to utility-consistent consumption weights (EPM 2010)—EPM—CPI** | | | | | | | |
| Food and beverages | −11.1 | −22.3 | −13.7 | −12.4 | −7.7 | −14.9 | −15.9 |
| Clothing and footwear | 3.2 | 7.1 | 5.4 | 5.9 | 0.7 | 3.3 | 3.3 |
| Housing, water, electricity, gas, and other fuels | 13.1 | 13.3 | 8.2 | 9.3 | 8.6 | 15.2 | 13.2 |
| Furnishings, household equipment, and routine house items | 1.2 | 2.4 | 0.8 | 1.0 | 0.8 | 0.2 | 1.1 |
| Health | 1.6 | 2.6 | 1.9 | 3.5 | 1.0 | 0.4 | 1.6 |
| Transport | 3.3 | 1.0 | 1.3 | −0.1 | 2.4 | 3.2 | 4.0 |
| Recreation and culture | 1.8 | 2.2 | 3.8 | 2.1 | 1.3 | 0.7 | 2.0 |
| Education | −0.5 | 2.7 | 0.8 | −1.0 | 0.8 | 0.0 | 0.2 |
| Restaurants and hotels | −0.6 | −0.2 | 0.0 | −0.6 | 0.4 | −0.6 | 0.1 |
| Miscellaneous goods and services | −11.9 | −8.7 | −8.5 | −7.8 | −8.4 | −7.4 | −9.7 |

*Sources*: Authors' elaboration based on data from INSTAT and authors' calculations based on data from EPM 2010

how the trends in these estimates differ substantially. In the case of Madagascar in 2001, 2005, and 2010, the source of the differences between the utility-consistent and INSTAT approaches is the handling of the poverty lines and deflation of the household consumption aggregates. Although differing region-specific calorie requirements contribute partly to the disparity among the poverty lines of the two approaches, the differing compositions of the baskets used to value these calorie requirements play a more important role. The utility-consistent consumption baskets place more weight on non-food items compared to the CPI baskets used by INSTAT, thus offsetting the higher calorie requirements of the former. The specificity of these utility-consistent weights, based on consumption patterns of the poor in the spatial domains, is a strength of this approach compared to the previous approach taken by INSTAT.

## References

Amendola, N. and G. Vecchi (2007). 'Growth, Inequality and Poverty in Madagascar, 2001–2005'. Mimeo. Antananarivo, Madagascar: World Bank.

Arndt, C., U. R. Beck, M. A. Hussain, K. Simler, and F. Tarp (2013). 'User Guide to Poverty Line Construction Toolkit: Version 2.0'. Denmark: Development Economics Research Group, University of Copenhagen.

Arndt, C. and K. Simler (2010). 'Estimating Utility-Consistent Poverty Lines with Applications to Egypt and Mozambique', *Economic Development and Cultural Change*, 58(3): 449–74.

Deaton, A. and S. Zaidi (2002). 'Guidelines for Constructing Consumption Aggregates for Welfare Analysis', Living Standards Measurement Study Working Paper No. 135. Washington, DC: World Bank.

Foster, J., J. Greer, and E. Thorbecke (1984). 'A Class of Decomposable Poverty Measures', *Econometrica*, 52: 761–6.

INSTAT (2002). 'Enquete aupres des Menages 2001: Rapport Principal'. Antananarivo: Ministere de l'Economie, Des Finances et du Budget.

INSTAT (2006). 'Enquete aupres des Menages 2005: Rapport Principal'. Antananarivo: Ministere de l'Economie, Des Finances et du Budget.

INSTAT (2011). 'Enquete aupres des Menages 2010: Rapport Principal'. Antananarivo: Ministere de l'Economie, Des Finances et du Budget.

Paternostro, S., J. Razafindravonona, and D. Stifel (2001). 'Changes in Poverty in Madagascar: 1993–1999', Africa Region Working Paper Series No. 19. Washington, DC: World Bank.

Pradhan, M. (2000). 'How Many Questions Should be in a Consumption Questionnaire? Evidence from a Repeated Experiment in Indonesia', Cornell Food and Nutrition Policy Program Working Paper No. 112. Ithaca, NY: Cornell University.

Ravallion, M. (1998). 'Poverty Lines in Theory and Practice', Living Standards Measurement Study Working Paper No. 133. Washington, DC: World Bank.

Ravallion, M. and B. Bidani (1994). 'How Robust Is a Poverty Profile?', *World Bank Economic Review*, 8: 75–102.

Scott, C. and B. Amenuvegbe (1990). 'Effect of Recall Duration on Reporting of Household Expenditures: An Experimental Study in Ghana', Social Dimensions of Adjustment in Sub-Saharan Africa Working Paper No. 6. Washington, DC: World Bank.

# 7

# Methods Matter

## The Sensitivity of Malawian Poverty Estimates to Definitions, Data, and Assumptions

*Ulrik Beck, Richard Mussa, and Karl Pauw*

## 7.1 Introduction

In principle, the poverty headcount is a trivial statistic to compute: it requires an estimate of per capita consumption for every person in the country and a poverty line that represents a minimum level of disposable income needed to secure basic necessities. In practice, however, estimating per capita consumption and computing a poverty line—typically using household expenditure survey data—is not trivial at all. The analyst must make many methodological choices and assumptions, for some of which there is no consensus on what constitutes the best approach. In this chapter, using Malawi as a case study, we demonstrate how poverty estimates can be highly sensitive to these choices. In doing so, we carefully document the implications of various assumptions underlying the poverty analysis by Pauw, Beck, and Mussa (2016) (referred to as PBM in the remainder of the chapter), which yielded very different estimates of poverty compared to official ones prepared by Malawi's National Statistical Office (NSO 2012).

Somewhat contrary to expectations, Malawi's official poverty estimates suggested that the national poverty headcount rate declined by only 1.8 percentage points between 2004/5 and 2010/11, while rural poverty increased marginally (NSO 2012). The analysis was based on two national Integrated Household Surveys of Malawi (IHS2 and IHS3). By contrast, using the same datasets and a largely comparable cost-of-basic-needs methodology, PBM estimate a substantial 8.4 percentage point decrease in national poverty, driven by equally sharp declines in rural and urban poverty rates. PBM interpret these findings by comparing them to non-monetary poverty indicators as well as placing them in a larger, macroeconomic context of rapid, smallholder-led agricultural growth. This technical analysis delves deeper into the methodological choices made by PBM to show how alternative assumptions influence estimates of poverty lines and, ultimately, poverty rates.

For their analysis, PBM apply the PLEASe toolkit. However, PLEASe is not overly prescriptive, but rather provides guidelines in the form of a sequence of steps that can be followed to estimate poverty. Within each of these steps, certain assumptions must be made. At least as far as some of the more fundamental decisions are concerned—such as minimum calorie requirements—PBM tried to ensure consistency with the approach used by the NSO. However, various other choices remain, and this chapter explores the impact of some of these in more detail. That being said, the analysis is not exhaustive; instead, we focus on some of the more important choices that poverty analysts are confronted with, and particularly those that have non-trivial implications for results.

## 7.2 Comparing Methodologies

### 7.2.1 *Areas of Methodological Consistency*

Several fundamental methodological choices made by PBM are consistent with those of the NSO (see NSO 2005a, 2005b, and 2012 for details). First, PBM adopted the same monthly price indices as the NSO to ensure temporal consistency of consumption across different months within the same survey. While this is a deviation from the PLEASe default guideline—that methodology proposes the use of survey prices to estimate inter-survey temporal deflation rates—the existence of missing price information for major products in some regions/months made this a sensible choice.

Second, PBM follows the approach of the NSO in using median prices to calculate implicit unit prices used to value consumption of own production. The default behaviour of PLEASe is to use average prices.

Third, PBM adopts the NSO approach of estimating the non-food poverty line as an average of non-food consumption for households whose food consumption is near the food poverty line. The default PLEASe method is to use households whose total consumption is near the poverty line.

Fourth, the caloric requirement used for estimating the poverty line is the same as that of the NSO, i.e. 2400 kilocalories (kcal) per person per day. Finally, since the estimation of non-food consumption is potentially a source of contention—for example, due to the multi-year use of durable goods,

**Table 7.1.** Overview of the sets of methodological choices investigated

| | Baseline | Modify conversion factors | Use regional poverty lines | Use survey-based prices | Allow change in food basket | Allow change in non-food shares |
|---|---|---|---|---|---|---|
| Assumption | (1) | (2) | (3) | (4) | (5) | (6) |
| Conversion factors | NSO | IFPRI | IFPRI | IFPRI | IFPRI | IFPRI |
| Poverty lines | National | National | Regional | Regional | Regional | Regional |
| Inflation estimate | CPI-based | CPI-based | CPI-based | Survey-based | Survey-based | Survey-based |
| Fixed food bundle | Yes | Yes | Yes | Yes | No | No |
| Fixed non-food share | Yes | Yes | Yes | Yes | Yes | No |

*Source*: Constructed by the authors using information from NSO (2005a, 2012).

the need to estimate rental value of housing, and so on—PBM opted to use the NSO's published non-food consumption aggregate. As we highlight in section 7.2.2, the food consumption component, however, was estimated separately by using a revised set of food consumption conversion factors.

### 7.2.2 *Areas of Methodological Differences*

In order to examine the effect of methodological differences between NSO and PBM, we introduce some of these differences in a sequence of six steps. Table 7.1 summarizes these steps. In the first step, we provide a set of 'baseline' estimates (1) which aim to remove some of the most important differences between our results and those of the NSO. Subsequent steps bring the underlying methodology closer to the results of PBM. The second step introduces a modified set of food consumption conversion factors (2); in the third step we adopt regional poverty lines (3); next implicit survey prices are used in the estimation of the poverty line inflation rate (4); fifth, we permit changes in the underlying food consumption basket (5); and finally, a flexible non-food consumption share is introduced (6). Changes in results can thus be directly attributed to the methodological changes introduced at each step of the decomposition exercise. Although the decomposition allows us to isolate the effect of several methodological differences, the comparison of poverty results is still not straightforward since each change may affect either the estimated poverty line, the estimated consumption aggregate, or both. Subsections 7.2.2.1–7.2.2.6 provide further details on the methodological changes introduced at each point in the decomposition exercise.

---

**Box 7.1.** ADJUSTMENTS OF THE PLEASe METHODOLOGY

---

The code used for this chapter employs the PLEASe toolkit with some modifications. The code stream in the 'do'-folders reproduces the results of PBM. The folder do_0tech in the IHS3 folder produces the results of this chapter, including results based on various assumption sets (see Box 7.2). The file '000_master.do' runs the entire code stream. This box documents five important changes PBM made to obtain their results, compared to the default behaviour of the PLEASe code stream.

First, PBM uses a temporal price index supplied with the surveys to ensure temporal consistency. This is implemented in the 090_temp_index.do-files.

Second, PBM use median prices instead of mean prices to estimate implicit unit prices. This is done by using the median price which is already estimated in the 110_price_unit. do and 140_iterate.do files.

Third, the non-food poverty line of PBM is estimated based on the consumption of households whose food consumption is close to the food poverty line. This is in contrast with the default PLEASe behaviour, where the non-food poverty line is based on those households whose total consumption is close to the food poverty line. This is implemented by changing the estimation of the weighting kernel 'triwt' in the three different do-files:

```
replace triwt = 11 − round(50*abs(food_pc_tpi/povline_f_flex−1)
+0.5) if abs(food_pc_tpi/povline_f_flex−1)<=0.2
```

Fourth, PBM uses a caloric requirement of 2400 calories for all households. This is implemented in the 4_calpp.do-file:

```
gen calpp2=2400
replace calpp=calpp2
```

Fifth, the iterative method of poverty line estimation was modified. The default behaviour of PLEASe is to estimate an initial poverty line based on the consumption structure of those whose consumption is below some percentile of the consumption structure. The poverty line is then re-estimated using the consumption structure of those found to be poor using the initial poverty line. PBM keeps using the lowest 60 per cent of the consumption distribution, but the iterative procedure is used to deflate consumption by region, and the resulting poorest 60 per cent of the deflated consumption distribution are used to re-estimate poverty lines in order to achieve convergence. Five iterations are run. This is implemented by keeping the original cut-off across iterations in 140_iterate.do:

```
local cutpt= $bottom
```

### 7.2.2.1 BASELINE ESTIMATES

In the first step we aim to get close to the methodology described by the NSO. This set of results therefore serves as a 'baseline' against which successive steps in the decomposition exercise can be compared. This is not an attempt to replicate official figures as there are still some remaining differences between the method employed to construct the baseline results and the method outlined by the NSO. Perhaps most importantly, PBM uses the consumption structure of the poorest 60 per cent of the consumption distribution to construct initial regional poverty lines using an iterative procedure (see Boxes 7.1 and 7.2 for details). By contrast, the NSO's poverty line in 2004/5 is derived on the basis of consumption structures of the fifth and sixth consumption deciles only. Therefore, in the results presented in section 7.3, we also include the official estimates—labelled column (0) in each instance. However, for comparative purposes with the subsequent models the baseline (1) serves as the reference case.

### 7.2.2.2 THE CHOICE OF CONVERSION FACTORS

Food consumption conversion factors are used to convert non-standard measurement units often employed in household consumption surveys (e.g. cups, plates, pails, sachets, or cups) into standard metric units, i.e. grams (g). Conversions are necessary in order to calculate standardized unit prices and to estimate the calorie contents of foods consumed. The latter involves two further conversion steps. For those purchased foods that contain non-edible portions (e.g. bananas or maize on the cob) the weight is first converted to an edible portion equivalent. Next, the calorie content is calculated by multiplying the weight by the typical number of kilocalories contained per edible gram. Poverty lines are essentially calculated as the cost of achieving a certain number of calories per day, and hence getting the unit prices, edible portions, and calorie contents right is crucial.

Analysis by Verduzco-Gallo et al. (2014) of the International Food Policy Research Institute (IFPRI) complemented by further investigations by PBM revealed various inconsistencies in the sets of conversion factors provided with the IHS2 and IHS3 datasets. Verduzco-Gallo et al. (2014) subsequently released modified sets of weight conversion factors for both the IHS2 and IHS3 in which commodity-specific inconsistencies were identified systematically on the basis of unit price outliers. As a first explicit deviation from the official poverty estimation procedure, PBM adopt the modified 'IFPRI' conversion factors as the main source of conversion factors. PBM also apply the same set of conversion factors across all regions rather than attempting to reconcile some of the regional inconsistencies.

One example of a commodity-specific inconsistency is the official conversion factor for sachets of cooking oil in the IHS2. These small plastic containers are typically around 8–10 cm in height and around 3 cm in diameter, and therefore weigh approximately 50 g. However, the IHS2 conversion factor is 456 g. Double-checking the price per gram paid for sachets confirms that the official conversion factor deviates by a factor of approximately ten. Another example is the excessive calorie content for sugar cane (purported to be

---

**Box 7.2.** ADJUSTMENTS TO THE CODE TO IMPLEMENT DIFFERENT ASSUMPTION SETS

---

In the following, we describe how each of the assumption sets detailed in section 7.2 was implemented. We take the final set of methodological choices (6) as the point of departure since this is the scenario implemented by PBM and is the one which is closest to the default PLEASe code.

Moving to choice set (5), we fix the non-food share at the IHS2 levels. This is done simply by disregarding the IHS3 non-food estimation and instead using the share of non-food consumption from IHS2. The code used to generate these poverty lines is (in 050_gen.do):

```
gen nfsh=povline_nf/(povline_nf+food_povline_ent) if ihs==2
foreach sp of numlist 1 2 3 4 {
        sum nfsh if spdomain==`sp' & ihs==2, meanonly
        replace nfsh=r(mean) if spdomain==`sp' & ihs==3
        }
gen povline_nffix=food_povline_ent/(1-nfsh) if ihs==3
```

In choice set (4), we fix the food bundle of IHS3 to the food bundle estimated using IHS2. This poverty line is built into PLEASe as food_povline_fix, so generating the total poverty line is a simple matter of (in 050_gen.do):

```
gen povline_fix=food_povline_fix/(1-nfsh) if ihs==3
```

For choice set (3), we switch to using the CPI estimate of NSO instead of the survey-based measure to update the poverty line from IHS2 to IHS3. This means that while the IHS2 poverty lines do not change, the IHS3 poverty lines are now simply estimated as (in 050_gen.do):

```
foreach sp of numlist 1 2 3 4 {
        sum povline_ent_m if ihs==2 & spdomain==`sp'
        replace povline_nsoinfl=r(mean)*(1+1.289) if ihs==3 &
        spdomain==`sp'
        }
```

To implement choice set (2), we switch from regional poverty lines to a single, national poverty line. This is done simply by letting all households belong to a single spatial region (in 1_household_2.do in the do_2nat-subfolder):

```
gen spdomain=1
```

Finally, choice set (1) is implemented by switching conversion factor set. This is implemented by loading a different set of conversion factors (in the 2_food_2.do and 1b_consumption_aggregate_ihs2.do files in the do_1cf-subfolder):

```
use "in\kgfactor04.dta",clear
```

400 kcal/100 g serving) in the official sets of conversion factors. Following the food composition tables by Lukmanji et al. (2008), a calorie content of 260 kcal per serving is applied instead.

There are three channels through which conversion factors affect poverty estimation. First, since the food poverty line is the cost of achieving a certain number of calories per day, based on the observed consumption structure of the poor, the conversion of consumption into calories matters for the composition of the food poverty line bundle since the caloric contents of food items are usually only available in standard weight units such as grams or litres. Second, unit prices are used to price the food poverty line bundle, and conversion factors will affect this valuation since unit prices are expressed in standard units. Third, since products which were not home-produced or received as in-kind transfers or gifts are priced using the median unit price of products which were bought, the choice of conversion factors also impacts the consumption aggregates of individual households.

### 7.2.2.3 REGIONAL POVERTY LINES AND UTILITY CONSISTENCY

Malawi's official poverty statistics for 2004/5 and 2010/11 compare per capita consumption levels against a single national poverty line. This approach may not be adequate to capture differences in consumption structures across different regions and between urban and rural areas (see Tarp et al. 2002; Arndt and Simler 2007). Following in the tradition of the Malawian poverty analysis for 1997/8 (see NSO 2001), PBM estimate regional poverty lines for four regions: three rural regions (North, Central, and South) as well as an urban region, comprised of urban areas (cities) across the country.

The introduction of region-specific poverty lines gives rise to the problem that different poverty bundles may not equate to the same level of welfare. Hence, following Arndt and Simler (2007), PBM adjust the regional bundles using a maximum-entropy approach that ensures utility consistency. This entropy procedure is also the default procedure in the PLEASe toolkit. The next step in the decomposition exercise therefore introduces the region-specific and utility-consistent poverty bundles.

### 7.2.2.4 USE SURVEY PRICES TO UPDATE THE FOOD POVERTY LINE

Up to this point, we have used a CPI-based measure of inflation to adjust the estimated 2004/5 poverty line to comparable 2010/11 prices. The inflation rate used (128.9 per cent) is a national average inflation estimate used by the NSO in their poverty analysis, which was derived from a 'revised' CPI series constructed especially for the poverty analysis (see PBM for a more detailed discussion). The alternative method adopted by PBM, and introduced as the next step here, is to use survey unit prices to update poverty lines. Importantly, rather than estimating a national average inflation rate, region-specific rates are estimated from the survey to adjust poverty lines. Unit prices are based on the consumption patterns of poor households and are calculated as expenditure on a given item divided by quantity. Once again, this is also the default option of the PLEASe toolkit. Using implicit survey prices has several advantages: first, it allows us to explicitly use prices faced by poor consumers when calculating the poverty line inflation rate (Günther and Grimm 2007); second, the method is transparent in the sense that the underlying data used is available in the survey rather than obtained from an external source that uses a different data collection and aggregation methodology.

### 7.2.2.5 ALLOWING FOR TEMPORAL CHANGES IN THE COMPOSITION OF THE FOOD BASKET

The rationale for accounting for regional differences in food baskets can also be applied temporally. While poverty analyses assume a consistent set of preferences over time, it is reasonable to expect that consumers change their consumption bundles over time in response to relative price changes. If ignored, this could lead to an overestimation of the poverty line in subsequent periods of analysis.

Just as spatial utility consistency between regions can be imposed, it is also possible to impose intertemporal utility consistency (Arndt and Simler 2005). This means that the changes in the food basket of the poverty line are bounded by a utility consistency requirement in order to ensure that poverty lines are consistent, not just between regions, but also between surveys. The next step in our decomposition exercise therefore simultaneously allows for intertemporal changes in the food basket of the poverty line (i.e. flexible food poverty lines), subject to a minimum caloric requirement, and imposes intertemporal utility consistency restrictions.

### 7.2.2.6 ALLOWING FOR CHANGES IN NON-FOOD CONSUMPTION SHARES OVER TIME

PBM find that the non-food share of consumption, somewhat counter-intuitively considering general improvements in welfare, declined between 2004/5 and 2010/11 in all three rural regions and over a wide range of the consumption distribution. Figure 7.1 plots estimated non-food expenditure shares (vertical axis) for urban and rural households for different chosen food poverty lines (e.g. a value of 80 per cent means '80 per cent of the actual food poverty line' as per Table 7.2). The dashed horizontal line represents the 38 per cent non-food expenditure share estimated by the NSO in its 2004/5 poverty assessment and subsequently maintained in their estimation of the 2010/11 poverty line.

The figure is interesting in several respects. Firstly, if Engel's Law holds, the estimates of non-food expenditure shares would rise as we move to higher

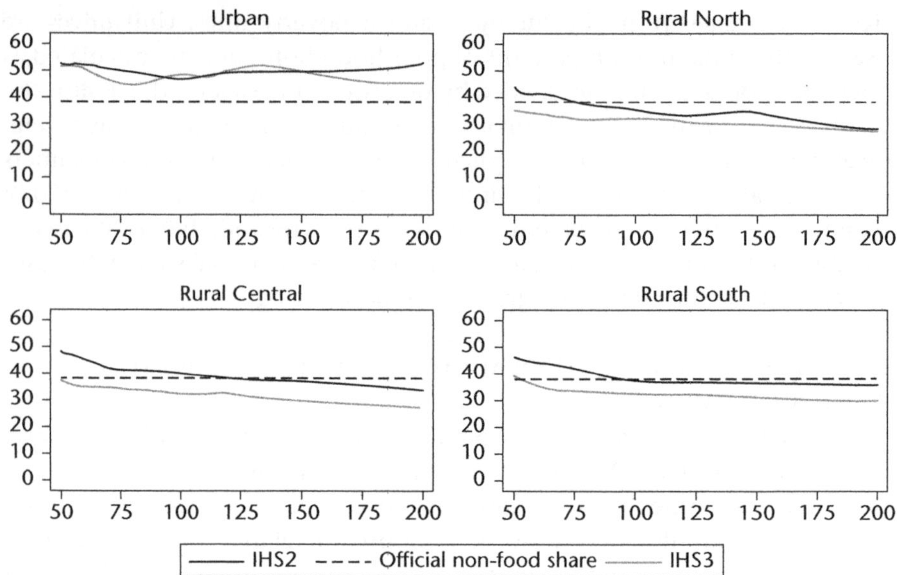

**Figure 7.1.** Estimated non-food share of total expenditure for different food poverty lines

*Note*: In all panels the horizontal axis represents the share of the estimated food poverty lines in the final model, i.e. the one used by PBM.

*Source*: Authors' calculations based on data from IHS2, IHS3, and NSO (2005, 2012)

poverty lines, simply because given the estimation procedure we would then be evaluating non-food expenditures of slightly wealthier households. It appears this only holds for urban households in 2004/5. In all other instances, the non-food share declines or is constant as we move to higher food poverty lines, which suggests extra income earned by the poor is initially spent on more (or better-quality) food rather than non-food expenditures (see further analysis by Pauw et al. 2015).

Secondly, while NSO assumed a constant non-food expenditure share of 38 per cent, we find this rate to be only reasonably close to our own non-food shares in 2004/5 in Central and southern rural areas. The non-food shares increased between the two surveys across the entire range of poverty lines considered in the rural South and Central regions, and for a wide range of possible poverty lines in the rural North. The official poverty line has a constant non-food share in the two surveys. As discussed earlier, NSO used an inflation factor of 128.9 per cent to update both the food and non-food poverty lines (NSO 2013). PBM estimated a similar non-food poverty line in 2004/5 in rural areas but a substantially lower inflation over time (on average 75.1 per cent).

On the other hand, PBM found a higher non-food poverty line for urban areas in 2004/5 as well as a higher poverty line inflation rate for non-food (133.4 per cent). The higher level of non-food consumption of the poor in urban areas is consistent with the literature where urban households are often found to consume fewer and more expensive calories (Tarp et al. 2002). This inflationary wedge is found to be consistent with the Malawi CPI information for this period. The choice to inflate both the food and non-food parts of the bundle by the weighted average of food and non-food inflation is problematic since the differential inflation will change the relative shares of food and non-food consumption moving forward. In reality, the differential food and non-food inflation rates would have resulted in a lower share of non-food items in the poverty line, even if the total poverty line did not change. The figure shows that in urban areas and for both surveys, the share is well above 38 per cent for a wide range of poverty lines. This finding should therefore also be reflected in the estimated poverty line for urban areas.

In summation, the regional and time-specific approach to poverty line estimation appears to be important in the present setting: consumption patterns, even the crude non-food shares shown here, differ substantially across regions and shift over time. Therefore, the final change we consider in our decomposition exercise is to allow the non-food consumption share to be independently determined by the actual consumption shares in both surveys, not just in the IHS2.

## 7.3 Comparison of Results

The poverty headcount rate is the share of people, nationally or in a population subgroup or region, whose per capita expenditure falls below the relevant poverty line. Since in each of our decomposition exercises, we introduce changes to consumption aggregates and/or poverty lines, we start by presenting the different poverty lines and show density plots of the different consumption aggregates. We then proceed to present the poverty results.

### 7.3.1 *Poverty Lines*

Table 7.2 shows the different poverty lines used and/or estimated. The baseline estimation (model 1) gives poverty lines, which are about 6 per cent lower than the official poverty line (model 0). Since the IHS2 poverty line is inflated by 128.9 per cent in the baseline scenario, this difference carries through to IHS3 poverty lines. Switching to the IFPRI set of conversion factors (model 2) lowers the IHS2 poverty line slightly.

**Table 7.2.** Poverty lines under different sets of methodological choices

| | Official poverty estimates (NSO) | Baseline | Modify conversion factors | Use regional poverty lines | Use survey-based prices | Allow change in food basket | Allow change in non-food shares |
|---|---|---|---|---|---|---|---|
| | (0) | (1) | (2) | (3) | (4) | (5) | (6) |
| *IHS2* | | | | | | | |
| Urban | 44.3 | 41.8 | 40.8 | 57.0 | 57.0 | 57.0 | 57.0 |
| Rural | 44.3 | 41.8 | 40.8 | 41.5 | 41.5 | 41.5 | 41.5 |
| Rural North | 44.3 | 41.8 | 40.8 | 46.1 | 46.1 | 46.1 | 46.1 |
| Rural Central | 44.3 | 41.8 | 40.8 | 43.8 | 43.8 | 43.8 | 43.8 |
| Rural South | 44.3 | 41.8 | 40.8 | 38.2 | 38.2 | 38.2 | 38.2 |
| National | 44.3 | 41.8 | 40.8 | 43.2 | 43.2 | 43.2 | 43.2 |
| *IHS3* | | | | | | | |
| Urban | 101.4 | 95.7 | 93.5 | 130.5 | 166.6 | 123.2 | 127.5 |
| Rural | 101.4 | 95.7 | 93.5 | 95.2 | 152.6 | 94.8 | 86.2 |
| Rural North | 101.4 | 95.7 | 93.5 | 105.5 | 122.3 | 100.2 | 95.6 |
| Rural Central | 101.4 | 95.7 | 93.5 | 100.2 | 164.5 | 100.1 | 88.4 |
| Rural South | 101.4 | 95.7 | 93.5 | 87.4 | 150.3 | 88.1 | 81.3 |
| National | 101.4 | 95.7 | 93.5 | 100.5 | 154.7 | 99.1 | 92.5 |
| *Poverty line inflation* | | | | | | | |
| Urban | 128.9 | 128.9 | 128.9 | 128.9 | 192.4 | 116.1 | 123.8 |
| Rural | 128.9 | 128.9 | 128.9 | 129.5 | 268.0 | 128.7 | 108.0 |
| Rural North | 128.9 | 128.9 | 128.9 | 128.9 | 165.5 | 117.5 | 107.6 |
| Rural Central | 128.9 | 128.9 | 128.9 | 128.9 | 275.8 | 128.8 | 102.1 |
| Rural South | 128.9 | 128.9 | 128.9 | 128.9 | 293.7 | 131.0 | 113.1 |
| National | 128.9 | 128.9 | 128.9 | 132.6 | 257.9 | 129.3 | 114.0 |

*Note*: The poverty lines are reported in Malawian Kwacha per day per person. The national poverty line is a population-weighted average of the regional poverty lines. The fact that national poverty line inflation differs from regional poverty line inflation factors in column 3 is due to population shifts between the regions in the timespan between the two surveys.

*Source*: Authors' calculations based on data from IHS2, IHS3, and NSO (2005a, 2012)

The introduction of regional poverty lines (model 3) raises most of the estimated regional poverty lines for 2004/5. However, the estimated national poverty line, which is a population-weighted average of the regional lines, is remarkably close to the official national poverty line (43.2 vs 44.3 MWK per day). Differences in regional poverty lines vary between 2 per cent in the rural Central region and 40 per cent in the urban areas. The urban region is where we would expect to see the largest increase due to the higher non-food consumption share documented in Figure 7.1. Differences in the structure of food consumption of the poor or the prices they face are strong justifications for the use of regional poverty lines. We return to the structure of the consumption bundles later. The remaining steps involve updating the poverty line from IHS2 to IHS3. Thus, the IHS2 poverty line does not change in these steps.

The next change is to update the poverty line using the survey prices of IHS3 (model 4) instead of exogenously imposing an inflation rate of 128.9 per cent. This change increases the poverty lines of IHS3 in all four regions substantially; for example, compared to the original estimate (model 3), the national poverty line for 2010/11 is now 54 per cent higher. This implies that the prices of the IHS2 poverty bundles rose faster than 128.9 per cent. One potential explanation for these large increases is that the IHS2 bundles were no longer representative of the consumption structure of the poor in 2010/11 when IHS3 was collected. When relative prices shift, substitution towards relatively cheaper goods means that a Laspeyres price index tends to overestimate increases in the cost of living. Using the fixed quantities of the IHS2 poverty line and updating with the IHS3 prices essentially corresponds to employing a Laspeyres price index. The implication is that the use of survey prices may be somewhat nonsensical if the consumption bundles are not updated at the same time. In fact, the use of actual (flexible) consumption bundles (model 5) brings the IHS3 poverty lines back to levels that are comparable to those in column (3). In all rural regions, the rural poverty lines are still slightly higher than the official line, while the urban poverty line is substantially higher than both the rural and official poverty lines.

The final change brings us to the set of poverty lines presented in PBM (model 6). Here the share of non-food consumption is now permitted to vary between the two survey periods. This lowers the poverty lines in all regions except the urban region. This reflects the finding reported in PBM that the non-food share of consumption fell between the two surveys in the three rural regions.

### 7.3.2 Consumption Aggregates

We now turn to the consumption aggregates used for calculating the poverty rates. Figure 7.2 shows the distribution of the different consumption aggregates used for the two surveys.

While the changes in consumption aggregates appear small due to the use of a log scale on the horizontal axis, the differences between consumption aggregates are in fact substantial, particularly for IHS3. Moreover, even if changes were small, they can have a big effect on estimated poverty rates since the density of observations is high in the region of the poverty line. Using the conversion factors supplied by NSO, we did not replicate the NSO consumption aggregate—our estimate has a lower mean. However, switching to the IFPRI conversion factors reverses this: the distribution of the consumption aggregate using the IFPRI conversion factors is right-shifted, compared to the NSO consumption aggregate.

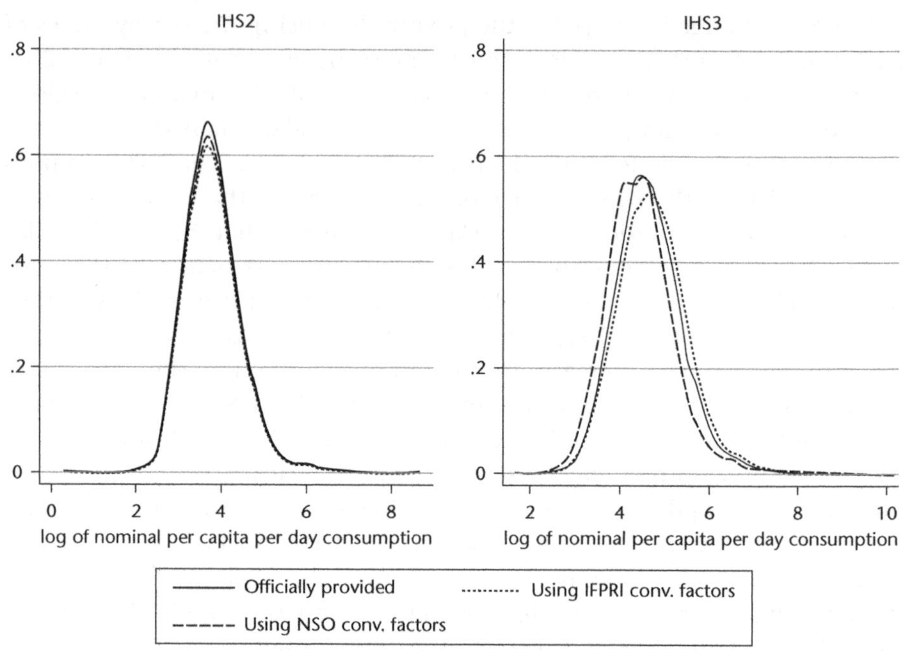



**Figure 7.2.** Kernel density plots of consumption aggregates using different conversion factor sets

*Source*: Authors' calculations based on data from IHS2 and IHS3

### 7.3.3 *Poverty Headcount Rates*

Table 7.3 shows the poverty headcount rates under different sets of methodological choices. There are two noticeable differences between the official figures (model 0) and our baseline estimates (model 1). First, the baseline poverty lines are slightly lower. Since the IHS3 poverty line in the baseline scenario is simply 128.9 per cent higher than the IHS2 poverty line, the differences carry through to IHS3 poverty lines. Second, while the IHS2 consumption aggregates are quite similar, baseline estimation of the IHS3 consumption aggregate gives somewhat lower values for a large proportion of households. In total, this means that in this baseline estimation, poverty is found to increase from IHS2 to IHS3.

The poverty headcount is always a result of combining the consumption aggregates and the poverty lines such as those presented in Figure 7.2 and Table 7.2. The rest of the results in Table 7.3 are therefore unsurprising given the discussion in sections 7.3.1 and 7.3.2. Using the IFPRI set of conversion factors (model 2) lowers poverty rates substantially since poverty lines are mostly unchanged while the IHS3 consumption distribution shifts to the

**Table 7.3.** Poverty headcounts under different sets of methodological choices

| | Official poverty estimates (NSO) | Baseline | Modify conversion factors | Use regional poverty lines | Use survey-based prices | Allow change in food basket | Allow change in non-food shares |
|---|---|---|---|---|---|---|---|
| | (0) | (1) | (2) | (3) | (4) | (5) | (6) |
| *IHS2* | | | | | | | |
| Urban | 25.5 | 22.6 | 20.4 | 37.6 | 37.6 | 37.6 | 37.6 |
| Rural | 55.9 | 51.2 | 47.0 | 48.2 | 48.2 | 48.2 | 48.2 |
| Rural North | 56.3 | 56.0 | 50.8 | 59.4 | 59.4 | 59.4 | 59.4 |
| Rural Central | 46.7 | 39.1 | 35.3 | 40.0 | 40.0 | 40.0 | 40.0 |
| Rural South | 64.4 | 61.3 | 57.0 | 53.1 | 53.1 | 53.1 | 53.1 |
| National | 52.4 | 47.9 | 43.9 | 47.0 | 47.0 | 47.0 | 47.0 |
| *IHS3* | | | | | | | |
| Urban | 17.3 | 28.5 | 14.6 | 28.7 | 38.9 | 26.0 | 27.3 |
| Rural | 56.6 | 63.1 | 45.1 | 46.2 | 71.3 | 45.9 | 40.6 |
| Rural North | 59.9 | 68.1 | 47.1 | 54.9 | 64.5 | 50.6 | 48.0 |
| Rural Central | 48.7 | 55.4 | 36.8 | 40.6 | 67.9 | 40.6 | 33.7 |
| Rural South | 63.3 | 69.1 | 52.4 | 49.1 | 76.5 | 49.6 | 45.1 |
| National | 50.7 | 57.9 | 40.4 | 43.6 | 66.4 | 42.9 | 38.6 |
| *Change in poverty headcount, percentage points* | | | | | | | |
| Urban | −8.2* | 6.0 | −5.8 | −8.9 | 1.3 | −11.6* | −10.3* |
| Rural | 0.8 | 12.0* | −1.9 | −1.9 | 23.1* | −2.3 | −7.5* |
| Rural North | 3.6 | 12.1* | −3.7 | −4.5 | 5.1 | −8.8* | −11.4* |
| Rural Central | 2.0 | 16.3* | 1.5 | 0.6 | 27.9* | 0.6 | −6.3* |
| Rural South | −1.1 | 7.8* | −4.5* | −4.0 | 23.5* | −3.5 | −8.0* |
| National | −1.8 | 10.0* | −3.5* | −3.4* | 19.4* | −4.1* | −8.4* |

*Note*: Asterisks indicate that the poverty change is statistically significant at the 5% level. The confidence interval is used to determine the statistical significance of the difference in the poverty rate between 2004/5 and 2010/11. Since the distribution of the poverty rate is unknown we follow Arndt and Simler (2007) in defining the confidence interval as plus or minus twice the standard error.

*Source*: Authors' calculations based on data from IHS2 and IHS3

right. We now have a statistically significant decrease in poverty of 3.5 percentage points at the national level.

Imposing regional poverty lines and utility consistency (model 3) raises the poverty levels of all four regions, which explains the increases in the level of poverty in 2004/5, compared to the previous model. Since the poverty line inflation is still imposed exogenously to be 128.9 per cent, it also raises the level of poverty in 2010/11. At the national level, the decline in poverty is practically unchanged. When we allow for a flexible bundle that changes between survey rounds, however, we find a moderate decrease in poverty of 4.1 per cent at the national level (model 5). Finally, allowing the non-food share to change over time (model 6) contributes substantially to the decline in poverty, which relates to the declining non-food shares over the period, as discussed earlier and in detail by PBM. This change gives us the final result reported by PBM: a decrease in the poverty rate of 8.4 percentage points.

### 7.3.4 Robustness of the Underlying Food Bundles

The underlying food bundle used for constructing poverty lines is crucial for poverty line construction. Yet this matter is rarely discussed in poverty analyses. One reason for this might be that there is no formula for determining what a reasonable food bundle looks like: typically, it is very country-specific and may also reflect economic conditions particular to the survey year. As a result, poverty analysts often have to make judgement calls as to whether a given bundle seems 'reasonable'. Explicit presentation of the food bundle opens up for discussion the question of whether the food bundle is reasonable. Of course, the lack of a gold standard to compare food bundles does not mean that this step should be overlooked when constructing poverty lines. As the results of Table 7.3 show, changes in how the food bundle is constructed can change poverty rates substantially. And the structure of the food bundles contain useful information which can help explain spatial and temporal differences in poverty lines.

Table 7.4 presents shares of calories in the food bundles of IHS2 before regional bundles are allowed and utility consistency is imposed (i.e. as in model 2 in Table 7.1) and after (as per models 3–6). Table 7.5 presents the utility-consistent bundles of IHS2 and IHS3 (this corresponds to model 6 in Table 7.1). The seven most important items in terms of caloric contribution to the poverty lines of model 6 in each region in each year were selected. Only

**Table 7.4.** Caloric shares of most important food items in national and regional poverty lines in 2004/5

| | National | Regional bundles | | | Differences | | | |
|---|---|---|---|---|---|---|---|---|
| | Bundle | Urban | Rural North | Rural Central | Rural South | Urban | Rural North | Rural Central | Rural South |
|---|---|---|---|---|---|---|---|---|---|
| Maize flour | 68.7 | 73.6 | 54.4 | 65.6 | 71.3 | 4.9 | −14.3 | −3.1 | 2.6 |
| —normal | 43.1 | 39.0 | 16.7 | 31.1 | 54.4 | −4.2 | −26.4 | −12.1 | 11.2 |
| —refined | 25.5 | 34.6 | 37.7 | 34.6 | 16.9 | 9.1 | 12.1 | 9.0 | −8.6 |
| Cassava tubers | 3.1 | 2.2 | 4.0 | 2.6 | 3.5 | −0.8 | 1.0 | −0.4 | 0.4 |
| Cassava flour | 2.5 | 0.0 | 12.9 | 2.3 | 0.0 | −2.5 | 10.4 | −0.2 | −2.5 |
| Bean, brown | 1.9 | 2.1 | 2.4 | 3.0 | 1.6 | 0.2 | 0.5 | 1.1 | −0.4 |
| Groundnut | 3.4 | 1.4 | 4.3 | 6.9 | 1.2 | −2.0 | 1.0 | 3.5 | −2.2 |
| Sugar | 1.8 | 4.3 | 3.3 | 1.4 | 1.6 | 2.5 | 1.5 | −0.4 | −0.2 |
| **Total** | **81.4** | **83.6** | **81.4** | **81.8** | **79.1** | **2.3** | **0.1** | **0.5** | **−2.3** |

*Note*: All numbers are in %.

*Source*: Authors' calculations based on data from IHS2

**Table 7.5.** Caloric shares of most important food items in entropy-adjusted poverty line

| | IHS2 | | | | IHS3 | | | | Differences | | | |
| --- | --- | --- | --- | --- | --- | --- | --- | --- | --- | --- | --- | --- |
| | Urban | Rural North | Rural Central | Rural South | Urban | Rural North | Rural Central | Rural South | Urban | Rural North | Rural Central | Rural South |
| Maize flour | 73.6 | 54.4 | 65.6 | 71.3 | 72.7 | 70.9 | 77.6 | 73.6 | −0.9 | 16.5 | 12.0 | 2.3 |
| —Normal | 39.0 | 16.7 | 31.1 | 54.4 | 39.4 | 20.9 | 34.6 | 56.4 | 0.4 | 4.1 | 3.6 | 2.1 |
| —Refined | 34.6 | 37.7 | 34.6 | 16.9 | 33.2 | 50.0 | 43.0 | 17.1 | −1.4 | 12.3 | 8.4 | 0.2 |
| Cassava tubers | 2.2 | 4.0 | 2.6 | 3.5 | 1.0 | 2.0 | 0.9 | 1.7 | −1.2 | −2.0 | −1.7 | −1.8 |
| Cassava flour | 0.0 | 12.9 | 2.3 | 0.0 | 0.0 | 7.1 | 1.2 | 0.0 | 0.0 | −5.8 | −1.1 | 0.0 |
| Bean, brown | 2.1 | 2.4 | 3.0 | 1.6 | 1.6 | 3.0 | 1.7 | 0.9 | −0.6 | 0.6 | −1.3 | −0.6 |
| Groundnut | 1.4 | 4.3 | 6.9 | 1.2 | 1.7 | 1.5 | 3.1 | 1.8 | 0.3 | −2.8 | −3.8 | 0.6 |
| Sugar | 4.3 | 3.3 | 1.4 | 1.6 | 4.0 | 2.8 | 1.5 | 1.7 | −0.3 | −0.5 | 0.2 | 0.1 |
| **Total** | **83.6** | **81.4** | **81.8** | **79.1** | **80.9** | **87.4** | **86.0** | **79.6** | **−2.8** | **6.0** | **4.2** | **0.5** |

*Note*: The food bundles shown in this table are the final bundles which were used in Pauw et al. (2015). They correspond to assumption set 6 in Table 7.1.

*Source*: Authors' calculations based on data from IHS2 and IHS3

items which showed up in three or more region-years were included. The focus on caloric contributions means that a few items such as salt which do not provide calories but are still part of the food bundles will not feature in this table. Alternatively, one could have picked products based on expenditure shares of the food bundle, but by using caloric contributions we are able to abstract from prices and still compare food bundles in a meaningful way. This procedure resulted in a total list of seven food products which make up at least 79 per cent of the caloric contents of the food poverty lines in all regions in both years.

Table 7.4 reveals some differences in the composition of the food consumption of the poor between the four regions. In the Urban and Rural South regions over 70 per cent of calories come from maize flour, where this share is only 54 per cent in the Rural North region. Here, cassava and cassava flour provide 17 per cent of calories. The national bundle caloric shares are bounded by the lowest and highest shares in each region but the regional differences are substantial and are missed using this approach. Table 7.4 therefore provides supporting evidence that estimating regional poverty lines may be important to capture spatial differences in the consumption structure of the poor.

In general, the caloric structure of the regional IHS2 food bundles look reasonable. Verduzco-Gallo et al. (2014) found that different types of maize makes up between 63 and 72 per cent of caloric consumption for the three poorest quintiles. Our food bundle has a somewhat lower maize consumption share for Rural North but this is largely made up for by cassava consumption, another cheap source of calories.

The consumption structure derived from IHS2 and IHS3 is shown in Table 7.5. The structure exhibits a great deal of consistency over time. Also in IHS3, maize flour was by far the most important source of calories and it appears to have increased in importance in all rural areas. This is perhaps not surprising as FISP (the Farm Input Subsidy Programme) is thought to have increased maize yields significantly. The official statistics report more than a doubling of maize yields in the years between the two surveys. Even though the maize production statistics have been questioned, it is still reasonable to expect that maize consumption of the poor would have increased over this period, particularly in the Rural North and Rural Central where the contribution of maize to the caloric contents of the poverty lines was relatively lower in 2004/5. A natural next question is what are the products in 2004/5 that were substituted for the additional calories covered by maize in 2010/11. This substitution cannot be attributed to one single product; instead, there are smaller decreases in many reported products as well as in other products in the poverty lines with caloric shares too low to be featured in the table (this is evident from the increases in the 'total' row).

The changes over time are consistent with the observation by Verduzco-Gallo et al. (2014) who find that while dietary diversity increased for the rich and middle-income quintiles, dietary diversity decreased from 2004/5 to 2010/11 for the poorest quintiles, partly due to an increase in consumption of maize.

In conclusion, the food bundles exhibit a great deal of consistency over time and correspond with what can be called stylized facts about the consumption structure of the poor in Malawi, including decreasing dietary diversity over time and a high and increasing degree of dependence on maize to meet caloric needs. Table 7.5 therefore provides supporting evidence that the changes in food bundles over time seem reasonable.

## 7.4 Concluding Remarks

This chapter considered a set of methodological choices for estimating poverty using the two Integrated Household Surveys of Malawi, collected in 2004/5 (IHS2) and 2010/11 (IHS3). Different methodological choices were found to matter for both the level of poverty and evolution over time. However, the various results based on what we deem reasonable sets of assumptions (models 0, 2, 3, 5, and 6) all agree that poverty declined in this period in Malawi. Of these, the models estimated by us (2, 3, 5, and 6) show a statistically significant decline in poverty at the national level. The magnitude varies between 3.4 and 8.4 percentage points, which are all larger than the officially reported poverty decrease. In this sense, the main result that poverty decreased significantly in Malawi over the period is characterized by a high degree of robustness—even though the actual numbers are quite sensitive to the specific assumptions made.

In what sense is it reasonable to re-estimate the poverty line bundle for IHS3? One might argue that despite entropy adjustments made to ensure utility consistency, we cannot guarantee welfare equivalence. If the same bundle is used in both periods, at least we are sure that at the poverty line, people can buy a well-defined and unchanging bundle. There are two problems with this argument. First, as shown by Arndt and Simler (2005) and reiterated by PBM, changing prices mean that the IHS2 bundle priced at IHS3 prices is most likely overvaluing the cheapest way to obtain a welfare-equivalent bundle at the time IHS3 was collected. Second, the poverty line was updated by exogenously imposing an inflation rate of 128.9 per cent. It is not clear how this inflation rate is connected to the IHS2 poverty line bundle, so the welfare equivalence of the IHS2 and the IHS3 poverty line, even in the interpretation that the same bundle should be affordable at the poverty line, cannot be taken for granted. The fact that the food and the non-food poverty lines were inflated by the same factor is almost certainly incorrect, considering the large increases in food prices over the period as well as the observed decline of non-food consumption as a share of total consumption. The food bundle analysis of this chapter lends additional credibility to temporal re-estimation of poverty line food bundles, as the bundles appear quite stable over time except for the increase in maize consumption, which most likely reflects a real change due to the introduction of the FISP programme, and which is corroborated by other evidence (Verduzco-Gallo et al. 2014).

Ultimately, as far as poverty analysis is concerned, there is no single set of methodological choices that can be deemed 'most correct' or appropriate. However, the relatively large changes in results obtained from one method to another underline the importance of clearly articulating these choices and their implications to ensure that results are transparent. This ensures that discussions can be fruitfully focused on what poverty estimates imply for past and future policy rather than whether the numbers can be trusted or not.

# References


Arndt, Channing and Kenneth R. Simler (2005). 'Estimating Utility-Consistent Poverty Lines', Food Consumption and Nutrition Division Discussion Paper No. 189, International Food Policy Research Institute, Washington, DC.

Arndt, Channing and Kenneth R. Simler (2007a). 'Consistent Poverty Comparisons and Inference', *Agricultural Economics*, 37(2–3): 133–9.

Günther, Isabel and Michael Grimm (2007). 'Measuring Pro-Poor Growth When Relative Prices Shift', *Journal of Development Economics*, 82(1): 245–56.

Lukmanji, Zohra, E. Hertzmark, N. Mlingi, V. Assey, G. Ndossi, and W. Fawzi (2008). 'Tanzania Food Composition Tables'. Dar es Salaam, Tanzania: MUHAS, TFNC, HSPH.

NSO (National Statistics Office) (2001). 'The Determinants of Poverty in Malawi, 1998: An Analysis of the Malawi Integrated Household Survey, 1997/98'. Zomba, Malawi: National Statistical Office.

NSO (2005a). 'Integrated Household Survey 2004–2005, Volume I: Household Socio-Economic Characteristics. Zomba, Malawi: National Statistical Office.

NSO (2005b). 'Note on Construction of Expenditure Aggregate and Poverty Lines for IHS2'. Unpublished documentation.

NSO (2012). 'Integrated Household Survey 2010–2011: Household Socio-Economic Characteristics Report'. Zomba, Malawi: National Statistical Office.

NSO (2013). Price Index Excel sheet received from NSO.

Pauw, Karl, Ulrik Beck, and Richard Mussa (2016). 'Did Rapid Smallholder-Led Agricultural Growth Fail to Reduce Rural Poverty?', in Channing Arndt, Andy McKay, and Finn Tarp (eds), *Growth and Poverty in Sub-Saharan Africa*. Oxford: Oxford University Press, 89–111.

Pauw, Karl, Iñigo Verduzco-Gallo, and Olivier Ecker (2015). 'Poverty, Food Prices, and Dietary Choices in Malawi', in Noora Aberman, Todd Benson, and Janice Meerman (eds), Mapping the Linkages between Agriculture, Food Security and Nutrition in Malawi. Washington, DC: Malawi Strategy Support Program, International Food Policy Research Institute, ch. 3.

Tarp, Finn, Kenneth Simler, Cristina Matusse, Rasmus Heltberg, and Gabriel Dava (2002). 'The Robustness of Poverty Profiles Reconsidered', *Economic Development and Cultural Change*, 51(1): 77–108.

Verduzco-Gallo, Íñigo, Olivier Ecker, and Karl Pauw (2014). 'Changes in Food and Nutrition Security in Malawi: Analysis of Recent Survey Evidence', International Food Policy Research Institute (IFPRI) Malawi Strategy Support Program, Working Paper 06.

# 8

# A Review of Consumption Poverty Estimation for Mozambique

*Channing Arndt, Sam Jones, Kristi Mahrt,*
*Vincenzo Salvucci, and Finn Tarp*

## 8.1 Introduction and Context

Since the end of the civil war in 1992, Mozambique has registered significant progress across a range of monetary and non-monetary poverty indicators at both national and regional levels. This conclusion of material progress draws from a large array of nationally representative datasets that became available starting from 1996. A detailed discussion of the evolution of welfare conditions in Mozambique can be found in Arndt, Jones, and Tarp (2016), which is the Mozambique chapter of the companion volume to this book.

In this chapter, we are concerned with the estimation of consumption poverty rates. Four national household budget surveys have been carried out in Mozambique: 1996/7, 2002/3, 2008/9, and 2014/15. The most recent survey has yet to be analysed as of this writing. Official poverty estimates were computed in a series of national poverty assessments (MPF/DNPO 1998; MPF/DNPO 2004; MPD/DNEAP 2010). Main results from these analyses indicate that consumption poverty (as measured by the headcount rate) fell significantly from 1996/7 to 2002/3 at the national level, whereas more recent data from 2008/9 show that consumption poverty was essentially the same as in 2002/3 at the national level.

This chapter begins by broadly reviewing the challenges encountered and choices made in the national assessments. Efforts to maintain consistency with the previous survey imply that prior choices tend to be adopted in subsequent analyses. At the same time, the practice of consumption poverty analysis is not static. Because 'best practice' evolves (and hopefully improves) with time, there arises a natural tension between the desire to follow best practice and the desire to maintain consistency with previous analyses. In section 8.3, we present new consumption poverty estimates for 2002/3 and 2008/9 using the default PLEASe software stream.[1] Principal differences between the PLEASe software and the methodologies employed in the national assessments are discussed.

A final section discusses in more detail the gradual accretion of tensions between consistency with previous analyses and evolving practice in both data collection and analysis, and concludes that the major findings from the three national assessments are robust. The results also point to the strong benefits of applying consistent methods over time, implying a need to re-estimate existing results as data collection methods, circumstances, and analytical techniques evolve.

## 8.2 Challenges and Choices

When the civil war finally ended in 1992, Mozambique was labelled the 'poorest country in the world' (Arndt, Jensen, and Tarp 2000). Remarkably, the 1996/7 household consumption survey (IAF96) was in the field only four years later. Not surprisingly, the survey that underpinned Mozambique's first national poverty assessment faced considerable challenges. Challenges encountered in the field included but were not limited to:

i. degraded or absent infrastructure as a consequence of more than ten years of civil war;

ii. widespread prevalence of landmines that demanded care while travelling in rural areas;

iii. major flooding in Sofala province that disrupted data collection;

iv. a vast array of non-standard units, which varied drastically across space and significantly complicated the estimation of quantities; and

v. the lack of a census sample frame.

Despite these barriers, a sample was obtained (largely relying on electoral lists from the 1994 election) and more than 8000 households were interviewed. The questionnaire contained a detailed consumption module alongside a series of other modules, including a community questionnaire. These modules gathered, among other items, market price information and

---

[1] As emphasized in Chapter 1, we do not pretend to label the default PLEASe as 'best practice', and certainly not in every case. Nevertheless, the defaults are certainly not manifestly inappropriate for Mozambique and serve as a convenient reference point. Also, as will be discussed, the complete code stream is only applied to the 2002/3 and 2008/9 data.

anthropometrics for children under five years of age. The resulting report was comprehensive and set a high standard for consumption poverty analysis in a low-income context given the knowledge base at the time.

The first assessment adopted a 'cost of basic needs' approach (see Chapters 2 and 4). Analysis of consumption patterns and food prices revealed pronounced differences across regions as well as between rural and urban zones. In a choice that was novel for the time period, the team charged with the first assessment elected to develop separate consumption bundles by region in order to accommodate this variation in consumption patterns and prices. Thirteen spatial domains were identified, of which six were rural and seven urban.[2]

The team conducting the analysis of the 1996/7 survey was well aware of the ongoing debates relating to consistency versus specificity discussed in Chapter 2. The team was also large and diverse, containing economists as well as specialists in nutrition and agriculture. Substantial efforts were made to arrive at bundles for the thirteen spatial domains that provided a similar level of welfare. This occurred through a series of ad hoc adjustments to the bundles underlying the poverty lines. Revealed preference conditions were not evaluated or imposed in the development of the official poverty rates.

As shown in Table 8.1, the first assessment estimated quite high consumption poverty rates almost everywhere, with more than 69 per cent of the population failing to consume more than the very basic standard of living implied by the poverty lines. As one might expect, significant shares of the population clustered near the poverty line. For example, while the estimated rural poverty rate at the full poverty line amounted to more than 71 per cent of the population, the rural population living below the food poverty line (which sits at about 80 per cent of the full poverty line) amounted to 56 per cent of the population.

Moving to the 2002/3 survey, a number of the major logistical challenges facing the survey team had been relieved compared with 1996/7. A census in 1997 provided a sample frame.[3] While infrastructure remained poor in an absolute sense, substantial efforts had been made to improve roads and other key infrastructure. Landmines remained a threat, but de-mining activities had been successfully ongoing for years with literally millions of landmines removed and remaining areas with landmines largely cordoned off. Climatic conditions were generally favourable both for crop production and for the conduct of the survey. Problems with non-standard units were mitigated by

---

[2] The domains consist of Maputo City plus separate domains for the rural and urban zones of Niassa and Cabo Delgado, Nampula, Sofala and Zambezia, Manica and Tete, Gaza and Inhambane, and Maputo Province.

[3] The 1997 census adopted a broader definition of urban than had been applied to IAF96. In particular, IAF96 defined 20 percent of the population as urban while the 1997 census defined about 30 per cent of the population as urban.

**Table 8.1.** Comparison of official and PLEASe poverty estimates

| Area | Official Estimates | | | RP Consistent | PLEASe Estimates | |
|---|---|---|---|---|---|---|
| | 1996/7 | 2002/3 | 2008/9 | 1996/7 | 2002/3 | 2008/9 |
| National | 69.4 | 54.1 | 54.7 | 69.7 | 52.8 | 51.7 |
| Urban | 62.0 | 51.5 | 49.6 | 61.8 | 48.2 | 46.8 |
| Rural | 71.3 | 55.3 | 56.9 | 71.8 | 55.0 | 53.8 |
| North | 66.3 | 55.3 | 46.5 | 67.3 | 51.9 | 45.1 |
| Centre | 73.8 | 45.5 | 59.7 | 74.1 | 49.2 | 57.0 |
| South | 65.8 | 66.5 | 56.9 | 65.5 | 59.9 | 51.2 |
| Niassa | 70.6 | 52.1 | 31.9 | 71.9 | 48.3 | 33.0 |
| Cabo Delgado | 57.4 | 63.2 | 37.4 | 59.1 | 60.3 | 39.0 |
| Nampula | 68.9 | 52.6 | 54.7 | 69.4 | 49.1 | 51.4 |
| Zambézia | 68.1 | 44.6 | 70.5 | 67.6 | 49.7 | 67.2 |
| Tete | 82.3 | 59.8 | 42.0 | 81.9 | 60.5 | 41.0 |
| Manica | 62.6 | 43.6 | 55.1 | 62.4 | 44.7 | 52.8 |
| Sofala | 87.9 | 36.1 | 58.0 | 87.8 | 41.3 | 54.4 |
| Inhambane | 82.6 | 80.7 | 57.9 | 83.0 | 78.1 | 54.6 |
| Gaza | 64.7 | 60.1 | 62.5 | 64.8 | 55.4 | 61.0 |
| Maputo Province | 65.6 | 69.3 | 67.5 | 65.6 | 59.0 | 55.9 |
| Maputo City | 47.8 | 53.6 | 36.2 | 47.1 | 42.9 | 29.9 |

*Sources:* Ministry of Planning and Finance/DNPO (1998); Ministry of Planning and Finance/DNPO (2004); Ministry of Planning and Development/DNEAP (2010); and authors' calculations

providing enumerator teams with portable scales such that a local unit (e.g. a can) could be converted to grams or litres or some other standard measure.

The team engaged in the analysis of the 2002/3 survey maintained the essential structure of the analysis from 1996/7. As noted, the 1996/7 analysis set a high standard for comprehensiveness and quality, especially in light of the difficulties encountered by enumerators in the field. Hence, the choice to maintain the essential structure followed logically.

Maintaining exact coherence was difficult, however. Consistent with standard practice at the time, the capability to reproduce the 1996/7 analysis from the raw data had not been preserved. A series of coding files had been used to generate a series of databases; however, the exact mapping between coding files and databases had been only loosely documented. To compound matters, analysis took place in two separate computer languages—SPSS and STATA. Finally, the data itself underwent a prolonged cleaning process that continued through the process of analysis.

The inability to reproduce the 1996/7 analysis implied that, for 2002/3, the series of choices necessary to, for example, produce the nominal consumption aggregate or to estimate prices were made frequently on the basis of recall by team members from the first assessment. To prevent recurrence of this situation, the second assessment constructed a continuous code stream that began with the raw data files as obtained from the statistics service and progressed through to final results. This guaranteed the ability to reproduce results and provided complete documentation of all decisions. This code also turned out to be an antecedent of PLEASe.

For 2002/3, a series of additional choices were required. The simplest approach to estimating poverty would have been to use the bundles derived in 1996/7 and price them in 2002/3 (implicitly assuming an elasticity of substitution in consumption of zero). This approach yielded a decline in poverty to about 63 per cent (MPF/DNPO 2004). However, an analysis of the poverty rate that would have prevailed, assuming a Cobb–Douglas utility function (assuming an elasticity of substitution equal to one), yielded a poverty rate of about 52 per cent (Arndt and Simler 2010). This analysis implied that substitution across foods in consumption was potentially important given observed changes in relative prices. Hence, the decision was made to re-estimate the bundles.

Consistent with best practice at the time, the team charged with the second assessment adopted a version of the iterative approach to estimating poverty lines discussed in Chapters 2 and 4. Once again, consistency of this approach with the one applied in 1996/7 was achieved mainly via recall. In addition, analysis conducted after the publication of the first assessment indicated revealed preference violations for some of the final bundles derived in 1996/7. Violations were also detected for many of the initial bundles emanating from the iterative approach used in 2002/3. As a result, the approach for estimating utility-consistent poverty lines discussed in Chapters 2 and 4 was applied to 2002/3 food bundles.

Spatial utility consistency was only imposed on estimated poverty lines for 2002/3 but not retroactively to the bundles derived in 1996/7. As shown in Table 8.1, application of spatial utility consistency to 1996/7 would have changed the published poverty estimates for that survey year. For the Mozambican government and statistics service, any change in existing official poverty estimates was unacceptable. The decision to leave 1996/7 estimates alone had implications for the application of temporal conditions. Specifically, the temporal conditions applied in 2002/3 were made relative to bundles from 1996/7 that were themselves revealed-preference-inconsistent (though not dramatically so). In addition, the first assessment team had encountered serious problems in estimating food bundles in the urban zone of the province of Maputo, which contains the capital city. These bundles were also estimated to fail spatial revealed preference conditions. The complexities of Maputo were also evident in 2002/3 with high-quality bundles emerging from the iterative procedure.

In the end, for 2002/3, the fixed bundle approach was imposed on Maputo (three spatial domains) by bringing forward the 1996/7 bundles and pricing them in 2002/3. This choice was pragmatic at the time, given the demand for published results. Nevertheless, it did set the poverty lines and hence rates in

Maputo to their maximum level consistent with temporal revealed preferences and ignored the spatial failure of revealed preference conditions (too high quality) of these bundles in 1996/7. The bundles for the remaining ten spatial domains were estimated using an iterative procedure similar to the one described in Chapter 4. Spatial and temporal revealed preference conditions were applied to these ten spatial domains.

Results for 2002/3 indicated a substantial decline in poverty. At the national level, the poverty rate declined by fifteen percentage points to about 54 per cent (see Table 8.1). These results were attributed to a return to a more normal living standard relative to the very low standards prevailing in the immediate post-civil-war period, climatic conditions reasonably favourable to agricultural production, and positive underlying development dynamics. The relative weights across these factors are essentially impossible to ascertain.

Turning to 2008/9, the survey was conducted on a sample derived from a new population census carried out in 2007. For this third assessment, the analytical team had the possibility to begin from the code stream developed for the second assessment in 2002/3. This constituted a considerable advantage (similar to PLEASe). As care had been exercised to maintain comparability of questionnaires across all the surveys, the mechanics of the analysis were simplified, and the approach applied in 2008/9 was essentially identical to the one applied in 2002/3. This included continued special treatment of Maputo with respect to revealed preference conditions and the imposition of utility consistency.[4]

With the advantage of an established approach, more detailed analysis and cross-checking became possible. The third assessment contains a large array of cross-checks and sensitivity analyses using data from both the 2008/9 budget survey and across alternative sources of information (MPD/DNEAP 2010). For example, the rate of price inflation implied by the poverty lines over the period 2002/3 to 2008/9 was compared with the rates implied by price data from the agricultural market information system and detailed consumer price index data. In addition, a macroeconomic analysis was undertaken in order to establish broad consistency with national accounts (Arndt, Jones, and Tarp 2016; Arndt et al. 2012).

For the third assessment, the potential for undercounting of consumption, essentially exclusively in urban zones and mainly in the South, also came to the fore (see section 10.6 of MPD/DNEAP 2010). This issue had been flagged in 2002/3 but not analysed in detail in order to produce the 2002/3 report in a

---

[4] Specifically, revealed preference conditions (both spatial and temporal) were applied within the three Maputo domains and within the ten remaining domains outside of Maputo. But, as with all earlier assessments, higher-quality bundles (e.g. revealed preference failures) for the three Maputo domains relative to the ten non-Maputo domains were permitted.

timely fashion. In both 2002/3 and 2008/9, median household consumption of calories in urban zones, mainly in the South, was implausibly low.

While the official data remained the source for official poverty rates, a large variety of approaches were used to impute potential missing consumption in 2002/3 and in 2008/9 (see MPD/DNEAP 2010: section 10.6) as a form of sensitivity analysis. These and other analyses confirmed a stagnation in poverty rates at the national level. Urban rates declined while rural rates increased. These essential conclusions pertained regardless of the calorie correction procedure employed (MPD/DNEAP 2010).[5] The combination of the global food and fuel price shocks of 2008 and a weather-induced decline in agricultural production, particularly in the Central provinces, drove the results (Arndt et al. 2012; Arndt, Jones, and Tarp 2016).

## 8.3 PLEASe Estimates

As shown in Table 8.1, the PLEASe estimates are qualitatively very similar to the official results. At the national level, a substantial fall in poverty occurred between 1996/7 and 2002/3. For both approaches, this decline was led by rural zones though poverty rates also fell substantially in urban zones. Between 2002/3 and 2008/9, the rate of poverty reduction levelled off with both the official data and the estimates based on PLEASe exhibiting an essential stagnation in poverty rates at the national level. The point estimates for the official data suggest a slight rise while the estimates from PLEASe suggest a small decline in national poverty rates. In neither case is there a statistically significant change in poverty at the national level (for the procedure for computing standard errors on poverty rates, see Simler and Arndt 2007). For rural and urban zones, the approaches point to a mixture of relatively small changes in poverty.

At the provincial level, poverty levels and trends are also quite similar. Table 8.2 shows correlations between the official estimates and PLEASe. For both poverty levels and poverty trends, correlations of at least 0.91 and normally much more are obtained for all possible comparisons when calculated across provinces. PLEASe does result in lower estimates of poverty rates in Maputo Province and Maputo City with a shift from a rise in poverty point estimate between 1996/7 and 2002/3 to a decline. Neither the rise (official) nor the decline (PLEASe) in Maputo between 1996/7 and 2002/3 is statistically

---

[5] Calorie corrections do substantially influence the regional poverty profile with urban areas exhibiting lower poverty rates, particularly in the South. This issue is discussed in detail in MPD/DNEAP (2010). Nevertheless, in order to facilitate comparison with official estimates, all subsequent analysis is conducted using the official data.

**Table 8.2.** Correlations in levels and trends between official and PLEASe estimates

|              | Provinces | |
|--------------|-----------|---------|
|              | Levels    | Changes |
| 1996/7       | 0.998     | —       |
| 2002/3       | 0.911     | 0.972   |
| 2008/9       | 0.965     | 0.980   |
| 1996/7–2008/9 | —        | 0.980   |

*Note*: Correlations are calculated across the ten provinces plus Maputo City as shown in Table 8.1.

*Sources*: Ministry of Planning and Finance/DNPO (1998); Ministry of Planning and Finance/DNPO (2004); Ministry of Planning and Development/DNEAP (2010); and authors' calculations

significant. The measured decline is more consistent with other analyses (e.g. Arndt, Hussain, Salvucci, Tarp, and Østerdal 2016).

While the spatial poverty profile is remarkably similar between official and PLEASe estimates as indicated by the correlation analysis shown in Table 8.2, the PLEASe approach generates somewhat lower estimates of poverty in both years, which cumulate to a 3.0 percentage point reduction in the national poverty rate relative to the official estimates in 2008/9. This cumulative differential of about three percentage points is distributed roughly equally between rural and urban zones.

As noted, the code streams applied to produce the official Mozambican poverty results are antecedents to PLEASe. As such, the official and PLEASe approaches are quite similar, particularly with respect to broad strategic choices. Specifically, both approaches adopt a 'cost of basic needs' approach. Both preserve the division of the country into the thirteen spatial domains developed in 1996/7. Both employ an iterative approach to arriving at initial poverty lines from the 2002/3 and 2008/9 surveys. These poverty lines are then adjusted to conform to revealed preference conditions using the basic approach applied by Arndt and Simler (2010). The main differences between the official approach and the PLEASe estimates presented in Table 8.1 stem from the operational application of this basic approach. These differences are as follows.

As noted, in 1996/7, code was not made available to reproduce the full analysis. Hence, for 1996/7, the only change is to impose revealed preference consistency on the official bundles from 1996/7. This results in mild changes to the estimated poverty rates for 1996/7 as shown in Table 8.1.

Turning to 2002/3 and 2008/9, the main differences in the methods underlying the official numbers and those underlying the results presented under the PLEASe columns in Table 8.1 are as follows (with the text referring to the official approach as the baseline). First, the iterative estimation procedure for determining initial poverty lines is modified to account more completely for spatial variations in the cost of living in the first iteration. Specifically, in the official approach, the iterative procedure is applied nationally with an initial spatial price index determined in a preliminary round of poverty estimations and an initial cut-point identifying relatively poor households that is set at 60 per cent. In PLEASe, the iterative procedure is applied by spatial domain with both the initial spatial price index and initial cut-points taken from the preliminary round. Second, food items lacking corresponding prices or calories are dropped prior to food basket estimations as opposed to dropping items after estimating the basket. Third, for consistency between surveys, the basket employed for calculating the 2002/3 temporal index within the survey year is expanded. Fourth, an improved procedure is employed for estimating prices of items with few observations in the spatial revealed preference calculations. Finally, spatial revealed preference conditions are imposed nationally with no special treatment for Maputo. An additional difference in the 2008/9 estimations involves the treatment of receipts in kind. In response to changes in survey design, the official methodology imputes receipts in kind based on 2002/3 patterns of receipts. The PLEASe methodology aims for consistency with 2014/15 and makes full use of available 2008/9 survey data.

In 2002/3, these changes result in an estimated national poverty rate prior to the imposition of revealed preference conditions of about 46.4 per cent in PLEASe versus about 48 per cent using the official methodology (derived principally from the first three changes). The procedure for imposing spatial and temporal revealed preference conditions then drives up the national poverty rate by essentially the same amount (about six percentage points) in both the official and PLEASe approaches. The main driver of this increase in poverty rates relative to the value derived directly from the iterative procedure, in both instances, is a strong failure of revealed preference conditions in rural Nampula, which is the most populous province (MPF/DNPO 2004). As noted, the poverty profile does shift. The inclusion of the Maputo spatial domains in the correction procedure in PLEASe tends strongly to lower the quality of the bundles in Maputo, resulting in lower poverty rates in Maputo Province and City. The poverty rate in Maputo is about ten percentage points lower in PLEASe versus the official numbers, almost entirely as a consequence of the imposition of revealed preference conditions on the three Maputo spatial domains.

In terms of changes from the iterative procedure poverty rates at the national level, the lowering of rates in Maputo in PLEASe is offset by slightly greater increases in rural poverty, which is also a consequence of the inclusion of Maputo domains in the revealed preference adjustment. In both the official approach and in PLEASe, the imposition of revealed preference conditions on the poverty lines derived from the iterative procedure increases national poverty rates by about six percentage points. Hence, the less than two-point difference in the poverty rate obtained from the iterative procedure persists in the post-adjustment numbers with the official rate at about 54 per cent and the new PLEASe estimate at about 53 per cent.

Moving on to 2008/9, the poverty rates obtained prior to the imposition of revealed preference conditions are a bit more than one point apart with the official estimate of 53.6 per cent compared to the PLEASe estimates of 54.9 per cent. In addition, when only spatial revealed preference conditions are applied to the PLEASe estimates, the resulting national poverty rate is 56.7 per cent, which is two points greater than the official national estimate. However, the somewhat lower poverty lines developed for 2002/3 are now also imposed as temporal conditions on the estimation of the 2008/9 poverty lines. The imposition of these temporal conditions shifts the national poverty rate downward by about five percentage points to the level of 51.7 per cent shown in Table 8.1. So, the principal effect driving the difference in the national poverty rate between the official and PLEASe estimates in 2008/9 is the lower welfare anchor (i.e. somewhat lower poverty lines) derived from the 2002/3 estimates via the temporal revealed preference conditions.

To recap, the default iterative procedure employed in PLEASe results in a national poverty rate in 2002/3, derived from the iterative procedure, that is less than two percentage points lower than the value derived from the iterative pro- cedure employed for the official analysis (the first three differences in methods discussed earlier in this section). After correction for revealed preference violations, the level of poverty rises in both cases with the differential between the official national poverty estimate (54.1) and PLEASe (52.8) slightly decreasing.

The somewhat lower poverty rates derived from PLEASe in 2002/3 corres- pond to somewhat lower poverty lines (note that nominal consumption estimates for each household are the same in the official and PLEASe approaches). These somewhat lower poverty lines are then employed as tem- poral conditions in 2008/9. These temporal conditions are binding and hold national poverty rates to lower levels. In other words, the bundles emerging from the PLEASe iterative procedure in 2008/9 are of somewhat higher quality than the final bundles from 2002/3. While the official estimates produce a slight rise in poverty at the national level (0.6 points) between 2002/3 and 2008/9, the PLEASe estimates produce a small decline ($-1.1$ points).

It is worthwhile to emphasize that the differentials in poverty rates dis- cussed here are not large relative to standard deviations for national poverty rates, which are estimated at about 1.7 or 1.8 percentage points (MPD/DNEAP 2010; Simler and Arndt 2007), and well within a confidence interval of about two standard deviations. Nevertheless, the differentials do accumulate, result- ing in a poverty rate in 2008/9 for PLEASe that is 3.0 percentage points below the official estimate for the same year.[6]

---

[6] Whether this differential is statistically significant is complex due to dependence between the 2002/3 and 2008/9 final rates. This dependence comes about through the temporal revealed

As the correlations in Table 8.2 illustrate, the poverty profiles are very similar between the two sets of estimates. As expected, imposition of revealed preference conditions on the domains in Maputo reduce estimated poverty rates in Maputo Province and City in PLEASe relative to the official numbers. Once the national-level difference of 3.0 percentage points is accounted for in 2008/9, differences in provincial poverty rates between the official estimates and PLEASe amount to much less than one standard deviation for all provinces, excepting Maputo, and for rural and urban domains.

## 8.4 Discussion and Conclusions

Poverty analysis is conducted mainly for the purpose of making robust comparisons. Often, comparisons through time generate the greatest level of interest. These comparisons respond to the key question: Are living standards improving/stagnating/deteriorating through time? As poverty estimates are sensitive to the methods employed for deriving them, there is great value in applying fully consistent methods. At the same time, data collection approaches, the practice of poverty analysis, and the circumstances under which the analysis is conducted, evolve through time. While considered the most appropriate at the time, choices made in past analyses may not correspond to current 'best practice' and/or may not be as suitable to current circumstances.[7] There is, as a result, a natural tension between maintaining consistency, and hence comparability, with previous analyses and the desire to obtain the best possible estimates of welfare given the state of knowledge of practice of poverty analysis as well as current circumstances.

To our knowledge, there is no established procedure for coping with this tension even though it is appearing with increasing frequency. For example, in Tanzania, changes to survey design and methodological approach were introduced with the 2011/12 survey (World Bank 2015; Arndt, Demery, McKay, and Tarp 2016) creating issues of comparability with earlier work. In order to attempt to develop comparable numbers with the preceding survey conducted in 2007, revisions were imposed on measured consumption and associated poverty lines. As a consequence of these revisions, estimated consumption per adult equivalent in 2007 rose by almost one-third with a similar

---

preference conditions. Under an assumption of independence, the standard deviation of the difference in national poverty rates between 2002/3 and 2008/9 is about 2.45 (MPD/DNEAP 2010). Accounting for dependence would likely reduce this standard error, meaning that the difference between the official 2002/3 national estimate and the PLEASe 2008/9 estimate would likely be near the edge of the confidence interval.

[7] Changes in data collection approaches likely present even greater conundrums (Deaton and Kozel 2005).

increase imposed on the poverty lines.[8] The end result was only a minor shift in measured poverty at the national level (World Bank 2015).

In assessing long-run poverty trends for Tanzania, Arndt, Demery, McKay, and Tarp (2016) present two poverty estimates for 2007, one of which is meant to be comparable with earlier surveys in 2001 and 1992 and the other comparable with the subsequent survey in 2011/12. The recent poverty assessment for Tanzania (World Bank 2015) copes with the issue principally by refraining from mentioning measured poverty rates in 2001 and 1992, ostensibly due to comparability issues.

For this chapter, we present new estimates for all three survey years with available data for Mozambique, though, as in Tanzania, the focus is on more recent survey years. We find that the essential conclusions of the three poverty assessments undertaken to date are maintained. To wit, poverty rates were uniformly high in 1996/7. Poverty rates reduced dramatically between 1996/7 and 2002/3 with particularly strong decreases registered in rural areas. Between 2002/3 and 2008/9, poverty at the national level stagnated with relatively small changes also occurring in rural and urban zones.

The estimates obtained via the default PLEASe software code indicate a larger decline in consumption poverty between 1996/7 and 2002/3 than the official estimate. Between 2002/3 and 2008/9, point estimates from PLEASe register a small decline as opposed to the very small increase in the official numbers. None of these differences is even close to statistically significant. Nevertheless, the cumulative effect results in an estimated poverty rate at the national level derived from PLEASe that is 3.0 percentage points below the official estimate for 2008/9. Regional poverty profiles are qualitatively similar between the two sets of estimates with lower rates registered in the South, particularly Maputo Province.

The results illustrate the value of the application of a consistent approach with this need for consistency in approach applying to essentially all calculations rather than just the broad strategies (e.g. cost of basic needs) employed. In updating methods and survey approaches over time, there appears to be no substitute for returning to the original data and re-estimating previous surveys in order to maintain consistency through time.

---

[8] This is a very large increase. According to World Bank (2015: 2), the increases are partly due to the inclusion of education, health, and communication expenditures, which were previously excluded, and 'partly due to a different way of drawing on the diary and recall data for non-food spending'. The magnitude of these shifts indicates that one can really only hope to detect gross trends in consumption poverty. Arndt, Leyaro, Mahrt, and Tarp (2017) provide further analysis for Tanzania.

## References


Arndt, C., L. Demery, A. McKay, and F. Tarp (2016). 'Growth and Poverty Reduction in Tanzania', in C. Arndt, A. McKay, and F. Tarp (eds), *Growth and Poverty in Sub-Saharan Africa*. Oxford: Oxford University Press, 238–62.

Arndt, C., M. A. Hussain, E. S. Jones, V. Nhate, F. Tarp, and J. Thurlow (2012). 'Explaining the Evolution of Poverty: The Case of Mozambique', *American Journal of Agricultural Economics*, 94(4): 854–72.

Arndt, C., M. A. Hussain, V. Salvucci, F. Tarp, and L. P. Østerdal (2016). 'Poverty Mapping Based on First-Order Dominance with an Example from Mozambique', *Journal of International Development*, 28: 3–21.

Arndt, C., H. T. Jensen, and F. Tarp (2000). 'Stabilization and Structural Adjustment in Mozambique', *Journal of International Development*, 12: 299–323.

Arndt, C., E. S. Jones, and F. Tarp (2016). 'Mozambique: Off-Track or Temporarily Sidelined?', in C. Arndt, A. McKay, and F. Tarp (eds), *Growth and Poverty in Sub-Saharan Africa*. Oxford: Oxford University Press, 190–217.

Arndt, C., V. Leyaro, K. Mahrt, and F. Tarp (2017). 'Growth and Poverty: A Pragmatic Assessment and Future Prospects', in C. Adam, P. Collier, and B. Ndulu (eds), *Tanzania: The Path to Prosperity*. Oxford: Oxford University Press.

Arndt, C. and K. Simler (2010). 'Estimating Utility-Consistent Poverty Lines', *Economic Development and Cultural Change*, 58: 449–74.

Deaton, A. and V. Kozel (2005). 'Data and Dogma: The Great Indian Poverty Debate', *The World Bank Research Observer*, 20(2): 177–99.

Ministry of Planning and Development/DNEAP (2010). 'Poverty and Wellbeing in Mozambique: Third National Poverty Assessment'. Maputo: Ministry of Planning and Development/DNEAP.

Ministry of Planning and Finance/DNPO (1998). 'Understanding Poverty and Wellbeing in Mozambique: The First National Assessment, 1996–97'. Maputo: Ministry of Planning and Finance/DNPO.

Ministry of Planning and Finance/DNPO (2004). 'Poverty and Wellbeing in Mozambique: Second National Poverty Assessment'. Maputo: Ministry of Planning and Finance/DNPO.

Simler, K. R. and C. Arndt (2007). 'Poverty Comparisons with Endogenous Absolute Poverty Lines', *Review of Income and Wealth*, 53: 275–94.

World Bank (2015). *Tanzania Mainland Poverty Assessment*. Washington, DC: World Bank.

# 9

# Poverty Trends in Pakistan

*Edward Whitney, Hina Nazli, and Kristi Mahrt*

## 9.1 Introduction

A large number of studies have attempted to estimate the incidence of poverty in Pakistan since the government started collecting nationally representative data on household expenditures in 1963–4. Early studies (Allaudin 1975; Naseem 1973) computed poverty lines on the basis of arbitrarily fixed per capita income or expenditure required by a household to fulfil its minimum food needs. By the mid-1970s and through the early 1990s, the focus of work shifted to estimating the extent of as well as the trends in poverty in terms of the absorption of a minimum diet based on nutritional requirements. Most of the studies conducted during this period computed poverty lines on the basis of the food energy intake (FEI) method that relies on the required daily allowance (RDA) of calorie intake[1] (Ahmad and Allison 1990; Ahmad and Ludlow 1989; Akhtar 1988; Allaudin 1975; de Kruijk and Leeuwen 1985; Ercelawn 1989, 1990; Irfan and Amjad 1984; M. H. Malik 1988; S. J. Malik 1993, 1994; Naseem 1973, 1977).

Poverty estimates are generally quite sensitive to the choice of various factors such as minimum calories required, scale of measurement (per capita or per adult equivalent), and the choice of welfare measure (income or expenditure). Since these early studies do not apply a uniform methodology, the poverty measures are not comparable and cannot be used to determine poverty trends over time (Arif 2006; Cheema 2005; GoP 2008a, 2008b; S. J. Malik 2005). Studies conducted from the 1990s onwards attempt to

---

[1] Poverty is defined with reference to the recommended calorie intake of a person. To adjust for the size and age composition of a household, an adult equivalent scale is used. Calorie requirements are then converted into minimum food expenditure in accordance with the expenditure patterns of the poor.

prepare a consistent time series so that poverty trends can be examined (Anwar and Qureshi 2002; Anwar et al. 2005; Arif et al. 2000; Cheema 2005; S. J. Malik 1993, 1994, 2005; Malik et al. 2014b; Jafri 1999; SPDC 2005; World Bank 2002). The results of these studies indicate that Pakistan experienced high levels of poverty in the 1960s which declined considerably during the 1970s and 1980s; the 1990s witnessed a sharp increase in poverty, and this increasing trend continued until 2001–2.

Starting from 1998–9, the government of Pakistan began estimating official poverty lines using the FEI methodology applied to the Household Integrated Economic Survey (HIES) for that year. Subsequent poverty lines were derived by scaling the previous year's line by the inflation rate as determined by the consumer price index (CPI) (Cheema 2005). The resulting estimates of poverty rates are problematic in a number of ways. First and most notably, the resulting poverty headcount estimates have shown a remarkable and consistent decline in poverty since 2001–2. This result is in stark contrast to evidence of deteriorating trends derived from other measures of welfare, even those based on the same data sources. For instance, Jamal (2012) and Malik et al. (2014b) re-estimated the poverty line and found not only a considerably higher incidence of poverty in 2010–11 but also a rising trend in poverty after 2004–5. Second, Malik et al. (2014b) point out that, owing to a variety of factors, the CPI may not represent the true cost of living for those living near the poverty line and thus the subsequent poverty lines may not accurately reflect living standards. Third, as discussed in Beck et al. (2015), inflating a fixed poverty line over time rather than re-estimating flexible poverty lines in each survey year ignores the substitution effects in consumption that may occur from variation in relative prices of essential commodities over time. Finally, estimating a single national poverty line fails to account for the possibility of regional differences in prices and consumption patterns.

Recently, the government of Pakistan, in recognition of the shortcomings in its poverty estimates, made plans to revise them. The revised estimates address regional, especially rural/urban, price gaps and also allow the consumption basket to evolve through time so that substitution effects are incorporated. In this study, we re-estimate poverty in Pakistan using the official methodology and a modified version of the Poverty Line Estimation Analytical Software (PLEASe). Across the alternatives employed, poverty trends differ drastically from the current official figures. The alternative methods employed are variants of the FEI and cost of basic needs (CBN) approaches to poverty measures. For the main alternatives, flexible bundles are developed that account for variations in consumption patterns and prices across space and through time. The CBN approach, as implemented using PLEASe, is an attractive option as it allows for utility-consistent estimates of consumption poverty rates.

The remainder of this chapter is structured as follows. Section 9.2 discusses the methodologies employed. Section 9.3 presents the data employed. Section 9.4 presents results. A final section concludes and looks ahead to future trends.

## 9.2 Methods

At the time of writing, the official methodology for estimating consumption poverty rates is based on an application of the FEI method to the HIES data for 1998–9. Adult-equivalent consumption aggregates (see section 9.3) are used as the welfare indicator in the estimation of an official poverty line. A single goods basket is assumed in all the provinces. However, in view of different prices across provinces and rural/urban areas, the poverty line is adjusted with Paasche price indices calculated at the primary sampling unit level by using the median prices and average budget shares in each unit. The first three per-adult equivalent consumption expenditure quintiles are used, so that the consumption patterns of the relatively well-off do not affect the determination of the FEI poverty line. Details can be found in GoP (2003) and Cheema (2005). Poverty lines are then adjusted in subsequent years by the CPI-based inflation rate between the household survey years. This means that poverty lines in each year are based on the same fixed consumption bundle. The Foster–Greer–Thorbecke class of poverty measures is used to measure poverty headcounts, poverty gaps, and the severity of poverty (Foster et al. 1984).

In response to the concerns about the use of the CPI raised in Malik et al. (2014a) and elsewhere, we apply the FEI approach, first nationally and then regionally, to all surveys since 2000. In other words, rather than update the 1998–9 consumption bundle based on the CPI, new bundles are calculated for each additional survey. This is done using the same approach as applied in 1998–9 and by calculating separate FEI lines by spatial domain.

There are also general concerns about the FEI approach. Ravallion and Bidani (1994) point out that because of higher relative prices for food and systematic differences in consumption patterns and activity levels across regions and survey years, the FEI method may be biased towards relatively rich regions (e.g. towards urban areas relative to rural areas). In addition, this method does not capture the true effect of price increases. Ravallion (1998) argues that an increase in prices may increase or decrease the poverty line depending on how the consumption patterns change (normal versus inferior goods).

The CBN approach provides an alternative to FEI (Ravallion 1994, 1998; Ravallion and Bidani 1994; Ravallion and Sen 1996; Wodon 1997). In common practice, the CBN approach identifies a single national consumption bundle satisfying minimum calorie requirements and evaluates this bundle at region-specific prices. However, if the consumption patterns of the poor vary by region and preferences permit substitution, the use of a single national consumption bundle may yield inconsistent poverty measures (Tarp et al. 2002). To address this issue, recent studies suggest the use of region-specific consumption bundles and region-specific prices to estimate poverty lines (Arndt and Simler 2010; Datt and Jolliffe 2005; Gibson and Rozelle 2003; Mukherjee and Benson 2003; Ravallion and Lokshin 2006; Tarp et al. 2002).

A difficulty found in both the FEI and the CBN approaches with using different bundles for each region is that the bundles may violate utility consistency of poverty lines, with some bundles being preferred to others (Ravallion and Lokshin 2006), thus rendering the associated poverty measures incomparable. In others words, an estimated increase in poverty may occur purely because the quality of the bundles underlying the poverty line improves over time, driving up the real value of the poverty line and hence the poverty rate. In order to allow comparability over time and space, Ravallion and Lokshin (2006) suggested applying the revealed preference criteria to assess the utility consistency of poverty lines. Subsequently, Arndt and Simler (2010) proposed a maximum-entropy approach to impose revealed preference conditions across consumption bundles, thus ensuring the existence of utility-consistent preference sets associated with the estimated consumption bundles. Here, we employ the basic approach suggested by Arndt and Simler (2010) via implementation of the PLEASe methodology with a series of modifications appropriate to the case of Pakistan.


## 9.3 Data

The official estimates, revised FEI estimates, and PLEASe estimates are generated using nationally representative household survey data collected between 2001 and 2011 by the government of Pakistan. The relevant survey modules and steps taken in preparing the data are described in this section. Additionally, we discuss issues related to the representativeness and quality of the data.

The Pakistan Bureau of Statistics (PBS) conducted the first Household Income and Expenditure Survey in 1963; it has been repeated periodically since then. To address the requirements of a new system of national accounts, the questionnaire was revised in 1990. The surveys conducted in 1990, 1992–3, 1993–4, and 1996–7 used the revised questionnaire. The scope of the survey was expanded in 1998 when it was merged with the Pakistan Integrated Household Survey (PIHS) that collects information on social indicators. This combined survey retained the acronym HIES, with 'Household Integrated Economic Survey' as the updated name. (The HIES acronym used herein refers to this updated name.) Also at that time, the questionnaire was further improved and was split into male and female sub-questionnaires.

This analysis employs data from five HIES conducted in 2001–2, 2004–5, 2005–6, 2007–8, and 2010–11 (see GoP 2001b, 2005, 2006, 2008b, 2011). These five surveys collected data on household characteristics, consumption patterns, household income by source, and social indicators. Data from these surveys enable researchers to estimate poverty at the national and subnational (urban–rural and provincial) levels. The population sample for the HIES consists of all urban and rural areas of the four provinces (Punjab, Sindh, Khyber Pakhtunkhwa (KPK), and Balochistan) and the capital territory (Islamabad) of Pakistan. It excludes the protected areas of KPK and military restricted areas.

In all surveys, a two-stage stratified random sample design is adopted to select the households. In the first stage, primary sampling units (enumeration blocks) are selected in the urban and rural areas of all four provinces. In the second stage, the sample of households is randomly selected from these primary sampling units. In this study, using a random systematic sampling scheme with a random start, either sixteen or twelve households were selected from each primary sampling unit.[2] The sample sizes for the five surveys were 16,182 (2001–2), 14,708 (2004–5), 15,543 (2005–6), 15,512 (2007–8), and 16,341 (2010–11) households.[3]

Data on household expenditures are critical sources of information for consumption-based poverty estimation as real consumption expenditure is the welfare indicator for measurement of the poverty status of a household. For Pakistan, the consumption aggregate includes not only actual purchases but also self-produced and consumed items, consumption of items received as gifts, and items provided in place of monetary compensation. The HIES provides detailed information on the consumption of food and non-food items. Consumption data consists of food items, fuel and utilities, housing (rent, imputed rent, and minor repair), frequent non-food expenses (household laundry and cleaning, personal care products and services), and other non-food expenses (clothes, footwear, education, and health-related expenses). Expenses such as taxes, fines, and expenses on marriages and funerals are not included in the consumption aggregate as they are judged to be

---

[2] According to the summary reports for each of the five survey years, the sampling design is based on the most recent population census from 1998–9. The number of villages (also referred to as *mouzas* or *dehs*), which informs the sampling frame for the rural areas, remains constant at 50,588 for all five years. As Malik et al. (2014b) explain, there are several problems associated with the fact that the sampling frame has not been updated since the most recent census, leading to questionable representativeness of the data for each of the years.

[3] Although designed to be nationally representative, military restricted areas were excluded from the sampling universe for each of the five surveys. For all years except 2001–2, Azad Jammu and Kashmir, Federally Administered Tribal Area, and Northern Areas were excluded from the scope of the survey. For 2001–2, removal of observations from these areas (1351 households) results in an adjusted sample size of 14,697.

insufficiently related to current living standards. The official methodology also excludes estimated use values for durable goods. For purposes of consistency in this study, the same exclusion was maintained for all the methods employed.

Survey data on some of the food items (quantities and expenditures) are collected on a recall period of fourteen days and others on a recall period of one month. Non-food expenditures are collected in either monthly or annual recall. Care was taken in data preparation in this study to ensure data across all items were calibrated to daily values. For food items, most of the quantities have been reported in kilograms or grams or as number of items. To make food consumption consistent, the consumed quantities are converted into grams and all quantities and expenditures are converted to daily values. Using the food composition tables for Pakistan (GoP 2001a), these quantities are then converted into calories.

Following GoP (2003), we assigned an adult equivalence factor to each individual in the household on the basis of a 2350 calorie threshold and the individual's gender and age. Exclusion of durable goods and use of an adult equivalence factor are departures from the default PLEASe methodology to maintain consistency with the official methodology.

As noted in section 9.2, the revised FEI and PLEASe methodologies allow for the estimation of distinct poverty lines by spatial domain. In all cases where separate poverty lines are calculated across space, eight spatial domains are employed. These spatial domains correspond to the rural and urban zones of the four provinces. Even though the sample frame represents Islamabad, it is incorporated into the urban zone of the province of Punjab.

In this study, data preparation involved an extensive cleaning process for each dataset. For each year of data, outliers for food items were replaced as follows: for each item, a median and standard deviation was calculated separately for each spatial domain for both total value and total quantity. Values greater than the sum of the median and three times the standard deviation were replaced with the median value for that item in that spatial domain. For 2001–2, we dropped observations for 182 households, or 1.2 per cent of the total sample, from the analysis as a result of missing (121 households) or incomplete (63 households) consumption data. For subsequent years, we dropped 1.4 (2004–5), 0.51 (2005–6), 0.46 (2007–8), and 0.28 (2010–11) per cent of households as a result of missing or incomplete consumption data.

To address the issue of seasonality, HIES collects data over a period of one year. Data for the survey years 2005–6, 2007–8, and 2010–11 identify the quarter in which data were collected. This enables us to identify seasonal price differences during the survey year. Unfortunately, the same is not true for 2001–2 and 2004–5. For these years, we assume no seasonal differences.

**Table 9.1.** Trends in poverty indicators based on the official poverty line (1992–3 to 2010–11)

| Year | Poverty headcount | | | Poverty gap | | | Severity of poverty | | |
|---|---|---|---|---|---|---|---|---|---|
| | urban | rural | national | urban | rural | national | urban | rural | national |
| 1992–3 | 20.0 | 27.6 | 25.5 | 3.4 | 4.6 | 4.3 | 0.9 | 1.2 | 1.1 |
| 1993–4 | 15.9 | 33.5 | 28.2 | 2.7 | 6.3 | 5.2 | 0.7 | 1.8 | 1.4 |
| 1996–7 | 15.8 | 30.2 | 25.8 | 2.4 | 5.3 | 4.4 | 0.6 | 1.4 | 1.1 |
| 1998–9 | 20.9 | 34.7 | 30.6 | 4.3 | 7.6 | 6.4 | 1.3 | 2.4 | 2.0 |
| 2001–2 | 22.7 | 39.3 | 34.5 | 4.6 | 8.0 | 7.0 | 1.4 | 2.4 | 2.1 |
| 2004–5 | 14.9 | 28.1 | 23.9 | 2.9 | 5.6 | 4.8 | 0.8 | 1.8 | 1.5 |
| 2005–6* | 13.1 | 27.0 | 22.3 | 2.1 | 5.0 | 4.0 | 0.5 | 1.4 | 1.1 |
| 2007–8 | 10.0 | 20.6 | 17.2 | — | — | — | — | — | — |
| 2010–11 | 7.1 | 15.1 | 12.4 | — | — | — | — | — | — |

*Note*: '—' indicates that these results were not published for that year.

*Source*: Based on Cheema (2005) and Government of Pakistan (2008a, 2014)

## 9.4 Analytical Steps and Results

### 9.4.1 *Official Methodology: A Fixed FEI Bundle across Space and Time*

The official measures of poverty show a considerable decline in the poverty headcount during the past decade. The incidence of poverty, according to official estimates, declined from 34.5 per cent in 2001–2 to 12.4 per cent in 2010–11. A twenty-four percentage point decline is observed in the rural poverty headcount during the same period—a decline much greater than the corresponding decline in the urban poverty headcount (GoP 2013, 2014). Official poverty rates are shown in Table 9.1.

As mentioned, the decline in official poverty estimates from 1998–9 does not correspond well with other welfare measures. For example, average real household consumption expenditure has remained more or less stagnant since 2001, whereas the average share of food expenditure in total household consumption has increased sharply since 2005–6.[4]

This contrasting situation has raised concerns about Pakistan's poverty figures and trends (Jamal 2012; Malik et al. 2014b). Using the 2010–11 HIES data and applying the official methodology, Malik et al. (2014b) re-estimated the poverty line by incorporating provincial and urban–rural price variations, finding a poverty headcount for 2010–11 of 45.6 per cent, much higher than the official estimate of 12.4 per cent.[5]

---

[4] For details, see the official survey reports on the HIES between years 2004 and 2012 (GoP 2015).

[5] Jamal (2012) also re-estimated poverty rates using the 2010–11 HIES and arrived at an estimate of 36.6 per cent. The approach employed used different calorie thresholds for urban (2230) and rural (2550) areas and estimated different calorie expenditure functions for rural and urban areas by incorporating provincial dummies. Jamal (2012) also estimated the consumption basket using households in the bottom quartile of per capita consumption expenditure.

As discussed earlier, the official poverty line was originally estimated using the 1998–9 HIES data and extrapolated for subsequent years by adjusting for inflation using the CPI. Malik et al. (2014a) highlighted two major inadequacies in the measurement of the CPI: (i) under-coverage of the data on prices, and (ii) underestimation of food shares in total household budget. The PBS, which is responsible for computing and disseminating the CPI and inflation rate in the country, collects data on prices only from urban areas. The food share is estimated through the Family Budget Survey, which is also conducted in urban areas. Therefore, the CPI has an inherent urban bias that may not reflect the changes in the consumption baskets of rural households.

Using HIES data, Malik et al. (2014a) demonstrate significant differences in the prices of different food and non-food items not only across provinces but also across urban and rural areas of provinces. As one might expect, items that are produced in rural areas, such as cereals, pulses, meat, and milk, are more expensive in urban areas. Processed items, such as edible oil/ghee and sugar, are more expensive in rural areas. In addition, Malik et al. (2014a) highlight differences in the food budget shares across urban and rural areas and point out that the current CPI only reflects the consumption patterns of the urban population.

### 9.4.2 Revised FEI Results

To overcome the issue of urban bias in the CPI and to allow poverty lines to vary over time and space, we estimated regional poverty lines for five rounds of the HIES: 2001–2, 2004–5, 2005–6, 2007–8, and 2010–11. In an attempt to isolate the impact of methodological changes, the poverty numbers were estimated with three different methods. First, we estimated a national poverty line in 2001–2 using the official FEI methodology and obtained poverty lines for subsequent years via CPI adjustments. Second, we estimated a single national poverty line for each year using the official FEI methodology. Third, we followed the official FEI methodology; however, we estimated different poverty lines in each year and for urban and rural areas of each province. In total, eight poverty lines were estimated in each year. The national and provincial poverty lines were calculated as the weighted average of these spatial lines, where spatial population was used as weights.

Results are presented in Figure 9.1. The figure illustrates declining poverty rates of the CPI-adjusted poverty lines, as per official reports and as estimated in the present study. In contrast with the official trend of decreasing poverty incidence, using a national and a regional and time-specific form of the official methodology, this study demonstrates that poverty incidence rose steadily between 2001–2 and 2010–11. Poverty incidence is found to be higher in rural areas than in urban areas in all of the estimates. The CPI-adjusted poverty lines

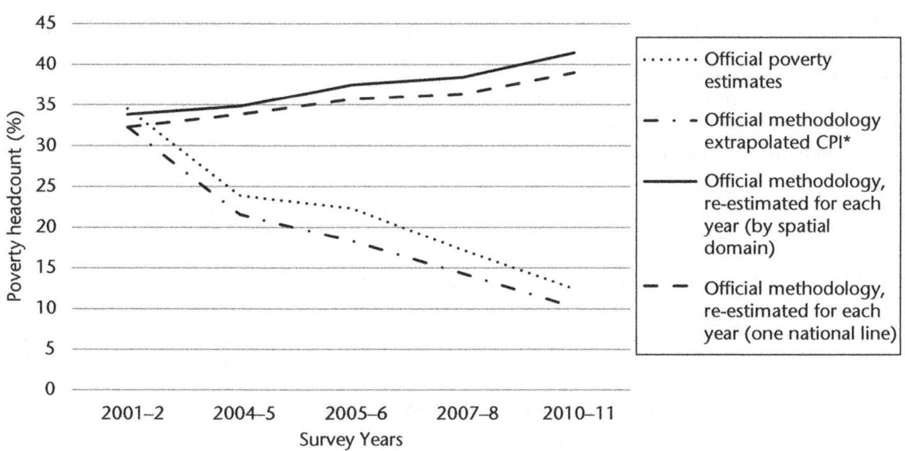

**Figure 9.1.** Poverty estimates using food energy intake (FEI) methodologies

*Note*: *Official methodology applied to 2001–2 survey data and updated for subsequent years using official consumer price index (CPI) data published in various economic surveys.

*Source*: Based on Cheema (2005), GoP (2008a, 2014), and authors' calculations using Household Integrated Economic Survey (HIES) data

show that the gap between rural and urban poverty incidence has reduced over time. However, the opposite is true when poverty lines are estimated for each year.

It is interesting to note that the gap between urban and rural areas is larger when one poverty line, instead of spatial poverty lines, is used to draw poverty estimates. This may be because cost of living varies across areas. Therefore, using one poverty line may overestimate or underestimate poverty across spatial domains. This is confirmed by looking at the provincial estimates of poverty. Poverty incidence is observed to be highest in the province of Punjab when one poverty line is used. However, Sindh and KPK appear the poorest when spatial poverty lines are used. Similar differences can be observed across the rural and urban areas of each province. Although rural poverty incidence is higher than urban poverty incidence, the gap between these two is greater when one poverty line is used (Table 9.2; Appendix Table 9.A1).

### 9.4.3 *PLEASe Approach and Results*

As discussed, the FEI approach may not be utility-consistent. This is particularly true when multiple FEI bundles are estimated across space and time. While we do not attempt to address these concerns in the context of the FEI approach, we do address these concerns by following a CBN approach that ensures utility consistency using a modified version of PLEASe.

**Table 9.2.** Poverty estimates using the food energy intake (FEI) methodology by urban and rural areas

|  | 2001–2 | 2004–5 | 2005–6 | 2007–8 | 2010–11 |
|---|---|---|---|---|---|
| Official methodology, extrapolated CPI* | | | | | |
| national | 32.3 | 21.6 | 18.3 | 14.3 | 10.2 |
| urban | 17.6 | 11.3 | 8.7 | 6.2 | 5.0 |
| rural | 38.2 | 26.4 | 23.1 | 18.2 | 12.7 |
| Official methodology, re-estimated for each year (by spatial domain) | | | | | |
| national | 33.9 | 34.8 | 37.5 | 38.4 | 41.4 |
| urban | 25.2 | 24.4 | 29.2 | 30.1 | 33.9 |
| rural | 37.4 | 39.7 | 41.7 | 42.4 | 45.1 |
| Official methodology, re-estimated for each year (one national line) | | | | | |
| national | 32.3 | 33.8 | 35.7 | 36.3 | 39.0 |
| urban | 17.6 | 19.1 | 20.9 | 22.6 | 24.1 |
| rural | 38.2 | 40.7 | 43.2 | 43.0 | 46.4 |

*Source*: GoP (2014) and authors' calculations using HIES data

We have already mentioned exclusion of asset use values and calculation of household consumption per adult equivalent as opposed to per capita as modifications imposed to ensure maximum possible consistency with the official methodology in terms of data treatment. We also applied two additional modifications to the default PLEASe code in terms of data processing/ analysis: the first relates to the calorie requirement calculation and the second to the sample population used to calculate the poverty line. In the default PLEASe code, a method to calculate the calorie requirement for each spatial domain based on household demographics is applied. In place of this approach, we applied the method for calculating adult equivalence described in GoP (2003). Following this official methodology, we assigned an adult equivalence factor to each individual in the household and multiplied this factor by the calorie threshold of 2350 daily adult equivalent calories (GoP 2003). The weighted average of this value gave the calorie requirement for each spatial domain. Food baskets in each domain were then scaled to attain this calorie requirement.

The second modification relates to the reference population used to construct the food baskets and poverty lines. In the default code, an iterative process is employed in order to arrive at poverty lines based on the consumption patterns of those households living at or below the poverty line. For Pakistan, we simply used the consumption patterns of the bottom 60 per cent of households, ranked by nominal per capita expenditures in each spatial domain. This modification was undertaken to retain greater comparability with the official methodology.

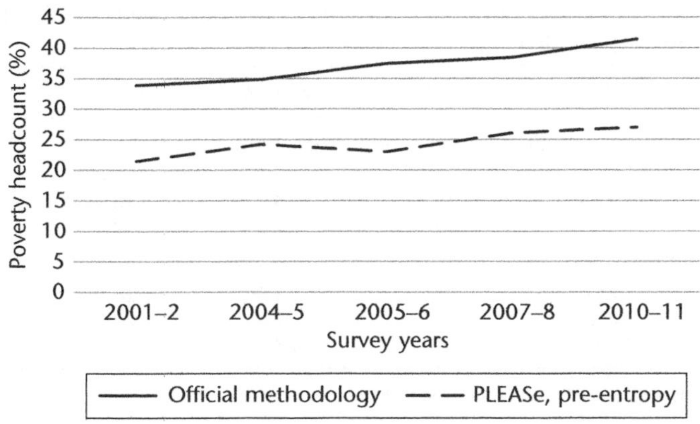


**Figure 9.2.** National poverty headcounts for cost of basic needs (CBN) and FEI bundles without controlling for utility consistency

*Source*: Authors' calculations using HIES data

This approach, deriving bundles based on the consumption patterns of the bottom 60 per cent of households in each domain and then scaling those bundles to strike calorie targets, yields a first set of poverty lines. National poverty rates from this simple approach, prior to any corrections for utility consistency, are shown in Figure 9.2. The figure also illustrates the rates obtained from the FEI approach as applied by spatial domain. Both approaches yield qualitatively similar results in terms of trends. In both cases, poverty rates are observed to increase over the period of study. The FEI approach results in a higher poverty line corresponding to a higher level of welfare that marks the (arbitrary) cut-off between poor and non-poor households. In addition, the FEI approach results in a slightly larger increase in the poverty rate.

Examining rural–urban differences, rural poverty incidence is observed to be consistently higher than urban poverty incidence in the FEI approach (Table 9.3). However, poverty estimates using the PLEASe code indicate that poverty incidence in urban areas is not much different from that in rural areas. Urban poverty incidence is observed to be higher than rural poverty incidence for 2001–2 and 2007–8, and a rise in poverty overall over the study period. However, looking across provinces, this trend holds only for Punjab (see Appendix Table 9.A2). This indicates that the overall trends are mainly driven by the largest province.

In Figure 9.3, utility consistency is ensured via entropy adjustments imposing revealed preference conditions across space for each survey year. This is shown alongside poverty rates derived from the unadjusted poverty lines (pre-entropy) shown in Figure 9.2. With the spatial adjustment imposed

**Table 9.3.** Poverty estimates using the FEI and PLEASe methodologies without controlling for utility consistency by rural and urban areas

|  | 2001–2 | 2004–5 | 2005–6 | 2007–8 | 2010–11 |
|---|---|---|---|---|---|
| Official methodology, re-estimated for each year (by spatial domain) | | | | | |
| national | 33.9 | 34.8 | 37.5 | 38.4 | 41.4 |
| urban | 25.2 | 24.4 | 29.2 | 30.1 | 33.9 |
| rural | 37.4 | 39.7 | 41.7 | 42.4 | 45.1 |
| PLEASe, pre-entropy | | | | | |
| national | 21.4 | 24.2 | 23.0 | 26.0 | 27.0 |
| urban | 23.8 | 23.5 | 22.8 | 27.0 | 26.1 |
| rural | 20.4 | 24.5 | 23.1 | 25.6 | 27.4 |

*Source*: GoP (2014) and authors' calculations using HIES data

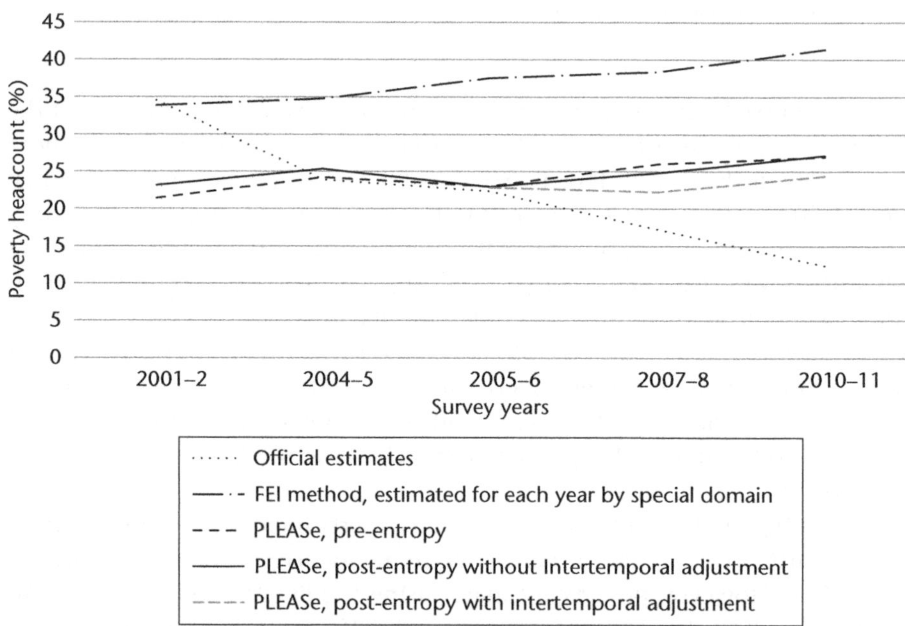


**Figure 9.3.** Poverty rates from official estimates, official methodology (FEI), and unadjusted and spatially adjusted CBN bundles
*Source*: Authors' calculations using HIES data

(post-entropy without intertemporal adjustment), poverty rates are observed to still increase over the period of study, although the magnitude of the increase is somewhat reduced. Figure 9.3 reveals that poverty incidence increased at a higher rate during 2007–8 compared to 2010–11 when revealed preference conditions were imposed. Most of this increase occurred in the

**Table 9.4.** Poverty estimates using the official and spatially/temporally adjusted PLEASe methodologies (2010–11)

| | Official methodology | PLEASe methodology | | | | |
|---|---|---|---|---|---|---|
| | national | national | Punjab | Sindh | KPK | Balochistan |
| Overall | 12.4 | 24.4 | 23.2 | 26.0 | 24.8 | 28.9 |
| Urban | 7.1 | 17.7 | 17.2 | 16.8 | 21.4 | 26.1 |
| Rural | 15.1 | 27.7 | 25.9 | 34.7 | 25.5 | 29.8 |

*Source*: GoP (2014) and authors' calculations using HIES data

rural areas of Punjab and KPK (Appendix Table 9.A3). This result is consistent with the economic situation within the country after the food price hike. For example, the price of wheat, the major staple of the country, rose by more than 200 per cent. The real wages of agricultural and non-agricultural workers declined. This resulted in a worsening situation for net buyers of food and net sellers of labour, especially in rural areas. We re-estimated poverty lines to now impose spatial and temporal revealed preference constraints in entropy adjustments (post-entropy with intertemporal adjustment). In these estimates, the magnitude of poverty declined but did not change the trend (Figure 9.3). A comparison of the FEI spatial domain method and the CBN method with and without spatial and temporal adjustments indicates that poverty estimates differ in magnitude, but they move in the same direction over time. However, the official estimates show contrasting results.

In Table 9.4, official estimates of national-level urban and rural poverty incidence for 2010–11 are compared alongside utility-consistent estimates for both national-level and province-level urban and rural poverty incidence (official estimates within provinces are not reported). These estimates indicate that poverty estimates with spatial and intertemporal adjustments are nearly two times higher than the official estimates. Poverty is higher in rural areas than in urban areas according to both the official and the PLEASe code estimates. Within the provinces, estimates using the PLEASe code show poverty to be consistently worse in rural areas than in urban areas. The gap between urban and rural poverty incidence is largest in Sindh.

## 9.5 Conclusions

In this study, we explored trends in poverty between 2001 and 2011 in Pakistan using two distinct methods of estimating poverty incidence. Working with nationally representative household data, we estimated poverty lines using both the official methodology and a modified version of the PLEASe code, the latter providing utility-consistent poverty lines. Evidence from both methods suggests that trends in poverty incidence in Pakistan between 2001 and 2010–11 did not follow the path indicated in the official estimates provided by the government of Pakistan.

Official estimates of poverty incidence suggest a downward trend from 2001–2 at an annual rate of approximately 2.2 percentage points per year countrywide, with substantial reductions in both rural and urban areas. In contrast with this trend, estimates obtained by applying the government's official methodology to estimate annual, regional poverty lines suggest a steady increase. Further, utility-consistent estimates obtained using the PLEASe code suggest that poverty levels have remained steady over the period of study. Poverty incidence is higher in rural areas than in urban areas according to results of nearly all methods described here. Data from the most recent year of study, 2010–11, show the divide between rural and urban poverty incidence is most pronounced in the Sindh province.

## Acknowledgement

The authors would like to acknowledge Channing Arndt for his technical and conceptual guidance with the software code applied herein and Sohail Malik and Paul Dorosh for their guidance on poverty analysis in Pakistan.

# Appendix 9.A

**Table 9.A1.** Poverty estimates using the food energy intake (FEI) methodology by spatial domain

|  | 2001–2 | 2004–5 | 2005–6 | 2007–8 | 2010–11 |
|---|---|---|---|---|---|
| **Official methodology, extrapolated CPI*** |  |  |  |  |  |
| Punjab | 34.1 | 23.7 | 15.8 | 14.4 | 11.0 |
| urban | 20.4 | 13.7 | 7.4 | 6.7 | 5.5 |
| rural | 39.6 | 28.3 | 19.7 | 18.0 | 13.6 |
| Sindh | 32.1 | 16.2 | 20.8 | 14.3 | 9.7 |
| urban | 12.9 | 7.0 | 8.3 | 4.5 | 4.1 |
| rural | 44.3 | 23.0 | 33.0 | 22.9 | 14.9 |
| KPK | 28.3 | 24.1 | 18.1 | 9.1 | 8.6 |
| urban | 19.7 | 12.7 | 14.6 | 3.6 | 5.7 |
| rural | 29.8 | 26.3 | 18.8 | 10.2 | 9.2 |
| Balochistan | 22.9 | 18.0 | 35.1 | 27.3 | 7.0 |
| urban | 15.9 | 11.7 | 22.1 | 18.7 | 4.7 |
| rural | 24.4 | 19.5 | 39.2 | 30.7 | 7.7 |
| **Official methodology, re-estimated for each year (by spatial domain)** |  |  |  |  |  |
| Punjab | 33.3 | 33.7 | 32.7 | 33.7 | 40.3 |
| urban | 28.2 | 26.2 | 27.4 | 27.9 | 35.0 |
| rural | 35.3 | 37.3 | 35.1 | 36.3 | 42.8 |
| Sindh | 35.0 | 34.3 | 43.5 | 46.9 | 44.4 |
| urban | 19.5 | 19.4 | 28.3 | 31.4 | 30.7 |
| rural | 44.9 | 45.5 | 58.4 | 60.3 | 57.3 |
| KPK | 35.0 | 39.1 | 39.0 | 37.5 | 40.4 |
| urban | 29.9 | 33.2 | 37.1 | 32.1 | 36.4 |
| rural | 35.8 | 40.2 | 39.3 | 38.6 | 41.3 |
| Balochistan | 31.3 | 37.5 | 57.4 | 55.9 | 42.2 |
| urban | 24.9 | 26.7 | 49.9 | 46.7 | 43.5 |
| rural | 32.7 | 40.3 | 59.7 | 59.6 | 41.8 |
| **Official methodology, re-estimated for each year (one national line)** |  |  |  |  |  |
| Punjab | 34.1 | 35.8 | 32.0 | 33.5 | 38.0 |
| urban | 20.4 | 21.7 | 19.7 | 21.5 | 23.5 |
| rural | 39.6 | 42.3 | 37.9 | 39.0 | 44.9 |
| Sindh | 32.1 | 27.5 | 37.5 | 39.7 | 39.7 |
| urban | 12.9 | 13.4 | 19.0 | 21.8 | 23.0 |
| rural | 44.3 | 37.9 | 55.6 | 55.3 | 55.3 |
| KPK | 28.3 | 39.1 | 39.7 | 34.5 | 41.5 |
| urban | 19.7 | 25.9 | 31.9 | 24.2 | 31.2 |
| rural | 29.8 | 41.7 | 41.1 | 36.5 | 43.6 |
| Balochistan | 22.9 | 29.0 | 56.9 | 59.4 | 39.8 |
| urban | 15.9 | 18.1 | 40.1 | 41.9 | 30.7 |
| rural | 24.4 | 31.7 | 62.1 | 66.3 | 42.6 |

*Source*: GoP (2014) and authors' calculations using HIES data

**Table 9.A2.** Poverty estimates using the FEI and PLEASe methodologies without controlling for utility consistency by spatial domain

|  | 2001–2 | 2004–5 | 2005–6 | 2007–8 | 2010–11 |
|---|---|---|---|---|---|
| *Official methodology, re-estimated for each year (by spatial domain)* | | | | | |
| Punjab | 33.3 | 33.7 | 32.7 | 33.7 | 40.3 |
| urban | 28.2 | 26.2 | 27.4 | 27.9 | 35.0 |
| rural | 35.3 | 37.3 | 35.1 | 36.3 | 42.8 |
| Sindh | 35.0 | 34.3 | 43.5 | 46.9 | 44.4 |
| urban | 19.5 | 19.4 | 28.3 | 31.4 | 30.7 |
| rural | 44.9 | 45.5 | 58.4 | 60.3 | 57.3 |
| KPK | 35.0 | 39.1 | 39.0 | 37.5 | 40.4 |
| urban | 29.9 | 33.2 | 37.1 | 32.1 | 36.4 |
| rural | 35.8 | 40.2 | 39.3 | 38.6 | 41.3 |
| Balochistan | 31.3 | 37.5 | 57.4 | 55.9 | 42.2 |
| urban | 24.9 | 26.7 | 49.9 | 46.7 | 43.5 |
| rural | 32.7 | 40.3 | 59.7 | 59.6 | 41.8 |
| *PLEASe, pre-entropy* | | | | | |
| Punjab | 19.6 | 22.2 | 18.7 | 22.4 | 25.5 |
| urban | 22.7 | 21.5 | 19.2 | 23.7 | 24.6 |
| rural | 18.3 | 22.6 | 18.5 | 21.8 | 25.9 |
| Sindh | 25.8 | 28.7 | 32.0 | 34.8 | 33.5 |
| urban | 26.0 | 27.6 | 26.9 | 32.9 | 29.0 |
| rural | 25.6 | 29.5 | 37.0 | 36.4 | 37.7 |
| KPK | 19.3 | 21.9 | 17.8 | 20.4 | 21.7 |
| urban | 20.8 | 18.9 | 21.0 | 19.9 | 22.9 |
| rural | 19.1 | 22.5 | 17.1 | 20.5 | 21.4 |
| Balochistan | 25.4 | 29.8 | 41.1 | 42.8 | 27.5 |
| urban | 25.9 | 26.8 | 37.6 | 35.2 | 28.7 |
| rural | 25.3 | 30.5 | 42.2 | 45.8 | 27.2 |

*Source*: GoP (2014) and authors' calculations using HIES data

**Table 9.A3.** Poverty estimates using the PLEASe methodology with and without spatial and intertemporal adjustment

|  | 2001–2 | 2004–5 | 2005–6 | 2007–8 | 2010–11 |
|---|---|---|---|---|---|
| *Post-entropy, spatially adjusted but no intertemporal adjustment* | | | | | |
| Punjab | 22.6 | 26.3 | 19.6 | 21.8 | 26.2 |
| urban | 22.3 | 20.6 | 14.1 | 17.1 | 20.1 |
| rural | 22.8 | 28.9 | 22.1 | 23.9 | 29.1 |
| Sindh | 24.6 | 21.6 | 26.3 | 28.3 | 27.9 |
| urban | 18.2 | 17.0 | 15.4 | 21.3 | 18.6 |
| rural | 28.7 | 25.0 | 37.0 | 34.5 | 36.7 |
| KPK | 21.8 | 27.1 | 22.6 | 21.8 | 27.5 |
| urban | 20.2 | 22.8 | 21.1 | 18.5 | 23.4 |
| rural | 22.1 | 28.0 | 22.9 | 22.5 | 28.4 |
| Balochistan | 25.5 | 28.5 | 32.7 | 53.9 | 32.7 |
| urban | 21.3 | 25.9 | 36.0 | 42.6 | 28.9 |
| rural | 26.4 | 29.1 | 48.7 | 58.3 | 33.8 |
| *Pre-entropy, with spatial and intertemporal adjustment* | | | | | |
| Punjab | 22.6 |  | 19.6 | 19.6 | 23.2 |
| urban | 22.3 |  | 14.1 | 14.9 | 17.2 |
| rural | 22.8 |  | 22.1 | 21.8 | 25.9 |
| Sindh | 24.6 |  | 26.0 | 25.2 | 26.0 |
| urban | 18.2 |  | 15.0 | 18.3 | 16.8 |
| rural | 28.7 |  | 36.7 | 31.2 | 34.7 |

| KPK | 21.8 | | 22.4 | 18.8 | 24.8 |
|---|---|---|---|---|---|
| urban | 20.2 | | 20.7 | 15.5 | 21.4 |
| rural | 22.1 | | 22.7 | 19.5 | 25.5 |
| Balochistan | 25.5 | | 45.4 | 49.5 | 28.9 |
| urban | 21.3 | | 36.0 | 37.7 | 26.1 |
| rural | 26.4 | | 48.3 | 54.1 | 29.8 |

*Source*: GoP (2014) and authors' calculations using HIES data

## References


Ahmad, E. and C. Allison (1990). 'Poverty, Growth and Public Policy in Pakistan'. Unpublished draft paper. Islamabad: Pakistan Institute of Development Economics.

Ahmad, E. and S. Ludlow (1989). 'Poverty, Inequality and Growth in Pakistan'. Background paper for the 1990 World Development Report. Washington, DC: World Bank. Available at <http://www.pide.org.pk/pdf/PDR/1989/Volume4/831-850.pdf>, accessed 22 December 2015.

Akhtar, S. (1988). 'Poverty in Pakistan'. Draft mimeo. Islamabad: World Bank.

Allaudin, T. (1975). 'Mass Poverty in Pakistan: A Further Study', *Pakistan Development Review*, 14(4): 431–50.

Anwar, T. and S. K. Qureshi (2002). 'Trends in Absolute Poverty in Pakistan: 1990–91 and 2001', *Pakistan Development Review*, 41(4, Part II): 859–78.

Anwar, T., S. K. Qureshi, and H. Ali (2005). 'Landlessness and Rural Poverty in Pakistan'. Paper presented at the 20th Annual General Meeting and Conference of Pakistan Society of Development Economists (PIDE), Islamabad, 10–12 January. Available at <http://www.pide.org.pk/pdf/psde20AGM/Landlessness%20and%20Rural%20Poverty%20in%20Pakistan.pdf>, accessed 22 December 2015.

Arif, G. M. (2006). 'Poverty, Economic Growth, and Inequality: A Review of Pakistan's Poverty Literature'. Background Paper 1. Islamabad: Asian Development Bank.

Arif, G. M., H. Nazli, and R. Haq (2000). 'Rural Non-Agriculture Employment and Poverty in Pakistan', *Pakistan Development Review*, 39(4, Part II): 1089–110.

Arndt, C. and K. R. Simler (2010). 'Estimating Utility-Consistent Poverty Lines with Applications to Egypt and Mozambique', *Economic Development and Cultural Change*, 58(3): 449–74.

Beck, U., K. Pauw, and R. Mussa (2015). 'Methods Matter: The Sensitivity of Malawian Poverty Estimates to Definitions, Data, and Assumptions', WIDER Working Paper 2015/126. Helsinki: UNU-WIDER.

Cheema, I. A. (2005). *A Profile of Poverty in Pakistan*. Islamabad: Centre for Research on Poverty Reduction and Income Distribution Planning Commission.

Datt, G. and D. Jolliffe (2005). 'Poverty in Egypt: Modeling and Policy Simulations', *Economic Development and Cultural Change*, 53(2): 327–46.

Ercelawn, A. A. (1989). 'Poverty in Pakistan: Choice of Poverty Criteria'. Draft paper. Islamabad: Federal Bureau of Statistics, Government of Pakistan.

Ercelawn, A. A. (1990). 'Absolute Poverty in Pakistan: Poverty Lines, Incidence, Intensity'. Draft paper. Karachi: Applied Economics Research Centre, University of Karachi.

Foster, J., J. Greer, and E. Thorbecke (1984). 'A Class of Decomposable Poverty Measures', *Econometrica*, 52(3): 761–6.

Gibson, J. and S. Rozelle (2003). 'Poverty and Access to Roads in Papua New Guinea', *Economic Development and Cultural Change*, 52(1): 159–86.

GoP (2001a). *Food Consumption Table for Pakistan (Revised 2001)*. Islamabad/Peshawar: Ministry of Planning and Development, Government of Pakistan (GoP) and UNICEF/ Department of Agricultural Chemistry, NWFP Agriculture University. Available at <http://www.fao.org/fileadmin/templates/food_composition/documents/regional/ Book_Food_Composition_Table_for_Pakistan_.pdf>, accessed 22 December 2015.

GoP (2001b). *Household Integrated Economic Survey 2001–02*. Islamabad: Federal Bureau of Statistics, Government of Pakistan (GoP).

GoP (2003). 'Accelerating Economic Growth and Reducing Poverty: The Road Ahead'. Poverty Reduction Strategy Paper. Islamabad: Ministry of Finance, Government of Pakistan (GoP). Available at: <http://www.embassyofpakistanusa.org/forms/Accelerating %20Economic%20Growth%20and%20Reducing%20Poverty–The%20Road%20Ahead %20%5BPRSP-2003%5D.pdf>, accessed 22 December 2015.

GoP (2005). *Household Integrated Economic Survey 2004–05*. Islamabad: Federal Bureau of Statistics, Government of Pakistan (GoP).

GoP (2006). *Household Integrated Economic Survey 2005–06*. Islamabad: Federal Bureau of Statistics, Government of Pakistan (GoP).

GoP (2008a). *Economic Survey 2007–08*. Islamabad: Ministry of Finance, Government of Pakistan (GoP).

GoP (2008b). *Household Integrated Economic Survey 2007–08*. Islamabad: Federal Bureau of Statistics, Government of Pakistan (GoP).

GoP (2011). *Household Integrated Economic Survey 2010–11*. Islamabad: Federal Bureau of Statistics, Government of Pakistan (GoP).

GoP (2013). *Economic Survey 2012–13*. Islamabad: Ministry of Finance, Government of Pakistan (GoP).

GoP (2014). *Economic Survey 2013–14*. Islamabad: Ministry of Finance, Government of Pakistan (GoP).

GoP (2015). 'Household Integrated Economic Survey Report 2004–05, 2005–06, 2007–08, 2010–11, 2011–12', in *Pakistan Social and Living Standards Measurement*. Islamabad: Ministry of Finance, Government of Pakistan (GoP). Available at <http://www.pbs.gov.pk/content/pakistan-social-and-living-standards-measurement>, accessed 22 December 2015.

Irfan, M. and R. Amjad (1984). 'Poverty in Rural Pakistan', in A. R. Khan and E. Lee (eds), *Poverty in Rural Asia*. Geneva: International Labour Office (ILO)/ARTEP, 19–47.

Jafri, S. M. Y. (1999). 'Assessing Poverty in Pakistan', in *A Profile of Poverty in Pakistan*, HDC Report. Islamabad: Mahbub ul Haq Human Development Centre (HDC). Available at <http://mhhdc.org/?p=54>, accessed 22 December 2014.

Jamal, H. (2012). 'Pakistan Poverty Statistics: Estimates for 2011', Research Report No. 84. Karachi: Social Policy Development Centre (SPDC). Available at <http:// www.spdc.org.pk/Data/Publication/PDF/RR84.pdf>, accessed 22 December 2015.

Kruijk, H. de and M. van Leeuwen (1985). 'Changes in Poverty and Income Inequality in Pakistan During the 1970s', *Pakistan Development Review*, 24(3–4): 407–22.

Malik, M. H. (1988). 'Some New Evidence on the Incidence of Poverty in Pakistan', *Pakistan Development Review*, 27(4): 509–15.

Malik, S. J. (1993). 'Poverty in Pakistan, 1984–85 to 1987–88', in M. Lipton and J. van der Gaag (eds), *Including the Poor: Proceedings of a Symposium Organized by the World Bank and the International Food Policy Research Institute*. Washington, DC: World Bank Regional and Sectoral Studies, 422–54.

Malik, S. J. (1994). 'Poverty in Pakistan: 1984–85, 1987–88 and 1990–91'. Mimeo. Washington, DC: International Food Policy Research Institute.

Malik, S. J. (2005). 'Agricultural Growth and Rural Poverty in Pakistan: A Review of the Evidence', Pakistan Resident Mission Working Paper 2. Islamabad: Asian Development Bank/Pakistan Resident Mission.

Malik, S. J., H. Nazli, A. Mehmood, and A. Shahzad (2014a). 'Issues in the Measurement and Construction of the Consumer Price Index in Pakistan', PSSP Working Paper 020. Islamabad: Pakistan Strategy Support Program, International Food Policy Research Institute.

Malik, S. J., H. Nazli, and E. Whitney (2014b). 'The Official Estimates of Poverty in Pakistan: What Is Wrong and Why? Illustrations Using the Government of Pakistan's Household Integrated Economic Survey 2010–11', PSSP Working Paper 26. Islamabad: Pakistan Strategy Support Program (PSSP), International Food Policy Research Institute.

Mukherjee, S. and T. Benson (2003). 'The Determinants of Poverty in Malawi, 1998', *World Development*, 31(2): 339–58.

Naseem, S. M. (1973). 'Mass Poverty in Pakistan: Some Preliminary Findings', *Pakistan Development Review*, 12(4): 317–60.

Naseem, S. M. (1977). 'Rural Poverty and Landlessness in Pakistan', ILO Report on Poverty and Landlessness in Asia. Geneva: International Labour Office (ILO).

Ravallion, M. (1994). *Poverty Comparisons*. Chur: Harwood Academic Publishers.

Ravallion, M. (1998). 'Poverty Lines in Theory and Practice', LSMS Living Standards Measurement Study Working Paper 133. Washington, DC: World Bank. Available at: <http://documents.worldbank.org/curated/en/1998/07/438657/poverty-lines-theory-practice>, accessed 22 December 2015.

Ravallion, M. and B. Bidani (1994). 'How Robust Is a Poverty Profile?', *World Bank Economic Review*, 8(1): 75–102.

Ravallion, M. and M. Lokshin (2006). 'Testing Poverty Lines', *Review of Income and Wealth*, 52(3): 399–421.

Ravallion, M. and B. Sen (1996). 'When Method Matters: Monitoring Poverty in Bangladesh', *Economic Development and Cultural Change*, 44(4): 761–92.

SPDC (2005). *Combating Poverty: Is Growth Sufficient? Social Development in Pakistan, Annual Review 2004*. Karachi: Social Policy and Development Centre (SPDC). Available at: <http://www.spdc.org.pk/Data/Publication/PDF/AR-6.pdf>, accessed 22 December 2015.

Tarp, F., K. R. Simler, C. Matusse, R. Heltberg, and G. Dava (2002). 'The Robustness of Poverty Profiles Reconsidered', *Economic Development and Cultural Change*, 51(1): 77–108.

Wodon, Q. (1997). 'Food Energy Intake and Cost of Basic Needs: Measuring Poverty in Bangladesh', *Journal of Development Studies*, 34(2): 66–101.

World Bank (2002). 'Poverty in Pakistan: Vulnerabilities, Social Gaps, and Rural Dynamics', Report 24296-PAK. Washington, DC: Poverty Reduction and Economic Management Sector Unit, South Asia Region, World Bank.

# 10

# Uganda

## A New Set of Utility-Consistent Poverty Lines

*Bjorn Van Campenhout, Haruna Sekabira, and Fiona Nattembo*

## 10.1 Introduction

During the past few decades, Uganda has experienced substantial economic growth. Especially during the nineties, Uganda outperformed other economies in Southern and Eastern Africa. Part of this accelerated growth is likely to be a peace dividend after years of civil war during the Amin and Obote regimes. However, some of this growth is also attributed to the far-reaching economic reforms implemented by the new government, transforming Uganda into one of the most liberal economies in sub-Saharan Africa (World Bank 1993). This growth has been accompanied by equally impressive social progress. Indeed, Uganda used to be considered a showcase when it comes to reducing poverty, fighting HIV/AIDS, and promoting social development (Dijkstra and van Donge 2001). According to official figures, poverty fell from about 56 per cent in 1992/3 to around 20 per cent in 2012/13 (UBOS 2006; Ssewanyana and Kasirye 2014). These days, in terms of economic growth, Uganda has been overtaken by some of the neighbouring countries, such as Tanzania and Ethiopia. While GDP growth shows a marked slowdown from 2005/6 onward (Duponchelle et al. 2014), official poverty statistics seem to persist in their downward trend.

However, research has cautioned that the positive aggregate trends may hide less positive dynamics at a more disaggregate level (Lawson et al. 2006). For instance, Emwanu et al. (2006) find that poverty reductions in the North were much less pronounced, and today, poverty levels in for example Karamoja remain disturbingly high. More recent research on poverty dynamics using a recently constructed panel data survey also points out stagnation or even a reversal in some areas (Ssewanyana and Kasirye 2014; Duponchelle et al. 2014). More worrying is that as of late, some have started to call the actual numbers into question. Levine (2012) points out significant divergence between the level and evolution of poverty figures reported by the government of Uganda and those published by the World Bank. Both qualitative and quantitative research on asset accumulation and non-monetary poverty indicators also suggest much more modest progress (Daniels and Minot 2015; Kakande 2010). Some scholars argue that the use of a single national poverty line may bias estimates in certain areas (Appleton 2003; Jamal 1998).

In this chapter, we explore some of the causes of these diverging views by estimating poverty using PLEASe and the most recent available dataset for Uganda. We feel that one of the major problems with the official poverty estimates is that they are based on an outdated basic-needs basket that is unlikely to adequately reflect current consumption patterns. In addition, we appreciate the fact that Uganda has an unusual dietary diversity (Benson et al. 2008; Appleton 2003), with for example people in the North consuming relatively more sorghum and cassava and those in the West more matooke.[1] It is well known that in many instances—for example, if relative prices of basic commodities vary by region (or through time) and preferences permit substitution—the use of a single consumption bundle may result in inconsistent poverty comparisons (Tarp et al. 2002). We estimate a new set of utility-consistent poverty lines taking into account the spatial variation in the cost of basic needs within Uganda and compare this to results using official Ugandan poverty lines.

The rest of this chapter is organized as follows. Section 10.2 describes official poverty in Uganda and discusses some of the issues that have been raised with respect to these figures. This is followed by a reassessment of poverty in Uganda (section 10.3). We first briefly introduce the data we will use in this reassessment and then describe in detail how we construct the welfare indicator. Next, we describe how we construct consumption bundles that correspond to basic needs in different locations, after which we discuss how we ensure these bundles provide the same basic needs. We then present the poverty estimates using the new poverty lines. A final section (10.4) concludes.

## 10.2 Poverty in Uganda

According to official estimates, poverty has decreased substantially since the 1990s in Uganda. Table 10.1 draws from various reports of large-scale household budget surveys that are periodically carried out by the Uganda Bureau of

---

[1] Matooke is a variety of starchy banana, commonly referred to as cooking bananas.

**Table 10.1.** Official poverty in Uganda

|  | 1992/3 | 1999/2000 | 2002/3 | 2005/6 | 2009/10 | 2012/13 |
|---|---|---|---|---|---|---|
| National | 55.5 | 33.8 | 38.8 | 31.1 | 24.5 | 19.7 |
| Central | 45.6 | 19.7 | 22.3 | 16.4 | 10.7 | 5.1 |
| East | 58.8 | 35.0 | 46.0 | 35.9 | 24.3 | 24.1 |
| West | 53.1 | 26.2 | 32.9 | 29.5 | 21.8 | 7.6 |
| North | 72.2 | 63.7 | 63.0 | 60.7 | 46.2 | 43.7 |
| Kampala |  |  | 4.7 | 4.4 | 4.0 | 0.7 |
| Central 1 |  |  | 22.0 | 18.8 | 11.2 | 3.7 |
| Central 2 |  |  | 30.0 | 19.7 | 13.6 | 7.3 |
| East Central |  |  | 42.6 | 32.7 | 21.4 | 24.3 |
| Eastern |  |  | 48.4 | 39.2 | 26.5 | 24.7 |
| Mid-Northern |  |  | 57.4 | 61.1 | 40.4 | 35.4 |
| North-East |  |  | 82.8 | 79.3 | 75.8 | 74.2 |
| West Nile |  |  | 62.8 | 55.3 | 39.7 | 42.3 |
| Mid-Western |  |  | 37.9 | 23.2 | 25.3 | 9.8 |
| South-Western |  |  | 29.0 | 18.7 | 18.4 | 7.6 |

*Source*: Uganda Bureau of Statistics (2010), Uganda Bureau of Statistics (2014), and Levine (2012)

Statistics (UBOS) to monitor poverty. At the national level, we see that poverty has been declining steadily over time, with the exception of 2002/3 when poverty increased slightly. The long-run downward trend in poverty, from 55.5 per cent to 19.7 per cent in just twenty years translates into an average yearly reduction in headcount poverty of more than 3 per cent.

However, the aggregate trend hides quite some variation in poverty reduction rates at a more disaggregate level. For example, if we restrict attention to the Central region, headcount poverty reduced from 45.6 per cent to just 5.1 per cent. This is partly because the Central region includes Kampala, and poverty fell much faster in urban areas than in rural areas. The reduction in the Central region over the twenty-year period amounts to a 4.4 per cent reduction per year. At the other extreme, the drier and more remote Northern region started off with poverty that was already about 60 per cent higher than headcount poverty in the Central region. Poverty reduced from 72.2 per cent to 43.7 per cent over the course of twenty years, which amounts to an annual rate of poverty reduction of less than 2 per cent.

The contrast becomes more pronounced with increasing disaggregation. If we go down to the sub-regional level, the lowest level at which the data is deemed representative, we find that for example poverty in Kampala has been reduced from about 5 per cent at the turn of the century to about 0.7 per cent at the latest survey, corresponding to an impressive annual poverty reduction rate of 8.5 per cent. The North-East, which covers one of the poorest districts in Uganda, Karamoja, started the new century with headcount poverty at a staggering 82.8 per cent. By 2012/13, still around three quarters of the population in this sub-region live below the national poverty line. The annualized rate of poverty reduction in this region was a mere 1 per cent per year.

Naturally, the divergence in rates of poverty reduction means that inequality has worsened over time. While the Northern region was only 60 per cent poorer than the Central region in 1992/2003, it was already 2.7 times poorer than Central in 2002/3 and more than eight times poorer in 2012/13. Again, this increasing inequality in wellbeing is amplified at lower levels of disaggregation. While at the beginning of the twentieth century the poorest sub-region was about twenty times as poor as Kampala, the North-East is more than 100 times poorer than the capital in 2012/13. This illustrates that Uganda has been much less successful in reducing poverty in poor and remote areas. This fact was already noted in Okidi and McKay (2003) who found that, using panel data, the chronic poor did not benefit from market-oriented reforms that seem to drive poverty reduction at the aggregate level. Recent work using newly available panel data seems to confirm this (Ssewanyana and Kasirye 2014).

Apart from the above qualifications, researchers have also raised methodological issues with the way poverty is measured in Uganda. In particular, official estimates in Uganda rely on a single national poverty line that is based on a nationally representative food consumption bundle of the poor.[2] While the continued use of this poverty line is defended as key to the comparability of poverty over time, it also means that today's welfare is compared to the cost of a basket of goods that may not adequately reflect the consumption patterns of the poor today. In addition, Appleton (2003) and Jamal (1998) argue that a single poverty line that does not take into account spatial heterogeneity in the diets of the population cannot adequately identify the poor. When they allow for spatial heterogeneity in the composition of the basic-needs basket, they find that the Western region is poorer than official statistics suggest, reflecting the relatively high price of matooke as a source of energy.

Official figures have also been challenged recently when compared to alternative methods of estimating poverty. For instance, Levine (2012) compares the official poverty estimates with the poverty estimates using the World Bank's 'a dollar a day' international poverty line.[3] He finds that absolute poverty is higher according to the World Bank, and also that reduction in poverty is substantially slower than official numbers suggest. The author identifies adjustments to account for urban and rural price differences, adjustments to account for household composition, and statistical weighting as potential causes for the divergence.

---

[2] The national poverty line does allow for some spatial heterogeneity in the non-food component of the poverty line. Spatial price heterogeneity is also incorporated in the official poverty estimates through deflation of the welfare indicator, although the exact details (what prices are used to make the adjustments) are lacking.

[3] This is done using PovcalNet, the online tool for poverty measurement developed by the Development Research Group of the World Bank (http://iresearch.worldbank.org/PovcalNet/).

Studies that employ alternative welfare indicators also paint a less optimistic picture. For example Daniels and Minot (2015) use information on asset ownership, access to water and sanitation, and other non-monetary indicators of wellbeing to predict poverty using Demographic and Health Surveys (DHS) data. Using methods related to poverty mapping and small area estimation, they find that poverty has reduced much slower than official figures suggest. The similar conclusions are reached in studies that use more qualitative methods to assess poverty and wellbeing (Krishna et al. 2006; Kakande 2010).

## 10.3 A Reassessment of Poverty in Uganda

Poverty measurement generally involves three steps. The first two steps are often referred to together as the *identification* stage and the last step involves *aggregation*. The first step in the identification stage consists of the construction of a welfare indicator and in the second step one agrees on a poverty line. The welfare measure from the first step is used to rank units according to wellbeing.[4] Ideally, this should be a measure that reflects the multidimensional nature of wellbeing, but in general, one settles for a money metric measure that is correlated with wellbeing. In practice, preference is given to consumption expenditure above income, as the first tends to be less susceptible to fluctuations over time and less prone to measurement error.

The poverty line is then used to delineate the poor from the rest of the population. There are two common ways to fix poverty lines. The cost of basic needs (CBN) method assembles a basket of goods typically consumed by the poor that generates a minimum necessary energy level (e.g. 3000 kcal per adult) that is deemed sufficient, and a non-food allowance is added. Alternatively, using the food energy intake (FEI) method, the poverty line is derived from a regression of food expenditure on caloric intake at the individual level, which is then used to predict expenditure needed to yield a particular minimum necessary energy level. The advantage of this method is that a non-food allowance is automatically included in the predicted expenditure, but the disadvantage is that one needs detailed data on food energy intake to estimate the regression.

In the aggregation step, the information pertaining to the position of the units in terms of welfare with respect to the poverty line is summarized at a particular level of aggregation. For instance, one can simply count the number of households that fall below the poverty line and express this as a proportion of the total number of households at a national level. This would be the

---

[4] Often these units are households due to the nature of surveys, but can also be individuals, countries, and regions.

poverty headcount, and this is usually what people refer to when they talk about the level of poverty in a particular country. An often used poverty measure, that encompasses the poverty headcount, is the Foster–Greere–Thorbecke (FGT) indicator (Foster et al. 1984). For more information on poverty measurement and analysis in practice, the reader is referred to Ravallion (1994).

### 10.3.1 *The Data*

Uganda has been lauded for its efforts to monitor poverty and wellbeing. At the basis of this achievement is a fairly well functioning statistics agency, the Uganda Bureau of Statistics (UBOS), which collects information on socio-economic characteristics at the household and community levels for monitoring development performance. As such, researchers that want to work on poverty measurement and comparisons have a range of data they can work with. The first household budget survey since the end of the civil war was done in 1989/90 and smaller surveys have been done at varying time intervals. From 1999/2000 onward, the format of the survey was adapted. The survey was modelled to conform to the Living Standards Measurement Survey (LSMS) and was held every three years. This first survey is popularly known as the Uganda National Household Survey 1999/2000 or UNHS-I. In this study, we will present results based on the UNHS 2012/13, the latest UNHS available. It covers about 6888 households, a sufficient numbers of observations to allow us to estimate poverty lines at a sufficiently disaggregated level.

While it is difficult to assess the quality of the data without a proper benchmark, internal inconsistencies within other datasets collected by UBOS have been documented in the past. For example, in the Uganda National Panel Survey (UNPS) wave of 2010/11, a similar but smaller LSMS-type dataset that is part of an ongoing panel, there is a gigantic unexplained drop in the number of people reporting to consume sweet potatoes (and to a lesser extent cassava). While in all other rounds of the UNPS about 1500 households report non-zero consumption of sweet potatoes, this is less than 300 households in the 2010/11. Duponchelle et al. (2014) also find suspicious patterns of attrition in the UNPS, consistent with declining motivation of interviewers, something not unusual in government organizations like UBOS that grapple with funding issues. There is no reason to believe that the UNHS 2012/13 does not suffer from similar problems.

### 10.3.2 *Constructing the Welfare Indicator*

The datasets that are disseminated by UBOS often have an extra file that can be used to replicate the official poverty numbers. For instance, the UNHS

2012/13 has a file called *Poverty2012.dta*. In this file, one will find a variable called *welfare*, which is the welfare indicator used for official poverty estimates.[5] One also needs the poverty lines (called *spline*) and the weights called *hmult*. Poverty can then simply be obtained as the weighted mean of a dummy that indicates if *welfare* is smaller than *spline*.

The consumption aggregate supplied by UBOS is convenient to replicate official estimates. However, often one would like to re-run the analysis with slight modifications to check robustness. For instance, one may want to check if scaling household consumption by household size would lead to different conclusions than scaling by the number of adult-equivalent units within the household. This is often difficult as there is no detailed information available on how the consumption aggregate has been constructed and the code that is used to generate the welfare variable is not in the public domain. Furthermore, while some datasets have a range of seemingly intermediate variables, such as the Poverty2012.dta file that we referred to, others have only a few intermediate variables.[6]

PLEASe contains modules to construct a consumption aggregate. Although it would be possible to use the consumption aggregate supplied by UBOS to rank households and compare them to a new set of poverty lines, the construction of the poverty lines itself using PLEASe requires more detailed consumption information than just the welfare indicator. Therefore, we decided to reconstruct our own welfare indicator from the raw consumption data.

One of the first things we do is merge household size from the household roster in section 2 of the UNHS questionnaire with the identifying information in section 1 which we will use to classify households into different spatial domains. To determine household size, we only incorporate usual or regular members present or absent, which leads to an average household size of about five members. Already, due to undocumented data cleaning and/or a different definition of what constitutes a household, our household size differs slightly from the one reported in the Poverty2012.dta dataset.

To calculate the welfare indicator at the household level, we start in section 6B and we simply sum all quantities consumed out of purchases at home, consumed out of purchases away from home (such as in restaurants), consumed out of home production, and quantities received in kind or for free.

---

[5] The data should be requested in writing from the director of the UBS. However, a reference to the content of the file is available on the website of the international household survey network: <http://catalog.ihsn.org/index.php/catalog/4620/datafile/F18>. The questionnaires can also be found on that website: <http://catalog.ihsn.org/index.php/catalog/4620>.

[6] Such as, for instance, the file kwelfare.dta that holds information to calculate poverty in the UNHS2009/10. The reference is <http://catalog.ihsn.org/index.php/catalog/2119/data_dictionary#page=F21&tab=data-dictionary>.

These amounts are divided by seven to get average daily consumption for each consumption item at household level.

A typical issue encountered in household budget surveys is that food consumption is often recorded in non-standard units. Some may be relatively straightforward to convert to kilograms, such as a 1 kg kimbo of maize grains, where kimbo is a well-known type of cooking fat that comes in 1 or 2 kg plastic containers, and so standard conversion factors are available for each crop.[7] Others are less precisely defined, such as a bunch of bananas or a bundle of fish. We convert non-standard units using a set of conversion factors that UBOS assembled during the Uganda Census of Agriculture 2008/9 (UCA), and for missing conversion factors in the UCA we use conversion factors provided for the UNHS 2012/13. But even then, for about 7 per cent of the households, item-level observations cannot be converted into kilograms because of missing conversion factors. In most cases, these are foodstuffs that are not well defined, such as 'other fruits'.

Section 5 of the UNHS 2012/13 provides information on health, with a single question on the cost of consultation. However, section 6C, on expenditures on Non-Durable Goods and Frequently Purchased Services also asks about health and medical expenses. This is done in a much more detailed way than in section 5, explicitly probing for traditional doctor's fees and in-kind or received-for-free services. We therefore include medical expenditures as non-durable goods and frequently purchased services. Other categories under this heading are (imputed) rent and fuel such as charcoal; non-durable and personal goods such as soap; transport and communication such as air time; and other services such as barber. As this was recorded during the last thirty days we converted to daily averages and aggregated to total household expenditures.

Section 4 records education for household members above the age of 5 and has a question on expenditures. However, section 6D on expenditures on semi-durable and durable goods and services that were purchased during the last year also includes questions on expenditure for education. To maintain uniformity with health, we therefore decided to use the figures from section 6D rather than those in section 4. Other semi-durable and durable goods include clothing and footwear; furniture; household appliances and equipment; utensils and others. Finally, there is a separate section for non-consumption expenditure, which collects tax payments, interests, funerals, and other functions.

The resulting welfare indicator is quite close to the official consumption aggregate that is in the Poverty2012.dta. The official welfare measure is

---

[7] For instance, a 1 kg kimbo of maize would hold 0.8 kg of maize.

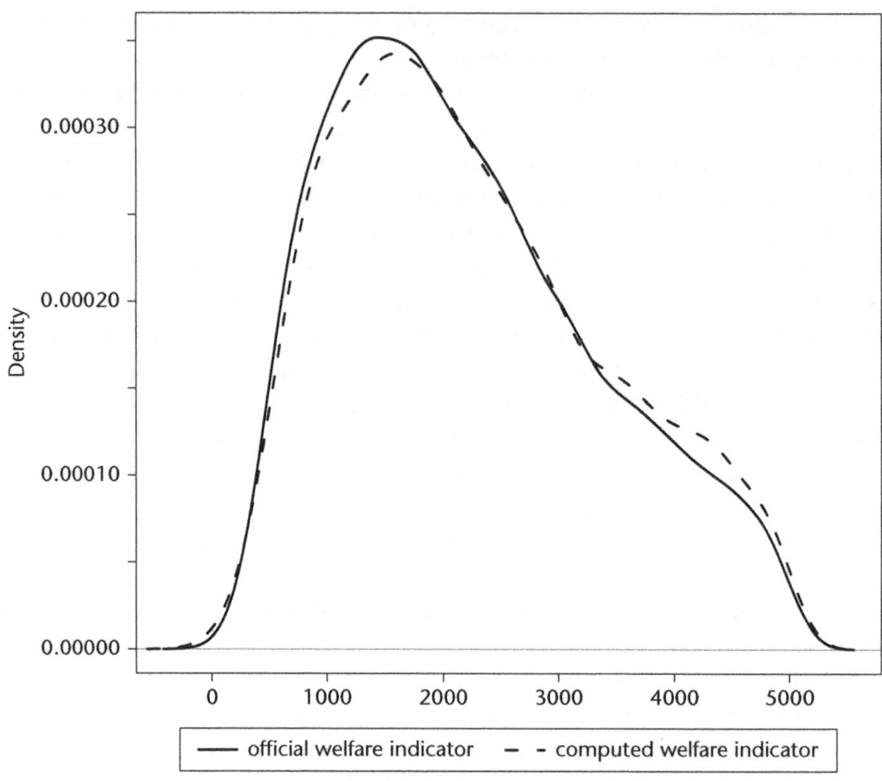



**Figure 10.1.** Density estimates for welfare indicators
*Source*: Authors' calculations based on UNHS 2012/13

expressed on a monthly basis and scaled by number of adult equivalents (Appleton et al. 1999). We therefore divided it by thirty and multiplied it by the number of adult equivalents and then divided it again by the number of household members to make it comparable to our daily consumption per capita measure. In addition, the welfare variable is expressed in 2005/6 prices, so we multiplied it by 1.85, which is the Consumer Price Index (CPI) that is implied by the poverty lines. We then find that our measure has a median value of about 2700 Ugandan shillings per day per capita, while the official estimate is slightly lower at about 2530.

Figure 10.1 shows in more detail how the distributions of the two welfare indicators compare to each other. The solid line represents a kernel density estimate of the distribution of the official welfare indicator, and the dashed line is the one we computed from the raw data. As you can see, they are very close, although the distribution of our welfare indicator suggests a slightly higher degree of inequality. The reason for the difference is most likely because of the way UBOS adjusts the welfare indicator in various ways.

For instance, Appleton et al. (1999) mention that the welfare indicator is adjusted for spatial price differences. However, it is not documented how this actually happens, so it is impossible to replicate.

### 10.3.3 *Cost of Basic Needs*

The official poverty estimates are based on poverty lines that are rooted in a single national food consumption bundle, derived from 1993/4 Monitoring Survey data. In particular, a single food basket was identified at the national level with twenty-eight of the most frequently consumed food items by households with less than the median income. The items in this food basket were then converted into caloric equivalents and scaled to generate 3000 calories per adult equivalent per day using the World Health Organization (WHO) estimates for an 18–30-year-old male as a reference. Next, a non-food allowance was added. Non-food requirements were estimated as the average non-food expenditure of those households whose total expenditure was around the food poverty line. The non-food requirements do allow for spatial heterogeneity, as separate averages were calculated for urban and rural locations interacted with the four regions (Central, Eastern, Northern, and Western), using the method described in Ravallion and Bidani (1994). These poverty lines have since been updated by the official inflation figures each time a new household survey has come out. More information can be found in Appleton et al. (1999).

Following the PLEASe methodology, we use a slightly different approach in that we first calculate the average per person caloric requirement and use this as the basis of our poverty line. If one uses the average caloric requirement of the population instead of, for instance, the caloric requirement of an 18–30-year-old male reference, one does not need to adjust the welfare indicator for nutritional requirements anymore, such as through adult equivalence scales. One can just use consumption expenditure per capita, which is then compared to the cost of obtaining the energy needed by the average person within the population. Specifically, we find the calories needed for each person given their age, gender, likelihood of being pregnant, and likelihood of breastfeeding.[8] If we calculate average caloric requirement for the entire sample, we find this to be about 2184 kcal per day.

However, we allow for spatial heterogeneity in the average caloric requirements. For instance, it may be that fertility rates are lower in urban areas or that rural areas host a disproportionate amount of elderly people. We use the

---

[8] The likelihood of being pregnant is estimated using fertility rates in Uganda.

**Table 10.2.** Average caloric requirement by spatial domain

| Spatial domain | Caloric requirement |
| --- | --- |
| Kampala | 2222.19 |
| Central Rural | 2145.17 |
| East Rural | 2114.05 |
| North Rural | 2111.02 |
| West Rural | 2138.29 |
| Other Urban | 2160.56 |

*Source*: Authors' calculations on the basis of UNHS 2012/13

same spatial domains as we use for the consumption baskets. The resulting caloric requirements are in Table 10.2.

In addition to heterogeneity in basic needs caused by demographics, Uganda has a very diverse diet. While in most of East and Southern Africa, diets are heavily skewed towards maize, there are at least four other staples that are widely consumed within Uganda: matooke, cassava, sweet potatoes, and sorghum. In addition to these staples, Ugandans also derive a lot of energy from beans, and in some parts, millet is also considered a staple. Rice is becoming more important, but mostly at the upper end of the welfare distribution.

To illustrate the unusual variation in diets in Uganda, we have selected the five most consumed staple crops in terms of calories in Uganda by the poor. We have then calculated how many calories a typical poor person derives from each of these crops in rural areas of each of the four regions (Central, Eastern, Northern, and Western). This is illustrated in the dot chart in Figure 10.2. The chart shows that people in Western rely heavily on matooke to obtain their calories. However, people in the rural areas in Northern and Eastern do not consume matooke. People in Northern mainly consume sorghum and cassava, as matooke has a hard time growing in these drier areas. In Eastern, there is a relatively higher reliance on maize.

Differences in diets would not really be a problem for poverty measurement and analysis if the cost of arriving at a specified level of calories would be the same regardless of the diet. However, different products often differ widely in terms of what they cost to generate a given amount of food energy. This is illustrated in the bar chart in Figure 10.3, which shows the average price per kilo calorie for each of the five important staple crops consumed in Uganda. The bar chart shows that matooke is rather inefficient as a source of calories, a point also made by Appleton (2003). The same amount of calories can be obtained at less than half of the cost of matooke by choosing to consume sorghum and cassava.

Referring back to Figure 10.2, we found that people living in the Western region of Uganda derive almost all their calories from matooke. People in the Northern region, on the other hand, have diets that are dominated by sorghum. A basic-needs basket that takes into account local diets will therefore

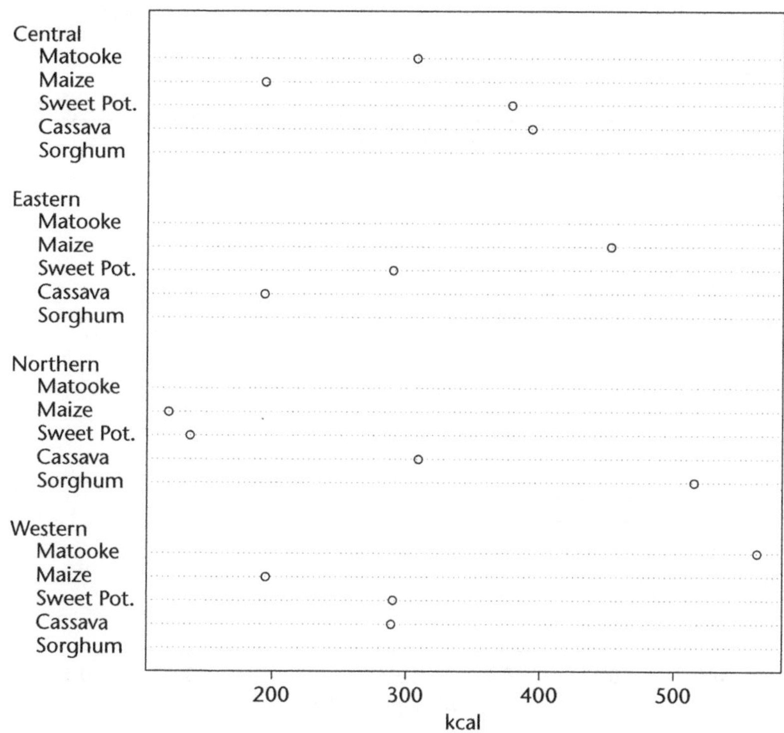



**Figure 10.2.** Calories derived by the poor from different crops per region
*Source*: Authors' calculations on the basis of UNHS 2012/13

differ in cost. In particular, the cost of obtaining a given amount of food energy in the Western region will be much higher than the cost of obtaining this same amount of energy using the Northern diet. Failure to account for this may lead to inconsistent poverty comparisons (Tarp et al. 2002).

While differences in prices in different locations are usually incorporated in poverty measurement by adjusting the welfare indicator to reflect prices used in the construction of the poverty lines (or by adjusting the poverty lines to reflect prices used in the construction of the welfare indicator), it is becoming more and more common to also account for spatial heterogeneity in consumption patterns. Specificity, as defined by Ravallion and Bidani (1994), means that poverty lines should reflect local perceptions of what constitutes poverty. Turning this around, specificity requires that a locally irrelevant basket of goods should not be imposed. In an effort to increase specificity, studies have started using consumption bundles that are disaggregated over spatial domains (e.g. Ravallion and Lokshin 2006; Mukherjee and Benson 2003).

Given the diversity in diets in Uganda, we feel the current official poverty line that is rooted in a single national food basket is inadequate. Following the

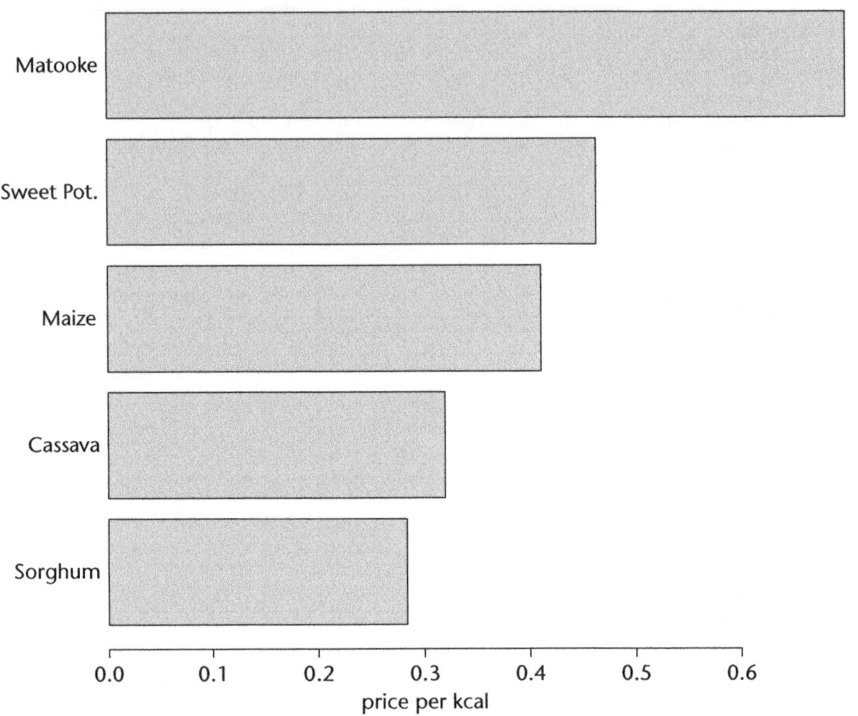



**Figure 10.3.** Average price per kcal for different crops
*Source*: Authors' calculations on the basis of UNHS 2012/13

PLEASe methodology, we therefore construct new poverty lines that allow consumption bundles to vary by location. In particular, we define six spatial domains within Uganda that each have their own basic-needs bundle. The domains are: Kampala, Central Rural, Eastern Rural, Northern Rural, Western Rural, and Other Urban. While these spatial domains are obviously not perfect, and higher specificity would be desirable, one also needs to make sure there are sufficient observations in each domain.

### 10.3.4 *Utility Consistency*

Allowing for different basic-needs bundles in each location improves on specificity. But how can we be sure that two different consumption bundles provide the same basic needs? Or, in the language of Ravallion and Bidani (1994), how do we ensure consistency?[9] Consistency is necessary to allow poverty comparisons across time or space. Poverty measurement and analysis

---

[9] A poverty measure is consistent if two individuals at the same welfare level are considered equally poor.

derives from welfare economics, where utility is maximized given a budget constraint. A poverty line is then defined as the cost of a consumption bundle that yields utility associated with the minimally acceptable standard of living. In other words, two bundles of goods are consistent if they yield the same utility.

To make sure that all basic-needs bundles correspond to the same utility level, we use a revealed preference approach (Ravallion and Lokshin 2006). The underlying assumption is that a rational consumer always prefers consuming more, sometimes referred to as the principle of non-satiation. Therefore, a particular bundle in a spatial domain will only be chosen if it minimizes expenditure. As such, we need to compare the cost of all other bundles evaluated at a given domain's prices to the cost of the bundle in that domain. If a bundle of the other domains turns out to be cheaper in that particular domain, it means it must provide lower utility, otherwise the rational consumer would have chosen it. Thus, a particular bundle in a spatial domain is utility-consistent if and only if all bundles in the other spatial domains' values at the prices of the particular domain turn out to be equally or more expensive.

As mentioned above, we have six spatial domains. This means that each of the six bundles needs to be compared to five other bundles, making for a total of thirty comparisons. Of these thirty comparisons, only eight fail the revealed preference test. Also, seven comparisons are mutually consistent, meaning that the revealed preference conditions are satisfied both when the two bundles, A and B, are evaluated at region B's prices and when the same bundles are evaluated at region A's prices. As there are fifteen such mutual possibilities, this means that almost 50 per cent are mutually consistent. This seems to be remarkable, as other studies suggest failures of revealed preference conditions occur more often than not. For example, Ravallion and Lokshin (2006) find that in Russia, revealed preference conditions are violated almost half of the time and only find 1 per cent of comparisons to involve mutually consistent bundles. Arndt and Simler (2010) find that conditions are less violated in Egypt, but more problematic in Mozambique. In case revealed preference conditions fail, adjustments need to be made to the bundles involved until they pass the test. We use a minimum cross-entropy framework to adjust consumption shares in such a way that revealed preference conditions are satisfied. The details of this procedure are described in Arndt and Simler (2010).

It can be instructive to have a closer look at the poverty lines. After all, poverty lines are not only useful to separate the rich from the poor, but also serve as deflators for cost-of-living differences, permitting interpersonal welfare comparisons when the cost of acquiring basic needs varies over time and/or space (Ravallion 1998). Table 10.3 presents the resulting region-specific poverty lines after adjustments to render the different bundles utility-consistent. We see that

**Table 10.3.** Estimated poverty lines for each spatial domain

| Spatial domain | Non-food component | Food component | Poverty line | Food share |
|---|---|---|---|---|
| Kampala | 576.41 | 1759.64 | 2336.05 | 0.75 |
| Central Rural | 695.51 | 1418.86 | 2114.37 | 0.67 |
| East Rural | 477.68 | 1144.39 | 1622.07 | 0.71 |
| North Rural | 454.78 | 1141.45 | 1596.23 | 0.72 |
| West Rural | 577.66 | 1425.65 | 2003.31 | 0.71 |
| Other Urban | 579.04 | 1354.06 | 1933.10 | 0.70 |

*Source*: Authors' calculations based on UNHS 2012/13

the poverty line in Kampala is highest and the poverty line in Northern Rural regions is the lowest. The difference between these two poverty lines is substantial. The poverty line for Kampala is almost 50 per cent higher than the one estimated for the rural areas in the Northern region.

The reason why the poverty line in the Northern Rural is much lower than the poverty line in the Central or Western region is evident from Figures 10.2 and 10.3. In the Northern region, the preferred diet contains mainly sorghum and cassava, which are relatively more cost-effective in generating the necessary food energy.[10] In the Central and Western regions, relatively less cost-effective staples are preferred, such as matooke and sweet potatoes.

While Table 10.3 reports the poverty lines at the level of disaggregation that they were estimated, Table 10.4 compares official and region-specific utility-consistent poverty lines at the same level of disaggregation. The official updated poverty line has been converted to yield the average minimum caloric requirement of the sample to make it comparable to the utility-consistent line.[11] It is about 26 per cent lower than the utility-consistent poverty line. If we disaggregate by region, the official poverty line does not vary a lot, except for Central, where it is a little higher due to the presence of Kampala in that region. The utility-consistent poverty line is higher everywhere, but it varies significantly by region. Thus, we find that while the official poverty line for the Northern region is 20 per cent lower than the utility-consistent poverty line, the difference increases to 33 per cent in the Western region. This is again consistent with Appleton (2003) who also finds a large difference with the official poverty line in the Western region.

[10] Which, as it happens, is also the lowest among the six spatial domains according to Table 10.2. However, the differences with other spatial domains are small and unlikely to be the main driver of the large differences found in the poverty lines.

[11] The scaling was done for the national sample; regional differences are the result of the non-food component of the poverty line.

**Table 10.4.** Estimated versus official poverty lines

|  | Official poverty line | Utility-consistent poverty line |
|---|---|---|
| National | 1361.59 | 1851.53 |
| Central | 1447.33 | 2099.43 |
| East | 1329.98 | 1668.08 |
| North | 1335.73 | 1652.78 |
| West | 1330.49 | 1989.51 |
| Kampala | 1553.45 | 2336.05 |
| Central 1 | 1443.36 | 2047.72 |
| Central 2 | 1415.68 | 2076.53 |
| East Central | 1332.40 | 1674.42 |
| Eastern | 1328.32 | 1663.75 |
| Mid-Northern | 1339.08 | 1664.25 |
| North-East | 1331.23 | 1637.39 |
| West Nile | 1331.91 | 1639.70 |
| Mid-Western | 1334.74 | 1987.03 |
| South-Western | 1326.25 | 1991.98 |

*Source*: Authors' calculations based on UNHS 2012/13

### 10.3.5 *Aggregation*

The final step in poverty measurement is aggregation. In this step, information from the relative position of the welfare indicator of the units is compared to the poverty line and summarized at different levels of aggregation. The simplest and most common method of aggregation is just to calculate the proportion of units that fall below the poverty line. This measure is often referred to as headcount poverty (P0). One can also calculate the average shortfall of welfare to the poverty line as a share of the poverty line. This is often referred to as the poverty gap (P1). Alternatively, one can square the gap to give a higher weight to households or individuals that fall further below the poverty line to make the measure sensitive to inequality. This is often referred to as the squared poverty gap index (P2). All three measures belong to the family of poverty measures introduced by Foster et al. (1984). The measures can be calculated at the national level, but also separately for different regions or different mutually exclusive groups within the sample. As such, one can construct a poverty profile, which identifies where the poor tend to live, what education levels they have, what their households look like in terms of number of children, elderly, etc.

Table 10.5 presents headcount poverty, the poverty gap index, and the squared poverty gap using utility-consistent poverty lines next to the official figures. As can be seen, in general, estimated poverty using utility-consistent poverty lines is much higher than official reported poverty.[12] If we disaggregate

---

[12] But pretty close to the estimates using the US$1.25 dollar a day international poverty line of 37.8 per cent as reported by the World Bank (http://iresearch.worldbank.org/PovcalNet/).

**Table 10.5.** Poverty headcount estimates

| | Utility-consitent poverty lines | | | Official poverty lines | | |
| --- | --- | --- | --- | --- | --- | --- |
| | P0 | P1 | P2 | P0 | P1 | P2 |
| National | 33.0 | 9.3 | 3.9 | 19.47 | 5.2 | 2.0 |
| Central | 17.3 | 4.0 | 1.4 | 4.7 | 1.0 | 0.3 |
| Eastern | 40.8 | 10.3 | 3.8 | 24.5 | 5.3 | 1.7 |
| Northern | 51.2 | 18.7 | 9.1 | 43.7 | 14.1 | 6.2 |
| Western | 24.2 | 5.7 | 2.0 | 8.7 | 1.7 | 0.5 |
| Kampala | 2.5 | 1.1 | 0.7 | 0.7 | 0.0 | 0.1 |
| Central 1 | 14.1 | 3.4 | 1.3 | 3.7 | 0.2 | 0.4 |
| Central 2 | 25.5 | 5.5 | 1.8 | 7.3 | 2.0 | 0.4 |
| East Central | 35.7 | 8.6 | 3.0 | 24.3 | 2.7 | 1.4 |
| Eastern | 44.2 | 11.4 | 4.3 | 24.7 | 11.3 | 2.0 |
| Mid-North | 44.3 | 14.5 | 6.4 | 35.4 | 18.9 | 3.9 |
| North East | 78.5 | 37.8 | 21.5 | 74.2 | 22.0 | 17.0 |
| West Nile | 49.0 | 15.8 | 7.0 | 42.3 | 21.2 | 4.7 |
| Mid-West | 27.4 | 6.6 | 2.4 | 9.8 | 13.9 | 0.6 |
| South-Western | 21.2 | 4.8 | 1.6 | 7.6 | 4.6 | 0.4 |

*Source:* Authors' calculations based on UNHS 2012/13

by region, we find that the higher utility-consistent poverty lines did not increase the poverty headcount that much in the Northern region. A virtually equal increase in the poverty line in the Eastern region had a much larger effect on poverty. This seems to suggest that the bulk of the people in the Northern region are concentrated at the lower end of the welfare distribution, which is confirmed by the relatively high P2. Central and West both have significantly higher poverty measures when using utility-consistent poverty lines. This was to be expected given the higher poverty lines caused by the less cost-effective diets people have in these regions.

The regional results are again magnified at the sub-regional level. In the North-Eastern sub-region, poverty is extremely high regardless of the poverty line used. In the South-Western, Mid-Western, and Central sub-regions, the difference between official poverty and poverty using utility-consistent poverty lines is very large. The use of different poverty lines also reduces differences in poverty estimates between the regions. For instance, while, according to the official poverty estimates, the Northern region is about ten times as poor as the Central region, it is only about three times as poor using utility-consistent poverty lines.

## 10.4 Conclusion

Since the government of Yoweri Museveni took over in 1986, Uganda has seen impressive economic growth. The growth also seemed to be particularly pro-poor, leading to large reductions in headcount poverty. However, over time, studies have pointed out substantial heterogeneity in the dynamics of poverty, with some areas such as North-Eastern lagging in poverty reduction. The government's market-oriented development policy that was credited for most of the poverty reductions in the nineties did not seem to work for the chronic poor (Okidi and McKay 2003). In addition, while alternative welfare measures and qualitative studies pointed to a stagnation or even regression of wellbeing, official poverty estimates continued their downward trend.

In this chapter, we have used the UNHS 2012/13 to estimate a new set of utility-consistent poverty lines based on current and region-specific food bundles. The lines, which are differentiated by six spatial domains, result in higher poverty estimates, nationally at around 33 per cent, and less extreme poverty differences between (sub-)regions. While the North-Eastern sub-region remains the poorest sub-region, higher poverty lines in Kampala and areas that rely on matooke as their main source of food energy appear to have done less well over time in terms of poverty reduction than official figures suggest.

Finding that poverty levels are higher when taking into account regional-specific poverty lines does not automatically mean that the officially reported downward trend in poverty is wrong. It is likely that utility-consistent poverty lines using past rounds of the UNHS would also result in substantially higher poverty lines and poverty, resulting in equally impressive poverty reductions. In fact, poverty reductions may even be more impressive when using utility-consistent poverty lines, as fixed poverty lines tend to overestimate poverty by ignoring substitution effects.

We feel that a poverty line rooted in a basic-needs bundle derived from consumption patterns of the poor more than twenty years ago is bound to result in misleading poverty estimates. In addition, the theory of poverty measurement and analysis has progressed since the first poverty estimates, and it is now common to allow for heterogeneity in the underlying consumption bundles to increase specificity. We feel it is time the government of Uganda updates the food bundles forming the basis of its poverty line. The argument for estimating a single national poverty line and holding on to the original 1993 poverty line to ensure spatial and temporal comparability does not make much sense.[13] Maintaining a fixed food bundle after more than two decades of rapid economic growth in a volatile macroeconomic environment, including two food price crises, surely ignores important changes in the consumption patterns of poor households.

---

[13] Especially since the method of using utility-consistent poverty lines explained in this chapter can not only be used to ensure consistency over space but also across time (Arndt and Simler 2010).

## References


Appleton, S. (2003). 'Regional or National Poverty Lines? The Case of Uganda in the 1990s', *Journal of African Economies*, 12(4): 598–624.

Appleton, S., T. Emwanu, J. Kagugube, and J. Muwonge (1999). 'Changes in Poverty in Uganda, 1992–1997', CSAE Working Paper No. 1999–22, Centre for the Study of African Economies, University of Oxford.

Arndt, C. and K. R. Simler (2010). 'Estimating Utility-Consistent Poverty Lines with Applications to Egypt and Mozambique', *Economic Development and Cultural Change*, 58(3): 449–74.

Benson, T., S. Mugarura, and K. Wanda (2008). 'Impacts in Uganda of Rising Global Food Prices: The Role of Diversified Staples and Limited Price Transmission', *Agricultural Economics*, 39: 513–24.

Daniels, L. and N. Minot (2015). 'Is Poverty Reduction Overstated in Uganda? Evidence from Alternative Poverty Measures', *Social Indicators Research*, 212(1): 115–33.

Dijkstra, A. G. and J. K. van Donge (2001). 'What Does the "Show Case" Show? Evidence of and Lessons from Adjustment in Uganda', *World Development*, 29(5): 841–64.

Duponchelle, M., A. McKay, and S. Ssewanyana (2014). 'The Dynamics of Poverty in Uganda, 2005/6 to 2011/12: Has the Progress Stalled?'. Paper presented at the CSAE conference 2015.

Emwanu, T., J. Hoogeveen, and P. O. Okwi (2006). 'Updating Poverty Maps with Panel Data', *World Development*, 34(12): 2076–88.

Foster, J., J. Greer, and E. Thorbecke (1984). 'A Class of Decomposable Poverty Measures', *Econometrica*, 52: 761–6.

Jamal, V. (1998). 'Changes in Poverty Patterns in Uganda', in H. B. Hansen and M. Twaddle (eds), *Developing Uganda*. Kampala: Fountain Publishers, 73–97.

Kakande, M. (2010). 'Poverty Monitoring', in F. Kuteesa, E. Tumusiime-Mutebile, A. Whitworth, and T. Williamson (eds), *Uganda's Economic Reforms: Insider Accounts*. Oxford: Oxford University Press, 226–45.

Krishna, A., D. Lumonya, M. Markiewicz, F. Mugumya, A. Kafuko, and J. Wegoye (2006). 'Escaping Poverty and Becoming Poor in 36 Villages of Central and Western Uganda', *Journal of Development Studies*, 42(2): 346–70.

Lawson, D., A. McKay, and J. Okidi (2006). 'Poverty Persistence and Transitions in Uganda: A Combined Qualitative and Quantitative Analysis', *Journal of Development Studies*, 42(7): 1225–51.

Levine, S. (2012). 'Exploring Difference in National and International Poverty Estimates: Is Uganda on Track to Halve Poverty by 2015?', *Social Indicators Research*, 107(2): 331–49.

Mukherjee, S. and T. Benson (2003). 'The Determinants of Poverty in Malawi, 1998', *World Development*, 31(2): 339–58.

Okidi, J. A. and A. McKay (2003). 'Poverty Dynamics in Uganda: 1992 to 2000', CPRC Working Paper No. 27.

Ravallion, M. (1994). *Poverty Comparisons*. Fundamentals of Pure and Applied Economics 56. Chur, Switzerland: Harwood Academic Press.

Ravallion, M. (1998). *Poverty Lines in Theory and Practice*. Washington, DC: World Bank.

Ravallion, M. and B. Bidani (1994). 'How Robust Is a Poverty Profile?', *World Bank Economic Review*, 8(1): 75–102.

Ravallion, M. and M. Lokshin (2006). 'Testing Poverty Lines', *Review of Income and Wealth*, 52(3): 399–421.

Ssewanyana, S. N. and I. Kasirye (2014). 'Uganda's Progress towards Poverty Reduction during the Last Decade 2002/3–2012/13: Is the Gap between Leading and Lagging Areas Widening or Narrowing?', EPRC Research Series No. 118.

Tarp, F., K. R. Simler, C. Matusse, R. Heltberg, and G. Dava (2002). 'The Robustness of Poverty Profiles Reconsidered', *Economic Development and Cultural Change*, 51(1): 77–108.

Uganda Bureau of Statistics (2006). *Uganda National Household Survey 2005/2006: Report on the Socioeconomic Module*. Kampala, Uganda: UBS.

Uganda Bureau of Statistics (2010). *Uganda National Household Survey 2009/10*. Kampala, Uganda: UBS.

Uganda Bureau of Statistics (2014). *Uganda National Household Survey 2012/13*. Kampala, Uganda: UBS.

World Bank (1993). *Uganda—Growing Out of Poverty*. World Bank Country Study. Washington, DC: World Bank.

# 11

# Estimating Multidimensional Childhood Poverty in the Democratic Republic of Congo

## 2007 through 2013

*Kristi Mahrt and Malokele Nanivazo*

### 11.1 Introduction

The Democratic Republic of Congo (DRC) has endured decades of conflict, corruption, political and legal instability, poor infrastructure, and substandard macroeconomic policies. Given this volatile environment, it is not surprising that the DRC is among the poorest countries in the world based on both its GPD per capita and Human Development Index scores. Despite this unfavourable history, evidence suggests that the DRC has begun a path to recovery through a sustained average annual growth rate of 6 per cent since 2002 (World Bank 2014). Nonetheless, though estimated monetary poverty has fallen during this period of recovery from 71 per cent in 2005, nearly two-thirds of the population (63 per cent) remained poor in 2012 (UNDP 2014). Broader measures of welfare also continue to register low levels as evidenced by the DRC's likely failure to achieve any of the eight Millennium Development Goals (MDGs) (UNDP 2014).

This chapter continues the work of Nanivazo and Mahrt (2016) in seeking to provide a broader understanding of non-monetary welfare in the DRC. For this purpose, Arndt et al.'s (2012) first-order dominance (FOD) approach is used to evaluate the distribution and evolution of multidimensional welfare of school-aged children in the eleven provinces of the DRC. The analysis spans the years 2007 to 2013, a period of ongoing localized conflict but overall increased political stability as well as strong economic growth. In addition to presenting

FOD analysis, this chapter delves into the possibility of FOD comparisons not determining dominance between two areas. Indeterminate outcomes may result from areas being very similar or very different across time and space. Understanding this distinction may be quite useful in evaluating FOD results.

The organization of this chapter is as follows. Section 11.2 discusses indeterminate outcomes in FOD. Section 11.3 presents the data, discusses sampling issues, and defines the FOD indicators. Section 11.4 presents the FOD results and sensitivity analysis. Finally, section 11.5 provides a concluding discussion.

## 11.2 Indeterminate FOD Outcomes

The analysis presented in this chapter employs the FOD approach to empirically evaluate the wellbeing of school-aged children in the eleven provinces and three aggregate areas (national, urban, and rural) in the DRC in 2007, 2010, and 2013. The FOD methodology is presented in detail in Chapter 3 and discussed intuitively in Chapter 15. In this section, we consider the possibility of FOD not establishing dominance between two populations over time or space. In general, indeterminate outcomes are likely when populations have very similar or very different welfare profiles; the latter is the focus of this discussion.

Given two populations A and B, the FOD criterion can be described as follows: population A first-order dominates population B if one can generate distribution B by transferring probability mass (i.e. moving individuals) from better to unambiguously worse outcomes within A. FOD dominance requires better welfare outcomes to be manifested throughout the population and across indicators. Indeterminate outcomes could stem from poor outcomes in a single indicator within a small subset of the population. Therefore, a dominant result provides a robust and broad-based indication of greater welfare through time or across space.

When welfare outcomes are not at all similar between areas or within the same area over time, FOD comparisons may result in indeterminate outcomes. We illustrate two scenarios involving two populations, A and B. In both scenarios, 50 per cent of population A and 30 per cent of population B are not deprived in each indicator; however, the distribution of populations between welfare outcomes differs in each population and in each scenario. In Scenario 1 (see Figure 11.1), populations A and B are similar in welfare patterns; however, fewer shares of population A fall into deprived welfare combinations and none of population B is not deprived in any indicator. In this scenario, dominance of A over B is easily established. By transferring shares of population A from a strictly better outcome (1,1,1) to strictly worse outcomes (1,0,0), (0,1,0), (0,0,1), and (0,0,0), the distribution of B is recreated.

Scenario 2 (Figure 11.2) illustrates the possibility of an indeterminate outcome even when population A outperforms population B on average in every

Population not deprived in each indicator (per cent)

|       | Water | Sanitation | Shelter |
|-------|-------|------------|---------|
| Urban | 50    | 50         | 50      |
| Rural | 30    | 30         | 30      |

Population shares with each combination of welfare indicators (per cent)

| Water | Sanitation | Shelter | A | B | A' |
|-------|------------|---------|---|---|----|
| 0 | 0 | 0 | 0 | 10 | 10 |
| 0 | 0 | 1 | 25 | 30 | 30 |
| 0 | 1 | 0 | 25 | 30 | 30 |
| 1 | 0 | 0 | 25 | 30 | 30 |
| 0 | 1 | 1 | 0 | 0 | 0 |
| 1 | 0 | 1 | 0 | 0 | 0 |
| 1 | 1 | 0 | 0 | 0 | 0 |
| 1 | 1 | 1 | 25 | 0 | 0 |
| | | Total | 100 | 100 | 100 |

**Figure 11.1.** Population A dominates population B (Scenario 1)
*Source*: Authors' illustration

Population not deprived in each indicator (per cent)

|       | Water | Sanitation | Shelter |
|-------|-------|------------|---------|
| Urban | 50    | 50         | 50      |
| Rural | 25    | 40         | 30      |

Population shares with each combination of welfare indicators (per cent)

| Water | Sanitation | Shelter | A | B | A' |
|-------|------------|---------|---|---|----|
| 0 | 0 | 0 | 0 | 5 | 5 |
| 0 | 0 | 1 | 0 | 30 | 25 |
| 0 | 1 | 0 | 50 | 40 | 45 |
| 1 | 0 | 0 | 0 | 25 | 25 |
| 0 | 1 | 1 | 0 | 0 | 0 |
| 1 | 0 | 1 | 50 | 0 | 0 |
| 1 | 1 | 0 | 0 | 0 | 0 |
| 1 | 1 | 1 | 0 | 0 | 0 |
| | | Total | 100 | 100 | 100 |

**Figure 11.2.** Population A and population B are indeterminate (Scenario 2)
*Source*: Authors' illustration

indicator (which precludes the possibility that B could dominate A). In this case, the distribution of population A and B falling into each combination of indicators is sufficiently different that population B's distribution cannot be created by moving shares of A to strictly worse outcomes. Specifically, because A's outcome (0,1,0) is no better or worse than B's outcomes (0,0,1) and (1,0,0), B's distribution cannot be recreated.

From an analytical perspective, it would be useful to understand if indeterminate outcomes have resulted from similarities or differences across time or space. While this distinction may not be immediately obvious, basic descriptive statistics may in some cases shed light on the inability of FOD to determine dominance. Section 11.3 evaluates descriptive statistics and section 11.4 applies these observations to the FOD results.


## 11.3 FOD Indicators

### 11.3.1 *Survey Data*

The FOD indicators are drawn from the 2007 and 2013 DRC Demographic and Health Surveys (DHS) and the 2010 DRC Multiple Indicator Cluster Survey (MICS), tabulated by the Ministry of Planning and Macro International Inc. (2008), and the National Institute of Statistics and UNICEF (2011), respectively. Both surveys are nationally representative household surveys that follow a similar sampling scheme with stratification by provinces as well as cities, towns, and rural areas. Sample sizes increase over time with 8886, 11,393, and 18,171 households included in the 2007 DHS, the 2010 MICS, and the 2013 DHS, respectively. The sample of school-aged children used in this analysis is restricted to children aged 7–17 with non-missing values for all indicators and the sample increases from 13,397 in 2007 to 17,351 in 2010 and 27,905 in 2013.

It is worth emphasizing that data collection is a challenging endeavour in the DRC. Given its recent tumultuous history, institutional weaknesses, and the lack of trust of the population vis-à-vis agents of the government (enumerators), the scope for non-sample error is large. Even sample biases are difficult to control. The most recent census was collected more than thirty years ago, in 1984. All recent national surveys, including the Demographic and Health Surveys, the Multiple Indicator Cluster Survey, and the Enquête 1-2-3 (the basis of national consumption poverty estimates), base their sample frames on a combination of the 1984 census and administrative censuses. This is well short of ideal. Consequently, figures derived from the three surveys in focus here should be interpreted with a degree of caution.

The lack of a proper sample frame becomes apparent in the fluctuation of the urban sample size from year to year. In the sample of all individuals, the urban sample fluctuates between 42.9, 30.3, and 34.5 per cent in 2007, 2010, and 2013. To reduce the influence of these ad hoc sample frame variations on outcomes, we reweight the sample in order to strike World Bank (2014) urban population share estimates of 38.5, 39.4, and 41.5 per cent in 2007, 2010, and 2013 respectively.

### 11.3.2 *Indicator Definitions*

The FOD methodology is rooted in measuring welfare profiles of populations based on a set of binary indicators. Given the deep and extensive nature of poverty in the DRC, we define child poverty as a severe lack of access to basic needs. Gordon et al. (2003a, 2003b) developed a set of indicators known as the 'Bristol Indicators'. Specifically severe deprivations are defined as 'circumstances that are highly likely to have serious adverse consequences for the health, wellbeing, and development of children' (Gordon et al. 2003b: 5). Closely following the Bristol Indicators, Nanivazo and Mahrt (2016) define five deprivation indicators for children aged 7–17,[1] which are adopted in this analysis. Each indicator is defined according to a deprivation threshold such that children with outcomes better than the threshold are considered not deprived. Deprivation thresholds are described below.

1. *Water deprivation*: Children with only access to surface water for drinking or for whom the nearest source of water is more than a 30-minute walking distance (one-way) from their dwellings.

2. *Sanitation deprivation*: Children with no access to any kind of latrines or toilets.

3. *Shelter deprivation*: Children living in dwellings with five or more people per room or with no flooring material (e.g. a mud floor).

4. *Health deprivation*: Children who did not sleep under a bed net the previous night.[2]

5. *Information deprivation*: Children who belong to a household where there is no access to a television, radio, or phone.[3]

6. *Education deprivation*: Children who have never been to at least primary school or are not currently attending school.

Table 11.1 reports the percentage of school-aged children not deprived in water, sanitation, shelter, health, information, and education by areas and years. Though the indicators provide mixed evidence of advancement and stagnation, the picture is typically one of progress when only averages are considered. All aggregate areas and provinces advanced in terms of bed net usage (the health proxy indicator), primary school enrolment, and access to information. National use of bed nets increased fivefold to 40.1 per cent in

---

[1] Nanivazo and Mahrt (2016) also define a set of indicators for children aged 0–5 that includes an indicator of malnutrition.

[2] The Bristol health indicator is defined in terms of immunizations. Due to the limited sample for which this data is drawn and the FOD requirement that no indicator should have missing values, we define health in terms of the use of bed nets.

[3] The Bristol Indicators incorporate access to newspapers and computers in the information indicator. These media sources were excluded due to data limitations.

**Table 11.1.** Children 7–17 not deprived by welfare indicator (per cent)

| | Water | | | Sanitation | | | Shelter | | | Health | | | Information | | | Education | | |
|---|---|---|---|---|---|---|---|---|---|---|---|---|---|---|---|---|---|---|
| | 2007 | 2010 | 2013 | 2007 | 2010 | 2013 | 2007 | 2010 | 2013 | 2007 | 2010 | 2013 | 2007 | 2010 | 2013 | 2007 | 2010 | 2013 |
| National | 42.9 | 49.7 | 49.9 | 90.7 | 87.9 | 88.4 | 19.6 | 22.8 | 19.6 | 8.1 | 20.6 | 40.9 | 52.1 | 58.4 | 64.2 | 82.4 | 87.6 | 93.2 |
| Rural | 21.1 | 30.5 | 32.5 | 86.8 | 82.0 | 83.1 | 3.4 | 4.2 | 3.2 | 5.3 | 17.8 | 40.7 | 36.6 | 41.6 | 47.6 | 77.0 | 82.9 | 90.3 |
| Urban | 77.0 | 78.5 | 74.6 | 96.9 | 96.7 | 95.8 | 45.0 | 50.6 | 42.8 | 12.5 | 24.9 | 41.2 | 76.5 | 83.7 | 87.7 | 91.0 | 94.7 | 97.2 |
| Bandundu | 24.3 | 19.4 | 31.1 | 87.8 | 86.1 | 85.3 | 13.1 | 4.2 | 6.4 | 5.8 | 26.2 | 59.7 | 39.0 | 39.4 | 48.4 | 77.9 | 90.4 | 94.1 |
| Bas-Congo | 42.8 | 40.2 | 58.2 | 81.9 | 76.7 | 79.8 | 25.6 | 30.0 | 32.3 | 20.9 | 12.9 | 43.3 | 69.2 | 77.5 | 80.0 | 84.8 | 90.8 | 95.8 |
| Équateur | 14.9 | 16.8 | 26.1 | 93.4 | 85.6 | 89.1 | 5.9 | 5.4 | 3.1 | 11.3 | 27.0 | 55.1 | 32.3 | 31.4 | 44.8 | 77.6 | 83.2 | 91.9 |
| K. Occidental | 26.6 | 16.8 | 31.5 | 76.7 | 62.7 | 74.9 | 7.1 | 3.8 | 9.6 | 2.6 | 5.7 | 20.9 | 47.7 | 38.5 | 53.3 | 78.9 | 82.9 | 92.3 |
| K. Oriental | 46.6 | 46.9 | 41.3 | 93.1 | 84.8 | 80.1 | 15.0 | 16.6 | 15.2 | 2.3 | 3.2 | 29.5 | 58.4 | 55.9 | 64.4 | 86.2 | 90.8 | 95.9 |
| Katanga | 55.1 | 60.3 | 53.8 | 86.1 | 84.7 | 85.4 | 24.0 | 15.5 | 25.3 | 12.3 | 12.6 | 48.9 | 51.4 | 56.7 | 70.0 | 81.7 | 80.7 | 93.3 |
| Kinshasa | 91.2 | 86.8 | 93.2 | 98.8 | 98.1 | 98.1 | 71.2 | 79.6 | 72.3 | 15.5 | 31.4 | 37.1 | 93.6 | 95.1 | 98.5 | 96.6 | 96.5 | 96.7 |
| Maniema | 26.9 | 32.8 | 51.8 | 92.5 | 90.7 | 89.6 | 5.7 | 4.5 | 5.3 | 6.9 | 40.7 | 27.9 | 56.4 | 56.1 | 64.6 | 84.6 | 91.1 | 93.6 |
| N. Kivu | 71.7 | 58.8 | 81.2 | 93.1 | 94.1 | 97.3 | 13.5 | 16.3 | 24.7 | 1.5 | 15.8 | 30.7 | 54.9 | 60.8 | 70.2 | 76.3 | 84.5 | 88.8 |
| Orientale | 34.4 | 58.3 | 41.3 | 95.6 | 97.0 | 94.2 | 5.6 | 8.2 | 11.2 | 5.0 | 34.0 | 28.4 | 37.7 | 52.9 | 64.4 | 79.4 | 88.7 | 92.0 |
| S. Kivu | 63.9 | 54.8 | 65.5 | 95.0 | 88.9 | 95.5 | 26.5 | 23.5 | 19.2 | 8.3 | 17.7 | 39.3 | 58.5 | 60.0 | 72.1 | 83.8 | 84.6 | 90.9 |

*Source*: Authors' calculations based on DHS and MICS data

2013 by which time they were used nearly equally in urban and rural areas. By 2013, more than 93 per cent of school-aged children had attended at least some primary school. Though this indicator measures severe deprivation and does not provide information as to primary school completion, rural children accessing primary school increased from 77 per cent in 2007 to 90 per cent in 2013.

Progress in attaining access to improved water, sanitation, and shelter varied. While sanitation and shelter declined for the nation, urban areas, and rural areas, water improved for the nation and rural areas but declined in urban areas. Progress in water, sanitation, and shelter outcomes within the provinces also varies. For example, access to water nearly doubled in Maniema while sanitation declined and shelter stagnated; in Sud Kivu, access to water and sanitation dropped and then bounced back to 2007 levels while shelter steadily declined; and Nord Kivu significantly improved in all three indicators.

## 11.4 Results

### 11.4.1 *Temporal FOD Comparisons*

Table 11.2 reports FOD temporal net domination results using the six indicators described in section 11.3.2. FOD comparisons are made using the original survey data and one hundred bootstrap samples; the former is referred to as the static approach. Bold values indicate domination in the static case. Bootstrap outcomes are measured as the average of domination across all bootstrap

**Table 11.2.** Temporal net FOD comparisons (bootstrap probabilities)

|  | Children 7–17 | | |
| --- | --- | --- | --- |
|  | 2010 FOD 2007 | 2013 FOD 2007 | 2013 FOD 2010 |
| National | 0.01 |  | 0.01 |
| Rural | 0.01 | 0.02 | 0.06 |
| Urban | 0.06 | 0.01 |  |
| Bandundu | 0.08 | 0.08 | 0.20 |
| Bas-Congo |  | 0.19 | 0.18 |
| Équateur |  | 0.01 | 0.01 |
| K. Occidental |  | 0.14 | **0.69** |
| K. Oriental |  |  | 0.05 |
| Katanga | 0.01 | 0.14 | 0.13 |
| Kinshasa | 0.01 | 0.03 |  |
| Maniema | 0.01 | 0.10 |  |
| N. Kivu | 0.04 | **0.58** | **0.45** |
| Orientale | **0.33** | 0.06 |  |
| S. Kivu |  |  | 0.15 |

*Note:* Figures in bold indicate domination in FOD comparisons using the static sample.
*Source:* Authors' calculations based on DHS and MICS data

samples and are interpreted as probabilities of domination. Temporal net domination measures the probability an area's welfare improves between two years minus any probability of regression. Positive values indicate the probability of advancement, blank cells stagnation, and negative values the probability of regression.

The temporal FOD comparisons do not indicate significant probabilities of improvement over time in the nation, urban areas, or rural areas. Nord Kivu is the only province with a significant probability of advancing over the full study period (58 per cent). Nord Kivu and Kasai Occidental are likely to have advanced between 2010 and 2013 with probabilities of 69 per cent and 45 per cent, respectively. Only the province of Orientale exhibited advancement in the static case between 2007 and 2010, though the probability of advancement is relatively low in the bootstrap (33 per cent). Each of the above-mentioned provinces improves on average in every indicator over the relevant timeframe. In contrast, Bas Congo improves in each indicator between 2010 and 2013 but the static FOD case does not provide evidence of welfare gains. Bas Congo illustrates that advancing in every indicator on average does not assure FOD advancement. A failure to achieve net temporal FOD dominance in such a case stems from an uneven distribution of gains among children. In other words, welfare gains are not broad-based.

The lack of widespread net temporal dominance can be attributed to regression and stagnation in the water, sanitation, and shelter deprivation indicators. Of the six indicators considered, health, information, and education exhibit a consistent pattern of improvement for nearly all areas. However, in each year, the direction of change in water, sanitation, and shelter welfare varies considerably. To explore the impact of each indicator on temporal results, FOD comparisons are re-evaluated excluding each indicator one by one. The results are presented in Table 11.3.

Evidence of advancement in Bas-Congo, Kasai Occidental, North Kivu, and Orientale is robust even when the strongly performing indicators, health, information, and education are individually excluded. Not surprisingly, excluding sanitation and shelter leads to significantly greater probability of welfare gains in both static and bootstrap FOD comparisons. Notably, excluding sanitation results in national, rural, and urban FOD advancement between 2007 and 2010, and excluding shelter results in rural advancement between 2010 and 2013. Bas-Congo appears to be quite sensitive to the distribution of gains. Though welfare gains are not registered in FOD comparisons using all six indicators, excluding education, information, shelter, sanitation, or water leads to 2013 dominating 2010 in the static sample and greater probabilities of domination in the bootstrap samples; this is particularly interesting as education and information are indicators that on average improved between 2010 and 2013.

**Table 11.3.** Temporal net FOD comparisons individually excluding each indicator

| | No Water | | | No Sanitation | | | No Shelter | | |
|---|---|---|---|---|---|---|---|---|---|
| | 2010 FOD 2007 | 2013 FOD 2007 | 2013 FOD 2010 | 2010 FOD 2007 | 2013 FOD 2007 | 2013 FOD 2010 | 2010 FOD 2007 | 2013 FOD 2007 | 2013 FOD 2010 |
| National | 0.01 | 0.04 | 0.02 | **0.82** | 0.39 | 0.03 | 0.01 | 0.07 | 0.39 |
| Rural | 0.01 | 0.03 | 0.17 | **0.64** | 0.36 | 0.15 | 0.01 | 0.08 | **0.56** |
| Urban | 0.31 | 0.04 | | **0.56** | 0.06 | | 0.05 | 0.02 | |
| Bandundu | 0.03 | 0.09 | 0.24 | 0.08 | 0.24 | **0.66** | 0.06 | 0.20 | 0.37 |
| Bas-Congo | 0.01 | 0.34 | **0.22** | 0.01 | **0.64** | **0.39** | | 0.29 | **0.23** |
| Équateur | | 0.02 | 0.01 | 0.06 | 0.10 | 0.01 | 0.01 | 0.15 | **0.63** |
| K. Occidental | | 0.20 | **0.81** | | 0.39 | **0.79** | | 0.21 | **0.94** |
| K. Oriental | | 0.01 | 0.09 | 0.02 | 0.15 | 0.11 | | 0.01 | 0.08 |
| Katanga | −0.03 | 0.28 | **0.44** | 0.01 | 0.32 | 0.19 | | 0.13 | 0.12 |
| Kinshasa | 0.02 | 0.07 | | 0.03 | 0.08 | | 0.02 | 0.14 | |
| Maniema | 0.03 | 0.16 | | 0.13 | 0.28 | | 0.13 | 0.26 | |
| N. Kivu | **0.36** | **0.80** | 0.46 | 0.06 | **0.68** | **0.51** | 0.06 | **0.71** | **0.76** |
| Orientale | **0.23** | 0.09 | 0.03 | **0.59** | **0.62** | 0.02 | **0.31** | 0.10 | 0.01 |
| S. Kivu | | 0.07 | 0.21 | 0.05 | 0.05 | 0.10 | | 0.10 | **0.67** |

| | No Health | | | No Information | | | No Education | | |
|---|---|---|---|---|---|---|---|---|---|
| | 2010 FOD 2007 | 2013 FOD 2007 | 2013 FOD 2010 | 2010 FOD 2007 | 2013 FOD 2007 | 2013 FOD 2010 | 2010 FOD 2007 | 2013 FOD 2007 | 2013 FOD 2010 |
| National | 0.01 | 0.02 | 0.01 | 0.01 | 0.02 | 0.01 | 0.01 | 0.02 | 0.01 |
| Rural | 0.01 | 0.02 | 0.12 | 0.01 | 0.02 | 0.13 | 0.02 | 0.02 | 0.13 |
| Urban | 0.02 | 0.01 | | 0.07 | 0.01 | | 0.10 | 0.02 | |
| Bandundu | 0.03 | 0.09 | 0.21 | 0.03 | 0.09 | 0.24 | 0.03 | 0.09 | 0.22 |
| Bas-Congo | 0.04 | 0.23 | 0.19 | 0.02 | 0.27 | **0.33** | | 0.23 | **0.28** |
| Équateur | 0.01 | 0.02 | 0.01 | | 0.02 | 0.01 | | 0.02 | 0.01 |
| K. Occidental | −0.09 | 0.17 | **0.71** | | 0.19 | **0.71** | | 0.17 | **0.74** |
| K. Oriental | | 0.01 | 0.02 | | 0.01 | 0.03 | −0.01 | 0.01 | 0.02 |
| Katanga | −0.01 | 0.12 | 0.12 | −0.06 | 0.13 | 0.13 | | 0.13 | 0.12 |
| Kinshasa | 0.02 | 0.05 | | 0.02 | 0.10 | | 0.03 | 0.15 | |
| Maniema | 0.04 | 0.10 | 0.08 | 0.06 | 0.10 | | 0.05 | 0.10 | |
| N. Kivu | 0.05 | **0.63** | **0.68** | 0.05 | **0.63** | **0.51** | 0.05 | **0.62** | **0.53** |
| Orientale | **0.20** | 0.07 | 0.01 | **0.28** | 0.07 | | **0.31** | 0.11 | 0.01 |
| S. Kivu | −0.13 | 0.01 | 0.12 | | 0.01 | 0.11 | | 0.01 | 0.11 |

*Note*: Figures in bold indicate domination in FOD comparisons using the static sample.

*Source*: Authors' calculations based on DHS and MICS data

### 11.4.2 *Spatial FOD Comparisons*

Tables 11.4–11.6 report the results of the 2007, 2010, and 2013 spatial FOD bootstrap comparisons, with values in bold indicating domination in the static sample. Row (column) averages display the probability that an area first-order dominates (or is dominated by) other provinces. Therefore, provinces that are relatively better off have larger row and lower column averages.[4]

Spatial FOD comparisons result in a high degree of indeterminate outcomes. Focusing on dominance in the static case (bolded values) or on bootstrap probabilities greater than 10 per cent, nearly every dominant outcome occurs when Kinshasa, Sud Kivu, or urban areas dominate or when Kasai Occidental or rural areas are dominated. Indeterminacy in 2013 is even more extreme in that much of the dominance of Kinshasa, Sud Kivu, and urban areas falls out, particularly in the static case. The apparent failure of Kinshasa and urban areas to dominate poor provinces is counter-intuitive. For example, Kinshasa (the least poor province with a 2012 poverty rate of 37 per cent) not dominating Equateur (one of the poorest provinces with a poverty rate of 78 per cent) is quite surprising. Average welfare in each indicator (Table 11.1), provides insight into why this may be happening. The health indicator stands out as following a pattern distinctly different from other indicators. Specifically, in 2013, all aggregate areas and five provinces outperform Kinshasa compared to virtually no other area outperforming Kinshasa in any other indicator in any year. Once again, when welfare patterns are very different between populations, indeterminate outcomes are likely. To test the sensitivity of the results to bed net usage, FOD spatial comparisons are conducted excluding the health indicator; results are presented in Table 11.7. Without health, the counter-intuitive indeterminate outcomes are eliminated. This implies that the results are sensitive to choice of deprivation indicators as well as to their definitions. We further explore this sensitivity in section 11.4.3.

### 11.4.3 *Spatial Rankings*

Spatial net domination provides a basis for ranking provinces and conveniently presenting a more detailed perspective on the evolution of relative wellbeing. Net domination measures the probability that an area dominates other areas minus the probability it is dominated by other areas. Area rankings and net domination scores are reported in Table 11.8.

---

[4] Note that bootstrap sampling introduces a degree of randomness into the results and care must be taken not to place too much importance on very small probabilities.

**Table 11.4.** 2007 Bootstrap spatial FOD comparisons (probabilities)

| Areas/Provinces | NAT | RUR | URB | BDD | BCO | ETR | KOC | KOT | KTG | KSS | MNM | NKV | ORT | SKV | AVG |
|---|---|---|---|---|---|---|---|---|---|---|---|---|---|---|---|
| National (NAT) | | **1** | | **0.30** | | | **0.61** | | | | | | | | 0.15 |
| Rural (RUR) | | | | | | | | | | | | | | | 0.00 |
| Urban (URB) | 1 | 1 | | **0.98** | 0.01 | **0.63** | 1 | **0.85** | 0.49 | | **0.97** | **0.72** | **0.49** | **0.42** | 0.66 |
| Bandundu (BDD) | | 0.18 | | | | | 0.03 | | | | | | 0.01 | | 0.02 |
| Bas-Congo (BCO) | | 0.10 | | 0.04 | | | **0.67** | | 0.01 | | | | | | 0.06 |
| Équateur (ETR) | | | | | | | | | | | | | | | 0.00 |
| K. Occidental (KOC) | | | | | | | | | | | | | | | 0.00 |
| K. Oriental (KOT) | | | | 0.04 | | | 0.19 | | | | | | | | 0.02 |
| Katanga (KTG) | | 0.11 | | 0.08 | | | 0.27 | | | | | 0.01 | | | 0.04 |
| Kinshasa (KSS) | 1 | 1 | **0.51** | 1 | 0.12 | **0.84** | 1 | 1 | **0.82** | | 1 | **0.98** | **0.91** | **0.83** | 0.85 |
| Maniema (MNM) | | 0.20 | | 0.08 | | | 0.05 | | | | | | | | 0.03 |
| N. Kivu (NKV) | | 0.01 | | 0.03 | | | 0.06 | | | | | | | | 0.01 |
| Orientale (ORT) | | 0.09 | | 0.03 | | 0.01 | | | | | | | | | 0.01 |
| S. Kivu (SKV) | **0.26** | **0.92** | | **0.47** | | 0.20 | **0.81** | 0.02 | 0.05 | | 0.08 | 0.14 | 0.12 | | 0.24 |
| Average | 0.17 | 0.35 | 0.04 | 0.23 | 0.01 | 0.13 | 0.36 | 0.14 | 0.11 | 0.00 | 0.16 | 0.14 | 0.12 | 0.10 | 0.15 |

*Note*: Figures in bold indicate domination in FOD comparisons using the static sample. A '1' in the bootstrap FOD comparisons indicates that the row (column) province dominates (is dominated by) the column provinces 100 percent of the time. An empty cell indicates that the FOD comparison of the row and column provinces is always indeterminate.

*Source*: Authors' calculations based on DHS and MICS data

**Table 11.5.** 2010 Bootstrap spatial FOD comparisons (probabilities)

| Areas/Provinces | NAT | RUR | URB | BDD | BCO | ETR | KOC | KOT | KTG | KSS | MNM | NKV | ORT | SKV | Average |
|---|---|---|---|---|---|---|---|---|---|---|---|---|---|---|---|
| National (NAT) | | **1** | | | | | **0.99** | 0.01 | 0.03 | | | | | 0.02 | 0.16 |
| Rural (RUR) | | | | | | | 0.18 | | | | | | | | 0.01 |
| Urban (URB) | 1 | 1 | | 0.42 | **0.66** | 0.41 | 1 | 1 | **0.99** | | | **0.93** | | **0.99** | 0.65 |
| Bandundu (BDD) | | | | | | 0.02 | **0.21** | | | | | | | | 0.02 |
| Bas-Congo (BCO) | | 0.01 | | | | | **0.99** | | | | | | | | 0.08 |
| Équateur (ETR) | | | | | | | 0.01 | | | | | | | | 0.00 |
| K. Occidental (KOC) | | | | | | | | | | | | | | | 0.00 |
| K. Oriental (KOT) | | | | | | | | | | | | | | | 0.00 |
| Katanga (KTG) | | 0.01 | | | | | 0.30 | | | | | | | | 0.02 |
| Kinshasa (KSS) | 1 | 1 | **0.71** | **0.83** | 1 | **0.88** | 1 | 1 | 1 | | 0.05 | **0.98** | 0.32 | **1.00** | 0.83 |
| Maniema (MNM) | | 0.31 | | 0.09 | | 0.10 | 0.47 | | | | | | | | 0.07 |
| N. Kivu (NKV) | | 0.26 | | | | 0.01 | **0.77** | | 0.03 | | | | | 0.06 | 0.09 |
| Orientale (ORT) | | **0.90** | | 0.17 | | **0.71** | **0.84** | | | | | | | 0.01 | 0.20 |
| S. Kivu (SKV) | | 0.28 | | | | | **0.71** | | 0.14 | | | | | | 0.09 |
| Average | 0.15 | 0.37 | 0.05 | 0.12 | 0.13 | 0.16 | 0.57 | 0.15 | 0.17 | 0.00 | 0.00 | 0.15 | 0.02 | 0.16 | 0.16 |

*Note*: Figures in bold indicate domination in FOD comparisons using the static sample. A '1' in the bootstrap FOD comparisons indicates that the row (column) province dominates (is dominated by) the column provinces 100 percent of the time. An empty cell indicates that the FOD comparison of the row and column provinces is always indeterminate.

*Source*: Authors' calculations based on DHS and MICS data

**Table 11.6.** 2013 Bootstrap spatial FOD comparisons (probabilities)

| Areas/Provinces | NAT | RUR | URB | BDD | BCO | ETR | KOC | KOT | KTG | KSS | MNM | NKV | ORT | SKV | Average |
|---|---|---|---|---|---|---|---|---|---|---|---|---|---|---|---|
| National (NAT) | | **0.66** | | | | | **0.78** | | | | | | | | 0.11 |
| Rural (RUR) | | | | | | | | | | | | | | | 0.00 |
| Urban (URB) | **0.66** | **0.66** | | | 0.13 | | 1 | **0.99** | 0.01 | | **0.95** | | **0.86** | 0.03 | 0.41 |
| Bandundu (BDD) | | 0.04 | | | | | 0.04 | | | | | | | | 0.01 |
| Bas-Congo (BCO) | | 0.09 | | | | | **0.78** | 0.06 | | | 0.03 | | | | 0.07 |
| Équateur (ETR) | | | | | | | | | | | | | | | 0.00 |
| K. Occidental (KOC) | | | | | | | | | | | | | | | 0.00 |
| K. Oriental (KOT) | | | | | | | **0.57** | | | | | | | | 0.04 |
| Katanga (KTG) | | 0.12 | | | | | **0.54** | | | | 0.01 | | | | 0.05 |
| Kinshasa (KSS) | 0.19 | 0.22 | 0.01 | | 0.11 | | 1 | **0.82** | 0.02 | | **0.90** | **0.49** | **0.94** | 0.27 | 0.38 |
| Maniema (MNM) | | | | | | | 0.11 | | | | | | | | 0.01 |
| N. Kivu (NKV) | | 0.02 | | | | | 0.04 | | | | 0.01 | | 0.02 | | 0.01 |
| Orientale (ORT) | | | | | | | 0.21 | | | | | | | | 0.02 |
| S. Kivu (SKV) | 0.03 | 0.28 | | | | | 0.25 | | 0.01 | | 0.06 | 0.01 | 0.10 | | 0.06 |
| Average | 0.07 | 0.16 | 0.00 | 0.00 | 0.02 | 0.00 | 0.41 | 0.14 | 0.00 | 0.00 | 0.15 | 0.04 | 0.15 | 0.02 | 0.08 |

*Note*: Figures in bold indicate domination in FOD comparisons using the static sample. A '1' in the bootstrap FOD comparisons indicates that the row (column) province dominates (is dominated by) the column provinces 100 percent of the time. An empty cell indicates that the FOD comparison of the row and column provinces is always indeterminate.

*Source*: Authors' calculations based on DHS and MICS data

**Table 11.7.** 2013 Bootstrap spatial FOD comparisons excluding health (probabilities)

| Areas/Provinces | NAT | RUR | URB | BDD | BCO | ETR | KOC | KOT | KTG | KSS | MNM | NKV | ORT | SKV | AVG |
|---|---|---|---|---|---|---|---|---|---|---|---|---|---|---|---|
| National (NAT) | | 1 | | 0.08 | | 0.06 | **0.70** | | 0.02 | | | | | | 0.14 |
| Rural (RUR) | | | | | | | | | | | | | | | 0.00 |
| Urban (URB) | 1 | 1 | | 1 | **0.87** | **0.99** | 1 | **0.96** | 1 | | **0.96** | 0.01 | **0.85** | 0.04 | 0.74 |
| Bandundu (BDD) | | 0.09 | | | | 0.01 | 0.04 | | | | | | | | 0.01 |
| Bas-Congo (BCO) | 0.01 | 0.37 | | 0.18 | | 0.03 | **0.76** | 0.09 | 0.09 | | 0.02 | | | | 0.12 |
| Équateur (ETR) | | | | | | | | | | | | | | | 0.00 |
| K. Occidental (KOC) | | 0.01 | | | | | | | | | | | | | 0.00 |
| K. Oriental (KOT) | | 0.06 | | 0.04 | | | **0.59** | | | | | | | | 0.05 |
| Katanga (KTG) | | 0.21 | | 0.04 | | | **0.50** | | | | | | | | 0.06 |
| Kinshasa (KSS) | 1 | 1 | 0.18 | **0.99** | **0.89** | **0.99** | 1 | **0.73** | 1 | | **0.98** | **0.72** | **0.99** | **0.76** | 0.86 |
| Maniema (MNM) | | **0.49** | | 0.04 | | 0.16 | 0.15 | | | | | | | | 0.06 |
| N. Kivu (NKV) | | 0.23 | | | | 0.05 | 0.05 | | 0.02 | | | | 0.04 | 0.01 | 0.03 |
| Orientale (ORT) | | **0.81** | | 0.05 | | 0.23 | 0.29 | | | | | | | | 0.11 |
| S. Kivu (SKV) | 0.07 | **0.53** | | 0.08 | | 0.33 | 0.23 | | 0.05 | | 0.07 | | 0.12 | | 0.11 |
| Average | 0.16 | 0.45 | 0.01 | 0.19 | 0.14 | 0.22 | 0.41 | 0.14 | 0.17 | 0.00 | 0.16 | 0.06 | 0.15 | 0.06 | 0.16 |

*Note*: Figures in bold indicate domination in FOD comparisons using the static sample. A '1' in the bootstrap FOD comparisons indicates that the row (column) province dominates (is dominated by) the column provinces 100 percent of the time. An empty cell indicates that the FOD comparison of the row and column provinces is always indeterminate.

*Source*: Authors' calculations based on DHS and MICS data

**Table 11.8.** Area rankings by probability of net domination

| 2007 | | 2010 | | 2013 | | 2007–13 |
|---|---|---|---|---|---|---|
| Area | Net Dom. | Area | Net Dom. | Area | Net Dom. | Rank change |
| Kinshasa (KSS) | 0.85 | KSS | 0.83 | URB | 0.41 | −1 |
| Urban (URB) | 0.62 | URB | 0.59 | KSS | 0.38 | 1 |
| Sud Kivu (SKV) | 0.14 | ORT | 0.18 | BCO | 0.06 | −1 |
| Bas Congo (BCO) | 0.05 | MNM | 0.07 | KTG | 0.05 | −2 |
| National (NAT) | −0.03 | NAT | 0.00 | NAT | 0.04 | 0 |
| Katanga (KTG) | −0.07 | BCO | −0.05 | SKV | 0.03 | 3 |
| Orientale (ORT) | −0.11 | NKV | −0.06 | BDD | 0.01 | −5 |
| Kasai Oriental (KOT) | −0.13 | SKV | −0.07 | ETR | 0.00 | −1 |
| Équateur (ETR) | −0.13 | BDD | −0.10 | NKV | −0.03 | −2 |
| Maniema (MNM) | −0.13 | KTG | −0.14 | KOT | −0.10 | 2 |
| Nord Kivu (NKV) | −0.13 | KOT | −0.15 | ORT | −0.13 | 4 |
| Bandundu (BDD) | −0.22 | ETR | −0.16 | MNM | −0.14 | 2 |
| Rural (RUR) | −0.35 | RUR | −0.35 | RUR | −0.16 | 0 |
| Kasai Occidental (KOC) | −0.36 | KOC | −0.57 | KOC | −0.41 | 0 |

*Note:* Rankings within shaded groups are highly sensitive to small perturbations and should be interpreted with caution.
*Source:* Authors' calculations based on DHS and MICS data

It is worth noting that the difference between net domination scores is often not sufficiently large to distinguish robustly between differences in welfare outcomes and randomness introduced through bootstrapping. To avoid misinterpreting rankings, within the tables, shading identifies clusters with similar net domination scores. Within these clusters, ranks cannot be established with confidence. Furthermore, for areas with similar scores, small changes in bootstrap probabilities may lead to disproportionately large rank changes. This sensitivity to small perturbations is a likely explanation for some of the fluctuations in rank changes among provinces.

Despite the need for caution in interpreting rankings, several conclusions can be drawn. Kinshasa and urban areas are ranked first or second throughout the six-year period. Despite high probabilities of temporal welfare advancement in Kasai Occidental, these gains were insufficient to improve its ranking. Kasai Occidental is ranked last in all years and is solidly last in 2013. Consistent with temporal results, Orientale jumps towards the top of the rankings in 2010, but these gains do not persist into 2013 (Orientale registers no temporal improvement between 2010 and 2013; see Table 11.2). Bandundu experiences the greatest increase in welfare relative to other areas, climbing five places, which is an improvement robust to randomness introduced via bootstrapping.

The FOD rankings appear to suggest a narrowing in the welfare gap among provinces as seen in the decline of Kinshasa's net dominance over other areas from 0.85 in 2007 to 0.38 in 2013. However, this narrowing is a result of the indeterminacy between urban areas and Kinshasa and many provinces due to

**Table 11.9.** Area rankings by probability of net domination (no health)

| 2007 | | 2010 | | 2013 | | 2007–13 |
|---|---|---|---|---|---|---|
| Area | Net Dom. | Area | Net Dom. | Area | Net Dom. | Rank change |
| Kinshasa (KSS) | 0.95 | KSS | 0.96 | KSS | 0.86 | 0 |
| Urban (URB) | 0.74 | URB | 0.80 | URB | 0.73 | 0 |
| Sud Kivu (SKV) | 0.23 | ORT | 0.11 | SKV | 0.05 | 0 |
| Kasai Oriental (KOT) | 0.07 | NAT | 0.04 | BCO | −0.02 | −4 |
| National (NAT) | −0.03 | NKV | 0.04 | NAT | −0.02 | 0 |
| Nord Kivu (NKV) | −0.05 | KOT | 0.00 | NKV | −0.03 | 0 |
| Orientale (ORT) | −0.06 | SKV | −0.01 | ORT | −0.05 | 0 |
| Bas Congo (BCO) | −0.09 | BCO | −0.05 | KOT | −0.08 | 4 |
| Maniema (MNM) | −0.11 | MNM | −0.07 | MNM | −0.09 | 0 |
| Katanga (KTG) | −0.13 | KTG | −0.15 | KTG | −0.11 | 0 |
| Équateur (ETR) | −0.26 | BDD | −0.17 | BDD | −0.18 | −1 |
| Bandundu (BDD) | −0.29 | ETR | −0.37 | ETR | −0.22 | 1 |
| Kasai Occidental (KOC) | −0.43 | RUR | −0.48 | KOT | −0.41 | 0 |
| Rural (RUR) | −0.52 | KOC | −0.65 | RUR | −0.45 | 0 |

*Note*: Rankings within shaded groups are highly sensitive to small perturbations and should be interpreted with caution.
*Source*: Authors' calculations based on DHS and MICS data

the inclusion of the health indicator. When health is excluded, rather than a narrowing, the gap between Kinshasa and urban areas and all other areas is wider in all three years (Table 11.9). Furthermore, rankings become extremely stable between years, indicating that the health indicator drives much of the ranking variation seen in Table 11.8. Nonetheless, the ranking gain of Oriental between 2007 and 2010 is robust.

## 11.5 Discussion

This chapter provides an evaluation of multidimensional welfare across provinces in the DRC from 2007 to 2013, a time period corresponding to local turmoil, restoration, reformation, and growth as well as declining rural consumption poverty. Application of the FOD approach to the 2010 MICS and the 2007 and 2013 DHS survey data, allows the analysis of the welfare of children aged 7–17 in terms of water, sanitation, shelter, health, information, and education.

Despite positive economic growth and consumption poverty trends, FOD temporal comparisons do not indicate broad-based advancement of welfare at the national, urban, or rural levels over the six-year period. This lack of multidimensional welfare advancement is partially due to inconsistent progress in the water, sanitation, and shelter indicators. Nonetheless, all areas achieved significant reductions in the percentage of children deprived in bed net usage, access to information, and primary school enrolment. Only Nord

Kivu exhibits convincing evidence of advancement across all indicators and over the full period.

Spatial FOD results are sensitive to the inclusion of the health indicator, defined as children not sleeping under a bed net the previous night. Our analysis demonstrates that the failure of Kinshasa and urban areas to dominate the most impoverished provinces in 2013 is likely due to an uneven distribution of gains: specifically deprivation in health (as measured by bed net usage) is higher in Kinshasa and urban zones compared to a number of areas that are worse off in all other indicators. Given this sensitivity to the health indicator and its counter-intuitive pattern of deprivation, it is useful to consider if bed net usage is an informative indicator in spatial comparisons.

The value of the bed net indicator hinges on its ability to measure a reduction in children's exposure to malaria. Households in urban areas may opt to use bed nets less frequently than their rural counterparts if alternatives such as insecticide sprays are more widely available. Furthermore, households in less malaria-prevalent areas, such as the city centre of Kinshasa (Giovanfrancesco et al. 2012), may elect not to use bed nets without significantly increasing their exposure to malaria. In both scenarios, the bed net indicator is counting children as deprived who are not necessarily at greater risk of contracting malaria, and is therefore not an appropriate measure of deprivation in health and should not be included in FOD analysis. However, if alternative prevention measures and malaria prevalence are equal in rural and urban areas, then the lower bed net usage in Kinshasa and urban areas truly reflects a greater deprivation level. Unfortunately, the information required to assess the appropriateness of the health indicator is not available. Further data and research on household use of other malaria prevention strategies are needed in order to ascertain which of these scenarios holds.

## References


Arndt, C., R. Distante, M. A. Hussain, L. P. Østerdal, P. L. Huong, and M. Ibraimo (2012). 'Ordinal Welfare Comparisons with Multiple Discrete Indicators: A First-Order Dominance Approach and Application to Child Poverty', *World Development*, 40 (11): 2290–301.

Giovanfrancesco, F., H. Ntuku, S. Schmidlin, C. Lengeler, and A. Tshefu (2012). 'A comprehensive risk map for malaria in Kinshasa, Democratic Republic of Congo', *Malaria Journal*, 11(Suppl. 1): O8. Available at <http://www.malariajournal.com/content/11/S1/O8>.

Gordon, D., S. Nandy, C. Pantazis, S. Pemberton, and P. Townsend (2003a). *Child Poverty in the Developing World*. Bristol: Policy Press.

Gordon, D., S. Nandy, C. Pantazis, S. Pemberton, and P. Townsend (2003b). 'Using Multiple Indicator Cluster Survey (MICS) and Demographic and Health Survey (DHS) Data to Measure Child Poverty'. Paper presented at the UNICEF MICS conference.

Ministry of Planning and Macro International (2008). *Democratic Republic of Congo Demographic and Health Survey 2007*. Calverton, MD: Ministry of Planning and Macro International.

Ministry of Planning and Monitoring the Implementation of the Modernity Revolution (MPSMRM), Ministry of Public Health (MSP), and ICF International (2014). *Democratic Republic of Congo Demographic and Health Survey 2013–2014*. Rockville, MD: MPSMRM, MSP, and ICF International.

Nanivazo, M. and K. Mahrt (2016). 'Growth and Poverty in the Democratic Republic of Congo: 2001 through 2013', in C. Arndt, A. McKay, and F. Tarp (eds), *Growth and Poverty in Sub-Saharan Africa*. Oxford: Oxford University Press, 421–45.

National Institute of Statistics and UNICEF (2011). *Democratic Republic of Congo Multiple Indicator Cluster Survey 2010*. Kinshasa, DRC: National Institute of Statistics and UNICEF.

United Nations Development Programme (2014). 'Democratic Republic of Congo Millennium Development Goals Status Report 2012'. Kinshasa: United Nations Development Programme (UNDP).

World Bank (2014). 'World Development Indicators', available at <data.worldbank.org>, accessed on 18 May 2014.

# 12

# Child Deprivation and Income Poverty in Ghana

*Raymond Elikplim Kofinti and Samuel Kobina Annim*

## 12.1 Introduction

In spite of the evidence that global poverty is on the decline, disparities in rates of reduction across countries as well as large disparities in levels of living standards continue to cause concern among policy-makers, development partners, and researchers. In sub-Saharan Africa, 47.5 per cent of its population, representing approximately 386 million people, lived below the poverty line of US$1.25 a day in 2008, down from 51.5 per cent in 1981 (World Bank 2012). On the African continent, there are wide disparities in poverty over time as countries such as Ghana, Ethiopia, Cameroon, Senegal, Gambia, and Morocco have made significant strides towards poverty reduction, whereas the same cannot be said of others such as Côte d'Ivoire and Nigeria (Ajakaiye et al. 2014).

In Ghana, consumption expenditure poverty from the perspectives of incidence and depth has experienced a significant reduction in terms of absolute and extreme poverty. Even though the methods for estimating consumption expenditure poverty have differed slightly, making comparisons over time less robust, available evidence suggests a significant decrease of absolute poverty from about 52 per cent in 1991–2 to about 24 per cent in 2012–13. Over the same period, extreme poverty declined by thirty-one percentage points. With these reductions, Ghana surpassed the first Millennium Development Goal (MDG) of halving extreme poverty by 2015 (Ghana Statistical Service (GSS) 2014).

Poverty has many dimensions, and as such the measurement of poverty significantly influences the understanding, analyses, and policies needed to target its reduction. From the seminal work of Sen (1976) until now, the measurement of poverty can be divided broadly into unidimensional and multidimensional approaches (Alkire and Foster 2011). Consumption expenditure and income poverty are typically presented as unidimensional measures. The multidimensional approach seeks to incorporate additional dimensions such as malnutrition, ill-health, illiteracy, and insecurity. According to Gordon et al. (2003) and UNICEF (2007), the use of a unidimensional measurement of poverty using income or consumption expenditure is biased towards adults, with limited attention paid to children. In addition, Minujin et al. (2014) argue that conventional poverty measurements in monetary values do not capture how poverty affects children in physical, emotional, and social ways. It also fails to recognize that children experience poverty differently from adults due to specific and different needs.

While an adult may fall into poverty temporarily, the implications of falling into poverty in childhood can last a lifetime because short periods of deprivation can impact children's long-term development (Ortiz et al. 2012). UNICEF (2000) argues that poverty reduction must begin with children and this warrants methodologies that adequately evaluate the living conditions of children. However, the most widely used methods to measure poverty are based on income or consumption levels. While such measures engender a broad understanding of populations living in poverty, they provide a potentially blurred or even misleading picture of the multidimensional and the interrelated nature of poverty as experienced by children.

Not surprisingly, most of the studies on poverty in Ghana (Annim et al. 2012; Boateng et al. 1992; Coulombe and Wodon 2007) are adult-oriented, with limited attention paid to children. As argued by UNICEF (2007), these approaches can show a significant increase in the welfare of a given household, yet child deprivation(s) may persist in such households, since one may erroneously assume households prioritize children in the intra-household distribution of resources. It is worth noting that the few studies on child poverty in Ghana (Mba and Badasu 2010; Mba et al. 2009) employed the Bristol (headcount) approach to measure the spatial distribution of child poverty across the country at a point in time.

Methodology-wise, the Bristol approach belongs to the 'counting' tradition of poverty measures. It involves an identification stage where the poor are identified according to the total number of dimensions in which they are deprived. Then, there is an aggregation stage where the 'headcount' or percentage of children who have been identified as poor is reported as the final measure (Roelen and Gassmann 2008). According to Alkire and Roche (2012), even though the headcount measure is theoretically relevant, and easy and clear to compute and interpret, it provides no incentive for policy-makers to prioritize the poorest children. This is because the headcount approach does not consider the intensity of poverty that poor children may suffer.

In addition, the literature on multidimensional wellbeing has long advocated the comparison of populations with welfare functions that aggregate separate dimensions of wellbeing into a headcount ratio like the Bristol method or single indices like the Multidimensional Poverty Index (MPI) and Multiple Overlapping Deprivation Analysis (MODA). The aggregation of separate dimensions into a single composite index typically requires imposition of weighting schemes, which could affect the consistency of ranking.

One way to ensure consistent ranking of populations is provided by multidimensional stochastic dominance conditions, under which a broad class of welfare functions consistently rank multivariate distributions of groups or societies (Yalonetzky 2013). The methodology of first-order dominance (FOD) is in the family of multidimensional stochastic dominance and ensures consistent ranking of populations when the FOD conditions are satisfied. The FOD approach was operationalized by Arndt et al. (2012) to enable welfare comparisons between two or more populations with multidimensional discrete wellbeing indicators observed at the micro level. With this approach, each welfare indicator can be ranked ordinally from worse to better without recourse to an arbitrary weighting scheme and complementarity/substitutability relationships between dimensions. The method uses a standard linear programming algorithm for determining dominance, allowing the implementation of a bootstrap procedure that facilitates rankings of populations.

This study assesses the temporal and spatial distribution of child poverty and wellbeing for four sets of geographical groupings in Ghana, namely national, rural/urban, ecological zones, and administrative regions. It uses the Ghana Living Standards Survey (GLSS) rounds five and six. The study employs the FOD methodology in five deprivation indicators—water, sanitation, shelter, education, and information—to measure the poverty and wellbeing of children aged 7–17 years old. In addition, the study employs a monetary approach in income to measure the incidence of children living in low-income households. Finally, the study compares the distribution of child poverty from a multidimensional deprivation-based analysis using FOD with that of income poverty.

This study contributes by employing a robust methodology (the FOD approach) and by considering the evolution of child poverty over time. This information could help to evaluate the effectiveness of existing policies in improving the living conditions of children. Importantly, in applying two approaches, the study seeks to provide comprehensive findings concerning the living conditions of children in the country, thereby aiding social intervention.

The rest of the chapter is presented as follows: section 12.2 reviews related literature on child poverty. Methods of study and discussion of the results are presented in sections 12.3 and 12.4 respectively. The final section highlights the main findings and policy recommendations.


## 12.2 Review of Related Literature

### 12.2.1 *Empirical Literature Review*

The last decade has seen a proliferation of empirical studies on child poverty across the globe: Alkire and Roche (2012); Arndt et al. (2012); Gordon et al. (2003); Minujin (2011); Minujin et al. (2014); Minujin and Nandy (2012); and Roche (2013). This may be attributed to the development of the child deprivation model (Gordon et al. 2003), coupled with the launching of the Global Study on Child Poverty and Disparity by UNICEF in 2007.

In the context of Ghana, Mba et al. (2009) conducted a study on child poverty and disparity in Ghana. Several datasets were used for the study: population censuses (1960, 1984, 2000), Multiple Indicator Survey (MICS) 2006, GLSS5, and the Ghana Demography Health Survey (GDHS) 2003. Another study was conducted by Mba and Badasu (2010) on deprivations among children in Ghana using the 2006 MICS. Both studies employed the deprivation model of Gordon et al. (2003) in dimensions of water, sanitation, shelter, education, health, nutrition, and information for children between 0 and 17 years. In both studies, absolute poverty was defined as children having two or more severe deprivations in any of the mentioned deprivations.

Their main findings reveal the Northern region as the poorest region in Ghana. Upper East and Upper West follow while the Greater Accra region is the least poor region in terms of child poverty. In addition, their findings indicate that children are more deprived in sanitation than any other indicator of child deprivation. Furthermore, they identified correlates of child poverty such as household size, households in the poorest wealth quintile, and female-headed households.


## 12.3 Methods and Data

### 12.3.1 *Multidimensional FOD Approach*

Arndt et al. (2012) developed the FOD methodology for evaluating multidimensional welfare comparisons among populations. The approach makes minimal assumptions, and at the same time allows welfare comparisons between two populations on the basis of a series of discrete ordinal welfare indicators without recourse to arbitrary weighting schemes or conditions on the social welfare function. The method uses an efficient algorithm for determining dominance and employs a bootstrap approach that permits cardinal rankings of populations.

The FOD approach is well established in the theory of both unidimensional and multidimensional FOD. However, for this study, we focus on the latter. Hence, in the multidimensional case, suppose that $f$ and $g$ are multidimensional probability mass functions of some population over a finite subset X of $R^n$ Then, $f$ FOD $g$ if one of the following conditions holds:

A. $g$ can be obtained from $f$ by a finite number of shifts of density from one outcome to another worse outcome;

B. Social welfare is at least as high for $f$ as for $g$ for any non-decreasing additively separable social welfare function such that $\sum_{x \in X} f(x)w(x) \geq \sum_{x \in X} g(x)w(x)$ for any non-decreasing real function $w$;

C. $\sum_{x \in Y} g(x) \geq \sum_{x \in Y} f(x)$ for any comprehensive set $Y \subseteq X$.

From the three equivalent FOD conditions, the most intuitive condition is A. The implication is that if condition A is observed between two population distributions, the dominating distribution is unambiguously better off.

The FOD approach makes the very minimum assumption that it is better not to be deprived than deprived. Coupled with its general strict nature, the approach has two major flaws. The first is the possibility that FOD criteria cannot determine whether one population dominates or is dominated by another population. The second is that the extent to which one population dominates another cannot be identified.

The two flaws can be mitigated through bootstrap sampling. Consequently, this study compares repeated bootstrap sampling over 100 iterations. This enables us to obtain the empirical probability of domination, which gives the extent to which one population dominates another. More important is the probability of net dominance (ND), which is the probability that a population dominates all other populations less the probability that a population is dominated by all other populations, interpreted as the cardinal measure of child welfare which provides the basis to rank populations.

This study chooses five main indicators of welfare for children aged 7–17 years by following closely the severe deprivation model of Gordon et al. (2003) and taking into cognizance the availability of data.

**Water:** A child is not severely deprived in water if the child's main water source for drinking is piped water, borehole, protected well water, or rainwater.

**Sanitation:** A child is not severely deprived in sanitation if the child has access to a flush toilet, an improved ventilated pit latrine, or a composting toilet.

**Education:** A child is not severely deprived in education if the child is attending school.

**Shelter:** A child is not severely deprived in shelter if the child's shelter floor material is made of a material other than earth/mud.

**Information:** A child is not severely deprived in information if the child belongs to a household that owns either a television or a radio.

These indicators constitute a set of five binary child welfare indicators. The binary variables were created for each child in each of the five welfare indicators, where '1' is the good outcome corresponding to non-deprived and '0' is the bad outcome corresponding to deprived. Hence, there are $2^5=32$ possible combinations of welfare outcomes for each child. For example, welfare combination (1,1,1,1,1) means non-deprivation in all of the five dimensions, while welfare combination (0,0,0,0,0) indicates deprivation in the five indicators of wellbeing.

As noted, FOD can be checked using a linear program that has a feasible solution in General Algebraic Modelling Systems (GAMS). For this study, bootstrap sampling in 100 iterations was carried out in order to mitigate the possibility of indeterminate outcomes of dominance. Therefore, the final result can be interpreted as the empirical probability that population A dominates population B or vice versa. Furthermore, temporal FOD outcomes allow comparison between populations over time. For this study, the temporal FOD analysis measures domination of the recent year (2013) over the last year (2006), and vice versa, in each of the four sets of geographical groups: national, rural/urban, ecological zones, and administrative regions. The results will provide information on three probabilities of temporal domination of child welfare in the mentioned geographical areas: positive probabilities indicating gains over time; negative probabilities indicating regression over time; and a blank cell indicating neither gains nor regression over time.

### 12.3.2 *An Income-Based Approach*

The income approach for measuring child poverty conceptualizes child poverty as children living in low-income households. This monetary poverty approach takes the household as the unit of analysis. The poor are identified by setting a poverty line corresponding to a given threshold of household income (Roelen and Gassmann 2008). Children in households beneath a given threshold are taken to be poor. According to Ravallion (1994), an absolute poverty line and a relative poverty line are the two main forms of poverty lines used to set the dividing line between poor and non-poor. The former is based on the ability to purchase a certain quantity of goods and services, whereas the latter is relative to the income level in the specific country (UNICEF 2005). This study employs the latter poverty line to estimate the incidence of children living in low-income households. Specifically, children living in households beneath 50 per cent of median household income are taken to be poor.

### 12.3.3 *Data Sources and Processing*

For both approaches, the study employs the GLSS as its main data source. The GLSS is a nationwide survey carried out by the Ghana Statistical Service (GSS). The first round of the GLSS was conducted in 1987–8. Six rounds in total have been conducted, with the second, third, fourth, fifth, and sixth rounds conducted in 1988–99, 1991–2, 1998–9, 2005–6, and 2012–13 respectively. The two central objectives of the GLSS, among many, are to monitor the living conditions of Ghanaians and to provide information for updating the country's national accounts. Consequently, it focuses on the household as the socio-economic unit, but collects information on individuals within the household, including children, and on the communities in which the households are identified. The GLSS captures information on thematic issues such as demographic characteristics, education, health, economic activity, migration, and tourism.

This study focuses on the last two rounds of the GLSS (5 and 6), and the population in focus for the FOD methodology is children aged 7–17 years. The fifth round contains information on 8687 households, and in these households there were 10,515 children aged 7–17 years. The sixth round contains information on 16,772 households, and in these households there were 20,082 children between the ages of 7 and 17.

For the FOD analysis, after managing the data and accounting for missing values in each of the welfare indicators, the number of children used for the analysis in 2006 dropped to 10,150, registering an attrition rate of 3 per cent, whereas that for 2013 dropped to 19,927, registering an attrition rate of 1 per cent. For the income analysis, out of the 8687 households in 2006, there are 10,515 children (7–17 years) living in 4783 households, whereas for the GLSS6 in 2013, out of the 16,722 households in 2013, there were 20,082 children (7–17 years) living in 9278 households.

## 12.4 Results and Discussion

The analyses were conducted in four geographical areas: national, rural–urban, ecological zones, and the ten administrative regions in Ghana for children aged 7 to 17 years. Five binary welfare indicators were selected in water, sanitation, shelter, education, and information.

### 12.4.1 *Children According to Welfare Indicators*

Table 12.1 presents the proportion and percentage change of Ghanaian children not deprived in each dimension, over time and across space. Nationally, Table 12.1 indicates positive percentage change in all five welfare indicators at the national level. The rural and urban areas registered a negative change in information and sanitation of 3.64 and 3.66 percentage points respectively. All three ecological zones recorded positive change in the five welfare indicators, except the Savannah zone. Regionally, all ten administrative regions had at least one negative percentage change in one of the five welfare indicators, except the Eastern and the Brong Ahafo regions. Overall, children have higher welfare in education and shelter and the worst welfare in sanitation over the two periods. Children having the worst welfare in sanitation is consistent with other studies in the same domain by Mba et al. (2009) and Mba and Badasu (2010).

### 12.4.2 *Share of Children in Multidimensional Welfare Combinations*

Five binary indicators were selected as mentioned above, and the number of possible welfare combinations is $2^5=32$, giving us thirty-two welfare combinations. Table 12.2 presents the share of children at the national level that fall in each of the thirty-two welfare combinations and the percentage point change over time. The first row of the table shows the share of children characterized by deprivation in all dimensions (0,0,0,0,0). The children in this group are worse off. The bottom row illustrates non-deprivation in any dimension (1,1,1,1,1). These children are better off. The discussion focuses on these two extremes solely: worse-off and better-off children.

From Table 12.2, the proportion of worse-off children registered a negative percentage point change of 0.16 per cent. The decrease in this proportion of children at the national level is good for the country, whereas the proportion of better-off children registered an increase of 12.64 percentage points.

### 12.4.3 *Temporal FOD Comparisons*

Table 12.3 shows the temporal FOD comparisons between 2006 and 2013. One must note that a '1' in the static case indicates that the area's/region's recent (2013) year welfare level dominates the earlier (2006) year's welfare level, while an empty cell indicates no domination. In the bootstrap case, a '1' indicates that all 100 bootstrap replications resulted in domination, while an empty cell indicates no domination.

From the table, the advance in the wellbeing of children over the period between 2006 and 2013 is registered at the national level, the Coastal zone,

**Table 12.1.** Children not deprived by welfare indicator over time and across space (per cent) and percentage point change

| | Water | | | Sanitation | | | Shelter | | | Education | | | Information | | |
|---|---|---|---|---|---|---|---|---|---|---|---|---|---|---|---|
| | 2006 | 2013 | Change | 2006 | 2013 | Change | 2006 | 2013 | Change | 2006 | 2013 | Change | 2006 | 2013 | Change |
| National | 76.1 | 84.9 | 8.8 | 41.5 | 54.7 | 13.3 | 85.9 | 91.2 | 5.2 | 84.2 | 95.1 | 10.9 | 80.6 | 81.0 | 0.5 |
| Rural | 69.1 | 74.5 | 5.3 | 23.0 | 38.8 | 15.8 | 79.5 | 85.5 | 6.0 | 79.4 | 92.4 | 13.0 | 77.9 | 74.3 | −3.6 |
| Urban | 89.0 | 96.2 | 7.2 | 75.6 | 71.9 | −3.7 | 97.8 | 97.3 | −0.6 | 93.3 | 98.2 | 4.9 | 85.5 | 88.3 | 2.8 |
| Coastal | 77.7 | 89.4 | 11.6 | 56.5 | 68.0 | 11.5 | 92.1 | 95.4 | 3.3 | 92.1 | 98.3 | 6.1 | 85.6 | 87.2 | 1.6 |
| Forest | 76.5 | 83.1 | 6.6 | 43.7 | 57.9 | 14.2 | 87.1 | 90.1 | 3.0 | 89.7 | 97.2 | 7.5 | 79.8 | 80.6 | 0.9 |
| Savannah | 72.8 | 81.8 | 9.1 | 13.1 | 20.1 | 7.0 | 73.8 | 86.2 | 12.4 | 59.2 | 83.1 | 23.9 | 74.8 | 70.5 | −4.3 |
| Western | 71.5 | 84.8 | 13.3 | 40.6 | 64.9 | 24.2 | 87.1 | 95.8 | 8.7 | 89.3 | 98.7 | 9.4 | 87.0 | 86.4 | −0.6 |
| Central | 75.9 | 82.5 | 6.6 | 39.2 | 57.5 | 18.3 | 88.9 | 90.5 | 1.6 | 93.3 | 97.2 | 3.9 | 82.0 | 78.5 | −3.5 |
| Greater Accra | 84.5 | 97.1 | 12.6 | 82.7 | 77.1 | −5.6 | 98.8 | 98.3 | −0.5 | 93.8 | 98.7 | 4.9 | 86.9 | 93.4 | 6.6 |
| Volta | 62.0 | 64.1 | 2.1 | 29.8 | 42.0 | 12.2 | 78.8 | 89.0 | 10.2 | 84.2 | 92.6 | 8.4 | 81.7 | 73.2 | −8.5 |
| Eastern | 70.2 | 80.8 | 10.6 | 38.2 | 53.1 | 15.0 | 84.8 | 88.2 | 3.4 | 91.3 | 98.0 | 6.7 | 80.6 | 81.0 | 0.4 |
| Ashanti | 86.2 | 92.2 | 6.0 | 59.5 | 70.7 | 11.3 | 93.6 | 92.4 | −1.2 | 94.0 | 98.9 | 4.9 | 80.7 | 84.9 | 4.2 |
| Brong Ahafo | 79.2 | 83.5 | 4.3 | 34.3 | 51.1 | 16.9 | 85.1 | 88.5 | 3.5 | 84.2 | 96.9 | 12.7 | 75.4 | 78.2 | 2.8 |
| Northern | 63.0 | 75.1 | 12.1 | 16.9 | 26.4 | 9.4 | 78.8 | 90.7 | 11.8 | 56.5 | 76.2 | 19.6 | 74.9 | 73.3 | −1.6 |
| Upper East | 77.6 | 87.8 | 10.2 | 9.1 | 8.9 | −0.2 | 70.2 | 87.4 | 17.3 | 62.3 | 93.7 | 31.5 | 77.1 | 67.8 | −9.3 |
| Upper West | 98.3 | 95.2 | −3.1 | 6.2 | 15.3 | 9.1 | 62.3 | 70.5 | 8.2 | 63.8 | 90.8 | 27.0 | 71.4 | 65.0 | −6.4 |

*Source*: Authors' calculation based on GLSS5 (GSS 2007) and GLSS6 (GSS 2014)

**Table 12.2.** Children by combination of welfare indicators, national figures (per cent), and percentage point change

| Water | Sanitation | Shelter | Education | Information | 2006 | 2013 | Change |
|---|---|---|---|---|---|---|---|
| 0 | 0 | 0 | 0 | 0 | 0.31 | 0.16 | −0.16 |
| 0 | 0 | 0 | 0 | 1 | 1.62 | 0.23 | −1.39 |
| 0 | 0 | 0 | 1 | 0 | 0.58 | 0.44 | −0.14 |
| 0 | 0 | 0 | 1 | 1 | 3.04 | 1.47 | −1.57 |
| 0 | 0 | 1 | 0 | 0 | 0.58 | 0.44 | −0.14 |
| 0 | 0 | 1 | 0 | 1 | 2.44 | 0.77 | −1.66 |
| 0 | 0 | 1 | 1 | 0 | 1.91 | 1.74 | −0.17 |
| 0 | 0 | 1 | 1 | 1 | 9.2 | 5.82 | −3.38 |
| 0 | 1 | 0 | 0 | 0 | 0.02 | 0.03 | 0.02 |
| 0 | 1 | 0 | 0 | 1 | 0.12 | 0.01 | −0.11 |
| 0 | 1 | 0 | 1 | 0 | 0.06 | 0.16 | 0.10 |
| 0 | 1 | 0 | 1 | 1 | 0.17 | 0.49 | 0.32 |
| 0 | 1 | 1 | 0 | 0 | 0.05 | 0.04 | −0.02 |
| 0 | 1 | 1 | 0 | 1 | 0.23 | 0.12 | −0.11 |
| 0 | 1 | 1 | 1 | 0 | 0.87 | 0.72 | −0.15 |
| 0 | 1 | 1 | 1 | 1 | 2.70 | 2.46 | −0.24 |
| 1 | 0 | 0 | 0 | 0 | 0.74 | 0.36 | −0.38 |
| 1 | 0 | 0 | 0 | 1 | 1.55 | 0.31 | −1.24 |
| 1 | 0 | 0 | 1 | 0 | 1.22 | 1.12 | −0.10 |
| 1 | 0 | 0 | 1 | 1 | 3.40 | 1.90 | −1.50 |
| 1 | 0 | 1 | 0 | 0 | 1.74 | 0.57 | −1.17 |
| 1 | 0 | 1 | 0 | 1 | 4.15 | 1.05 | −3.10 |
| 1 | 0 | 1 | 1 | 0 | 5.37 | 6.08 | 0.710 |
| 1 | 0 | 1 | 1 | 1 | 20.72 | 22.84 | 2.110 |
| 1 | 1 | 0 | 0 | 0 | 0.20 | 0.05 | −0.16 |
| 1 | 1 | 0 | 0 | 1 | 0.11 | 0.02 | −0.09 |
| 1 | 1 | 0 | 1 | 0 | 0.32 | 0.79 | 0.47 |
| 1 | 1 | 0 | 1 | 1 | 0.61 | 1.32 | 0.71 |
| 1 | 1 | 1 | 0 | 0 | 0.44 | 0.14 | −0.30 |
| 1 | 1 | 1 | 0 | 1 | 1.49 | 0.58 | −0.92 |
| 1 | 1 | 1 | 1 | 0 | 5.04 | 6.15 | 1.11 |
| 1 | 1 | 1 | 1 | 1 | 29.01 | 41.65 | 12.64 |

*Source*: Authors' calculation based on GLSS5 (GSS 2007) and GLSS6 (GSS 2014)

and the Eastern region, using the static approach. However, bootstrapping at the national level, the Coastal zone, and the Eastern region results in fewer instances of 2013 dominating 2006 than instances of indeterminate outcomes, with probabilities of dominating of 0.41, 0.25, and 0.18, respectively. This implies that there is about a four out of ten probability of advance at the national level. At the Coastal zone, there is a one out of four probability of advance and the Eastern region recorded about a one out of five probability of advance in child welfare between the two periods.

Children in other areas such as the urban area, Forest zone, the Savannah zone, Brong Ahafo region, Northern region, and Western region recorded positive (empirical) probabilities of 2013 dominating 2006 of 0.01, 0.10, 0.01, 0.03, 0.05, and 0.11, respectively, albeit low probabilities. The results

**Table 12.3.** Temporal FOD comparisons between 2006 and 2013 (probabilities)

| | | Bootstrap | | | |
|---|---|---|---|---|---|
| | | 2013 FOD | | 2006 FOD | |
| | Static case | 2006 | Undecided | 2013 | Total |
|---|---|---|---|---|---|
| National | 1.00 | 0.41 | 0.59 | | 1.00 |
| Rural | | | 1.00 | | 1.00 |
| Urban | | 0.01 | 0.99 | | 1.00 |
| Coastal | 1.00 | 0.25 | 0.75 | | 1.00 |
| Forest | | 0.10 | 0.90 | | 1.00 |
| Savannah | | 0.01 | 0.99 | | 1.00 |
| Ashanti | | 0.01 | 0.99 | | 1.00 |
| Brong Ahafo | | 0.03 | 0.97 | | 1.00 |
| Central | | | 1.00 | | 1.00 |
| Eastern | 1.00 | 0.18 | 0.82 | | 1.00 |
| Greater Accra | | | 1.00 | | 1.00 |
| Northern | | 0.05 | 0.95 | | 1.00 |
| Upper East | | | 1.00 | | 1.00 |
| Upper West | | | 1.00 | | 1.00 |
| Volta | | | 1.00 | | 1.00 |
| Western | | 0.11 | 0.89 | | 1.00 |

*Source*: Authors' calculation based on GLSS5 (GSS 2007) and GLSS6 (GSS 2014)

from the table provide no evidence of regression in any area/region, as indicated by a blank column of cells in '2006 FOD 2013'.

These results provide broad-based evidence of no regression in child welfare over time. However, there is little to no evidence of advancement for most areas, except the national and Coastal zone. For the remaining areas, the probabilities are too low to indicate advancement with much confidence. The lack of advancement is likely due to the declines for many areas in sanitation and information.

### 12.4.4 *Spatial FOD Comparisons Using Net Dominance and Rank of Child Poverty*

The average probability of ND is the difference between the average probability of dominating and of being dominated by all other areas, i.e. the row average less the column average dominance. Table 12.4 shows the average ND and the rank of child welfare over time across the ten administrative regions. For the row and column average dominance of each region, see Kofinti and Annim (2015: tables 5 and 6). Regions with relatively lower ND and higher ranks correspond to poorer regions, whereas the opposite is true for better-off regions in terms of child poverty.

In 2006, Greater Accra has the best ranking, followed by the Ashanti region. The remaining rankings are shown by the 'Rank1' column in Table 12.4. The

**Table 12.4.** ND (probabilities) and rankings of deprivation child poverty across regions over time

| Regions | 2006 | | 2013 | | 2006–13 |
| --- | --- | --- | --- | --- | --- |
| | ND | Rank1 | ND | Rank2 | Differ |
| Greater Accra | 0.53 | 1 | 0.7 | 1 | 0 |
| Ashanti | 0.37 | 2 | 0.45 | 2 | 0 |
| Western | 0.06 | 4 | 0.33 | 3 | 1 |
| Central | 0.12 | 3 | 0.09 | 4 | −1 |
| Eastern | −0.03 | 6 | −0.09 | 5 | 1 |
| Upper West | 0.00 | 5 | −0.09 | 5 | 0 |
| Upper East | −0.19 | 8 | −0.21 | 7 | 1 |
| Brong Ahafo | −0.13 | 7 | −0.22 | 8 | −1 |
| Northern | −0.44 | 10 | −0.28 | 9 | 1 |
| Volta | −0.21 | 9 | −0.49 | 10 | −1 |

*Source*: Authors' calculation based on GLSS5 (GSS 2007) and GLSS6 (GSS 2014)

two worst regions, with higher rankings, are the Volta and the Northern regions: the likely reason is that Volta and Northern regions had the highest proportion of worse-off children (see Kofinti and Annim 2015: table 3).

The three worst regions (Upper East, Volta, and Northern regions) in terms of child welfare using the FOD approach are fairly different from other studies of child poverty (Mba and Badasu 2010; Mba et al. 2009) where the three worst regions were the three northern regions (Upper East, Upper West, and Northern regions). The reason could be in the different assumptions underlying the approaches used for these studies. The headcount approach considers children with two or more deprivations as poor, whereas the FOD is a strict procedure which considers the better-ranked population as unambiguously better off.

From the 2013 results, Greater Accra region is the best-ranked region. The remaining rankings are provided by the 'Rank2' column in Table 12.4. The two worst regions are the Northern and Volta regions, the likely reason being that Volta and Northern regions had the two highest proportions of worse-off children (see Kofinti and Annim 2015: table 3).

The three worst regions (Brong Ahafo, Northern, and Volta regions) in terms of child welfare using the FOD approach are reasonably different from other studies of child poverty (Mba and Badasu 2010; Mba et al. 2009), where the three worst regions were the three northern regions. The last column, 'Differ', indicates the difference between the rankings of 2006 and 2013.

### 12.4.5 Comparison between the Rankings of Deprivation Child Poverty, Income Child Poverty, and Consumption Expenditure Poverty

Tables 12.5 and 12.6 compare the multidimensional FOD (deprivation analyses) rankings with the income and consumption expenditure approaches at

**Table 12.5.** Comparison of rankings of child deprivation poverty, child income poverty, and consumption expenditure poverty in 2006

| Regions | Ranks of child deprivation poverty (R1) (2006) | Ranks of child income poverty (R2) (2006) | Differ1 R1–R2 | Ranks of consumption expenditure poverty (R3) (2006) | Differ2 R1–R3 |
|---|---|---|---|---|---|
| Western | 4 | 2 | 2 | 3 | 1 |
| Central | 3 | 4 | −1 | 4 | −1 |
| Greater Accra | 1 | 1 | 0 | 1 | 0 |
| Volta | 9 | 6 | 3 | 7 | 2 |
| Eastern | 6 | 3 | 3 | 2 | 4 |
| Ashanti | 2 | 4 | −2 | 5 | −3 |
| Brong Ahafo | 7 | 7 | 0 | 6 | 1 |
| Northern | 10 | 8 | 2 | 8 | 2 |
| Upper East | 8 | 10 | −2 | 9 | −1 |
| Upper West | 5 | 9 | −4 | 10 | −5 |

*Source*: Authors' derivation from GLSS5 (GSS 2007)

**Table 12.6.** Comparison of rankings of child deprivation poverty, child income poverty, and consumption expenditure poverty in 2013

| Regions | Ranks of child deprivation poverty in 2013 (R1) | Ranks of child income poverty 2013 (R2) | Differ1 R1–R2 | Ranks of consumption expenditure poverty in 2013 (R3) | Differ2 R1–R3 |
|---|---|---|---|---|---|
| Western | 3 | 1 | 2 | 4 | −1 |
| Central | 4 | 7 | −3 | 3 | 1 |
| Greater Accra | 1 | 2 | −1 | 1 | 0 |
| Volta | 10 | 6 | 4 | 7 | 3 |
| Eastern | 5 | 3 | 2 | 5 | 0 |
| Ashanti | 2 | 4 | −2 | 2 | 0 |
| Brong Ahafo | 8 | 5 | 3 | 6 | 2 |
| Northern | 9 | 8 | 1 | 9 | 0 |
| Upper East | 7 | 10 | −3 | 8 | −1 |
| Upper West | 5 | 9 | −4 | 10 | −5 |

*Source*: Authors' derivation from GLSS6 (GSS 2014)

the regional level in 2006 and 2013 respectively. For the incidence of consumption expenditure and child income poverty, see Kofinti and Annim (2015: table 8). One must note that the highest rank corresponds to the poorest region, whereas the lowest rank corresponds to the best region.

Table 12.5 compares child deprivation, child income, and consumption expenditure poverty in 2006. The column 'Differ1' indicates the differences in rankings between child deprivation and income poverty; only two regions, Greater Accra and Brong Ahafo, maintained the same rank out of the ten regions in 2006. On the other hand, the column 'Differ2' indicates the differences in rankings between deprivation child poverty and consumption expenditure poverty; only the Greater Accra region, the capital city, registered the same rank between both approaches.

Table 12.6 shows the comparison between the rankings of child deprivation, child income, and consumption expenditure poverty in 2013. The column 'Differ1' indicates the differences in rankings between child deprivation and income poverty; none of the regions registered the same rank using both approaches. This points to differences in regional distribution of child poverty using both approaches. On the other hand, the column 'Differ2' indicates the differences in rankings between child deprivation poverty and consumption expenditure poverty.

## 12.5 Conclusion

This chapter assesses the poverty of children aged 7 to 17 years across four geographical areas of Ghana, namely national, rural–urban, ecological zones, and administrative regions, and over time, between 2006 and 2013, using GLSS5 and GLSS6 respectively. The specific objectives addressed are: (1) determine the gains in wellbeing of children over time; (2) assess the spatial distribution of deprivation child poverty; (3) compare the spatial distribution of deprivation and income child poverty across the ten administrative regions.

The findings indicate that children are worse off in sanitation than any other welfare indicator. The temporal FOD comparisons robustly provide broad-based evidence of no regression over time. The spatial FOD comparisons indicate profound disparities in deprivation child poverty across the four sets of geographical groupings: (1) we observed that in both years the rural area and the Savannah zone were the worst-ranked in terms of the area of residence and the ecological zone respectively; (2) regionally, the results from the spatial comparisons in 2013 reveal the Brong Ahafo, the Northern, and Volta regions as the three worst regions in the country respectively; (3) the urban area, the Coastal zone, Greater Accra, and the Ashanti regions were the best-performing areas, zones, and regions in both years respectively. Finally, the comparison between deprivation and income child poverty across the ten regions reveals the following: in 2006, only two regions out of the ten maintained the same rank using both approaches, whereas no region maintained the same rank using both approaches in 2013.

The government should therefore focus more on children in the rural area, the Savannah zone, Brong Ahafo, Northern, and the Volta regions through the provision of social amenities such as improved ventilated latrines, boreholes, and schools to reduce the number of children in these areas facing severe deprivation in all five welfare indicators. In addition, the government should concentrate on reducing income poverty in the Upper West, Upper

East, and Northern regions. Finally, the differences in rank from the comparison between deprivation and income child poverty call for sustained efforts from the government to implement child-focused policies such as compulsory basic and senior high school education and enforcement of the rights of children.


# References


Ajakaiye, O., A. T. Jerome, O. Olaniyan, K. Mahrt, and O. A. Alaba (2014). 'Multidimensional Poverty in Nigeria: First-Order Dominance Approach', WIDER Working Paper 2014/143. Helsinki: UNU-WIDER.

Alkire, S. and J. Foster (2011). 'Understandings and Misunderstandings of Multidimensional Poverty Measurement', *The Journal of Economic Inequality*, 9(2): 289–314.

Alkire, S. and J. M. Roche (2012). 'Beyond Headcount: The Alkire–Foster Approach to Multidimensional Child Poverty Measurement', in I. Ortiz, L. Moreira Daniels, and S. Engilbertsdóttir (eds), *Child Poverty and Inequality: New Perspectives*. New York: UNICEF Division of Policy and Practice, 18–22.

Annim, S. K., S. Mariwah, and J. Sebu (2012). 'Spatial Inequality and Household Poverty in Ghana', *Economic Systems*, 36(4): 487–505.

Arndt, C., R. Distante, M. A. Hussain, L. P. Østerdal, P. L. Huong, and M. Ibraimo (2012). 'Ordinal Welfare Comparisons with Multiple Discrete Indicators: A First-Order Dominance Approach and Application to Child Poverty', *World Development*, 40(11): 2290–301.

Boateng, E. O., K. Ewusi, R. Kanbur, and A. McKay (1992). 'A Poverty Profile for Ghana, 1987–1988', *Journal of African Economies*, 1(1): 25–58.

Coulombe, H. and Q. Wodon (2007). 'Poverty, Livelihoods, and Access to Basic Services in Ghana', in *Ghana CEM: Meeting the Challenge of Accelerated and Shared Growth*. Washington, DC: World Bank, 1–86.

Ghana Statistical Service (2007). 'Ghana Living Standards Survey Round 5 (GLSS5)'. Available at <http://www.statsghana.gov.gh>, retrieved on 14 March 2015.

Ghana Statistical Service (2014). 'Ghana Living Standards Survey Round 6 (GLSS6) Main Report'. Available at <http://www.statsghana.gov.gh>, retrieved on 7 May 2015.

Gordon, D., S. Nandy, C. Pantazis, S. Pemberton, and P. Townsend (2003). 'The Distribution of Child Poverty in the Developing World'. Report to UNICEF. Bristol, UK: Centre for International Poverty Research, University of Bristol.

Kofinti, R. E. and S. K. Annim (2015). 'Child Deprivation and Income Poverty in Ghana', WIDER Working Paper 2015/150. Helsinki: UNU-WIDER.

Mba, C. J. and D. M. Badasu (2010). 'Deprivations among Children in Ghana: Evidence from the 2006 Multiple Indicator Cluster Survey', *The Social Sciences*, 5(5): 440–5.

Mba, C. J., S. O. Kwankye, D. M. Badasu, C. Ahiadeke, and J. Anarfi (2009). *Child Poverty and Disparities in Ghana*. Accra: UNICEF Ghana.

Minujin, A. (2011). 'Child Poverty in East Asia and the Pacific: Deprivations and Disparities. A Study of Seven Countries'. Bangkok: UNICEF East Asia and Pacific.

Minujin, A., C. McCaffrey, M. Patel, and Q. Paienjton (2014). 'Redefining Poverty: Deprivation among Children in East Asia and the Pacific', *Global Social Policy*, 14(1): 3–31.

Minujin, A. and S. Nandy (2012). *Global Child Poverty and Wellbeing: Measurement, Concepts, Policy and Action*. Bristol, UK: Policy Press.

Ortiz, I., L. Moreira Daniels, and S. Engilbertsdóttir (2012). *Child Poverty and Inequality: New Perspectives*. New York: UNICEF Division of Policy and Practice.

Ravallion, M. (1994). *Poverty Comparisons*, vol. 56. Chur, Switzerland: Harwood Academic Publishers.

Roche, J. M. (2013). 'Monitoring Progress in Child Poverty Reduction: Methodological Insights and Illustration to the Case Study of Bangladesh', *Social Indicators Research*, 112(2): 363–90.

Roelen, K. and F. Gassmann (2008). 'Measuring Child Poverty and Wellbeing: A Literature Review', Maastricht Graduate School of Governance Working Paper 001. Maastricht: Maastricht University.

Sen, A. (1976). 'Poverty: An Ordinal Approach to Measurement', *Econometrica: Journal of the Econometric Society*, 44(2): 219–31.

UNICEF (2000). *Poverty Reduction Begins with Children*. New York: UNICEF.

UNICEF (2005). 'Child Poverty in Rich Countries'. Report Card No. 6. Florence: UNICEF Innocenti Research Centre.

UNICEF (2007). 'Child Poverty in Perspective: An Overview of Child Wellbeing in Rich Countries'. Report Card 7. Florence: UNICEF Innocenti Research Centre.

World Bank (2012). *World Development Indicators*. Washington, DC: World Bank.

Yalonetzky, G. (2013). 'Stochastic Dominance with Ordinal Variables: Conditions and a Test', *Econometric Reviews*, 32(1): 126–63.

# 13

# Measuring Multidimensional Poverty in Nigeria

*Olu Ajakaiye, Afeikhena T. Jerome, Olanrewaju Olaniyan, Kristi Mahrt, and Olufunke A. Alaba*

## 13.1 Introduction

Though Nigeria has achieved rapid economic growth, the extent to which poverty reduction has accompanied this growth remains uncertain. The economy grew strongly at an average annual rate in excess of 6 per cent over the last decade, even during the global financial crisis (IMF 2013), ranking Nigeria as one of the fastest growing economies globally. In spite of this strong growth performance, poverty remains widespread. Nigeria's National Bureau of Statistics (NBS) estimated consumption poverty to have risen from 27 per cent in 1980 to 66 per cent in 1996. With the onset of higher growth rates, estimated poverty initially dipped to 54 per cent in 2004 but then peaked at 69 per cent in 2010 (NBS 2012).[1]

In response to questions regarding the underestimation of consumption and inconsistencies between per capita GDP and poverty rates, the World Bank re-estimated Nigeria's consumption poverty (World Bank 2014). These new estimates, which are significantly lower than NBS estimates, indicate national poverty rates of 35 per cent in 2011 and 33 per cent in 2013, respectively (World Bank 2014).[2] Though the NBS and World Bank estimates are not directly comparable, the World Bank estimates call into question the 2010 NBS estimates and the overall direction of change.

---

[1] Concerns have been expressed about the comparability of surveys through time, thus these figures should be interpreted with caution.

[2] The 2004 and 2010 NBS poverty estimates are based upon the 2003/4 and 2009/10 Nigerian Living Standard Surveys, while the World Bank estimates are based upon the 2010/11 and 2012/13 General Household Surveys.

In this context, where consumption poverty estimates do not provide a clear perspective on poverty levels and trends, triangulating poverty analysis with alternative measures could be particularly informative. Ajakaiye et al. (2016) advance the discussion by estimating multidimensional, non-income poverty within Nigeria's six geopolitical zones and rural and urban areas between 1999 and 2008 using the first-order dominance (FOD) method developed by Arndt et al. (2012). Their analysis lends support to the view that poverty reduction in Nigeria has not kept pace with the rapid economic growth attained in the last decade. The analysis further indicates that regional inequalities remain profound with huge disparities between the urban and rural sectors as well as between the southern and northern geopolitical zones of the country.

In this chapter we expand upon the work of Ajakaiye et al. (2016) by introducing state-level FOD analysis in 2008 and 2013. Additionally, we scrutinize indicator definitions and evaluate the sensitivity of outcomes to indicator welfare thresholds. The remainder of the chapter is structured as follows. Section 13.2 presents the FOD methodology, data, and FOD indicators. Section 13.3 analyses spatial and temporal FOD results. Finally, section 13.4 concludes.

## 13.2 Methodology

### 13.2.1 *FOD*

The FOD approach is adopted in this study to appraise multidimensional welfare in Nigeria across time and space. FOD analysis is a method of comparing populations using multiple, binary welfare indicators without imposing weighting schemes or making assumptions about the preferences for each indicator. Multidimensional welfare comparisons are based on the simple criterion that it is better to be not deprived than deprived in any indicator. FOD comparisons of population A and B result in one of three outcomes: population A dominates population B; population B dominates population A; dominance is indeterminate. Indeterminate outcomes occur when two populations are too similar or too different for comparisons to be made. For example, when comparing two individuals with outcomes (0,1,0) and (1,0,1), dominance cannot be established because we do not assume it is better to be not deprived in any given dimension. The same logic can be extended to populations. See Chapter 11 for a more detailed discussion of indeterminate outcomes.

Dominant outcomes are all or nothing, and thus provide no information about the extent of domination. To mitigate this shortcoming, we draw one hundred bootstrap samples and conduct FOD analysis for each sample.[3] The share of dominant outcomes for each pair of populations across all bootstrap samples can be interpreted as the probability of domination. Thus, while the welfare indicators are ordinal in nature, the application of bootstrap sampling produces probabilities of one population performing better than another. For greater detail on the FOD methodology, see Chapter 3 for a mathematical presentation and Chapter 15 for an intuitive discussion.

### 13.2.2 Data Sources

FOD analysis is based on the 1999, 2003, 2008, and 2013 Nigeria Demographic and Health Surveys (DHS). All surveys are nationally representative, covering both urban and rural households. The surveys follow a stratified cluster sampling design with the intention of statistical representation by zone and urban/rural area in 1999 and 2003 and state and urban/rural area in 2008 and 2013. Details of the sample design can be found in the final reports (NPC and ORC Macro 1999, 2004, NPC and IFC Macro 2009, and NPC and IFC International 2014). As indicated in the reports, 7647, 7225, 34,070, and 40,320 households were surveyed in 1999, 2003, 2008, and 2013, respectively. After eliminating households with missing values, 7323, 7115, 32,888, and 36,016 households in 1999, 2003, 2008, and 2013 were utilized for the analysis.

Nigeria is divided into thirty-six states plus the Federal Capital Territory (FCT), Abuja. Ideally, analysis would be conducted at the politically relevant state level. However, because the DHS sampling scheme only permits state-level analysis in 2008 and 2013, the analysis is conducted in two stages. First, spatial and temporal comparisons are made for the nation, urban and rural areas, and six geopolitical zones (North Central, North East, North West, South East, South South, and South West) for all years. See Figure 13.1 for a map of zones. Next, spatial and temporal FOD comparisons are made for the thirty-six states and the FCT in 2008 and 2013.

### 13.2.3 FOD Indicators

Poverty can be reflected in various broad dimensions and the selection of relevant indicators should be driven by the context and specificity of the exercise. The five welfare indicators chosen for this study reflect households' access to water, sanitation, energy, housing and education. Indicators and the associated poverty thresholds are motivated by the Nigerian context and internationally recognized standards such as those laid out in the Millennium Development Goals (MDGs). However, available data does not always allow

---

[3] Bootstrap sampling follows the same stratified cluster sample design used in the DHS sampling. Samples are drawn with replacement.

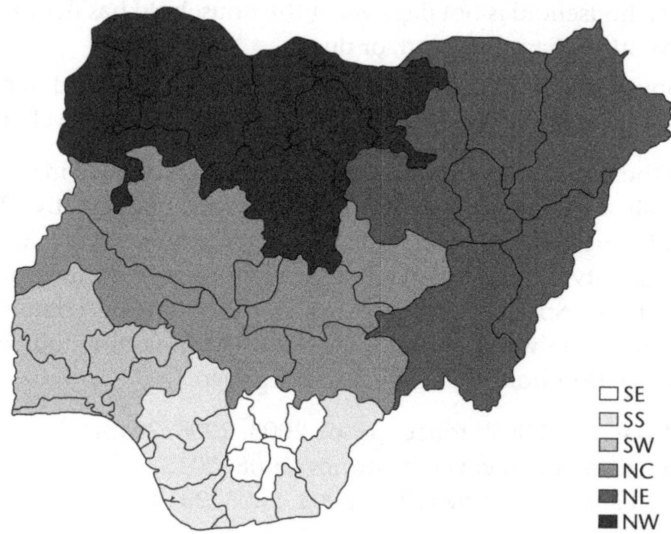


**Figure 13.1.** Zones of Nigeria
*Source*: Authors' compilation

indicators to be defined as would be preferred. Ideally, we would follow the MDG definition of improved water, where water obtained from piped sources, protected wells, protected springs, and rainwater are deemed improved (WHO/UNICEF JMP 2015).[4] Unfortunately, the 1999 DHS does not distinguish between protected and unprotected wells and the 1999 and 2003 DHS do not distinguish between protected and unprotected springs. Likewise, the MDGs define improved sanitation to include most flush toilets, ventilated improved pits, and covered latrines (WHO/UNICEF JMP 2015). Again, this definition was not feasible, as the 1999 and 2003 surveys do not distinguish between covered and uncovered latrines.

Given the data restrictions, household-level FOD welfare indicators are defined as follows, where all indicators are binary variables such that a '1' is assigned to households that are not deprived.[5]

Water: a household is not deprived if the household's water source is piped water, well water, or rainwater.

Sanitation: a household is not deprived if the household uses a flush toilet, a ventilated, improved pit (VIP) latrine, or a composting toilet.

Access to electricity: a household is not deprived if the household has access to electricity.

[4] See WHO/UNICEF JMP (2015) for more detailed descriptions of specific water and sanitation categorization.
[5] Population weights are used throughout the analysis.

Housing: a household is not deprived if the household has flooring made of a material other than dirt, sand, or dung.

Education: a household is not deprived if any household member has completed three or more years of schooling at the primary level or above.

Given that the water and sanitation indicators may be defined in several ways, we seek to gain a greater understanding of the impact of alternative definitions on FOD outcomes. We re-estimate FOD comparisons with the above definitions of electricity, housing, and education while varying the sanitation and water definitions. Specifically, we consider the following combinations of water and sanitation welfare thresholds such that household outcomes at or better than the threshold are deemed not deprived:

1. piped water and flush toilets (1999, 2003, 2008, 2013)
2. protected wells and covered latrines (2008, 2013)
3. any well and any latrine (1999, 2003, 2008, 2013)

## 13.3 Results

### 13.3.1 *Welfare Indicators*

Table 13.1 presents the mean welfare levels of each indicator for the nation, rural and urban areas, and the six zones. The overall picture varies considerably by area. As a whole, Nigeria achieved gains in water, sanitation, and electricity over the fourteen-year period, while both housing and education slightly deteriorated. Rural areas followed a similar pattern with more significant declines in housing and education. In contrast, urban areas achieved gains in sanitation, housing, and education but worsened in access to clean water and electricity.

Sanitation welfare increased substantially between 2003 and 2008. This apparent improvement is driven by the use of VIP latrines, which increased from 2.9 per cent in 2003 to 23.9 per cent in 2008. Comparing these figures to another nationally representative Nigerian household survey, the Multiple Indicator Cluster Survey (MICS), calls into question the likelihood of this large leap. In particular, MICS data indicate that household VIP latrine usage was merely 0.8 per cent in 2007 and 1.5 per cent in 2011 (NBS 2007, 2011). This uncertainty gives even greater importance to sensitivity analysis to evaluate the robustness of results.

Table 13.2 reports mean welfare levels for alternative water and sanitation thresholds and illustrates welfare sensitivity to these thresholds. Access to piped water greatly deteriorated over the full study period. However, the more relevant measure of poverty, *protected wells*, improved substantially between 2003 and 2013 in nearly every area—a pattern similar to our default

**Table 13.1.** Households not deprived, by welfare indicator and year (per cent)

| Area | Water | | | | Sanitation | | | | Electricity | | | | Housing | | | | Education | | | |
|---|---|---|---|---|---|---|---|---|---|---|---|---|---|---|---|---|---|---|---|---|
| | 1999 | 2003 | 2008 | 2013 | 1999 | 2003 | 2008 | 2013 | 1999 | 2003 | 2008 | 2013 | 1999 | 2003 | 2008 | 2013 | 1999 | 2003 | 2008 | 2013 |
| National | 68.9 | 70.0 | 73.5 | 79.1 | 18.6 | 15.8 | 40.2 | 41.4 | 44.7 | 51.1 | 47.8 | 51.1 | 61.4 | 64.4 | 61.8 | 59.7 | 78.9 | 78.0 | 78.9 | 77.1 |
| Rural | 59.8 | 64.9 | 68.1 | 73.9 | 9.6 | 7.3 | 30.2 | 28.9 | 28.0 | 34.4 | 29.8 | 32.5 | 50.4 | 52.6 | 48.5 | 44.8 | 74.4 | 72.5 | 72.2 | 67.2 |
| Urban | 90.9 | 80.0 | 84.7 | 87.8 | 40.6 | 32.5 | 60.6 | 61.9 | 85.3 | 83.9 | 84.6 | 81.8 | 88.1 | 87.6 | 88.9 | 84.1 | 90.1 | 88.9 | 92.5 | 93.5 |
| NC | 66.3 | 50.7 | 60.5 | 63.8 | 18.7 | 10.1 | 32.6 | 31.3 | 51.0 | 47.2 | 32.3 | 44.8 | 73.9 | 69.3 | 62.4 | 62.6 | 86.5 | 87.7 | 84.8 | 87.1 |
| NE | 76.7 | 68.9 | 71.9 | 75.6 | 10.6 | 5.6 | 25.3 | 34.4 | 23.1 | 34.4 | 24.7 | 30.7 | 32.5 | 39.4 | 30.8 | 44.5 | 57.2 | 61.7 | 57.0 | 55.6 |
| NW | 89.6 | 84.3 | 87.5 | 90.8 | 8.1 | 5.8 | 48.4 | 47.1 | 30.8 | 45.1 | 38.3 | 43.5 | 43.2 | 56.1 | 39.1 | 42.6 | 52.4 | 61.0 | 59.2 | 62.9 |
| SE | 44.5 | 73.7 | 70.8 | 71.3 | 18.6 | 37.1 | 44.2 | 43.2 | 43.9 | 66.0 | 64.4 | 63.2 | 76.6 | 85.4 | 84.4 | 73.9 | 95.2 | 96.3 | 95.6 | 96.2 |
| SS | 47.0 | 59.5 | 67.1 | 75.7 | 21.2 | 28.2 | 35.3 | 44.7 | 48.4 | 55.8 | 56.9 | 67.8 | 67.4 | 76.0 | 79.5 | 77.3 | 96.0 | 96.5 | 96.8 | 97.8 |
| SW | 74.6 | 76.2 | 72.5 | 81.8 | 34.5 | 31.4 | 46.4 | 43.5 | 67.3 | 80.7 | 71.2 | 77.9 | 77.3 | 87.4 | 85.9 | 89.8 | 94.1 | 93.4 | 92.2 | 92.9 |

*Source*: Authors' calculations based on the 1999, 2003, 2008, and 2013 Nigeria DHS

**Table 13.2.** Households not deprived, by alternative water and sanitation welfare indicator and year (per cent)

| Area | Piped Water | | | | Protected Wells | | | | Flush Toilet | | | | Covered Latrines | | | | Any Latrine | | | |
|---|---|---|---|---|---|---|---|---|---|---|---|---|---|---|---|---|---|---|---|---|
| | 1999 | 2003 | 2008 | 2013 | 1999 | 2003 | 2008 | 2013 | 1999 | 2003 | 2008 | 2013 | 1999 | 2003 | 2008 | 2013 | 1999 | 2003 | 2008 | 2013 |
| National | 24.1 | 16.3 | 10.3 | 9.6 | na | 39.6 | 55.0 | 61.2 | 12.2 | 12.9 | 16.2 | 19.3 | na | na | 53.5 | 53.1 | 73.3 | 75.4 | 67.3 | 69.1 |
| Rural | 13.2 | 8.0 | 5.2 | 5.5 | na | 28.1 | 44.1 | 48.0 | 3.8 | 5.6 | 5.8 | 6.4 | na | na | 41.8 | 38.7 | 67.4 | 67.5 | 57.8 | 60.2 |
| Urban | 50.7 | 32.6 | 20.7 | 15.8 | na | 62.4 | 77.5 | 83.1 | 32.5 | 27.2 | 37.5 | 38.8 | na | na | 77.3 | 76.7 | 87.7 | 91.1 | 86.6 | 83.7 |
| NC | 24.5 | 13.0 | 9.6 | 8.7 | na | 29.0 | 47.7 | 54.5 | 8.7 | 8.6 | 12.6 | 16.6 | na | na | 38.3 | 37.3 | 64.6 | 61.3 | 44.3 | 42.9 |
| NE | 23.8 | 13.7 | 5.5 | 7.3 | na | 22.6 | 32.6 | 48.9 | 7.9 | 4.6 | 1.7 | 7.5 | na | na | 34.3 | 45.3 | 71.8 | 81.8 | 65.4 | 73.0 |
| NW | 21.8 | 21.5 | 12.4 | 10.4 | na | 35.9 | 50.4 | 57.4 | 3.6 | 4.2 | 4.8 | 5.3 | na | na | 62.1 | 59.9 | 87.9 | 82.6 | 82.5 | 85.0 |
| SE | 14.9 | 18.5 | 4.3 | 5.7 | na | 69.0 | 68.8 | 70.5 | 16.2 | 36.4 | 25.1 | 32.0 | na | na | 64.7 | 57.2 | 76.4 | 79.0 | 77.1 | 64.8 |
| SS | 22.9 | 7.7 | 10.9 | 10.4 | na | 51.7 | 59.8 | 69.9 | 16.0 | 20.7 | 26.4 | 35.6 | na | na | 54.3 | 55.1 | 75.9 | 71.7 | 64.8 | 66.2 |
| SW | 32.8 | 23.6 | 14.3 | 13.2 | na | 53.7 | 70.4 | 78.5 | 23.1 | 26.0 | 31.2 | 41.6 | na | na | 59.4 | 59.3 | 60.6 | 70.0 | 61.6 | 62.2 |

*Source*: Authors' calculations based on the 1999, 2003, 2008, and 2013 Nigeria DHS

FOD water indicator, *any well* over the same time range. Access to flush toilets steadily improved, while the more relevant indicator, *covered latrines*, stagnated or declined between 2008 and 2013—again, a pattern similar to the default *VIP latrine* indicator across these years. Discouragingly, access to *any latrine* declined in nearly every area, including urban areas, and in some cases quite substantially.

Overall, southern zones outperform northern zones in the default FOD indicators (Table 13.1), though a few exceptions involving the North West zone stand out. North West zone has the highest average water welfare level in all years with 90.8 per cent of the population not deprived in water in 2013. This compares to 87.8 per cent in urban areas and 81.8 per cent in the next-best-performing zone, South West. Similarly, in 2008 and 2013 North West outperforms all zones in sanitation. These results are quite surprising given that the North West zone was one of the two poorest zones in terms of monetary poverty throughout the study period (NBS 2009, 2012). Turning to the alternative water and sanitation indicators (Table 13.2), North West's superior water performance does not hold up with either of the alternative water thresholds. However, North West's high sanitation performance does indeed remain with the *covered latrine* and *any latrine* indicators.

In order to gain greater understanding as to whether North West's relatively high sanitation performance is a robust outcome, applying the same definitions, we cross-check the sanitation indicators with the 2011 MICS data. In contrast to the DHS outcomes, the MICS data indicate that North West is outperformed by all southern zones using the default *VIP* indicator and the *covered latrine* indicator (NBS 2011). However, the 2011 MICS supports the finding that North West outperformed all zones in the *any latrine* indicator with 82 per cent of households in North West zone not deprived in sanitation compared to 76 per cent, 68 per cent, and 71 per cent in South East, South South, and South West zones, respectively (NBS 2011). In essence, both the MICS and the DHS report that fewer households in North West have no sanitation facility/open defecation than any other zone. Unfortunately, the inconsistency in the *VIP* and *covered latrines* indicator casts doubt on the validity of the sanitation data, and, consequently, results must be interpreted accordingly.

### 13.3.2 *Temporal FOD Results*

Examining average indicator gains and losses is a useful exercise. However, FOD analysis provides a more stringent measure of welfare advancement than can be gleaned from indicator averages. FOD domination requires improvements to be occurring throughout each population in every indicator. Thus, while the measure is quite strict and often results in indeterminate outcomes, a dominant outcome is robust.

**Table 13.3.** Temporal net FOD comparisons (probabilities)

| Area | 2003 FOD 1999 | 2008 FOD 1999 | 2008 FOD 2003 | 2013 FOD 1999 | 2013 FOD 2003 | 2013 FOD 2008 |
|---|---|---|---|---|---|---|
| National | 0.01 | 0.09 | | 0.04 | 0.01 | |
| Rural | 0.01 | 0.01 | | | | −0.01 |
| Urban | **−0.40** | | **0.40** | 0.01 | 0.04 | |
| NC | −0.06 | | | | | 0.09 |
| NE | 0.01 | | | 0.11 | 0.01 | 0.18 |
| NW | 0.02 | 0.02 | | 0.15 | | |
| SE | **0.45** | **0.47** | 0.05 | 0.20 | −0.08 | −0.03 |
| SS | **0.39** | **0.70** | 0.25 | **0.92** | **0.55** | 0.14 |
| SW | 0.04 | 0.03 | | 0.28 | 0.20 | 0.15 |

*Note*: Values in bold indicate domination in the static case (FOD without bootstrapping).
*Source*: Authors' calculations based on the 1999, 2003, 2008, and 2013 Nigeria DHS

Table 13.3 presents temporal net FOD results, which measure the likelihood an area advances between two time periods minus any probability of regression. Table values report the average outcome over one hundred bootstrap iterations, which can be interpreted as probabilities of advancement. Values in bold indicate net domination prior to bootstrapping, i.e. the static case.

Consistent with a lack of progress across all indicators, FOD comparisons do not suggest that the nation or rural areas have attained welfare gains or losses over the fourteen-year study period. Both static and bootstrap FOD comparisons suggest that urban welfare deteriorated between 1999 and 2003, improved between 2003 and 2008, and stagnated between 2008 and 2013. Within the zones, only South East and South South exhibit strong evidence, in both the bootstrap and static comparisons, of achieving welfare gains. Furthermore, South South is the only area likely to have improved between 1999 and 2013, with a probability of 92 per cent. The North East, North West, and South West zones have weak probabilities of gains in at least one period.

FOD comparisons in the South South zone illustrate the strength of a dominant outcome. Though average welfare in every indicator improves in each time period between 1999 and 2013, static net FOD gains are not registered between 2003 and 2008 or between 2008 and 2013. This failure to dominate in the static case indicates that though welfare improved on average, the improvements were not sufficiently distributed throughout the population to meet the FOD criterion.

### 13.3.3 *Temporal Sensitivity Analysis*

This section tests the sensitivity of FOD temporal results to the choice of water and sanitation indicator thresholds (Table 13.4). This exercise is motivated by data restrictions in defining the indicators, questionably high gains in the

**Table 13.4.** Temporal net FOD comparisons with alternative water and sanitation welfare indicator (probabilities)

| | Piped/Flush | | | | | | Protected wells/Covered latrines | Any well/Any latrine | | | | | |
| --- | --- | --- | --- | --- | --- | --- | --- | --- | --- | --- | --- | --- | --- |
| | 2003 FOD 1999 | 2008 FOD 1999 | 2008 FOD 2003 | 2013 FOD 1999 | 2013 FOD 2003 | 2013 FOD 2008 | 2013 FOD 2008 | 2003 FOD 1999 | 2008 FOD 1999 | 2008 FOD 2003 | 2013 FOD 1999 | 2013 FOD 2003 | 2013 FOD 2008 |
| National | | | −0.01 | | | | | 0.03 | | | | | 0.01 |
| Rural | −0.01 | −0.04 | −0.16 | −0.01 | −0.14 | | −0.01 | 0.04 | | −0.02 | | | |
| Urban | −**0.36** | | | | | −0.02 | | −0.01 | | | | | |
| NC | −0.07 | −0.02 | −0.02 | | | 0.15 | 0.10 | −0.05 | −**0.41** | −0.02 | −0.13 | | 0.11 |
| NE | 0.01 | −0.09 | −**0.59** | | 0.02 | 0.18 | 0.31 | 0.06 | −0.06 | −0.10 | 0.01 | | 0.18 |
| NW | 0.23 | −0.01 | −0.22 | | −0.02 | 0.02 | 0.02 | | −0.02 | −0.06 | 0.02 | −0.01 | **0.30** |
| SE | **0.31** | | −0.28 | | −0.21 | | −0.07 | 0.23 | 0.19 | −0.04 | | −0.19 | −0.07 |
| SS | −0.01 | | **0.28** | 0.01 | 0.35 | 0.01 | 0.20 | 0.05 | | −0.01 | 0.02 | 0.07 | 0.09 |
| SW | | | −0.09 | | | 0.25 | 0.22 | 0.17 | 0.03 | −**0.36** | 0.12 | −0.02 | **0.31** |

*Note*: Values in bold indicate domination in the static case (FOD without bootstrapping).

*Source*: Authors' calculations based on the 1999, 2003, 2008, and 2013 Nigeria DHS

sanitation indicator between 2003 and 2008, unexpectedly high welfare in the North West zone, and sensitivity of average welfare to indicator thresholds.

Changing the water and sanitation thresholds to *protected wells* and *covered latrines*, respectively, for the limited period for which data are available (2008 and 2013), FOD outcomes are similar to those with the default indicators (Table 13.3). However, now North East, South South, and South West have probabilities greater than 20 per cent of advancing. Lowering the sanitation threshold further to include *any latrine* and reverting to the original water indicator encompassing *any well*, temporal patterns are quite different. Now urban areas and South South are no longer likely to have advanced in any period and evidence of advancement and decline is isolated. Finally, increasing the water and sanitation thresholds to *piped water* and *flush toilets* produces fewer cases of domination, though more evidence of regression. The decline in urban areas (1999–2003) and advancements in South East (1999–2003) and South South (2003–8, 2003–13) are consistent with the default indicators.

### 13.3.4 *Spatial FOD Results*

Tables 13.5–13.8 present the results of spatial FOD comparisons. Table values display the probability that row areas dominate column areas. Row averages indicate the probabilities that row areas dominate all other areas and column averages indicate the probabilities that all other areas dominate column areas. In other words, relatively large row or column averages imply relatively better- or worse-performing areas.

In 1999, all domination in the static case and significant bootstrap probabilities of domination occur when rural areas are dominated or urban areas dominate. In 2003 zonal advantages and disadvantages emerge with nearly all

**Table 13.5.** 1999 Bootstrap spatial FOD comparisons (probabilities)

| Area | National | Rural | Urban | NC | NE | NW | SE | SS | SW | Avg. |
|---|---|---|---|---|---|---|---|---|---|---|
| National | | **1** | | | 0.03 | | | | | 0.13 |
| Rural | | | | | | | | | | 0.00 |
| Urban | 1 | 1 | | **0.85** | 1 | **0.59** | | | | 0.56 |
| NC | 0.02 | **0.63** | | | 0.04 | | | | | 0.09 |
| NE | | | | | | | | | | 0.00 |
| NW | | | | | | | | | | 0.00 |
| SE | | | | | | | | 0.01 | | 0.00 |
| SS | | 0.03 | | 0.01 | | | | | | 0.01 |
| SW | 0.25 | **0.81** | | 0.11 | 0.28 | 0.01 | 0.02 | 0.04 | | 0.19 |
| Average | 0.16 | 0.43 | 0.00 | 0.12 | 0.17 | 0.08 | 0.00 | 0.01 | 0.00 | 0.11 |

*Note:* Values in bold indicate domination in the static case (FOD without bootstrapping). A '1' in the bootstrap FOD comparisons indicates that the row (column) province dominates (is dominated by) the column provinces 100 per cent of the time. An empty cell indicates that the FOD comparison of the row and column provinces is always indeterminate.
*Source:* Authors' calculations based on the 1999 Nigeria DHS

**Table 13.6.** 2003 Bootstrap spatial FOD comparisons (probabilities)

| Area | National | Rural | Urban | NC | NE | NW | SE | SS | SW | Avg. |
|---|---|---|---|---|---|---|---|---|---|---|
| National | | **0.95** | | | 0.55 | | | | | 0.19 |
| Rural | | | | | 0.11 | | | | | 0.01 |
| Urban | **0.95** | **0.95** | | **0.52** | **1** | 0.15 | | | | 0.45 |
| NC | | | | | 0.02 | | | | | 0.00 |
| NE | | | | | | | | | | 0.00 |
| NW | | | | | 0.21 | | | | | 0.03 |
| SE | **0.65** | **0.86** | | **0.85** | **0.67** | | | 0.28 | | 0.41 |
| SS | 0.02 | 0.08 | | 0.33 | 0.1 | | | | | 0.07 |
| SW | **0.60** | **0.84** | | **0.54** | **0.85** | 0.04 | | | | 0.36 |
| Average | 0.28 | 0.46 | 0.00 | 0.28 | 0.44 | 0.02 | 0.00 | 0.04 | 0.00 | 0.17 |

*Note*: Values in bold indicate domination in the static case (FOD without bootstrapping). A '1' in the bootstrap FOD comparisons indicates that the row (column) province dominates (is dominated by) the column provinces 100 per cent of the time. An empty cell indicates that the FOD comparison of the row and column provinces is always indeterminate.

*Source*: Authors' calculations based on the 2003 Nigeria DHS

**Table 13.7.** 2008 Bootstrap spatial FOD comparisons

| Area | National | Rural | Urban | NC | NE | NW | SE | SS | SW | Avg. |
|---|---|---|---|---|---|---|---|---|---|---|
| National | | **1** | | | 0.71 | | | | | 0.21 |
| Rural | | | | | 0.09 | | | | | 0.01 |
| Urban | **1** | **1** | | **1** | **1** | 0.08 | | | **0.47** | 0.57 |
| NC | | | | | | | | | | 0.00 |
| NE | | | | | | | | | | 0.00 |
| NW | | | | | 0.65 | | | | | 0.08 |
| SE | 0.21 | **0.86** | | **0.97** | 0.46 | | | 0.01 | | 0.31 |
| SS | | 0.17 | | **0.74** | 0.09 | | | | | 0.13 |
| SW | 0.14 | **0.95** | | **0.98** | 0.59 | | | | | 0.33 |
| Average | 0.17 | 0.50 | 0.00 | 0.46 | 0.45 | 0.01 | 0.00 | 0.00 | 0.06 | 0.18 |

*Note*: A '1' in the bootstrap FOD comparisons indicates that the row (column) province dominates (is dominated by) the column provinces 100 per cent of the time. An empty cell indicates that the FOD comparison of the row and column provinces is always indeterminate.

*Source*: Authors' calculations based on the 2008 Nigeria DHS

domination resulting from urban areas, South East and South West dominating rural areas, North East, and North Central. Similar outcomes occur in 2008 and 2013 with increasing domination by South West and South South, and decreasing domination by South East. North West is only dominated in the static case or with substantial bootstrap probability in 1999 by urban areas. Though this outcome is not consistent with North West's relatively high poverty rate, it is consistent with its surprisingly high average welfare in sanitation and water. However, due to questions surrounding the sanitation data, this outcome should be interpreted with caution.

Turning to Table 13.8, we focus on the South South zone to illustrate the usefulness of bootstrap sampling in assessing the extent of domination. Using the static approach, South South dominates rural areas, North Central, and South East, yet we have no information as to whether South South dominates

**Table 13.8.** 2013 Bootstrap spatial FOD comparisons (probabilities)

| Area | National | Rural | Urban | NC | NE | NW | SE | SS | SW | Average |
|---|---|---|---|---|---|---|---|---|---|---|
| National | | **1** | | | 0.59 | | | | | 0.20 |
| Rural | | | | | | | | | | 0.00 |
| Urban | **1** | **1** | | **1** | **1** | 0.07 | | | | 0.51 |
| NC | | | | | | | | | | 0.00 |
| NE | | | | | | | | | | 0.00 |
| NW | | 0.01 | | | 0.13 | | | | | 0.02 |
| SE | | 0.2 | | **0.84** | 0.07 | | | | | 0.14 |
| SS | 0.05 | **0.69** | | 1 | 0.28 | | **0.24** | | | 0.28 |
| SW | **0.51** | **0.97** | | **0.95** | **0.73** | | | | | 0.40 |
| Average | 0.20 | 0.48 | 0.00 | 0.47 | 0.35 | 0.01 | 0.03 | 0.00 | 0.00 | 0.17 |

*Note*: A '1' in the bootstrap FOD comparisons indicates that the row (column) province dominates (is dominated by) the column provinces 100 per cent of the time. An empty cell indicates that the FOD comparison of the row and column provinces is always indeterminate.

*Source*: Authors' calculations based on the 2013 Nigeria DHS

each area with the same strength. Conducting FOD analysis on one hundred bootstrap samples reveals that South South dominates South East in twenty-four bootstrap samples, rural areas in fifty-nine samples, and North Central in every sample. As such, bootstrap sampling distinguishes between static results and establishes probabilities of domination, which provide an indication of quite varied degrees of domination.

### 13.3.5 *Spatial Sensitivity Analysis*

We continue our sensitivity analysis by employing the alternative water and sanitation indicators in spatial FOD comparisons. Table 13.9 presents 2013 net domination scores for the default indicators and for various combinations of alternative indicators. Net domination scores measure the extent to which an area dominates all other areas net any probability of being dominated (spatial FOD row averages minus column averages). Net domination scores in a sense summarize spatial FOD tables as well as provide a basis for ranking areas. Table 13.9 provides a fairly consistent pattern across all indicator combinations. In each case, urban areas are ranked first, rural areas are ranked at the bottom, and southern zones strongly outperform northern zones. The primary variation concerns the rankings of northern zones and the extent to which northern zones and the nation are dominated. For instance, North West, whose relative sanitation welfare is highly dependent on the choice of threshold, also exhibits net domination sensitivity to thresholds. North West has net domination scores close to zero for the *any well/VIP* and *any well/any latrine* thresholds. In contrast, the *piped/flush* and *protected well/covered latrine* thresholds produce net domination scores of −0.35 and −0.22, respectively,

**Table 13.9.** Areas ranked by net domination scores for various combinations of water and sanitation indicator thresholds, 2013

| Piped/flush | | | | Any well/VIP (default) | | | Protected wells/Covered latrines | | | Any well/Any latrine | | |
|---|---|---|---|---|---|---|---|---|---|---|---|---|
| Area | Net Dom. | Rank | 1999–2013 Change | Area | Net Dom. | 1999–2003 Change | Area | Net Dom. | 2008–13 Change | Area | Net Dom. | 1999–2013 Change |
| Urban | 0.62 | 1 | 0 | Urban | 0.51 | 0 | Urban | 0.63 | 0 | Urban | 0.50 | 0 |
| SW | 0.60 | 2 | 0 | SW | 0.40 | 0 | SW | 0.54 | −1 | SS | 0.23 | −2 |
| SS | 0.42 | 3 | 0 | SS | 0.28 | −1 | SS | 0.51 | −1 | SW | 0.20 | −2 |
| SE | 0.07 | 4 | 0 | SE | 0.11 | 1 | SE | 0.49 | 2 | SE | 0.11 | 1 |
| NC | −0.02 | 5 | 0 | NW | 0.01 | −2 | National | −0.20 | 0 | NW | 0.02 | −1 |
| National | −0.05 | 6 | 0 | National | 0.00 | 1 | NW | −0.22 | 0 | National | 0.00 | 4 |
| NW | −0.35 | 7 | −1 | NE | −0.35 | −1 | NC | −0.47 | 0 | NE | −0.14 | −1 |
| NE | −0.60 | 8 | 1 | NC | −0.47 | 2 | NE | −0.64 | −1 | Rural | −0.43 | −1 |
| Rural | −0.70 | 9 | 0 | Rural | −0.48 | 0 | Rural | −0.64 | 1 | NC | −0.48 | 2 |

*Note*: Rankings within shaded groups are highly sensitive to small perturbations and should be interpreted with caution.
*Source*: Authors' calculations based on the 1999, 2003, 2008, and 2013 Nigeria DHS

which are more in line with expectations based on monetary poverty. All in all, while overall spatial domination patterns are robust, specific figures and rankings should be interpreted with caution.

### 13.3.6 *State-Level FOD Results*

The 2008 and 2013 DHS surveys are stratified by state, allowing FOD comparisons to be made between Nigeria's thirty-six states and the Federal Capital Territory, Abuja. Maps provide a convenient method of displaying state-level results and have the advantage of highlighting regional trends. Figure 13.2 presents spatial FOD rankings derived from net domination scores where better rankings are represented by lighter shades. Based on consumption poverty figures, we would expect a dark band, representing the worst-ranked areas, to be present across the northern and central portions of the country. Rather, we find that states with the lowest welfare are most prevalent in eastern Nigeria, an area encompassing portions of North East, North Central, South South, and South East zones. As a whole, the southern band of the nation has the highest welfare. The relatively high rankings of the north-west states, particularly in 2008, suggest that unexpectedly high water and sanitation welfare in the North West zone is not dictated by a single state, but present throughout many north-west states.

Figure 13.3 presents the results of FOD comparisons using alternative water and sanitation indicator thresholds. FOD comparisons using the *piped/flush* water and sanitation indicators produce a welfare pattern more in line with monetary poverty figures with all states ranked in the bottom one third falling in northern zones and all states ranked in the top one third in southern zones, with the exception of Abuja (2008, 2013) and Kaduna (2008). The *protected wells/ covered latrines* combination also follows this pattern with the exception of Abuja, Cross River (2008), and Ebonyi. Recalling that the North West zone outperforms all other zones in the *any latrine* sanitation indicator, it is not surprising that the *any well/any latrine* FOD comparisons produce results similar to the default indicators, with higher deprivation concentrated in the east.

Figure 13.4 compares temporal changes to spatial rank changes using the default indicators. In both maps, lighter greys indicate higher probabilities of advancement. Note that in temporal comparisons, the lowest category (10 per cent to −10 per cent) essentially represents stagnation. No state has significant probability of regression. General trends are quite consistent across the maps, which indicates that areas that advanced between 2008 and 2013 also improved relative to other states. States with a probability of advancement greater than 50 per cent include Kwara, Osun, and Ekiti in the west and Adamawa in the north-east. Sensitivity results are not presented; however, these patterns are quite similar in the *covered/protected* and *any well/any latrine*

2008

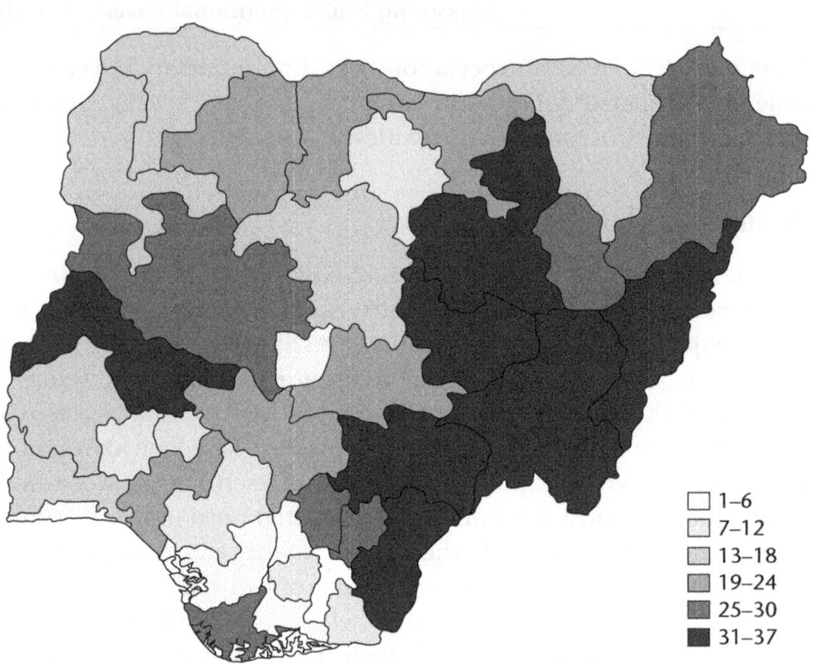


2013

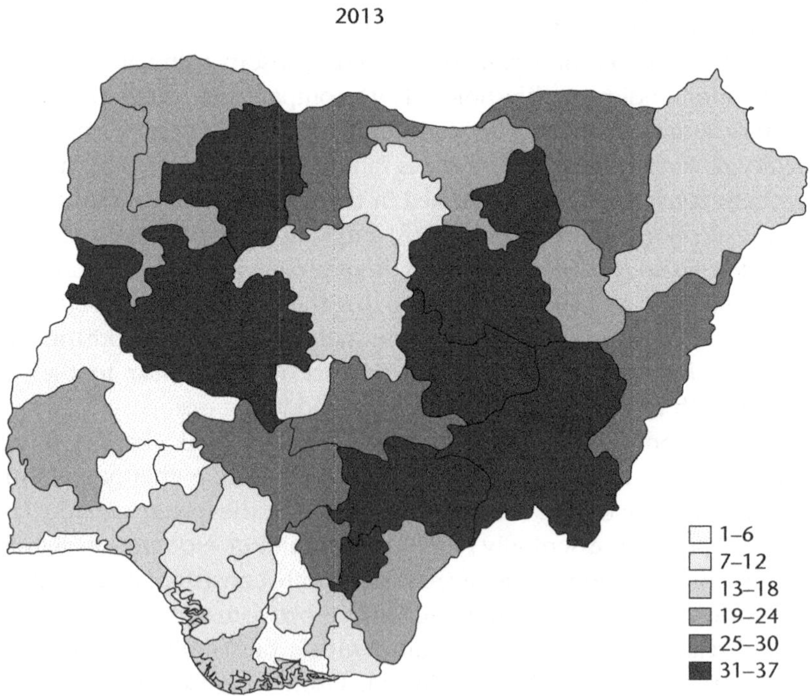


**Figure 13.2.** Spatial rankings by state

*Source*: Authors' calculations based on the 2008 and 2013 Nigeria DHS

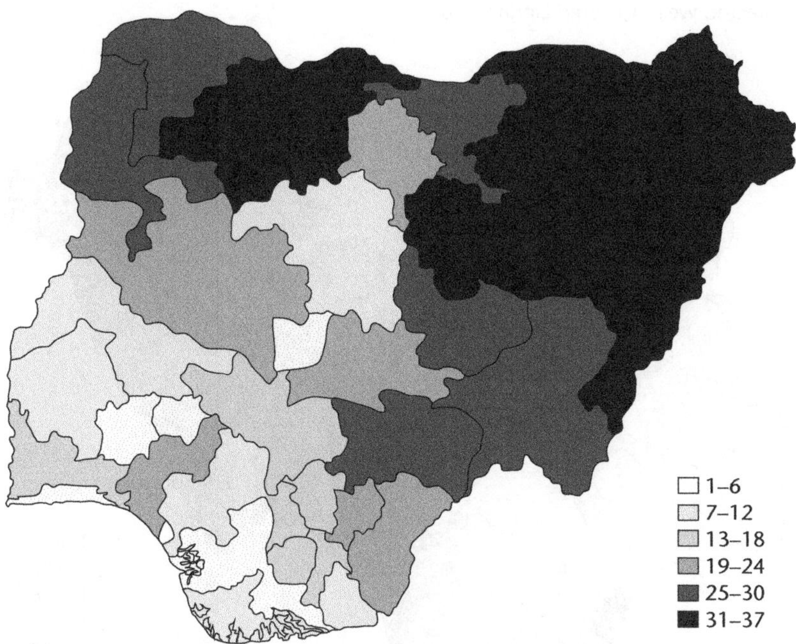



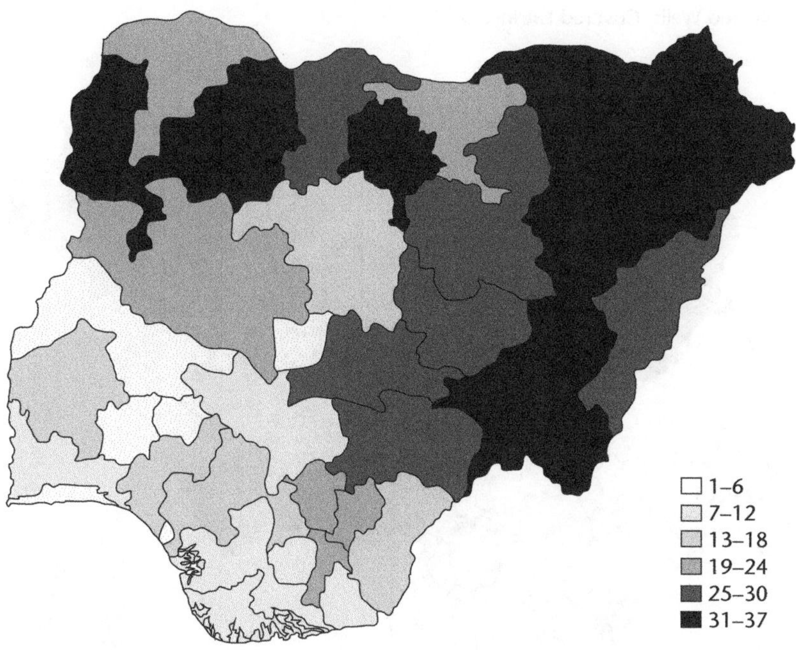



**Figure 13.3.** Sensitivity of spatial rankings to the water and sanitation indicators, by state

*Source*: Authors' calculations based on the 2008 and 2013 Nigeria DHS

Protected Wells, Covered Latrines, 2008

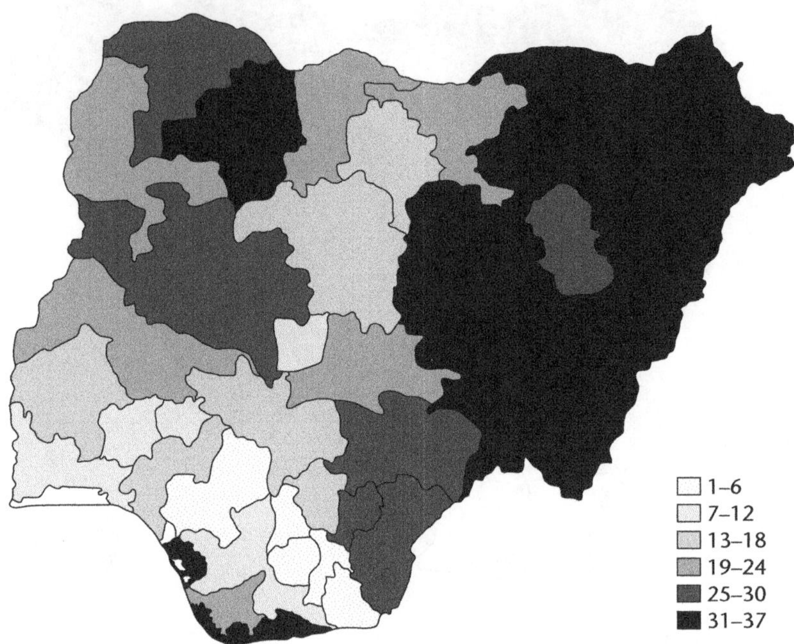


Protected Wells, Covered Latrines, 2013

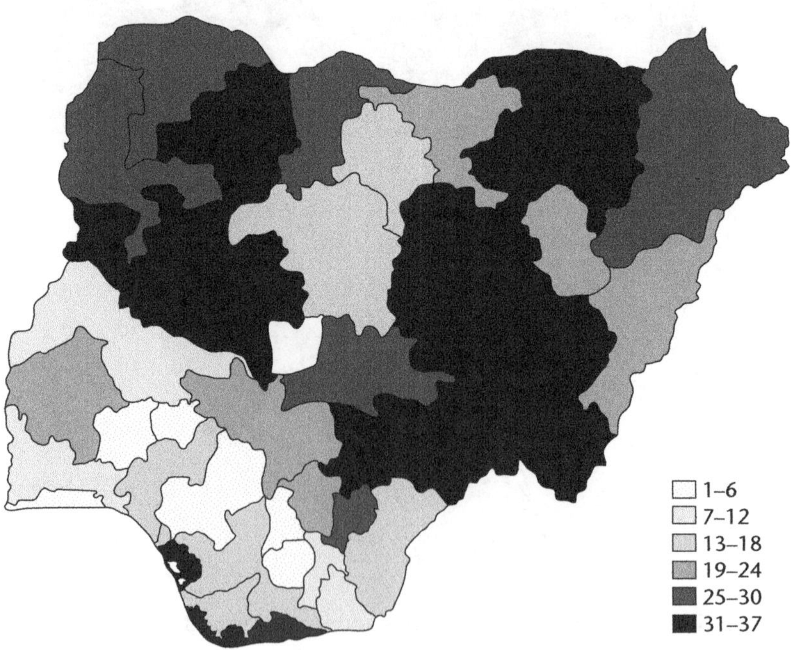


**Figure 13.3.** Continued

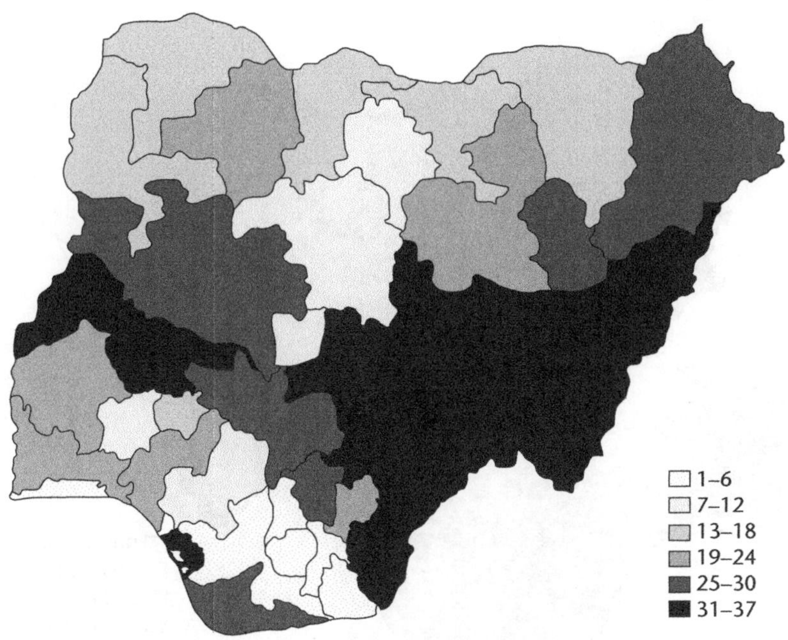




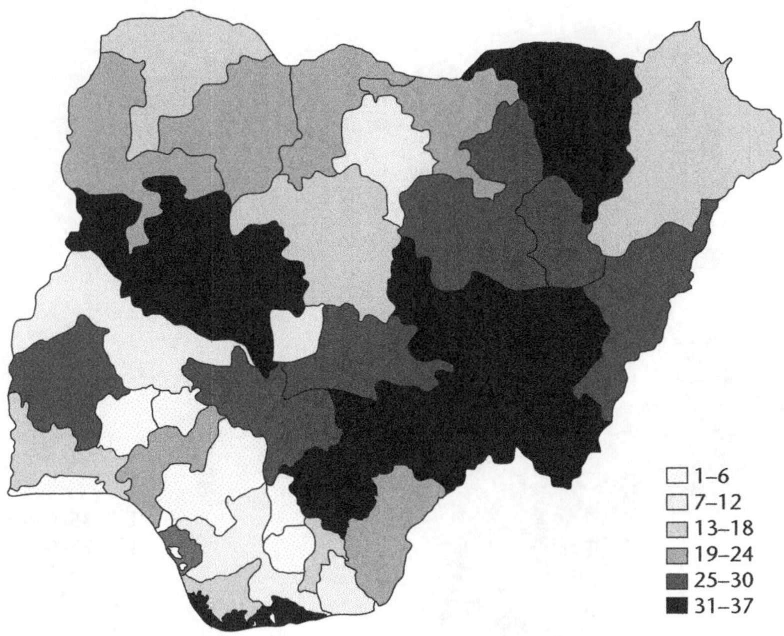


**Figure 13.3.** Continued

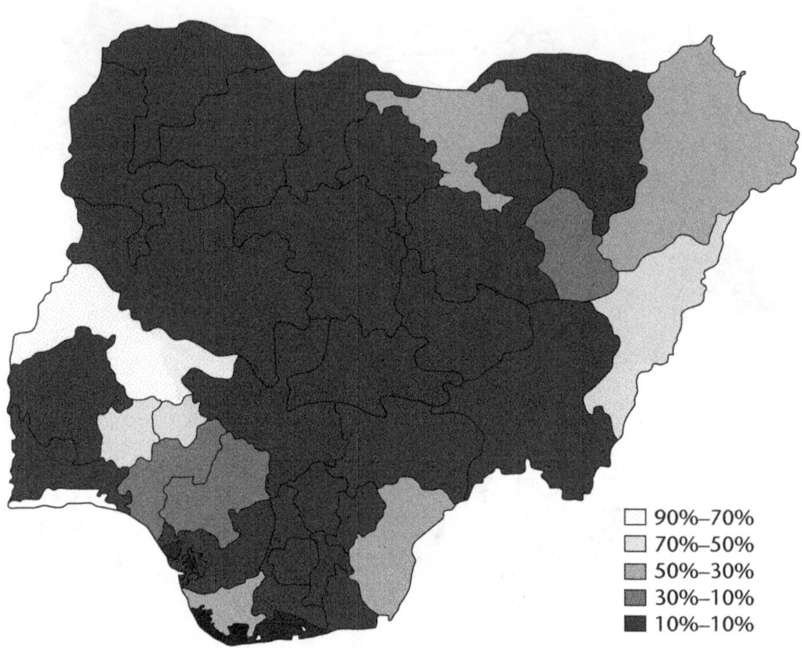



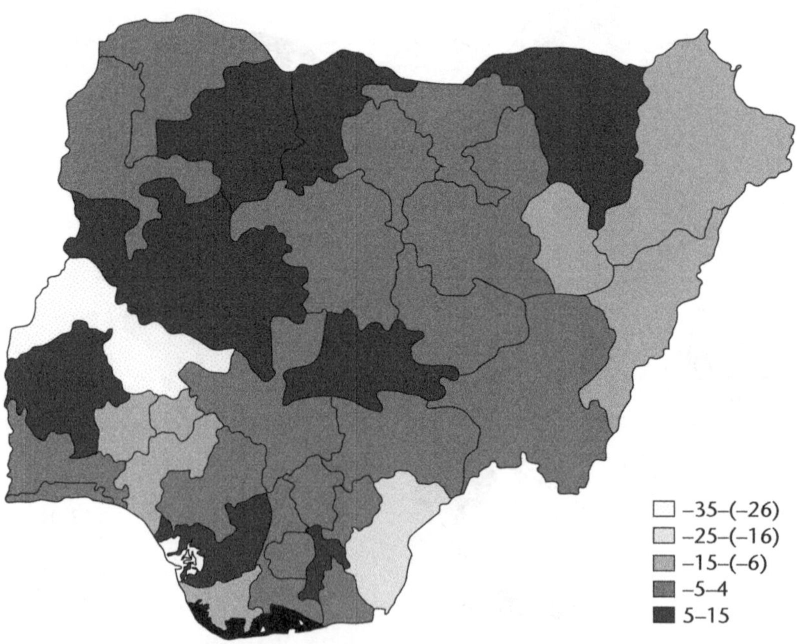



**Figure 13.4.** Temporal FOD change compared to spatial rank change by state, 2008–13

*Source*: Authors' calculations based on the 2008 and 2013 Nigeria DHS

comparisons, with the addition of Ogun and Borno showing greater likelihoods of advancing. FOD comparisons using the *piped/flush* thresholds indicate very little welfare advancement with only Lagos and Adamawa achieving probabilities of advancement greater than 50 per cent.


## 13.4 Conclusion

Despite recent high growth, trends in consumption poverty remain uncertain. This study set out to gain deeper insight into the evolution of Nigerian poverty between 1999 and 2013 by appraising multidimensional non-monetary poverty. Though the FOD approach produces a robust measure of broad-based multidimensional poverty, results may be sensitive to data issues and indicator choices. Motivated by data restrictions in defining the indicators, questionably high gains in the sanitation indicator between 2003 and 2008, unexpectedly high welfare in the North West zone, and sensitivity of average welfare to indicator thresholds, this chapter expanded upon the work of Ajakaiye et al. (2016) in its consideration of alternative water and sanitation indicators.

This analysis lends support to the view that poverty reduction in Nigeria has not kept pace with the rapid economic growth attained in the last decade. The distribution of positive economic performance has not translated to improvements in multidimensional welfare throughout the country over time. This conclusion is consistent with the lack of pro-poor growth observed by Ichoku et al. (2012). Nonetheless, a number of zones and states do display a positive probability of advancement over the study period, most notably the South South zone and Kwara, Osun, Ekiti, and Adamawa states. Sensitivity analysis also suggests the possibility of advancement in Borno, Lagos, and Ogun. While the evolution of state-level welfare using the MDG-inspired water and sanitation indicators (*protected wells/covered latrines*) and the lower thresholds (*any well/any latrine*) do not differ substantially from the default indicators, welfare dynamics are sensitive to the higher deprivation thresholds (*piped/ flush*). Nevertheless, the high degree of stagnation in welfare is the primary insight to be gleaned in every scenario.

The analysis further indicates that regional inequalities remain profound, with large disparities between the urban and rural sectors as well as between the southern and northern geopolitical zones of the country. However, the extent of domination over northern zones is sensitive to indicator choices. State trends reveal greater sensitivity to the water and sanitation indicators, with deprivation concentrated in either the north (*piped/flush* and *protected wells/covered latrines*) or the east (*any well/VIP latrine* or *any well/any latrine*). While specific state and zonal outcomes should be interpreted with a high degree of caution, the overall conclusion of limited welfare gains and vast regional disparities appears to be robust.

# References

Ajakaiye, O., A. Jerome, O. Olaniyan, K. Mahrt, and O. Alaba (2016). 'Spatial and Temporal Multidimensional Poverty in Nigeria', in C. Arndt, A. McKay, and F. Tarp (eds), *Growth and Poverty in Sub-Saharan Africa*. Oxford: Oxford University Press, 218–37.

Arndt, C., R. Distante, M. A. Hussain, L. P. Østerdal, P. Huong, and M. Ibraimo (2012). 'Ordinal Welfare Comparisons with Multiple Discrete Indicators: A First Order Dominance Approach and Application to Child Poverty', *World Development*, 40(11): 2290–301.

Ichoku, H. E., C. Agu, and J. E. Ataguba (2012). 'What Do We Know about Pro-Poor Growth and Regional Poverty in Nigeria?', *International Journal of Economic Sciences and Applied Research*, 5(3): 147–72.

IMF (International Monetary Fund) (2013). 'Nigeria: 2012 Article IV Consultation', Country Report 13/116. Washington, DC: IMF.

NBS (National Bureau of Statistics) (2007). 'Nigeria Multiple Indicator Cluster Survey 2007 Final Report'. Abuja, Nigeria: National Bureau of Statistics.

NBS (National Bureau of Statistics) (2009). 'Annual Abstract of Statistics'. Abuja, Nigeria: National Bureau of Statistics.

NBS (National Bureau of Statistics) (2011). 'Nigeria Multiple Indicator Cluster Survey 2011 Main Report'. Abuja, Nigeria: National Bureau of Statistics.

NBS (National Bureau of Statistics) (2012). 'Nigeria Poverty Profile 2010'. Abuja, Nigeria: National Bureau of Statistics.

NPC (National Population Commission) and ICF International (2014). 'Nigeria Demographic and Health Survey 2013'. Abuja, Nigeria and Rockville, MD: National Population Commission and ICF International.

NPC (National Population Commission) and ICF Macro (2009). 'Nigeria Demographic and Health Survey, 2008'. Abuja, Nigeria: National Population Commission and ICF Macro.

NPC (National Population Commission) and ORC Macro (1999). 'Nigeria Demographic and Health Survey, 1999'. Calverton, MD: National Population Commission and ORC Macro.

NPC (National Population Commission) and ORC Macro (2004). 'Nigeria Demographic and Health Survey, 2003'. Calverton, MD: National Population Commission and ORC Macro.

WHO/UNICEF Joint Monitoring Programme (JMP) for Water Supply and Sanitation (2015). 'Improved and Unimproved Water Sources and Sanitation Facilities', available at <www.wssinfo.org/definitions-methods/watsan-categories>.

World Bank (2014). 'Nigeria: Economic Report, No. 2'. Washington, DC: World Bank.

# 14

# Multidimensional Assessment of Child Welfare for Tanzania

*Channing Arndt, Vincent Leyaro, Kristi Mahrt, and Finn Tarp*

## 14.1 Introduction

Identifying trends in living standards in Tanzania has been a subject of considerable interest. Analysis of a household budget survey conducted in 2007 revealed consumption poverty rates approximately similar to the rates calculated from a comparable survey conducted in 2001 (Government of Tanzania 2009). This stagnation in consumption poverty occurred despite relatively high published rates of economic growth over the same period and little change in measured inequality. Price inflation over the same period as measured by the household budget survey also differed drastically from inflation rates derived from the published consumer price index (CPI) and the GDP deflator (Adam et al. 2012). The growth–poverty–inequality conundrum alongside the wide divergences in measured inflation provoked a great deal of analysis.[1]

More recently, the World Bank (2015) published a poverty assessment based on a household budget survey conducted in 2011/12. This recent assessment focused heavily on comparisons of the results from 2011/12 with the data available from the 2007 survey and found a reduction in consumption poverty of about six percentage points. In the companion volume to this book, Arndt et al. (2016a) draw upon this and other analyses to assess growth and poverty for Tanzania, and Arndt et al. (2017) conduct a macroeconomic assessment of the growth–poverty relationship using a structural model.

---

[1] Examples include Atkinson and Lugo (2010); Demombynes and Hoogeveen (2007); Hoogeveen and Ruhinduka (2009); Kessy et al. (2013); Mashindano et al. (2011); Mkenda et al. (2010); Osberg and Bandara (2012); and World Bank (2007, 2012, 2013).

They find that the six percentage point reduction in poverty from 2007 to 2011/12 lies at the optimistic end of a reasonable range.

The assessment of consumption poverty trends in Tanzania over this most recent period (2007–11/12) has been substantially complicated by changes in the data collection methods employed in 2011/12 compared with all earlier surveys. In their poverty assessment, the World Bank (2015) also took the opportunity to apply a series of methodological changes to the computation of the nominal consumption aggregate and the poverty lines. These differentials rendered the analyses of the 2011/12 survey non-comparable with published analyses from 2007 and earlier. In order to account for these differences, the World Bank (2015) took a series of steps to revise 2007 data and calculations.

The revisions to the 2007 data were considerable. World Bank (2015: 2) reports that 'consumption per adult rose by almost one-third'. The poverty line was also adjusted upward substantially, leaving the measured poverty rate at the national level essentially at the same value as reported in previously published assessments. Nevertheless, the issue of achieving comparability in data and methods clearly dominates any analysis of consumption poverty trends over the 2007 to 2011/12 period.

Rather than enter this fray, the work presented here seeks to analyse welfare trends from a multidimensional perspective, relying on data from four Demographic and Health Surveys conducted over the period 1991/2 to 2010. The chapter is structured as follows. Section 14.2 provides a brief review of multidimensional poverty measures. Both the first-order dominance (FOD) method and the Alkire–Foster (AF) approach are considered. Section 14.3 presents the datasets employed and the choices made to derive a set of comparable indicators. Section 14.4 presents results, including a comparison across the FOD and AF approaches. A final section concludes by highlighting the need for a collection of poverty tools to fully capture the complex nature of poverty dynamics.

## 14.2 Multidimensional Poverty Measurement

### 14.2.1 First-Order Dominance

The FOD methodology and implementation are described in detail in Chapters 3 and 4. They highlight that FOD analysis is an approach to comparing populations using multiple, binary welfare indicators without imposing weighting schemes or making assumptions about preferences for each indicator. Briefly, multidimensional welfare comparisons are based on the simple criterion that it is better to be not deprived than deprived in any indicator. FOD comparisons of population A and B result in one of three outcomes: population A dominates population B; population B dominates population A; dominance is indeterminate. Indeterminate outcomes occur when two populations are too similar or too different for definitive comparisons to be made (without further information or assumptions). For example, when comparing two individuals using three binary indicators with outcomes (0,1,0) and (1,0,1), dominance cannot be established because we do not assume it is better to be not deprived in any given dimension. The same logic can be extended to populations.[2]

Dominant outcomes are binary and thus provide no information about the extent of domination. To mitigate this shortcoming, we draw bootstrap samples from the surveys considered and conduct FOD analysis for each sample.[3] The share of dominant outcomes for each pair of populations across all bootstrap samples can be interpreted as a probability of domination. Thus, while the welfare indicators are ordinal in nature, the application of bootstrap sampling produces probabilities of one population performing better than another. Probability of net domination across all bootstraps is used to rank areas. The probability of net spatial domination of area $i$ is defined as the sum of the probability that $i$ dominates each other area minus the sum of the probability that each other area dominates $i$. This probability of net spatial domination can be linearly transformed into an index that falls in the interval $[-1,1]$ where higher values indicate that an area is better off. Analogously, bootstrap samples can be employed to calculate temporal net domination of a given area in time period $t$ relative to time period $s$.

### 14.2.2 Alkire–Foster Approach

Next, we consider an alternative approach to multidimensional analysis, the Alkire–Foster (AF) approach developed by Alkire and Foster (2007). The method is well known for its application to the Multidimensional Poverty Index of the United Nations Development Programme (UNDP) which assesses welfare in over one hundred countries (see for example, Alkire and Santos 2010). This section provides a brief overview of the methodology. Alkire et al. (2015) provide a recent and comprehensive discussion of an array of multidimensional poverty measures.

The AF approach to multidimensional analysis aggregates information obtained from a set of binary welfare indicators into a single index that captures both the incidence and intensity of multidimensional poverty. The process of defining this index can be described in two steps: identification and

---

[2] See Chapter 11 for a discussion of indeterminate outcomes.
[3] Bootstrap sampling follows the same stratified cluster sample design used in the DHS sampling. Samples are drawn with replacement.

aggregation. Identification is achieved in what Alkire and Foster (2007) refer to as a dual cut-off method. First, as with FOD, the approach begins with a set of binary welfare indicators, where in each dimension an individual is deemed to be deprived or not deprived according to a dimension-specific threshold. Second, an across dimension cut-off must be specified to distinguish the poor from the non-poor. In this context, the cut-off ($k$) identifies the poor as those with a weighted deprivation count greater than a cutoff level $k$. This provides a poverty headcount ($H$). When weights are equal across dimensions, $k$ can be expressed as a number of dimensions such that individuals who are poor in $k$ or more dimensions are considered poor.

Identification of the poor (via $H$) provides no information about the intensity of poverty. If an individual with a weighted deprivation count greater than $k$ (i.e. one who is defined as poor in the multidimensional sense) becomes poor in an additional dimension, the multidimensional headcount ratio would not reflect this increase in the intensity of poverty. Therefore, an additional aspect of poverty is introduced to reflect the intensity of poverty. Intensity is measured by the average weighted deprivation count among those who are identified as poor. The final AF poverty index is referred to as the adjusted headcount ratio ($M_0$) and is expressed as the product of the multidimensional headcount ratio ($H$) and the average deprivation count among the poor ($A$),

$$M_0 = HA$$

Thus, a change in $M_0$ cannot be understood without considering both $H$ and $A$. Though the method is sensitive to thresholds within and across dimensions as well as dimensional weights, the adjusted headcount ratio is simple to compute and convenient for comparisons across time and space.

### 14.2.3 *Comparison of the FOD and AF Approaches*

Two important differences between the FOD and AF methodologies could lead to dissimilar results. First, FOD results use information from the full distribution of outcomes whereas $M_0$ is the product of two averages: $H$ and $A$. For FOD, indeterminacy may result between two populations B and C when B outperforms C for all but a small segment of population B. In the same situation, AF is likely to clearly establish that population B outperforms C. Second, the use of weights allows the AF method to result in clear outcomes that may be indeterminate with FOD. As noted, because no assumptions are made about the relative importance of each dimension, FOD dominance cannot be established between pairs of welfare outcomes such as (0,1,0) and (1,0,1). However, with the AF method, the comparison is dependent upon how weights are assigned. For instance, with equal weighting the second pair is clearly superior to the first. On the other hand, with a weighting scheme (0.2, 0.6, 0.2) the first outcome is associated with greater welfare.

Results derived from FOD rely on few assumptions and strict criteria for establishing dominance. Thus, when dominance is established, the result is quite robust. AF, on the other hand, applies a weighting scheme and cut-off levels that may influence results. Despite this potential for different conclusions, in a comparison across thirty-eight countries Permanyer and Hussain (2015) find that the methodologies align closely with a correlation coefficient of 0.95. Arndt et al. (2016b) similarly find high correlations using census data for Mozambique. For these analyses, the indicators and thresholds determining deprived and not deprived in each dimension, which both FOD and AF are obliged to specify, were the same.

## 14.3 Data and Indicators

In this analysis, data from four Tanzania Demographic and Health Surveys (TDHS) are used to define five binary welfare indicators that allow multidimensional welfare to be estimated using both the FOD and AF methodologies in two subpopulations of children.

### 14.3.1 *Demographic and Health Survey*

The 1991/2, 1996, 2004/5, and 2010 TDHS provide the data used in this analysis (National Bureau of Statistics and Macro 1993, 1997, 2005, 2011). The TDHS aims to provide estimates for the entire country, for urban and rural areas, and regions. The 1991/2 and 1996 TDHS samples were drawn in a three-stage design, with the goal of selecting 500 households each in Dar es Salaam and Zanzibar, and 300 households in the remaining regions. Using the 1988 census sampling frame, 357 enumeration areas (EAs) were first selected from wards/branches and then within wards/branches such that rural and urban EAs were selected proportionally within each region. In the third sampling stage, households were selected from complete household listings in each EA. The sampling design for the 2004/5 and 2010 TDHS involved two stages where in the first stage 475 clusters were selected from a list of EAs based on the 2002 census with eighteen clusters selected in each region except Dar es Salaam where twenty-five clusters were selected. In the second stage, households were then systematically selected from complete household listings in each EA.

From this micro data, we capture the non-monetary multidimensional nature of poverty by defining two population groups: school-age children at least seven and less than eighteen years old and young children less than five years old. The 7–17 sample includes 13,608, 11,472, 14,357, and 14,687 children and the under-five sample includes 7287, 6080, 7461, and 7526 children for 1991/2, 1996, 2004/5, and 2010, respectively. In each population group, children's welfare is examined over time and across regions. Spatial areas include the nation, urban/rural areas, and geographical zones. Larger sample sizes for the 7–17 population group also allow analysis of administrative regions.[4]

### 14.3.2 *Indicators*

For each population group we identify a set of five binary welfare indicators based on the Bristol Indicators (Gordon et al. 2003); the indicators are presented in Table 14.1.

Ideally, the sanitation threshold would be specified such that children using unimproved sanitation (e.g. uncovered latrines or no facilities) would be considered deprived. However, in 1992, 1996, and 2004 the TDHS does not distinguish between covered and uncovered latrines. In 2010, 73 per cent of school-age children used latrines and of these children 89 per cent used uncovered latrines. It is logical then to classify all latrines to be a deprivation. In section 14.4, we examine the sensitivity to the sanitation indicator choice by considering an alternative sanitation threshold where the use of any kind of latrine is not deemed to be a deprivation.

Browsing household surveys, the possibilities of examining a rich variety of deprivations appear to be great. However, both the FOD and the AF methodologies require that all indicators be non-missing for every individual or household in the sample. Care must be taken in constructing indicators that apply to the full population being examined. For instance, immunization histories seem to provide a useful measure of the health of children under five. Yet, children under the age of one would not be fully immunized and therefore should not be deemed deprived based on incomplete immunization records. Consequently, the sample would need to be restricted to children aged one to five rather than zero to five.

Women's health indicators present similar difficulties. The Demographic and Health Surveys offer information on a wide range of family planning, fertility, and maternal health topics. However, these questions tend to be posed to a narrow range of women for whom these issues apply, and thus care must be taken to restrict the sample to the relevant population. For instance, maternal health issues would limit the population to not only

---

[4] The region of Manyara was created from Arusha in 2002. To maintain consistency throughout the survey, these regions are combined. To achieve minimum sample sizes, Pemba North and Pemba South are combined and Zanzibar North and Zanzibar South are combined into Zanzibar rural.

**Table 14.1.** Welfare indicators for children aged 7–17 and children aged 0–4

| Population | Indicator | Deprivation threshold |
| --- | --- | --- |
| Children aged 7–17 | Water | Water is not from a pipe, tap, or well. |
| | Sanitation | Sanitation facility is not a toilet or ventilated improved pit (VIP) latrine. |
| | Alternative sanitation | Sanitation facility is not a flush toilet or latrine of any kind. |
| | Housing | Floors are made of dirt, sand, dung, or planks. |
| | Education | The child has not completed at least primary school or is not in school. |
| | Information | The household does not have a radio or television. |
| Children aged 0–4 | Water | Water is not from a pipe, tap, or well. |
| | Sanitation | Sanitation facility is not a flush toilet or VIP latrine. |
| | Education | The child's mother has not completed at least primary school. |
| | Housing | Floors are made of dirt, sand, dung, or planks. |
| | Nutrition | The child is more than two standard deviations below the median of the reference population in at least one of the following anthropometric measures: weight for age, height for age, or weight for height. |
| | Delivery | The child was delivered at home. |

*Source*: Author's definitions

women of childbearing age, but also women who were pregnant in the recent past. Depending on sample sizes or analytical goals, necessary restrictions may render the inclusion of certain indicators impractical due to the concomitant restrictions on the sample.

### 14.3.3 *Descriptive Statistics*

Figure 14.1 presents mean deprivation trends for children aged 7–17 at the national and urban/rural level. Table 14.2 also reports deprivation at the zonal level for all indicators including the alternative sanitation indicator. Overall, Figure 14.1 exhibits positive signs of advancement in most indicators. School-age children make considerable progress in access to education and information with national deprivation in education reduced by more than half between 1992 and 2010. Similar trends are observed in rural and urban areas and in all zones.

Access to safe water follows the most variable pattern. Urban water deprivation is relatively low but increases over time from 9 to 14 per cent. While national and rural areas achieve gains over the entire period, welfare backslides somewhat between 2004 and 2010 to 29 per cent and 33 per cent, respectively. In the zones, only Western makes progress between each survey while Central, Eastern, and Southern Highlands deteriorate over the eighteen-year period.

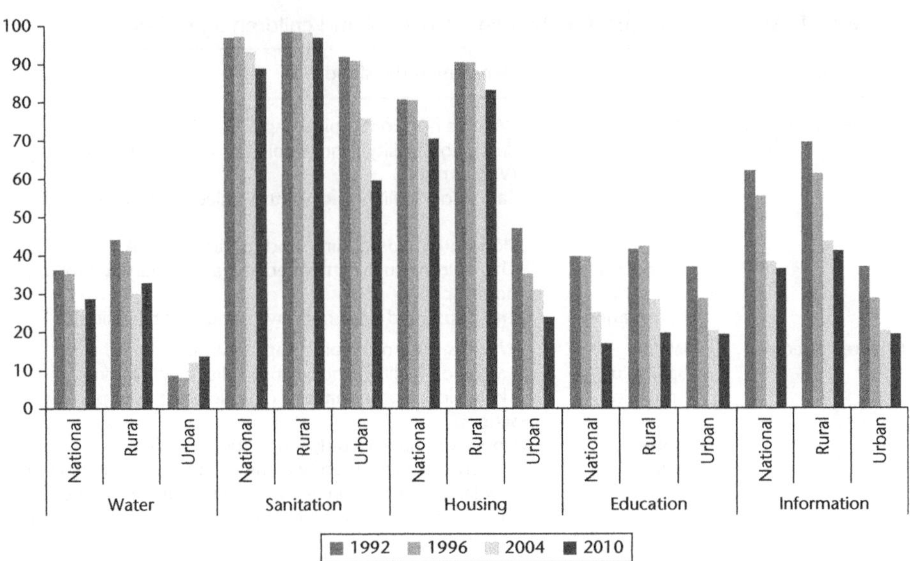



**Figure 14.1.** Children aged 7–17 deprived by welfare indicator (per cent)

*Source*: Authors' calculations based on the 1991/2, 1996, 2004/5, 2010 TDHS (National Bureau of Statistics and Macro 1993, 1997, 2005, 2011)

Urban areas progressed in terms of the housing and the primary sanitation indicator. Though access to urban sanitation improved by thirty-two percentage points over the study period, deprivation remained high at 60 per cent. In contrast, rural areas achieved little gains in either indicator with deprivations in sanitation and housing of 97 per cent and 83 per cent in 2010. Within the zones, Zanzibar, and Eastern zone follow urban patterns while the remaining zones generally mirror rural areas.

The vast majority of the population uses covered or uncovered pit latrines (83 per cent in 1992 and 73 per cent in 2010). The primary sanitation indicator classifies children using any pit latrines as deprived while the alternative sanitation indicator shifts this large percentage of children to being not deprived. As a result, deprivation in the alternative sanitation indicator (children with no sanitation facility) is extremely low. In contrast to the primary sanitation indicator, the percentage of children deprived in the alternative indicator increased at the national, rural, and urban areas, with more substantial increases in Central, Southern Highlands, and Western zones. Zanzibar is the only area to significantly reduce alternative sanitation deprivation.

Table 14.3 presents mean deprivation levels for children under five. Deprivations in water, sanitation, and housing closely follow the levels and trends seen with school-age children. Deprivation in education for under-fives measures whether children's mothers have completed primary school. Though

**Table 14.2.** Children aged 7–17 deprived by welfare indicator (per cent)

| | Water | | | | Sanitation | | | | Alternative Sanitation | | | |
|---|---|---|---|---|---|---|---|---|---|---|---|---|
| | 1992 | 1996 | 2004 | 2010 | 1992 | 1996 | 2004 | 2010 | 1992 | 1996 | 2004 | 2010 |
| Nation | 36 | 35 | 26 | 29 | 97 | 97 | 93 | 89 | 13 | 13 | 13 | 16 |
| Rural | 44 | 41 | 30 | 33 | 98 | 99 | 98 | 97 | 17 | 16 | 17 | 20 |
| Urban | 9 | 8 | 12 | 14 | 92 | 91 | 76 | 60 | 1 | 1 | 3 | 3 |
| Central | 27 | 27 | 34 | 35 | 97 | 96 | 97 | 95 | 8 | 10 | 9 | 17 |
| Eastern | 14 | 16 | 15 | 22 | 96 | 94 | 84 | 78 | 3 | 5 | 2 | 2 |
| Lake | 50 | 36 | 41 | 28 | 97 | 100 | 93 | 87 | 20 | 19 | 18 | 21 |
| Northern | 42 | 50 | 24 | 39 | 97 | 97 | 92 | 91 | 13 | 21 | 12 | 18 |
| S. Highlands | 30 | 37 | 23 | 32 | 98 | 99 | 95 | 93 | 7 | 4 | 9 | 14 |
| Southern | 43 | 36 | 26 | 34 | 98 | 99 | 96 | 91 | 5 | 3 | 4 | 8 |
| Western | 43 | 41 | 23 | 22 | 96 | 96 | 98 | 93 | 17 | 12 | 23 | 24 |
| Zanzibar | 8 | 5 | 1 | 1 | 97 | 96 | 85 | 73 | 57 | 45 | 32 | 25 |

*Source*: Authors' calculations based on the 1991/2, 1996, 2004/5, 2010 TDHS (National Bureau of Statistics and Macro 1993, 1997, 2005, 2011)

| | Housing | | | | Education | | | | Information | | | |
|---|---|---|---|---|---|---|---|---|---|---|---|---|
| | 1992 | 1996 | 2004 | 2010 | 1992 | 1996 | 2004 | 2010 | 1992 | 1996 | 2004 | 2010 |
| Nation | 81 | 81 | 75 | 71 | 40 | 40 | 25 | 17 | 62 | 56 | 38 | 36 |
| Rural | 91 | 91 | 88 | 83 | 42 | 43 | 28 | 20 | 70 | 61 | 44 | 41 |
| Urban | 47 | 35 | 31 | 24 | 34 | 28 | 14 | 7 | 37 | 29 | 20 | 19 |
| Central | 87 | 85 | 84 | 87 | 44 | 41 | 29 | 23 | 70 | 59 | 49 | 52 |
| Eastern | 62 | 56 | 46 | 46 | 41 | 36 | 16 | 11 | 48 | 41 | 28 | 24 |
| Lake | 88 | 91 | 81 | 74 | 44 | 42 | 24 | 20 | 66 | 59 | 35 | 36 |
| Northern | 72 | 80 | 70 | 64 | 31 | 39 | 18 | 11 | 51 | 52 | 37 | 39 |
| S. Highlands | 87 | 88 | 83 | 79 | 42 | 45 | 25 | 14 | 75 | 63 | 43 | 47 |
| Southern | 86 | 83 | 76 | 69 | 36 | 40 | 29 | 14 | 67 | 64 | 46 | 34 |
| Western | 89 | 86 | 90 | 84 | 42 | 39 | 33 | 24 | 68 | 58 | 41 | 35 |
| Zanzibar | 66 | 63 | 44 | 34 | 44 | 34 | 24 | 14 | 44 | 33 | 18 | 25 |

*Source*: Authors' calculations based on the 1991/2, 1996, 2004/5, 2010 TDHS (National Bureau of Statistics and Macro 1993, 1997, 2005, 2011)

**Table 14.3.** Children 0–4 deprived by welfare indicator (per cent)

| | Water | | | | Sanitation | | | | Housing | | | | Education | | | | Nutrition | | | |
|---|---|---|---|---|---|---|---|---|---|---|---|---|---|---|---|---|---|---|---|---|
| | 1992 | 1996 | 2004 | 2010 | 1992 | 1996 | 2004 | 2010 | 1992 | 1996 | 2004 | 2010 | 1992 | 1996 | 2004 | 2010 | 1992 | 1996 | 2004 | 2010 |
| Nation | 35.89 | 35.92 | 27.89 | 29.53 | 97.45 | 97.52 | 95.84 | 91.53 | 82.97 | 81.67 | 80.70 | 75.64 | 52.89 | 44.71 | 42.11 | 40.51 | 54.41 | 54.56 | 47.41 | 41.21 |
| Rural | 43.08 | 42.08 | 30.50 | 32.63 | 98.89 | 98.44 | 98.87 | 98.05 | 91.49 | 91.05 | 91.11 | 86.58 | 57.15 | 48.63 | 46.45 | 44.89 | 55.79 | 56.98 | 49.69 | 43.50 |
| Urban | 8.56 | 7.39 | 16.34 | 16.37 | 92.00 | 93.24 | 82.46 | 63.77 | 50.63 | 38.24 | 34.62 | 29.06 | 36.68 | 26.59 | 22.88 | 21.88 | 49.17 | 43.33 | 37.33 | 31.46 |
| Central | 27.79 | 27.08 | 34.68 | 41.02 | 98.28 | 97.82 | 98.07 | 97.18 | 90.48 | 85.65 | 91.18 | 89.54 | 48.68 | 41.46 | 43.64 | 42.24 | 58.75 | 54.13 | 50.70 | 50.90 |
| Eastern | 19.23 | 15.01 | 18.44 | 20.21 | 96.82 | 94.18 | 91.54 | 81.90 | 62.72 | 53.72 | 50.81 | 45.57 | 46.29 | 36.98 | 32.86 | 32.87 | 54.31 | 54.83 | 36.04 | 34.04 |
| Lake | 46.35 | 37.44 | 44.61 | 28.35 | 98.13 | 98.82 | 95.18 | 91.09 | 90.35 | 91.02 | 85.12 | 79.63 | 60.52 | 50.07 | 40.22 | 42.42 | 48.72 | 49.58 | 43.74 | 36.76 |
| Northern | 41.65 | 48.04 | 25.58 | 40.73 | 94.48 | 97.19 | 94.21 | 92.39 | 73.58 | 80.26 | 76.70 | 70.74 | 39.33 | 37.98 | 34.31 | 33.98 | 52.83 | 55.14 | 46.06 | 43.64 |
| S. Highlands | 38.37 | 35.77 | 25.64 | 34.44 | 98.79 | 98.66 | 97.47 | 90.74 | 86.71 | 82.27 | 82.37 | 71.71 | 49.44 | 42.64 | 47.66 | 34.12 | 59.19 | 63.66 | 53.48 | 47.48 |
| Southern | 26.56 | 35.89 | 24.50 | 29.00 | 99.29 | 99.15 | 97.92 | 94.11 | 86.95 | 86.72 | 84.71 | 82.32 | 52.32 | 39.75 | 42.34 | 34.42 | 65.85 | 65.57 | 58.95 | 44.77 |
| Western | 42.91 | 45.32 | 20.91 | 23.64 | 97.55 | 97.06 | 98.28 | 95.39 | 90.71 | 89.02 | 90.85 | 88.35 | 66.86 | 54.26 | 47.44 | 51.71 | 49.28 | 47.16 | 49.27 | 38.18 |
| Zanzibar | 11.13 | 3.25 | 1.32 | 1.72 | 97.25 | 94.95 | 82.89 | 73.58 | 68.63 | 64.32 | 42.99 | 35.21 | 57.16 | 58.48 | 51.35 | 42.75 | 60.89 | 49.85 | 35.91 | 39.11 |

*Source*: Authors' calculations based on the 1991/2, 1996, 2004/5, 2010 TDHS (National Bureau of Statistics and Macro 1993, 1997, 2005, 2011)

declining in every year, under-five education deprivation is greater than that of school-age children. Under-five nutrition, as evidenced by anthropometric measures, improved over the eighteen-year period. However, these figures remained high with 31 per cent and 41 per cent of urban and rural children nutritionally deprived in 2010. Though improvement occurred in all zones, as many as 51 per cent of children in Central were still nutritionally deprived in 2010.

## 14.4 FOD Results

### 14.4.1 *Temporal FOD Comparisons*

We begin by examining whether child welfare, as defined by our set of five indicators, improved between 1992 and 2010. FOD temporal analysis compares the performance of a given area between survey years and is reported as the average probability of net domination across 100 bootstrap iterations. Net probability of domination measures the probability that the welfare of an area improves between two years minus any probability of regression.

Table 14.4 reports the temporal FOD outcomes for school-age children. Both the static results and bootstrap probabilities provide strong evidence of welfare progress at the national level and in rural areas from 1992 or 1996 to 2004 or 2010. In contrast, urban areas advance between 1992 and 1996 and then stagnate in the remaining years. National and rural stagnation between 1992 and 1996 is consistent with very little to no change in the percentage of children who are deprived in sanitation, housing, and education. Urban stagnation across most years and national and rural stagnation between 2004 and 2010 are directly associated with decreasing welfare in the water indicator. Among the zones, only the Central zone shows little to no signs of advancement during the study period. In line with substantial improvements in all indicators, Zanzibar exhibits the greatest probability of advancement among the zones.

To evaluate the sensitivity of temporal outcomes to the sanitation threshold, FOD comparisons were re-estimated using the alternative sanitation indicator and reported in Table 14.5. Consistent with alternative sanitation deprivation increasing over time (Table 14.2), evidence of temporal advancement is drastically reduced. Notably, static advancement in national and urban areas disappears and only moderate bootstrap probabilities of welfare gains in national and rural areas remain between 1992 or 1994 and 2004. However, Zanzibar, where the alternative sanitation indicator improved in all years, exhibits strong probabilities of advancement.

Finally, the temporal FOD results for children under five are reported in Table 14.6. Though the indicator trends for school-age children are generally

**Table 14.4.** Temporal net FOD comparisons, children 7–17 years (probabilities)

| | 1996 FOD 1992 | | 2004 FOD 1992 | | 2010 FOD 1992 | | 2004 FOD 1996 | | 2010 FOD 1996 | | 2010 FOD 2004 | |
| --- | --- | --- | --- | --- | --- | --- | --- | --- | --- | --- | --- | --- |
| | Static | Boot | Static | Boot | Static | Boot | Static | Boot | Static | Boot | Static | Boot |
| National | | 0.03 | 1 | 1.00 | 1 | 0.98 | 1 | 0.97 | 1 | 0.97 | | 0.11 |
| Rural | | 0.04 | 1 | 0.51 | 1 | 0.97 | 1 | 0.53 | 1 | 0.90 | | 0.13 |
| Urban | 1 | 0.23 | | 0.28 | | 0.19 | | 0.17 | | 0.09 | | 0.07 |
| Central | | 0.13 | | 0.09 | | 0.09 | | 0.07 | | 0.03 | | 0.02 |
| Eastern | | 0.18 | | 0.54 | | 0.17 | 1 | 0.47 | | 0.20 | | 0.09 |
| Lake | | 0.00 | 1 | 0.67 | 1 | 0.99 | | 0.24 | 1 | 0.81 | | 0.15 |
| Northern | | −0.21 | 1 | 0.57 | 1 | 0.51 | 1 | 0.86 | 1 | 0.88 | | −0.01 |
| S. Highlands | | 0.03 | 1 | 0.66 | 1 | 0.82 | 1 | 0.61 | 1 | 0.67 | | 0.09 |
| Southern | | 0.03 | 1 | 0.49 | | 0.33 | 1 | 0.66 | 1 | 0.72 | | 0.03 |
| Western | | 0.19 | | 0.11 | 1 | 0.62 | | 0.09 | 1 | 0.53 | 1 | 0.34 |
| Zanzibar | | 0.17 | 1 | 0.92 | 1 | 0.92 | 1 | 0.82 | 1 | 0.81 | | 0.00 |

*Source*: Authors' calculations based on the 1991/2, 1996, 2004/5, 2010 TDHS (National Bureau of Statistics and Macro 1993, 1997, 2005, 2011)

**Table 14.5.** Temporal net FOD comparisons with the alternative sanitation indicator, children 7–17 years (probabilities)

| | 1996 FOD 1992 | | 2004 FOD 1992 | | 2010 FOD 1992 | | 2004 FOD 1996 | | 2010 FOD 1996 | | 2010 FOD 2004 | |
|---|---|---|---|---|---|---|---|---|---|---|---|---|
| | Static | Boot | Static | Boot | Static | Boot | Static | Boot | Static | Boot | Static | Boot |
| National | | 0.05 | | 0.39 | | 0.05 | | 0.39 | | 0.02 | | 0.00 |
| Rural | | 0.06 | 1 | 0.42 | | 0.08 | | 0.27 | | 0.00 | | 0.00 |
| Urban | | 0.18 | | 0.03 | | 0.00 | | 0.00 | | 0.00 | | 0.01 |
| Central | | 0.01 | | 0.14 | | 0.00 | | 0.12 | | 0.01 | | −0.08 |
| Eastern | | 0.01 | | 0.23 | | 0.09 | 1 | 0.41 | | 0.16 | | −0.01 |
| Lake | | 0.06 | 1 | 0.35 | | 0.32 | | 0.01 | | 0.06 | | 0.00 |
| Northern | −1 | −0.27 | | 0.40 | | 0.16 | 1 | 0.77 | 1 | 0.63 | | 0.00 |
| S. Highlands | | 0.06 | | 0.35 | | 0.18 | | 0.07 | | 0.05 | | 0.01 |
| Southern | | | 1 | 0.38 | | 0.03 | | 0.09 | | 0.00 | | 0.00 |
| Western | | 0.24 | | 0.04 | | 0.13 | | 0.00 | | 0.00 | | 0.02 |
| Zanzibar | | 0.34 | 1 | 0.94 | 1 | 0.95 | 1 | 0.79 | 1 | 0.88 | | 0.00 |

*Source*: Authors' calculations based on the 1991/2, 1996, 2004/5, 2010 TDHS (National Bureau of Statistics and Macro 1993, 1997, 2005, 2011)

**Table 14.6.** Temporal net FOD comparisons, children 0–4 years (probabilities)

| | 1996 FOD 1992 | | 2004 FOD 1992 | | 2010 FOD 1992 | | 2004 FOD 1996 | | 2010 FOD 1996 | | 2010 FOD 2004 | |
|---|---|---|---|---|---|---|---|---|---|---|---|---|
| | Static | Boot | Static | Boot | Static | Boot | Static | Boot | Static | Boot | Static | Boot |
| National | | 0.06 | 1 | 0.69 | 1 | 0.97 | | 0.35 | 1 | 0.89 | | 0.16 |
| Rural | | 0.04 | 1 | 0.23 | 1 | 0.88 | | 0.02 | | 0.40 | | 0.17 |
| Urban | | 0.07 | | 0.05 | | 0.03 | | 0.00 | | 0.01 | | 0.03 |
| Central | | 0.05 | | 0.05 | | 0.04 | | −0.05 | | −0.04 | | 0.00 |
| Eastern | | 0.30 | 1 | 0.37 | | 0.39 | | 0.12 | | 0.15 | | 0.06 |
| Lake | | 0.04 | 1 | 0.26 | 1 | 0.90 | | 0.02 | 1 | 0.75 | | 0.28 |
| Northern | | −0.03 | | 0.19 | | 0.23 | 1 | 0.55 | 1 | 0.52 | | −0.02 |
| S. Highlands | | 0.03 | | 0.18 | 1 | 0.62 | | 0.05 | 1 | 0.39 | | 0.06 |
| Southern | | 0.01 | | 0.22 | | 0.28 | | 0.13 | 1 | 0.61 | | 0.10 |
| Western | | 0.10 | | 0.05 | 1 | 0.46 | | 0.01 | 1 | 0.27 | | 0.04 |
| Zanzibar | | 0.10 | 1 | 0.77 | 1 | 0.94 | 1 | 0.62 | 1 | 0.71 | | 0.00 |

*Source*: Authors' calculations based on the 1991/2, 1996, 2004/5, 2010 TDHS (National Bureau of Statistics and Macro 1993, 1997, 2005, 2011)

comparable to under-fives deprived in water, sanitation, housing, and education, the under-five temporal results demonstrate the strict nature of the FOD criteria. For example, children under five and school-age children advance in all indicators between 1996 and 2004 nationally and between 1996 and 2010 nationally and in rural areas. However, unlike outcomes for school-age children, in the under-five static case, 2004 does not dominate 1996 for the nation or rural areas. In both periods, the probability of domination is lower than that of school-age children. This example demonstrates that the FOD criteria demand progress not only on average, but throughout the distribution (see Chapter 11 for more a more detailed discussion of indeterminacy).

### 14.4.2 *Spatial FOD Comparisons*

In each year, FOD comparisons are made between all areas to determine the degree of domination of each area and zone. Values in the inner table represent the probability that the row area dominates the corresponding column area.[5] Row averages measure the probability that the row population dominates all other populations, and column averages measure the probability that the column population is dominated by all other populations. In interpreting a population's relative wellbeing, both row and column averages should be considered.

The 1992 and 2010 spatial comparisons for school-age children are presented in Tables 14.7 and 14.8.[6] Within the tables, all domination in the static case (bold values) and significant bootstrap probabilities occur when urban areas, Eastern, Northern (1992), and Zanzibar dominate or when rural areas, Lake (1992), and Central (2010) are dominated. Column averages indicate that Southern Highlands, Southern, and Western zones also have moderate probabilities of being dominated in both years. Between the remaining areas, FOD is indeterminate or the probabilities of domination are quite low. Column averages for urban, Eastern, and Zanzibar and row averages for rural areas and Central increase considerably between 1992 and 2010, indicating a greater disparity between the welfare of the better-off and worst-off areas. In both years, the nation is nearly as likely to dominate other areas as it is to be dominated.

Tables 14.9 and 14.10 present the spatial results for children under five in 1992 and 2010. In 1992, significant domination occurs only when urban areas and Eastern dominate or rural areas are dominated. The remaining areas are

---

[5] Note that bootstrap sampling introduces a degree of randomness into the results and care must be taken in interpreting very small probabilities or small differences in probabilities.

[6] For both populations of children, spatial tables generally follow the trend seen between 1992 and 2010 and are therefore not presented.

**Table 14.7.** 1992 Bootstrap spatial FOD comparisons, children 7–17 years (probabilities)

| Area | National | Rural | Urban | C | E | L | N | SH | S | W | Z | Avg. |
|---|---|---|---|---|---|---|---|---|---|---|---|---|
| National | | 1 | | 0.03 | | 0.36 | | 0.05 | 0.02 | 0.19 | | 0.17 |
| Rural | | | | 0.02 | | | | | | | | 0.00 |
| Urban | 1 | 1 | | **0.94** | **0.69** | **0.97** | 0.28 | **0.78** | 1 | **0.96** | 0.11 | 0.77 |
| Central | 0.01 | 0.10 | | | | 0.07 | | 0.02 | 0.07 | 0.08 | | 0.04 |
| Eastern | 0.26 | **0.53** | | **0.39** | | **0.59** | | 0.09 | **0.50** | **0.31** | | 0.27 |
| Lake | | 0.01 | | | | | | | | 0.01 | | 0.00 |
| Northern | 0.12 | **0.49** | | 0.04 | | 0.36 | | **0.40** | 0.08 | 0.25 | | 0.17 |
| S. Highlands | | 0.10 | | 0.03 | | 0.02 | | | 0.01 | 0.04 | | 0.02 |
| Southern | | | | 0.01 | | | | | | | | 0.00 |
| Western | | 0.11 | | 0.04 | | 0.07 | | 0.02 | | | | 0.02 |
| Zanzibar | 0.17 | 0.29 | | 0.27 | 0.07 | **0.39** | 0.01 | 0.11 | 0.35 | 0.22 | | 0.19 |
| Average | 0.16 | 0.36 | 0.00 | 0.18 | 0.08 | 0.28 | 0.03 | 0.15 | 0.20 | 0.21 | 0.01 | 0.15 |

*Note*: Figures in bold indicate FOD in the static sample.
*Source*: Authors' calculations based on the 1991/2 TDHS (National Bureau of Statistics and Macro 1993)

**Table 14.8.** 2010 Bootstrap spatial FOD comparisons, children 7–17 years (probabilities)

| Area | National | Rural | Urban | C | E | L | N | SH | S | W | Z | Avg. |
|---|---|---|---|---|---|---|---|---|---|---|---|---|
| National | | 1 | | 0.87 | | 0.03 | | 0.01 | 0.08 | | | 0.20 |
| Rural | | | | 0.09 | | | | | | | | 0.01 |
| Urban | 1 | 1 | | 1 | **0.59** | 1 | 1 | **0.99** | **0.99** | **0.91** | | 0.85 |
| Central | | | | | | | | | | | | 0.00 |
| Eastern | **0.92** | **0.97** | | 0.95 | | **0.72** | 0.49 | **0.68** | **0.76** | 0.35 | | 0.58 |
| Lake | 0.02 | **0.42** | | 0.59 | | | | | 0.05 | | | 0.11 |
| Northern | | 0.04 | | 0.27 | | | | 0.01 | 0.08 | | | 0.04 |
| S. Highlands | 0.02 | 0.43 | | 0.54 | | 0.02 | 0.05 | | 0.17 | | | 0.12 |
| Southern | | 0.02 | | 0.34 | | | | | | | | 0.04 |
| Western | | | | 0.17 | | | | | | | | 0.02 |
| Zanzibar | **0.94** | 1 | | **0.98** | 0.02 | **0.94** | 0.11 | 0.39 | 0.43 | **0.99** | | 0.58 |
| Average | 0.29 | 0.49 | 0.00 | 0.58 | 0.06 | 0.27 | 0.17 | 0.21 | 0.26 | 0.23 | 0.00 | 0.23 |

*Note*: Figures in bold indicate FOD in the static sample.
*Source*: Authors' calculations based on the 2010 TDHS (National Bureau of Statistics and Macro 2011)

**Table 14.9.** 1992 Bootstrap spatial FOD comparisons, children 0–4 years (probabilities)

| Area | National | Rural | Urban | C | E | L | N | SH | S | W | Z | Avg. |
|---|---|---|---|---|---|---|---|---|---|---|---|---|
| National | | **0.94** | | 0.01 | | 0.02 | | 0.08 | | | | 0.11 |
| Rural | | | | | | | | | | | | 0.00 |
| Urban | **0.94** | **0.94** | | **0.97** | **0.81** | 0.53 | **0.60** | **0.97** | **1** | **0.60** | **0.50** | 0.79 |
| Central | | 0.14 | | | | 0.04 | | 0.04 | 0.02 | 0.02 | | 0.03 |
| Eastern | 0.34 | **0.59** | | 0.13 | | 0.15 | | 0.41 | 0.33 | 0.10 | 0.04 | 0.21 |
| Lake | | 0.02 | | | | | | | | 0.01 | | 0.00 |
| Northern | 0.07 | **0.42** | | 0.02 | | 0.07 | | 0.21 | 0.02 | 0.07 | | 0.09 |
| S. Highlands | | 0.02 | | | | | | | 0.01 | | | 0.00 |
| Southern | | | | | | | | | | | | 0.00 |
| Western | | | | | | 0.03 | | | | | | 0.00 |
| Zanzibar | 0.01 | 0.04 | | 0.03 | | | | 0.02 | 0.17 | | | 0.03 |
| Average | 0.14 | 0.31 | 0.00 | 0.12 | 0.08 | 0.08 | 0.06 | 0.17 | 0.16 | 0.08 | 0.05 | 0.11 |

*Note*: Figures in bold indicate FOD in the static sample.
*Source*: Authors' calculations based on the 1991/2 TDHS (National Bureau of Statistics and Macro 1993)

**Table 14.10.** 2010 Bootstrap spatial FOD comparisons, children 0–4 years (probabilities)

| Area | National | Rural | Urban | C | E | L | N | SH | S | W | Z | Avg. |
|---|---|---|---|---|---|---|---|---|---|---|---|---|
| National | | **1** | | **0.62** | | | | | 0.01 | | | 0.16 |
| Rural | | | | 0.03 | | | | | | | | 0.00 |
| Urban | **1** | **1** | | **1** | **0.47** | **0.75** | **0.98** | **1.00** | **0.91** | **0.79** | | 0.79 |
| Central | | | | | | | | | | | | 0.00 |
| Eastern | **0.76** | **0.88** | | **0.90** | | 0.24 | 0.50 | 0.43 | 0.35 | 0.37 | | 0.44 |
| Lake | 0.01 | **0.63** | | 0.41 | | | 0.01 | | 0.03 | 0.08 | | 0.12 |
| Northern | | 0.01 | | 0.34 | | | | 0.03 | | | | 0.04 |
| S. Highlands | | 0.02 | | **0.41** | | | | | 0.01 | | | 0.04 |
| Southern | | 0.18 | | **0.57** | | | 0.02 | 0.01 | | | | 0.08 |
| Western | | 0.02 | | | | | | | | | | 0.00 |
| Zanzibar | 0.29 | **0.70** | | 0.53 | 0.01 | 0.19 | 0.08 | 0.04 | 0.06 | 0.40 | | 0.23 |
| Average | 0.21 | 0.44 | 0.00 | 0.48 | 0.05 | 0.12 | 0.16 | 0.15 | 0.14 | 0.16 | 0.00 | 0.17 |

*Note*: Figures in bold indicate FOD in the static sample.
*Source*: Authors' calculations based on the 2010 TDHS (National Bureau of Statistics and Macro 2011)

essentially indeterminate with very low probabilities of domination. In 2010, the number of instances of static domination increases and domination now also occurs when Zanzibar dominates and when Central is dominated. Eastern and Zanzibar's row averages significantly increase between 1992 and 2010, indicating an increasingly greater welfare compared to all other areas. The probability that rural areas and Central are dominated, as indicated by column averages, also increases, suggesting that these areas are falling behind all other areas.

### 14.4.3 *Spatial FOD Rankings*

Net domination scores measure the average probability across all bootstrap samples that an area dominates all other areas less the probability that it is dominated by all other areas. Net domination can be interpreted as the probability of domination, and allows areas to be ranked. Zonal rankings based on school-age children are reported in Table 14.11 (for zones) and Table 14.12 (for regions).[7] It is worth noting that the difference in net domination scores is often insufficiently large to distinguish between differences in welfare outcomes and variability introduced through random bootstrapping. To avoid misinterpreting rankings within the tables, shading identifies clusters with similar net domination scores. Within these clusters, ranks cannot be established with confidence.

Across all four years, Zanzibar and Eastern outperform all areas with the probability of domination more than doubling between 1992 and the remaining years (Table 14.11). Though a number of zones seem to change rank from year to year, these changes are not robust due to small differences in the probabilities of domination. For example, Lake appears to improve from last to fifth, but given probabilities in 2010, a rank of fifth and seventh cannot be distinguished with confidence. However, the decline in Central province is robust. Not only was Central ranked last in 2010, but it has a probability of being dominated 0.38 greater than the seventh ranked zone, Western. The gap between the best-performing and worst-performing zones widened considerably from a range spanning [−0.21, 0.26] in 1992 to [−0.55, 0.56] in 2010.

Table 14.12 reports regional rankings in 1992 and 2010. In both years Zanzibar urban, Dar es Salaam, Kilimanjaro, and Zanzibar rural are the highest-ranked regions, with Zanzibar urban and Dar es Salaam decisively first and second. Consistent with strong temporal advancement, Zanzibar urban's net domination widens in 2010. In 1992, the remaining nineteen

---

[7] Zonal rankings for children under five are not presented. The results are similar to rankings for school-aged children but have a larger number of areas with net dominations scores too similar to distinguish with confidence.

**Table 14.11.** Spatial FOD ranking and probability of net domination by zone and year, children 7–17

| | 1992 | | | 1996 | | | 2004 | | | 2010 | | Rank Change |
| --- | --- | --- | --- | --- | --- | --- | --- | --- | --- | --- | --- | --- |
| | Domination | Rank | | Domination | Rank | | Domination | Rank | | Domination | Rank | |
| Eastern | 0.26 | 1 | Eastern | 0.57 | 1 | Eastern | 0.73 | 1 | Eastern | 0.56 | 1 | 0 |
| Zanzibar | 0.20 | 2 | Zanzibar | 0.55 | 2 | Zanzibar | 0.54 | 2 | Zanzibar | 0.55 | 2 | 0 |
| Northern | 0.16 | 3 | Central | −0.04 | 3 | Northern | 0.17 | 3 | Northern | −0.04 | 3 | 0 |
| S. Highlands | −0.08 | 4 | Western | −0.10 | 4 | Southern | −0.16 | 4 | S. Highlands | −0.04 | 4 | 0 |
| Central | −0.08 | 5 | Northern | −0.12 | 5 | Lake | −0.20 | 5 | Lake | −0.15 | 5 | −3 |
| Western | −0.11 | 6 | S. Highlands | −0.24 | 6 | S. Highlands | −0.26 | 6 | Southern | −0.16 | 6 | −1 |
| Southern | −0.14 | 7 | Lake | −0.26 | 7 | Western | −0.34 | 7 | Western | −0.17 | 7 | 1 |
| Lake | −0.21 | 8 | Southern | −0.35 | 8 | Central | −0.49 | 8 | Central | −0.55 | 8 | 3 |

*Note*: Rankings within shaded groups are highly sensitive to small perturbations and should be interpreted with caution.
*Source*: Authors' calculations based on the 1991/2, 1996, 2004/5, 2010 TDHS (National Bureau of Statistics and Macro 1993, 1997, 2005, 2011)

**Table 14.12.** Spatial FOD ranking and probability of net domination by region and year, children 7–17

| | 1992 | | | 2010 | | Rank Change |
|---|---|---|---|---|---|---|
| | Domination | Rank | | Domination | Rank | |
| Dar es Salaam | 0.64 | 1 | Zanzibar (Urban) | 0.74 | 1 | −1 |
| Zanzibar (Urban) | 0.60 | 2 | Dar es Salaam | 0.58 | 2 | 1 |
| Kilimanjaro | 0.20 | 3 | Zanzibar (Rural) | 0.28 | 3 | −1 |
| Zanzibar (Rural) | 0.09 | 4 | Kilimanjaro | 0.25 | 4 | 1 |
| Tanga | 0.02 | 5 | Pemba | 0.15 | 5 | −4 |
| Mbeya | −0.01 | 6 | Coast | 0.15 | 6 | −4 |
| Rukwa | −0.02 | 7 | Mbeya | 0.09 | 7 | 1 |
| Tabora | −0.02 | 8 | Mwanza | 0.04 | 8 | −3 |
| Pemba | −0.04 | 9 | Morogoro | 0.00 | 9 | −9 |
| Coast | −0.04 | 10 | Iringa | 0.00 | 10 | −9 |
| Mwanza | −0.05 | 11 | Ruvuma | −0.03 | 11 | −3 |
| Singida | −0.06 | 12 | Mara | −0.03 | 12 | −9 |
| Arusha & Manyara | −0.07 | 13 | Shinyanga | −0.07 | 13 | −3 |
| Ruvuma | −0.07 | 14 | Tabora | −0.09 | 14 | 6 |
| Lindi | −0.08 | 15 | Tanga | −0.13 | 15 | 10 |
| Shinyanga | −0.10 | 16 | Arusha & Manyara | −0.15 | 16 | 3 |
| Kgoma | −0.12 | 17 | Kgoma | −0.21 | 17 | 0 |
| Morogoro | −0.12 | 18 | Lindi | −0.21 | 18 | 3 |
| Iringa | −0.13 | 19 | Mtwara | −0.21 | 19 | −1 |
| Mtwara | −0.15 | 20 | Singida | −0.22 | 20 | 8 |
| Mara | −0.16 | 21 | Rukwa | −0.25 | 21 | 14 |
| Dodoma | −0.16 | 22 | Kagera | −0.28 | 22 | −1 |
| Kagera | −0.16 | 23 | Dodoma | −0.41 | 23 | 1 |

*Note*: Rankings within shaded groups are highly sensitive to small perturbations and should be interpreted with caution.
*Source*: Authors' calculations based on the 1991/2, 2010 TDHS (National Bureau of Statistics and Macro 1993, 2011)

regions have net domination scores falling in a narrow range between 0.02 and −0.16. Though many of the rank shifts between 1992 and 2010 rely on small differences in net domination scores, a few regions stand out. Pemba and Coast improve four places to ranks of fifth and sixth. Mororno, Mara, and Iringa all climb nine positions. Shidiga, Tanga, and Rukwu fall eight, ten, and fourteen places. Finally, Dodoma is decisively last in 2010.

### 14.4.4 *Alkire–Foster*

The AF approach provides, as noted, an alternative method for evaluating multidimensional poverty using the same set of binary indicators. In this analysis, a child is identified as multidimensionally poor when deprived in two or more equally weighted indicators. Recall that $M_0 = HA$, and thus the adjusted headcount ratio reflects the proportion of children who are multidimensionally poor ($H$) multiplied by the average intensity of deprivation among poor children ($A$).

**Table 14.13.** Multidimensional poverty in two dimensions

| Child Population | | | 1992 | 1996 | 2004 | 2010 | change | % change |
|---|---|---|---|---|---|---|---|---|
| 7–17 | Nation | $M_0$ | 0.61 | 0.60 | 0.49 | 0.45 | −0.16 | −26.2 |
| | | $H$ | 0.89 | 0.88 | 0.82 | 0.77 | −0.12 | −13.5 |
| | | $A$ | 0.69 | 0.68 | 0.60 | 0.59 | −0.10 | −14.7 |
| | Urban | $M_0$ | 0.38 | 0.31 | 0.24 | 0.17 | −0.21 | −54.2 |
| | | $H$ | 0.65 | 0.57 | 0.47 | 0.33 | −0.32 | −49.0 |
| | | $A$ | 0.58 | 0.54 | 0.51 | 0.52 | −0.06 | −10.3 |
| | Rural | $M_0$ | 0.68 | 0.66 | 0.57 | 0.53 | −0.15 | −22.3 |
| | | $H$ | 0.96 | 0.95 | 0.93 | 0.89 | −0.07 | −7.2 |
| | | $A$ | 0.71 | 0.69 | 0.61 | 0.59 | −0.12 | −16.3 |
| 0–4 | Nation | $M_0$ | 0.63 | 0.61 | 0.57 | 0.54 | −0.10 | −15.3 |
| | | $H$ | 0.92 | 0.91 | 0.89 | 0.85 | −0.07 | −7.5 |
| | | $A$ | 0.69 | 0.67 | 0.64 | 0.63 | −0.06 | −8.4 |
| | Urban | $M_0$ | 0.43 | 0.36 | 0.33 | 0.27 | −0.17 | −38.7 |
| | | $H$ | 0.75 | 0.67 | 0.61 | 0.48 | −0.26 | −35.3 |
| | | $A$ | 0.58 | 0.54 | 0.54 | 0.55 | −0.03 | −5.2 |
| | Rural | $M_0$ | 0.69 | 0.67 | 0.63 | 0.60 | −0.09 | −12.5 |
| | | $H$ | 0.97 | 0.96 | 0.96 | 0.94 | −0.03 | −2.9 |
| | | $A$ | 0.71 | 0.69 | 0.65 | 0.64 | −0.07 | −9.9 |

*Source*: Authors' calculations based on the 1991/2, 1996, 2004/5, 2010 TDHS (National Bureau of Statistics and Macro 1993, 1997, 2005, 2011)

Table 14.13 reports $M_0$ and its components, $H$ and $A$, for school-age children and children under five who are deprived in two or more dimensions. Nationally, the adjusted headcount ratio for school-age children has declined over the eighteen-year study period from 0.61 in 1992 to 0.45 in 2010. The proportion of school-age children who are multidimensionally poor fell twelve percentage points to 77 per cent and the intensity of poverty fell ten percentage points to 59 per cent. Thus, the decline in $M_0$ can be attributed roughly equally to incidence and intensity.

Rural areas experienced a similar reduction in the adjusted headcount ratio for schoolage children, which fell from 0.68 in 1992 to 0.52 in 2010. However, rural gains were driven primarily by a reduction in the intensity of poverty, which dropped twelve percentage points compared to only a seven-point decline in the headcount ratio. The proportion of schoolage children suffering two or more deprivations remained extremely high at 89 per cent in 2010. In contrast, the large reduction in the urban index from 0.38 to 0.17 was primarily due to a reduction in the poverty headcount, which at 33 per cent in 2010 was nearly cut in half over the study period. Moreover, the intensity of urban poverty declined by only six percentage points.

At the national, urban, and rural levels across years, a similar pattern occurs in children under five. However, all three measures, $M_0$, $H$, and $A$, are higher and decline less compared to outcomes for school-age children. This disparity in gains between the two populations of children is consistent with FOD temporal results.

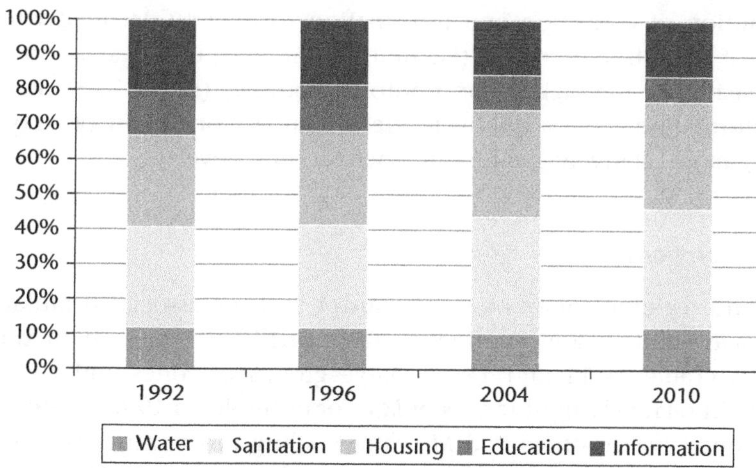

**Figure 14.2.** Relative contributions to the adjusted headcount ratio, $M_0$, for children aged 7–17 by year

*Source*: Authors' calculations based on the 1991/2, 1996, 2004/5, 2010 TDHS (National Bureau of Statistics and Macro 1993, 1997, 2005, 2011)

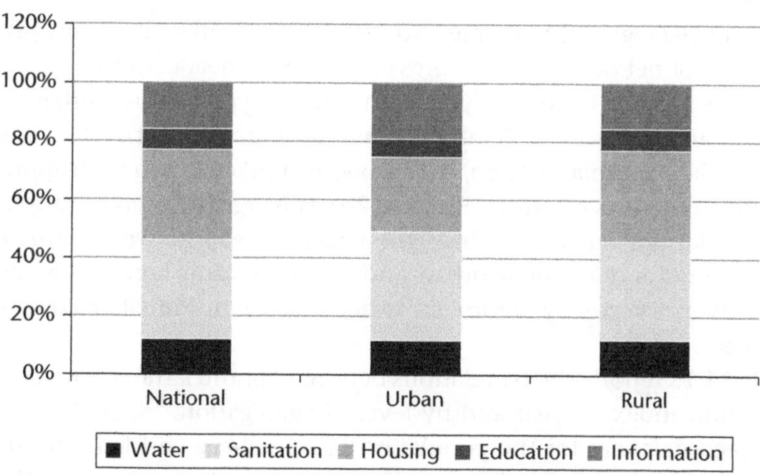

**Figure 14.3.** 2010 relative contributions to the adjusted headcount ratio, $M_0$, for children aged 7–17, by area

*Source*: Authors' calculations based on 2010 TDHS (National Bureau of Statistics and Macro 2011)

Figures 14.2 and 14.3 explore each indicator's relative contribution to the school-age adjusted headcount ratios over time and by aggregate areas, respectively. The most notable aspect of these figures is how stable the contribution of each indicator is over time and space. Nonetheless there are several subtle observations to be made. Between 1992 and 2010, the relative contribution of education and information to poverty declined while the impact of sanitation increased (Figure 14.2). Across all three areas, sanitation and housing are the biggest contributors to poverty (Figure 14.3). Sanitation and information have a relatively greater impact on urban poverty while housing has a relatively greater influence on rural poverty.

### 14.4.5 *Comparisons*

Zonal and regional values of $M_0$, $H$, and $A$ and the associated rankings for school-age children are reported in Table 14.14. As was seen in the FOD rankings (Tables 14.11 and 14.12), large groups of zones and regions are grouped in relatively tight ranges of $M_0$. For example, in 1992 regions ranked five through twenty-three had $M_0$ values falling in the range 0.57 to 0.71. Despite the very different approaches to comparing areas, FOD and AF produce similar spatial rankings. Zonal rankings based on the adjusted headcount ratio are nearly identical in 2010 to rankings based on net domination scores (Table 14.11). The notable exception is that Central is ranked last over the entire period based on the AF methodology, but declined over time with FOD (Table 14.11).

AF and FOD regional ranks are also remarkably similar, especially given the tight range of net domination scores and adjusted headcount ratios. In 2010, the top six regions have nearly the same rankings (Zanzibar (urban), Dar es Salaam, Zanzibar (rural), Pemba, Kilimanjaro, and Coast). The remaining regions follow a similar pattern, with Dodoma ranked last in both approaches. While the dynamics between 1992 and 2010 diverge between the approaches, some similarities remain, such as the widening gap between Zanzibar and Eastern zones and Zanzibar urban and Dar es Salaam regions—a gap most likely driven by greatly improved water quality in Zanzibar compared to other areas.

Table 14.15 reports the correlations between $M_0$ and a transformed FOD net domination index by year and by level of aggregation.[8] Spatial correlations across regions/zones for the population of school-age children are strikingly high and range between 0.96 and 0.99. This result is consistent with correlations reported in Permanyer and Hussain (2015) and Arndt et al. (2017). The correlations are somewhat lower in the population of children under five falling in the range 0.81 to 0.86.

Despite some similarities, FOD and AF also generate numerous dissimilar temporal outcomes, in contrast to the spatial analyses. The AF method indicates welfare improved in every year for the nation, urban areas, and rural

---

[8] In order to facilitate comparisons with $M_0$, the net domination score was transformed to a range of [0,1] such that low values are associated with higher welfare rates.

**Table 14.14.** Multidimensional poverty in two dimensions by zone and region, children 7–17 years

| | 1992 | | | | 2010 | | | | Change | | | |
|---|---|---|---|---|---|---|---|---|---|---|---|---|
| | $M_0$ | $H$ | $A$ | Rank | $M_0$ | $H$ | $A$ | Rank | $M_0$ | $H$ | $A$ | Rank |
| Zanzibar | 0.48 | 0.79 | 0.61 | 1 | 0.23 | 0.45 | 0.51 | 1 | 0.25 | 0.34 | 0.10 | 0 |
| Eastern | 0.48 | 0.77 | 0.63 | 2 | 0.30 | 0.55 | 0.55 | 2 | 0.18 | 0.22 | 0.08 | 0 |
| Northern | 0.56 | 0.86 | 0.65 | 3 | 0.45 | 0.75 | 0.60 | 3 | 0.11 | 0.11 | 0.06 | 0 |
| S. Highlands | 0.65 | 0.91 | 0.71 | 5 | 0.45 | 0.78 | 0.58 | 4 | 0.19 | 0.13 | 0.13 | 1 |
| Lake | 0.68 | 0.95 | 0.71 | 8 | 0.47 | 0.81 | 0.58 | 5 | 0.21 | 0.15 | 0.14 | 3 |
| Western | 0.67 | 0.94 | 0.71 | 7 | 0.50 | 0.86 | 0.58 | 6 | 0.17 | 0.07 | 0.13 | 1 |
| Southern | 0.65 | 0.94 | 0.69 | 6 | 0.51 | 0.85 | 0.60 | 7 | 0.15 | 0.09 | 0.10 | −1 |
| Central | 0.63 | 0.91 | 0.70 | 4 | 0.57 | 0.89 | 0.64 | 8 | 0.07 | 0.01 | 0.06 | −4 |
| Zanzibar (Urban) | 0.29 | 0.54 | 0.54 | 2 | 0.06 | 0.13 | 0.46 | 1 | 0.23 | 0.41 | 0.09 | 1 |
| Dar es Salaam | 0.26 | 0.54 | 0.48 | 1 | 0.11 | 0.23 | 0.48 | 2 | 0.15 | 0.30 | 0.01 | −1 |
| Zanzibar (Rural) | 0.46 | 0.80 | 0.57 | 3 | 0.28 | 0.56 | 0.50 | 3 | 0.18 | 0.24 | 0.07 | 0 |
| Pemba | 0.57 | 0.88 | 0.65 | 5 | 0.35 | 0.67 | 0.52 | 4 | 0.22 | 0.21 | 0.13 | 1 |
| Kilimanjaro | 0.50 | 0.87 | 0.58 | 4 | 0.36 | 0.68 | 0.53 | 5 | 0.14 | 0.19 | 0.04 | −1 |
| Coast | 0.61 | 0.94 | 0.65 | 9 | 0.39 | 0.76 | 0.52 | 6 | 0.22 | 0.18 | 0.13 | 3 |
| Mwanza | 0.64 | 0.93 | 0.69 | 15 | 0.42 | 0.75 | 0.57 | 7 | 0.22 | 0.18 | 0.12 | 8 |
| Iringa | 0.69 | 0.93 | 0.74 | 20 | 0.43 | 0.73 | 0.59 | 8 | 0.26 | 0.20 | 0.15 | 12 |
| Mbeya | 0.60 | 0.87 | 0.69 | 8 | 0.43 | 0.79 | 0.55 | 9 | 0.17 | 0.09 | 0.14 | −1 |
| Morogoro | 0.64 | 0.92 | 0.70 | 16 | 0.44 | 0.76 | 0.58 | 10 | 0.20 | 0.16 | 0.11 | 6 |
| Ruvuma | 0.63 | 0.93 | 0.67 | 12 | 0.46 | 0.81 | 0.57 | 11 | 0.16 | 0.12 | 0.10 | 1 |
| Mara | 0.71 | 0.98 | 0.73 | 23 | 0.47 | 0.82 | 0.57 | 12 | 0.24 | 0.17 | 0.15 | 11 |
| Tanga | 0.62 | 0.91 | 0.69 | 10 | 0.48 | 0.76 | 0.63 | 13 | 0.15 | 0.15 | 0.05 | −3 |
| Shinyanga | 0.68 | 0.92 | 0.74 | 18 | 0.48 | 0.83 | 0.58 | 14 | 0.20 | 0.09 | 0.17 | 4 |
| Arusha & Manyara | 0.57 | 0.82 | 0.70 | 6 | 0.48 | 0.79 | 0.61 | 15 | 0.09 | 0.03 | 0.10 | −9 |
| Tabora | 0.59 | 0.92 | 0.64 | 7 | 0.49 | 0.90 | 0.55 | 16 | 0.09 | 0.02 | 0.09 | −9 |
| Rukwa | 0.63 | 0.92 | 0.68 | 13 | 0.53 | 0.85 | 0.62 | 17 | 0.10 | 0.07 | 0.06 | −4 |
| Mtwara | 0.70 | 0.97 | 0.72 | 21 | 0.53 | 0.85 | 0.62 | 18 | 0.17 | 0.12 | 0.10 | 3 |
| Kagera | 0.70 | 0.96 | 0.73 | 22 | 0.53 | 0.89 | 0.60 | 19 | 0.17 | 0.07 | 0.13 | 3 |
| Singida | 0.65 | 0.91 | 0.71 | 17 | 0.54 | 0.89 | 0.61 | 20 | 0.11 | 0.03 | 0.10 | −3 |
| Kgoma | 0.68 | 0.97 | 0.70 | 19 | 0.55 | 0.89 | 0.61 | 21 | 0.14 | 0.08 | 0.09 | −2 |
| Lindi | 0.63 | 0.93 | 0.68 | 14 | 0.57 | 0.96 | 0.59 | 22 | 0.06 | −0.03 | 0.09 | −8 |
| Dodoma | 0.62 | 0.90 | 0.69 | 11 | 0.58 | 0.90 | 0.65 | 23 | 0.04 | 0.01 | 0.04 | −12 |

*Source*: Authors' calculations based on the 1991/2, 1996, 2004/5, 2010 TDHS (National Bureau of Statistics and Macro 1993, 1997, 2005, 2011)

**Table 14.15.** Correlation between FOD spatial domination score and $M_0$

|  |  | 1992 | 1996 | 2004 | 2010 |
|---|---|---|---|---|---|
| Children 7–17 | Zone | 0.97 | 0.99 | 0.96 | 0.97 |
|  | Regions | 0.96 | 0.98 | 0.98 | 0.98 |
| Children 0–4 | Zone | 0.86 | 0.81 | 0.82 | 0.86 |

*Source*: Authors' calculations based on the 1991/2, 1996, 2004/5, 2010 TDHS (National Bureau of Statistics and Macro 1993, 1997, 2005, 2011)

areas in both populations of children (Table 14.13). The per cent declines in the urban index was more than double that of rural areas. Welfare gains indicated by $M_0$ were driven by both reduced poverty headcounts, $H$, and reduced intensity, $A$. Though, in both populations of children, FOD indicates national and rural welfare are likely to have improved over the entire period, advancement between individual years is less conclusive, particularly in the under five years of age sample (Table 14.6). In contrast to AF outcomes, FOD provides evidence of urban advancement only in the school-age population between 1992 and 1996 (Table 14.4) and not at all in the under-five population.

Why the big temporal difference? The FOD criteria are strict and require advancement throughout the distribution of welfare states. Regression in a subset of the population may lead to indeterminate results. On the other hand, advancement using the AF method is based on average headcount and intensity values. If a subset of the population fails to advance, $M_0$ may still indicate the population as a whole is advancing. As noted in the discussion of FOD temporal results, temporal stagnation is likely to be associated with periods of regression in the water indicator and stagnation in the sanitation, housing, and education indicators. Given the equal weights applied in the AF method, the periodic lack of advancement in these indicators was offset by gains elsewhere, allowing advancement in the adjusted headcount measure.

## 14.5 Conclusion

Poverty analysis in Tanzania highlights the need for careful consideration of multiple welfare measures. With uncertainty surrounding consumption poverty estimations, multidimensional welfare analyses provide useful opportunities to supplement and cross-check these estimations.

In this chapter, we considered the FOD and AF approaches to multidimensional welfare analysis. In the Tanzanian context, the use of several methods shines a light on the limitations of any one approach to fully capture the complicated interactions of the many factors determining welfare.

The FOD and AF approaches provide similar stories across areas and most notably the large urban rural disparities that have increased between 1992 and 2010. The two methodologies result in remarkably similar rankings of zones and regions. These rankings suggest a widening gap between the best- and worst-performing areas and indicate that the majority of areas lie in a tight range in the middle.

In contrast, despite employing the same set of welfare indicators, the approaches do not provide a clear and simple story of welfare dynamics. AF outcomes reflect the overall trend of indicator advancement with great improvements in the adjusted headcount index across all years, particularly in urban areas and for the school-age population. FOD, however, suggests periods of advancement and stagnation.

The national-level and rural areas appear to achieve robust welfare gains; however, these results are sensitive to the population of children considered as well as how the sanitation indicator is defined. FOD outcomes also highlight the failure of several indicators to improve, particularly, urban water, which deteriorated, and rural sanitation, which stagnated (or deteriorated if considering the alternative indicator). As a result of deterioration in urban water access, urban areas exhibit few signs of advancement. Furthermore, FOD provides no evidence of advancement between 2004 and 2010.

These results contrast with the adjusted headcount index of AF and consumption poverty figures, which indicate the greatest gains occur in urban areas and, in the case of consumption poverty, the greatest poverty reduction occurs between 2007 and 2011. Nonetheless, rather than conflict, the two multidimensional approaches complement one another by highlighting different aspects of poverty dynamics. While AF focuses on population averages, FOD identifies advancement or regression found throughout the population. In a sense, the approaches provide upper (AF) and lower (FOD) bounds on welfare advancement in Tanzania over the eighteen-year period.

## References


Adam, C., D. Kwimbere, W. Mbowe, and S. O'Connell (2012). 'Food Prices and Inflation in Tanzania', International Growth Centre Working Paper, London and Oxford, July.

Alkire, S. and J. Foster (2007). 'Counting and Multidimensional Poverty Measurement', OPHI Working Paper 7. Oxford: University of Oxford.

Alkire S., J. Foster, S. Seth, M. Santos, J. Roche, and P. Ballon (2015). *Multidimensional Poverty Measurement and Analysis*. Oxford: Oxford University Press.

Alkire, S. and M. Santos (2010). 'Acute Multidimensional Poverty: A New Index for Developing Countries', OPHI Working Paper 38. Oxford: University of Oxford.

Arndt, C., L. Demery, A. McKay, and F. Tarp (2016a). 'Growth and Poverty Reduction in Tanzania', in C. Arndt, A. McKay, and F. Tarp (eds), *Growth and Poverty in Sub-Saharan Africa*. Oxford: Oxford University Press, 238–62.

Arndt, C., M. A. Hussain, V. Salvucci, F. Tarp, and L. P. Østerdal (2016b). 'Poverty Mapping Based on First-Order Dominance with an Example from Mozambique', *Journal of International Development*, 28: 3–21.

Arndt, C., V. Leyaro, K. Mahrt, and F. Tarp (2017). 'Growth and Poverty: A Pragmatic Assessment and Future Prospects', in C. Adam, P. Collier, and B. Ndulu (eds), *Tanzania: Policies for Prosperity*. Oxford: Oxford University Press.

Atkinson, A. B. and M. A. Lugo (2010). 'Growth, Poverty and Distribution in Tanzania', International Growth Centre Working Paper 10/0831, London and Oxford, November.

Demombynes, G. and J. G. Hoogeveen (2007). 'Growth, Inequality and Simulated Poverty Paths for Tanzania, 1992–2002', *Journal of African Economies*, 16: 596–628.

Gordon, D., S. Nandy, C. Pantazis, S. Pemberton, and P. Townsend (2003). *Child Poverty in the Developing World*. Bristol: Policy Press.

Government of Tanzania (2009). *Household Budget Survey 2007—Tanzania Mainland*. Dar es Salaam: National Bureau of Statistics.

Hoogeveen, J. and R. Ruhinduka (2009). 'Poverty Reduction in Tanzania since 2001: Good Intentions, Few Results'. Paper prepared for the Research and Analysis Working Group.

Kessy, F., O. Mashindano, A. Shepherd, and L. Scott (eds) (2013). *Translating Growth into Poverty Reduction: Beyond the Numbers*. Dar es Salaam: Mkuki na Nyota.

Mashindano, O., K. Kayunze, L. da Corta, and F. Maro (2011). *Agriculture Growth and Poverty Reduction in Tanzania 2000–2010: Where Has Agriculture Worked for the Poor and What Can We Learn from this?* Chronic Poverty Research Centre, Working Paper No. 208, June.

Mkenda, A., E. Luvanda, and R. Ruhinduka (2010). 'Growth and Distribution in Tanzania: Recent Experience and Lessons', Interim Report to REPOA.

National Bureau of Statistics (NBS) and ICF Macro (2011). *Tanzania Demographic and Health Survey 2010*. Dar es Salaam: NBS and ICF Macro.

National Bureau of Statistics (NBS) and Macro International Inc. (1993). *Tanzania Demographic and Health Survey 1991/1992*. Columbia, MD: NBS and Macro International.

National Bureau of Statistics (NBS) and Macro International Inc. (1997). *Tanzania Demographic and Health Survey 1996*. Calverton, MD: NBS and Macro International.

National Bureau of Statistics (NBS) and ORC Macro (2005). *Tanzania Demographic and Health Survey 2004-05*. Dar es Salaam: NBS and ORC Macro International.

Permanyer, I. and M. A. Hussain (2015). 'Multidimensional Poverty Indices and First Order Dominance Techniques: An Empirical Comparison of Different Approaches', EQUALITAS Working Paper 35. Spain: EQUALITAS.

Osberg, L. and A. Bandara (2012). 'Why Poverty Remains High in Tanzania: And What to Do About It?', Special Paper 12/3. Dar es Salaam: REPOA.

World Bank (2007). *Tanzania: Sustaining and Sharing Economic Growth* (CEM and Poverty Assessment). Washington, DC: World Bank (1 March).

World Bank (2012). *Spreading the Wings: From Growth to Shared Prosperity* (PREM Issue 2). Washington, DC: World Bank.

World Bank (2013). *Tanzania Economic Update: Raising the Game* (PREM Issue 4). Washington, DC: World Bank.

World Bank (2015). *Tanzania Poverty Assessment*. Washington, DC: World Bank.

# 15

# Estimating Multidimensional Poverty in Zambia

*Kristi Mahrt and Gibson Masumbu*

## 15.1 Introduction

Throughout the 2000s, Zambia achieved robust economic growth with real gross domestic product (GDP) growing at an average annual rate of 7 per cent, making Zambia one of the fastest-growing economies in southern Africa (World Bank 2014; AFDB 2013) and boosting Zambia from low-income to middle-income country status. This economic achievement is remarkable in that it follows more than twenty years of economic decline whereby GDP per capita fell from US$1,070 at independence to US$582 in 1994 (World Bank 2013), rural extreme consumption poverty peaked in 1993 at 84 per cent (UNDP 2013), and life expectancy fell from fifty-three years in 1987 to forty-eight years in 1992 (Bonnick 1997). The growth rebound is thus broadly welcomed. Nevertheless, the re-emergence of sustained, strong macroeconomic performance has not proven to be inclusive. While urban consumption poverty rates have fallen from as high as 56 per cent in 1998 to 28 per cent in 2010,[1] rural rates have hovered near 80 per cent since 1996 (World Bank 2014).

In this chapter, we continue the effort of Masumbu and Mahrt (2016) to better understand the nature of welfare dynamics during this period of high growth and relatively little rural consumption poverty reduction. Both analyses evaluate the evolution of non-monetary welfare in Zambia through an application of the first-order dominance (FOD) methodology. FOD comparisons generate information about the relative welfare of the nine provinces of Zambia and their

---

[1] The 2006 and 2010 poverty rates are not strictly comparable with earlier years. These rates were calculated using year-specific Engel ratios to derive food shares while previous years used a fixed ratio.

performance over time. In this chapter, we focus on an extension of the methodology to compare household welfare by rural economic activity and urban housing cost areas. Analysis by rural household stratum provides a more detailed perspective on rural welfare, which is particularly pressing in the Zambian context of only modest gains in rural consumption poverty. From the 1996, 2006, and 2010 Living Conditions Monitoring Surveys (LCMS), we define welfare in terms of five household-level binary indicators measuring deprivations in five basic needs: water, sanitation, shelter, energy, and education.

With welfare defined in terms of binary indicators based on categorical data, careful and purposeful attention must be given to defining cut-offs that determine which outcomes are deemed deprived or not deprived. In this chapter we focus on cut-off levels to illustrate two points. First, data restrictions often prohibit indicator definitions from aligning with development and policy goals. Second, FOD results are sensitive to variable definitions, not only because outcomes across populations are likely to differ with alternative definitions, but also within a given set of definitions too much similarity or too many differences among indicators in each population could prevent meaningful comparisons.

The chapter is structured as follows. Section 15.2 provides a brief contextual discussion of rural poverty. Section 15.3 presents the FOD methodology. Section 15.4 presents the data and addresses FOD indicator choices. Section 15.5 discusses spatial and temporal welfare comparisons for both provinces and rural and urban household strata, sensitivity to indicator choices, and indeterminate outcomes. Finally, section 15.6 concludes.

## 15.2 Context

The Zambian government has prioritized poverty reduction since the 2002 adoption of the interim Poverty Reduction Strategy Paper (PSRP), and the subsequent Fifth and Sixth National Development Plans (FNDP and SNDP). Yet despite targeted planning and robust growth, 2010 national monetary poverty lines indicate the Zambian population has not benefited equally. Figure 15.1 displays rural and urban poverty rates over the period 1996 to 2010. In 2010, 78 per cent of rural populations still live in poverty compared to only 28 per cent in urban areas. Furthermore, 90 per cent of Zambians living below the extreme poverty line reside in rural areas (CSO 2010).

Table 15.1 disaggregates urban and rural poverty trends by urban housing cost areas and rural economic activities.[2] These figures pinpoint the modest

---

[2] Small-, medium-, and large-scale farms are those achieving the greater of two criteria. Either households are cultivating less than 5 hectares, 5–20 hectares, and more than 20 hectares,

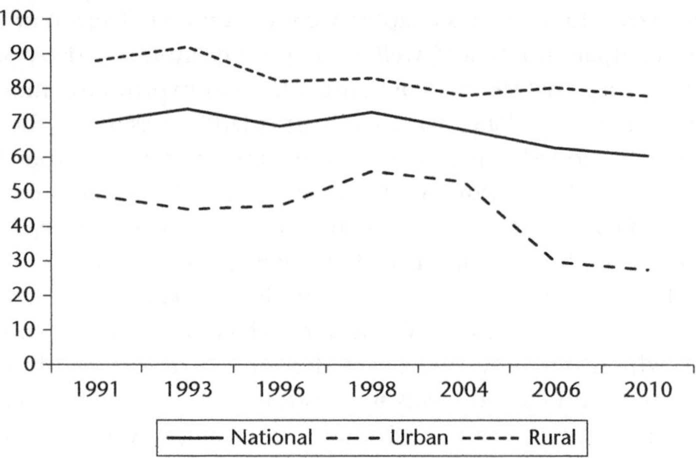


**Figure 15.1.** Urban and rural poverty, 1996–2010

*Note*: The 2006 and 2010 poverty rates are not strictly comparable with earlier years. These rates were calculated using year-specific Engel ratios to derive food shares while previous years used a fixed ratio.

*Source*: World Development Indicators (World Bank 2014)

**Table 15.1.** Consumption poverty headcount rates by stratum (per cent), 1996–2010

|  | 1996 | 1998 | 2004 | 2006* | 2010* | 2010 Population share | 2010 Contribution to national poverty |
|---|---|---|---|---|---|---|---|
| Low-cost housing | 58 | 61 | 58 | 35 | 35 | 26 | 15 |
| Medium cost | 43 | 50 | 46 | 14 | 9 | 6 | 1 |
| High-cost housing | 36 | 33 | 30 | 5 | 5 | 3 | < 1 |
| Small-scale farms | 88 | 84 | 79 | 82 | 80 | 59 | 78 |
| Medium-scale farms | 73 | 72 | 73 | 70 | 70 | 2 | 3 |
| Large-scale farms | 22 | 16 | 37 | 33 | 25 | < 1 | < 1 |
| Non-agricultural | 80 | 80 | 69 | 68 | 59 | 4 | 4 |

*Note*: * The 2006 and 2010 poverty rates are not strictly comparable with earlier years. These rates were calculated using year-specific Engel ratios to derive food shares while previous years used a fixed ratio.
*Source*: CSO (2005, 2012)

reductions in rural poverty to a failure of agricultural households to achieve substantial gains. Between 1996 and 2010, rural non-agricultural consumption poverty fell twenty-one percentage points to 59 per cent compared to reductions of eight and three percentage points to 80 per cent and 70 per cent in small- and medium-scale farm households, respectively. However, as non-agricultural households comprise only 6 per cent of rural households and

respectively, or they own at least a specified number of livestock or poultry. To be classified as small-scale farms, households must own fewer than five exotic dairy cows and no beef cattle, exotic pigs, broilers, or layers. See CSO (1997) for specific details.

4 per cent of all Zambian households, these significant gains had little impact on rural and overall poverty. On the other hand, small-scale farm households comprise 90 per cent of rural populations and account for 93 per cent of the rural poor, and comprise 59 per cent of Zambia's population and 78 per cent of the nation's poor.

Given the high percentage of poor households engaged in small-scale farming, attention to the polarized socioeconomic structure of the Zambian economy remains central to poverty reduction efforts. The primary push to reduce rural poverty has occurred through large government agricultural programmes. Subsidized seed and fertilizer distributed via the Farmer Input Support Programme (FISP), formally the Fertilizer Support Programme, and price supports via the Food Reserve Agency (FRA) account for the majority of agricultural spending under the Poverty Reduction Strategy (Mason et al. 2013). However, such programmes have been less effective at reaching the poorest subset of the population, small-scale and medium-scale farms. Only 9, 11, and 30 per cent of Zambian small-scale and medium-scale households received subsidized fertilizer through FISP in 2002/3, 2006/7, and 2010/11, respectively, and only 1, 10, and 27 per cent sold maize to the FRA in the 2003/4, 2007/8, and 2011/12 maize marketing years, respectively (Mason et al. 2015; Mason and Tembo 2014). Furthermore, wealthier households and households farming larger plots of land were more likely to participate in FISP; wealthier households on average received greater shares of fertilizer (Mofya-Mukuka et al. 2013; Mason and Tembo 2014).

In addition to agricultural supports, Zambia has made remarkable improvements in public service delivery in the last ten years. In 2005, the country benefited from substantial debt relief through the Heavily Indebted Poor Countries Initiatives that led to freeing of resources for poverty reduction programmes. The 2006 budgetary allocations to the social sectors stood at 30 per cent of the total budget, which was greater than any previous allocation (Zulu 2006) and has subsequently remained consistently high. Through the national development plans, the government of Zambia has implemented a number of strategies to enhance public service delivery. As a result, Zambia has achieved significant gains in wellbeing as seen in its climb from a low to a medium human development country in 2013 (UNDP 2014). Improvements have been recorded in dimensions such as infant mortality, under-five and maternal mortality rates, which have declined from 112,[3] 202,[4] and 650[5] in 1998 to 89, 93, and 440 (UNDP 2000, 2014). School enrolment has also increased over time although average years of schooling has remained stagnant at about 6 years by 2012 (UNDP 2014).

---

[3] Per 1,000 live births in 2012.    [4] Per 1,000 live births in 2012.
[5] Per 100,000 live births in 2010.

## 15.3 First-Order Dominance Methodology

First-order dominance (FOD) methodology is discussed in detail in Chapter 3, and thus this chapter provides an intuitive overview, drawing from Arndt et al. (2013). In brief, the FOD criterion asserts that it is better to be not deprived than deprived in any dimension. Consider a set of three ordinal, binary welfare indicators such that '0' indicates deprived and '1' indicates not deprived in each dimension. Each combination of welfare indicators is said to dominate, be dominated by, or be indeterminate relative to other combinations. The outcome (1,1,1) clearly is better than or dominates (0,0,0) since it is superior in every dimension. Furthermore, the outcome (1,1,0) dominates (0,1,0) because it is better to be not deprived than deprived in the first dimension. However, (1,1,0) and (0,0,1) are indeterminate outcomes. Without imposing assumptions regarding the relative importance of or substitutability between each outcome, it cannot be determined if it is better to be not deprived in the first two dimensions or in the third dimension.

Extending to two populations, A and B, consider the distribution of individuals falling into each combination of welfare indicators. The FOD criterion can be described as follows: population A first-order dominates population B if one can generate distribution B by transferring probability mass (i.e. moving individuals) from better to unambiguously worse outcomes within A, where better is defined as above.

Population groups are typically defined spatially to compare the welfare of geographic areas such as provinces or urban and rural areas. This study extends the FOD methodology to both compare welfare spatially and across household socioeconomic strata. The LCMS is stratified geographically and by rural household economic activity and urban housing cost areas, which allows welfare comparisons to be made between household strata and for each stratum over time.


## 15.4 Data

### 15.4.1 *LCMS Surveys*

FOD indicators are defined using the 1996, 2006, and 2010 Zambia LCMS conducted by the Central Statistical Office (CSO). These nationally representative surveys allow for welfare comparisons at the provincial and urban/rural levels. The sampling method also allows for analysis of households by urban housing cost areas (low-, medium-, and high-cost), and rural agricultural activities (non-agricultural, small-scale farm, medium-scale farm, and large-scale farm households). The total number of households surveyed increased over the study period from 11,787 in 1996 to 18,662 in 2006 and 19,397 in

2010. In urban areas 65, 20, and 15 per cent of the 2010 sample resides in low-, medium-, and high-cost areas, respectively. In rural areas, approximately 75, 10, and 15 per cent of the 2010 sample is engaged in small-scale farming, medium-scale farming, or non-agricultural activities, respectively. Fewer than sixty large-scale farming households were included in each sample, and therefore this stratum is excluded from analysis.

## 15.4.2 FOD Indicators

We aimed to define welfare in terms of five indicators inspired by the national development goals as outlined in the Fifth and Sixth National Development Plans (GRZ 2011a, 2011b) and Vision 2030 (GRZ 2006): water, sanitation, housing, energy, and education. For each indicator, a cut-off level of welfare was selected, which defines whether a household is deprived or not. The Millennium Development Goals provided guidance in selecting these cut-offs.[6] Table 15.2 presents each indicator and the corresponding definition of deprived.

In general, two issues may arise in defining indicators from survey data preventing the line between deprived and not deprived from being drawn as preferred. First, the questionnaire's response options pertaining to a given indicator may not closely align with policy goals. For instance, regarding the source of drinking water, response options might only broadly encompass water from any well as opposed to more detailed options such as water from a

**Table 15.2.** FOD indicators

| Indicators | Definitions |
| --- | --- |
| Water | Deprived if the main source of drinking water[1] is not supplied by a tap, pipe, protected well or spring, rainwater, or water kiosk.[2] |
| Sanitation | Deprived if the household does not use a flush toilet or a covered or uncovered latrine.[3] The use of communal or a neighbour's facilities is not considered a deprivation. |
| Housing | Deprived if the main flooring material is mud. |
| Fuel | Deprived if the household's cooking fuel source is firewood, charcoal, or crop/livestock material. |
| Education | Deprived if the household head has not completed primary school. |

*Note:* [1]The 1996 LCMS collected data on drinking water supply in the dry and wet seasons. The water indicator reflects drinking water supply in the dry season. [2]While water purchased from vendors is generally excluded from improved water sources, water kiosks differ in the formal provision of safe water at regulated prices. Only the 2010 LCMS reports drinking water supply from water kiosks; however, this does not create inconsistency since the kiosks were first introduced in 2006. [3]The use of uncovered latrines should be considered a deprivation; however, the 1996 and 2006 LCMS do not distinguish between covered and uncovered latrines.

*Source:* Authors' definitions

[6] MDG definitions of improved water and sanitation (WHO and UNICEF 2014) provided a framework for defining the water and sanitation indicators.

covered or water from an uncovered well. Development goals might focus on providing drinking water from a covered well or better. Second, though the questionnaire might identify useful categorizations, definitions may vary slightly or may not be interpreted similarly from year to year. For example, though the questionnaire distinguishes between covered and uncovered wells, the percentage of people responding that they obtain water from each source might be implausibly different from one year to the next. This chapter addresses the issue of response options defined more broadly than policy goals. The issue of seemingly unlikely changes in outcomes over time is addressed in terms of the sanitation indicator in Nigeria (Chapter 13 by Ajakaiye et al. in this volume).

The 1996 and 2006 LCMS questionnaires do not provide responses that permit the sanitation indicator to closely align with poverty reduction goals. Ideally, we would define the sanitation indicator to be consistent with the internationally recognized definition of improved sanitation laid out for the MDGs. In this definition, improved sanitation includes latrines covered with a slab but not open latrines. The MDGs' definition of improved sanitation further classifies all facilities shared among households to be unimproved. Unfortunately, the LCMS questionnaires prior to 2010 do not distinguish between covered and uncovered latrines. Though the LCMS distinguishes whether the household uses its own facilities or not, it does not identify if own facilities are shared. Given the data, the decision to define deprivation in sanitation as the lack of a flush toilet, covered latrine, or uncovered latrine was based on the more urgent priority of access to any latrine as opposed to access to flush toilets. Table 15.3 describes the sanitation indicator used in analysis and three alternative sanitation indicators. Section 15.4 will evaluate the sensitivity of FOD results to each sanitation indicator.

**Table 15.3.** Sanitation indicators

| Indicators | Definitions |
| --- | --- |
| Flush/any latrine | Deprived if the household does not use a flush toilet or a covered or uncovered latrine. |
| Own | Deprived if the household does not have a flush toilet or a covered or uncovered latrine. The use of a communal or a neighbour's facility is considered a deprivation. Sharing the household's own facilities with others is not a deprivation. |
| Flush | Deprived if the household does not use a flush toilet. |
| Flush/covered latrine | Deprived if the household does not use a flush toilet or a covered latrine. This definition is only possible with the 2010 LCMS. |

*Source*: Authors' definitions

## 15.5 Results

This section presents an assessment of Zambia's household welfare in 1996, 2006, and 2010.[7,8] We begin with a discussion of trends in each FOD indicator and then present temporal and spatial FOD results focusing on rural and urban welfare. Finally, we evaluate how each of the four sanitation definitions influences outcomes.

### 15.5.1 *Levels of Deprivation*

Table 15.4 presents deprivations across urban housing cost areas, rural agricultural strata, and all areas of analysis. Overall deprivation in access to water, sanitation, and education significantly declined over the period while only modest declines were registered in deprivation in shelter and cooking fuel. In contrast to monetary poverty trends, the indicators provide evidence of improved welfare in rural areas whereas urban welfare essentially stagnated in all indicators except education. Substantial gains in rural areas were concentrated in small-scale farm and non-agricultural households. Over the study period, a great disparity persisted in deprivation levels of households residing in urban low-cost housing areas compared to medium- and high-cost areas. However, low-cost areas outperformed all rural strata in every indicator by a large margin. Though rural areas achieved notable gains, both the deprivation rates and the gap between urban and rural deprivation levels remained high.

### 15.5.2 *Temporal FOD Comparisons*

Temporal FOD results are presented as the net probability of domination, which measures the probability that the welfare of an area or stratum improves between two years net of any probability of regression. Positive values indicate the probability of advancement in welfare and negative values indicate the probability of regression.

Table 15.5 displays the net temporal FOD results for each aggregate area, province, and stratum. At the national level, FOD comparisons indicate significant probabilities of advancement over time. National welfare advanced between 1996 and 2010 with a probability of 55 per cent and rural areas advanced with a probability of 87 per cent. Between 2006 and 2010, both urban and rural areas registered a 44 per cent probability of advancement. Provincial results also indicate rural advancement, in that predominately rural Central, Eastern, Northern, North-Western, and Southern provinces exhibit

---

[7] The use of updated 2010 weights resulted in slightly different figures than Masumbu and Mahrt (2016); however, overall trends and conclusions remain the same.

[8] Population weights are used throughout the analysis.

**Table 15.4.** Household deprivation by indicator (per cent)

| | Water | | | Sanitation | | | Shelter | | | Fuel | | | Education | | |
|---|---|---|---|---|---|---|---|---|---|---|---|---|---|---|---|
| | 1996 | 2006 | 2010 | 1996 | 2006 | 2010 | 1996 | 2006 | 2010 | 1996 | 2006 | 2010 | 1996 | 2006 | 2010 |
| National | 48 | 42 | 34 | 22 | 13 | 12 | 57 | 61 | 56 | 85 | 84 | 84 | 43 | 36 | 31 |
| Rural | 70 | 58 | 48 | 33 | 19 | 17 | 82 | 84 | 78 | 99 | 98 | 98 | 56 | 48 | 41 |
| Urban | 11 | 12 | 8 | 2 | 2 | 1 | 13 | 19 | 14 | 60 | 58 | 57 | 21 | 14 | 14 |
| Central | 47 | 39 | 31 | 16 | 5 | 4 | 62 | 71 | 56 | 87 | 91 | 89 | 42 | 37 | 26 |
| Copperbelt | 27 | 28 | 22 | 2 | 1 | 1 | 25 | 29 | 29 | 68 | 62 | 67 | 27 | 19 | 20 |
| Eastern | 56 | 41 | 24 | 43 | 22 | 26 | 79 | 79 | 72 | 97 | 97 | 96 | 60 | 57 | 52 |
| Luapula | 89 | 87 | 69 | 6 | 2 | 2 | 76 | 86 | 75 | 97 | 98 | 98 | 50 | 41 | 42 |
| Lusaka | 4 | 4 | 4 | 2 | 3 | 2 | 10 | 13 | 8 | 58 | 54 | 48 | 22 | 16 | 14 |
| Northern | 86 | 71 | 68 | 10 | 1 | 1 | 87 | 82 | 75 | 98 | 96 | 96 | 52 | 41 | 34 |
| N.-Western | 80 | 59 | 44 | 7 | 3 | 4 | 85 | 85 | 77 | 96 | 97 | 94 | 58 | 44 | 38 |
| Southern | 40 | 28 | 23 | 61 | 34 | 28 | 64 | 62 | 57 | 93 | 89 | 88 | 50 | 33 | 31 |
| Western | 68 | 57 | 50 | 63 | 56 | 42 | 84 | 88 | 84 | 97 | 97 | 98 | 55 | 52 | 35 |
| Low cost | 12 | 13 | 10 | 3 | 2 | 1 | 16 | 22 | 18 | 71 | 66 | 67 | 25 | 16 | 16 |
| Medium cost | 6 | 5 | 2 | 0 | 1 | 0 | 5 | 6 | 2 | 27 | 27 | 34 | 9 | 5 | 9 |
| High cost | 3 | 3 | 3 | 1 | 1 | 0 | 2 | 2 | 3 | 22 | 12 | 21 | 5 | 3 | 5 |
| Small-scale farms | 73 | 59 | 49 | 34 | 19 | 18 | 84 | 85 | 80 | 99 | 98 | 98 | 57 | 49 | 42 |
| Medium-scale farms | 52 | 47 | 50 | 28 | 15 | 17 | 60 | 62 | 62 | 97 | 97 | 97 | 40 | 33 | 31 |
| Non-agricultural | 43 | 42 | 28 | 25 | 14 | 11 | 58 | 72 | 61 | 97 | 91 | 86 | 50 | 42 | 30 |

*Source*: Authors' calculations based on the CSO 1996, 2006, and 2010 LCMS datasets

**Table 15.5.** Temporal net FOD comparisons by area and stratum (probabilities)

| | 2006 FOD 1996 | 2010 FOD 2006 | 2010 FOD 1996 |
|---|---|---|---|
| National | 0.20 | 0.45 | **0.55** |
| Rural | 0.09 | **0.44** | **0.87** |
| Urban | | **0.44** | 0.35 |
| Central | 0.02 | **0.51** | 0.22 |
| Copperbelt | 0.22 | −0.04 | 0.40 |
| Eastern | 0.43 | 0.03 | **0.47** |
| Luapula | | 0.07 | 0.20 |
| Lusaka | 0.06 | 0.19 | 0.29 |
| Northern | **0.80** | −0.02 | **0.93** |
| North-Western | 0.18 | 0.01 | **0.63** |
| Southern | **0.63** | 0.38 | **0.70** |
| Western | 0.07 | 0.32 | 0.22 |
| Urban low-cost housing | | 0.30 | 0.13 |
| Urban medium-cost housing | | 0.03 | |
| Urban high-cost housing | | | |
| Small-scale farms | 0.03 | 0.13 | **0.68** |
| Medium-scale farms | 0.05 | −0.04 | 0.02 |
| Rural non-agricultural | | **0.86** | 0.30 |

*Note*: Values in bold indicate domination in the static case (FOD without bootstrapping).
*Source*: Authors' calculations based on the CSO 1996, 2006, and 2010 LCMS datasets

notable probabilities of welfare improvements in 2010. The stronger evidence of rural compared to urban advancement stands in contrast to monetary trends over the same period, indicating significant reductions in urban poverty compared to only modest reductions in rural poverty (Figure 15.1).

This contrast between trends in multidimensional welfare and monetary poverty holds when FOD comparisons are decomposed by urban household stratum. Specifically, FOD results provide evidence that only low-cost housing areas improved with a probability of 30 per cent. However, welfare improvements in rural strata are more complex. Consistent with the 21 per cent decline in monetary poverty between 1996 and 2010 in non-agricultural households (Table 15.1), FOD results indicate an 86 per cent likelihood of welfare advancement between 2006 and 2010. Monetary poverty in medium-scale agricultural households stagnated at around 70 per cent over the study period, which is confirmed by the lack of evidence of advancement or regression in FOD comparisons. Despite a modest reduction in monetary poverty from 88 per cent to 80 per cent, small-scale farms achieved a 68 per cent likelihood of advancement in the FOD indicators between 1996 and 2010.

### 15.5.3 *Spatial FOD Comparisons*

In each year, FOD comparisons are made between all areas to determine the degree of domination of each aggregate area and province. In separate comparisons, the relative welfare of household strata is also evaluated. Spatial results are presented in two formats. First, spatial tables (Tables 15.6 and 15.7) present

**Table 15.6.** 1996 Bootstrap spatial FOD comparisons (probabilities)

| Areas | National | Rural | Urban | Central | Copperbelt | Eastern | Luapula | Lusaka | Northern | North-Western | Southern | Western | Avg. |
|---|---|---|---|---|---|---|---|---|---|---|---|---|---|
| National | | **1** | | | | 0.89 | | | | | 0.01 | **0.99** | 0.26 |
| Rural | | | | | | | | | | | | 0.02 | 0.00 |
| Urban | 1 | 1 | | **0.99** | 0.44 | 1 | 0.95 | | 1 | **0.99** | 1 | 1 | 0.85 |
| Central | 0.05 | 1 | | | | **0.84** | | | 0.02 | 0.01 | 0.13 | **0.99** | 0.28 |
| Copperbelt | 1 | 1 | | **0.96** | | **0.98** | 0.96 | | 1 | **0.96** | **0.98** | 1 | 0.80 |
| Eastern | | 0.01 | | | | | | | | | | 0.08 | 0.01 |
| Luapula | | | | | | | | | 0.14 | | | | 0.01 |
| Lusaka | 1 | 1 | 0.01 | 1 | 0.27 | 1 | **0.94** | | 1 | **0.99** | 1 | 1 | 0.84 |
| Northern | | 0.01 | | | | | | | | | | 0.01 | 0.00 |
| N.-Western | | | | | | | | | 0.04 | | | 0.01 | 0.00 |
| Southern | | | | | | | | | | | | **0.60** | 0.05 |
| Western | | 0.01 | | | | | | | | | | | 0.00 |
| Average | 0.28 | 0.46 | 0.00 | 0.27 | 0.06 | 0.43 | 0.26 | 0.00 | 0.29 | 0.27 | 0.28 | 0.52 | 0.26 |

*Note*: Values in bold indicate domination in the static case (FOD without bootstrapping).
*Source*: Authors' calculations based on the CSO 1996, 2006, and 2010 LCMS datasets

**Table 15.7.** 2010 Bootstrap spatial FOD comparisons (probabilities)

| Areas | National | Rural | Urban | Central | Copperbelt | Eastern | Luapula | Lusaka | Northern | N.- Western | Southern | Western | Avg. |
|---|---|---|---|---|---|---|---|---|---|---|---|---|---|
| National | | 1 | | | | | | | | | | **0.95** | 0.18 |
| Rural | | | | | | | | | | | | 0.06 | 0.01 |
| Urban | 1 | 1 | | **0.99** | **0.81** | 1 | **0.99** | | 0.98 | 1 | 1 | 1 | 0.89 |
| Central | 0.06 | 1 | | | | | 0.04 | | | 0.28 | 0.01 | **0.99** | 0.22 |
| Copperbelt | 1 | 1 | | **0.73** | | **0.96** | **0.75** | | 0.50 | 0.97 | 0.90 | **0.99** | 0.71 |
| Eastern | | | | | | | | | | | | | 0.00 |
| Luapula | | | | | | | | | | | | | 0.00 |
| Lusaka | 1 | 1 | 0.03 | **0.91** | 0.27 | 1 | **0.72** | | 0.46 | **0.97** | 1 | 1 | 0.76 |
| Northern | | | | | | | 0.15 | | | | | | 0.01 |
| N.-Western | | 0.31 | | | | | 0.01 | | | | | **0.58** | 0.08 |
| Southern | | 0.01 | | | | 0.32 | | | | | | **0.89** | 0.11 |
| Western | | | | | | | | | | | | | 0.00 |
| Average | 0.28 | 0.48 | 0.00 | 0.24 | 0.10 | 0.30 | 0.24 | 0.00 | 0.18 | 0.29 | 0.26 | 0.59 | 0.25 |

*Note*: Values in bold indicate domination in the static case (FOD without bootstrapping).
*Source*: Authors' calculations based on the CSO 1996, 2006, and 2010 LCMS datasets

the FOD outcome of each area compared to every other area. Second, area and household stratum rankings are presented based on spatial bootstrap outcomes (Tables 15.8 and 15.9). While spatial tables provide more detail, ranking tables conveniently summarize the welfare performance of each population relative to other populations.

Tables 15.6 and 15.7 present spatial FOD results for 1996 and 2010. Row by row, values in the inner table represent the probability that a population dominates the corresponding column population.[9] Higher row averages are associated with relatively better-off populations (populations likely to dominate) while higher column averages are associated with relatively worse-off populations (populations likely to be dominated). Outer row values present row averages, which measure the probability the row population dominates all other populations. Reading down the columns, inner values represent the probability that a population is dominated by the row population and outer values represent the probability that the population is dominated by all other populations. In interpreting a population's relative wellbeing, both row and column averages should be considered.

Net domination measures the probability that an area dominates other areas (row averages) minus the probability it is dominated by other areas (column averages). Net domination scores provide a basis for ranking provinces and conveniently presenting relative wellbeing. Table 15.8 presents area rankings and Table 15.9 presents urban and rural stratum rankings. It is worth noting that the difference in net domination scores is often insufficiently large to distinguish between differences in welfare outcomes and variability introduced through random bootstrapping. To avoid misinterpreting rankings within the tables, shading and lines identify clusters with similar net domination scores. Within these clusters, ranks cannot be established with confidence.

### 15.5.3.1 AREA COMPARISONS

Tables 15.6 and 15.7 present 1996 and 2010 area spatial results. In all three years, row averages indicate that urban areas, Copperbelt, and Lusaka dominated all other areas with a high degree of probability. Rural areas and Western province exhibit the highest average probability of being dominated (near 50 per cent or greater) in both 1996 and 2010. In all three years, virtually all FOD comparisons not involving one of the aforementioned areas result in indeterminate outcomes in the static case or low probabilities of domination in bootstrapping. In other words, nearly all FOD outcomes depend on the extent to which an area is dominated by urban areas, Lusaka, or Copperbelt, and the extent to which it dominates rural areas and Western province.

---

[9] Note that bootstrap sampling introduces a degree of randomness into the results and care must be taken in interpreting very small probabilities or small differences in probabilities.

**Table 15.8.** Area rankings by probability of net domination

| 1996 | Domination | Rank | 2006 | Domination | Rank | 2010 | Domination | Rank | 1996–2010 Change |
|---|---|---|---|---|---|---|---|---|---|
| Urban | 0.85 | 1 | Copperbelt | 0.73 | 1 | Urban | 0.89 | 1 | 0 |
| Lusaka | 0.84 | 2 | Urban | 0.68 | 2 | Lusaka | 0.76 | 2 | 0 |
| Copperbelt | 0.74 | 3 | Lusaka | 0.58 | 3 | Copperbelt | 0.61 | 3 | 0 |
| Central | 0.01 | 4 | Central | –0.01 | 4 | Central | –0.02 | 4 | 0 |
| National | –0.01 | 5 | Northern | –0.01 | 5 | National | –0.10 | 5 | 0 |
| Southern | –0.23 | 6 | National | –0.05 | 6 | Southern | –0.15 | 6 | 0 |
| Luapula | –0.25 | 7 | N.-Western | –0.14 | 7 | Northern | –0.16 | 7 | –2 |
| N.-Western | –0.26 | 8 | Southern | –0.14 | 8 | N.-Western | –0.21 | 8 | 0 |
| Northern | –0.29 | 9 | Luapula | –0.22 | 9 | Luapula | –0.24 | 9 | 2 |
| Eastern | –0.42 | 10 | Eastern | –0.37 | 10 | Eastern | –0.30 | 10 | 0 |
| Rural | –0.46 | 11 | Rural | –0.47 | 11 | Rural | –0.48 | 11 | 0 |
| Western | –0.52 | 12 | Western | –0.58 | 12 | Western | –0.59 | 12 | 0 |

*Note*: Rankings within shaded groups are highly sensitive to small perturbations and should be interpreted with caution.

*Source*: Authors' calculations based on the CSO 1996, 2006, and 2010 LCMS datasets

**Table 15.9.** Area rankings by probability of net domination

| 1996 | | | 2006 | | | 2010 | | | 1996–2010 |
|---|---|---|---|---|---|---|---|---|---|
| | Domination | Rank | | Domination | Rank | | Domination | Rank | Change |
| Medium-cost housing | 0.86 | 1 | High-cost housing | 0.96 | 1 | High cost housing | 0.87 | 1 | −1 |
| High cost housing | 0.79 | 2 | Medium-cost housing | 0.65 | 2 | Medium-cost housing | 0.86 | 2 | 1 |
| Urban | 0.55 | 3 | Urban | 0.55 | 3 | Urban | 0.51 | 3 | 0 |
| Low cost housing | 0.31 | 4 | Low-cost housing | 0.35 | 4 | Low cost housing | 0.27 | 4 | 0 |
| National | −0.23 | 5 | National | −0.20 | 5 | National | −0.21 | 5 | 0 |
| Medium-scale farms | −0.30 | 6 | Medium-scale farms | −0.30 | 6 | Non-agricultural | −0.22 | 6 | −1 |
| Non-agricultural | −0.35 | 7 | Non-agricultural | −0.33 | 7 | Medium-scale farms | −0.55 | 7 | 1 |
| Rural | −0.71 | 8 | Rural | −0.70 | 8 | Rural | −0.63 | 8 | 0 |
| Small-scale farms | −0.90 | 9 | Small-scale farms | −0.97 | 9 | Small-scale farms | −0.89 | 9 | 0 |

*Note*: Rankings within shaded groups are highly sensitive to small perturbations and should be interpreted with caution.

*Source*: Authors' calculations based on the CSO 1996, 2006, and 2010 LCMS datasets

Table 15.8 presents provincial rankings based on net domination scores. Keeping in mind that small differences in net domination scores may not be robust, Table 15.8 shows that little change in ranking occurs between 1996 and 2010. As seen in the spatial tables, urban areas, Lusaka, and Copperbelt are ranked at the top and rural areas and Western provinces are ranked at the bottom, in all three years. Though temporal results suggest advancement in rural areas and many rural provinces, these gains were not sufficient to improve their rankings, as rural provinces remain dominated by urban areas and urban provinces. With the exception of Central province, rural areas and provinces remain persistently and in most cases severely deprived.

### 15.5.3.2 HOUSEHOLD STRATUM COMPARISONS

The spatial FOD methodology applied to rural and urban household strata are more or less as one would expect and therefore FOD tables are not presented. In each year, all urban strata dominate all rural strata, rural areas, and the nation with probabilities at or near 100 per cent. Within urban strata, high and medium-cost areas dominate low-cost areas, but never dominate one another. Within the rural strata, both medium-scale agricultural households and non-agricultural households strongly dominate small-scale agricultural households in most cases but neither stratum ever dominates the other. These strata perform quite similarly in 1996 and 2006. However, in 2010 medium-scale agricultural households no longer dominate rural areas and dominate small-scale agricultural households to a much lesser degree while non-agricultural households dominate to a greater degree. This relative welfare improvement of non-agricultural households is consistent with temporal advancement between 2006 and 2010.

This reversal in the relative performance of medium-scale and non-agricultural households is also the most notable trend in the ranking table (Table 15.9). High-cost and medium-cost households also reverse. The remaining net domination scores and the resulting rankings are quite stable. Despite temporal evidence of welfare advancement in small-scale agricultural households and rural areas between 1996 and 2010 and non-agricultural households between 2006 and 2010, these advancements were insufficient to change rankings relative to the nation and urban populations. Small-scale agricultural households remain severely deprived relative to all other household strata as evidenced by net domination scores near −0.90 in 1996 and 2010.

### 15.5.4 *Indicator Sensitivity*

In this section we explore the sensitivity of temporal and spatial FOD outcomes to indicator definitions by exploring the impact of each of the four sanitation definitions presented in Table 15.3. This discussion is not intended

**Table 15.10.** Household deprivation by sanitation indicator (per cent)

| | Flush toilet or any latrine | | | Own flush toilet or any latrine | | | Flush toilet | | | Flush or covered latrine |
|---|---|---|---|---|---|---|---|---|---|---|
| | 1996 | 2006 | 2010 | 1996 | 2006 | 2010 | 1996 | 2006 | 2010 | 2010 |
| Nation | 22 | 13 | 12 | 33 | 26 | 31 | 79 | 85 | 87 | 67 |
| Rural | 33 | 19 | 17 | 42 | 29 | 33 | 98 | 98 | 99 | 85 |
| Urban | 2 | 2 | 1 | 18 | 20 | 26 | 46 | 62 | 64 | 33 |
| Central | 16 | 5 | 4 | 24 | 14 | 20 | 84 | 88 | 90 | 68 |
| Copperbelt | 2 | 1 | 1 | 10 | 7 | 13 | 42 | 51 | 58 | 42 |
| Eastern | 43 | 22 | 26 | 56 | 35 | 46 | 97 | 98 | 98 | 87 |
| Luapula | 6 | 2 | 2 | 18 | 15 | 17 | 96 | 96 | 99 | 86 |
| Lusaka | 2 | 3 | 2 | 25 | 34 | 41 | 60 | 76 | 75 | 28 |
| Northern | 10 | 1 | 1 | 21 | 9 | 12 | 97 | 96 | 96 | 85 |
| N.-Western | 7 | 3 | 4 | 18 | 13 | 29 | 95 | 96 | 97 | 81 |
| Southern | 61 | 34 | 28 | 67 | 49 | 49 | 90 | 89 | 91 | 65 |
| Western | 63 | 56 | 42 | 69 | 62 | 54 | 93 | 97 | 96 | 92 |
| Urban low-cost housing | 3 | 2 | 1 | 22 | 24 | 32 | 55 | 71 | 78 | 41 |
| Urban medium-cost housing | 0 | 1 | 0 | 4 | 8 | 11 | 21 | 26 | 25 | 10 |
| Urban high-cost housing | 1 | 1 | 0 | 6 | 4 | 10 | 10 | 12 | 21 | 9 |
| Small-scale farms | 34 | 19 | 18 | 43 | 29 | 33 | 98 | 98 | 99 | 86 |
| Medium-scale farms | 28 | 15 | 17 | 30 | 20 | 32 | 96 | 97 | 98 | 74 |
| Rural non-agricultural | 25 | 14 | 11 | 43 | 35 | 36 | 95 | 94 | 94 | 68 |

*Source*: Authors' calculations based on the CSO 1996, 2006, and 2010 LCMS datasets

to dig deeper into the sanitation indicator per se, but rather to illustrate the sensitivity of FOD outcomes to indicator definitions. We will also show that in some circumstances a single indicator choice can lead to a high degree of indeterminate outcomes, rendering FOD analysis much less effective.

Beginning with a look at descriptive statistics for each sanitation indicator, Table 15.10 highlights how different definitions can tell quite different stories about the level and degree of change in welfare. For instance, the percentage of households that do not use a *flush toilet* or *any latrine* declined significantly in rural areas but held steady in urban areas. Though the *own* indicator also suggests improvements in rural areas, urban areas backslid. Finally, the *flush* indicator suggests persistently high rural deprivation and significantly deteriorating conditions in in urban areas. In addition, patterns of deprivation differ with the *own* indicator driven by the prevalence of communal facilities in Lusaka. Compared to the large gap between urban and rural deprivation exhibited by other sanitation indicators, in 2010, own sanitation deprivation in the nation, rural areas, and urban areas is quite similar. Furthermore, deprivation in own sanitation is higher in Lusaka than the rural provinces of Central, Lupuala, Northern, and North-Western. Three of the poorest provinces, Lupuala, Northern, and North-Western, outperform almost all areas,

**Table 15.11.** Temporal net FOD comparisons by sanitation indicator (probabilities)

| | Flush toilet or any latrine | | | Own flush toilet or any latrine | | | Flush toilet | | |
|---|---|---|---|---|---|---|---|---|---|
| | 2006 FOD 1996 | 2010 FOD 2006 | 2010 FOD 1996 | 2006 FOD 1996 | 2010 FOD 2006 | 2010 FOD 1996 | 2006 FOD 1996 | 2010 FOD 2006 | 2010 FOD 1996 |
| National | 0.20 | 0.45 | **0.55** | 0.15 | | 0.16 | 0.03 | 0.24 | |
| Rural | 0.09 | **0.44** | **0.87** | 0.07 | 0.01 | **0.67** | 0.04 | 0.02 | 0.18 |
| Urban | | **0.44** | 0.35 | | | | | 0.15 | |
| Central | 0.02 | **0.51** | 0.22 | 0.02 | | 0.14 | −0.01 | 0.29 | 0.05 |
| Copperbelt | 0.22 | −0.04 | 0.40 | 0.23 | −0.03 | 0.05 | 0.10 | 0.12 | 0.03 |
| Eastern | 0.43 | 0.03 | **0.47** | 0.43 | | **0.38** | −0.01 | 0.20 | 0.10 |
| Luapula | | 0.07 | 0.20 | | 0.02 | 0.12 | | 0.01 | 0.06 |
| Lusaka | 0.06 | 0.19 | 0.29 | | −0.04 | | | 0.08 | |
| Northern | **0.80** | −0.02 | **0.93** | **0.79** | −0.01 | **0.88** | **0.66** | 0.25 | **0.64** |
| North-Western | 0.18 | 0.01 | **0.63** | 0.17 | | | 0.11 | 0.15 | 0.22 |
| Southern | **0.63** | 0.38 | **0.70** | **0.61** | 0.25 | **0.68** | 0.41 | 0.32 | 0.40 |
| Western | 0.07 | 0.32 | 0.22 | 0.06 | 0.31 | 0.22 | −0.03 | 0.29 | 0.05 |
| Urban low-cost housing | | 0.30 | 0.13 | | | | | | |
| Urban medium-cost housing | | 0.03 | | | −0.01 | | 0.11 | 0.01 | 0.02 |
| Urban high-cost housing | | | | | −0.02 | −0.01 | 0.08 | −0.01 | −0.07 |
| Small-scale farms | 0.03 | 0.13 | **0.68** | 0.02 | | **0.53** | 0.01 | | 0.02 |
| Medium-scale farms | 0.05 | −0.04 | 0.02 | 0.03 | −0.06 | | 0.02 | −0.08 | 0.02 |
| Rural non-agricultural | | **0.86** | 0.30 | | 0.14 | 0.01 | | **0.59** | 0.06 |

*Note*: Values in bold indicate domination in the static case (FOD without bootstrapping).
*Source*: Authors' calculations based on the CSO 1996, 2006, and 2010 LCMS datasets

including the urban area aggregate in many cases. Given the clear differences in the levels and dynamics of each sanitation indicator, it would be expected that FOD outcomes would also be sensitive to sanitation indicator choice.

Table 15.11 presents a comparison of temporal FOD outcomes using each sanitation indicator. Temporal results are sensitive to the sanitation indicator and generally mirror each indicator's pattern of deprivation. Temporal FOD comparisons using the *flush/any latrine* indicator point to a strong probability that national and rural welfare improved between 1996 and 2010. When the *own* indicator is used instead, only rural areas are likely to have improved over time. Finally, welfare is unlikely to have improved in any aggregate area with the *flush* indicator.

As with temporal FOD outcomes, spatial comparisons differ according to which sanitation indicator is included. In this discussion we will also consider the *flush/covered latrine* indicator, which was preferred but not used due to data limitations prior to 2010. Evaluating areas based on 2010 spatial net domination scores suggests that rankings do not differ substantially with the *flush/ any latrine*, *flush/covered latrine*, and the *flush* indicators (Table 15.12).

**Table 15.12.** 2010 Area rankings for each possible sanitation definition by probability of net domination

| Flush toilet or pit latrine of any kind | | | Flush toilet or covered latrrine | | | Flush toilet | | | Own flush toilet or own pit latrine of any kind | | |
|---|---|---|---|---|---|---|---|---|---|---|---|
| | Domination | Rank | | Domination | Rank | | Domination | Rank | | Domination | Rank |
| Urban | 0.89 | 1 | Lusaka | 0.92 | 1 | Urban | 0.82 | 1 | Copperbelt | 0.72 | 1 |
| Lusaka | | 2 | Urban | 0.89 | 2 | Lusaka | 0.82 | 2 | Urban | 0.51 | 2 |
| Copperbelt | 0.61 | 3 | Copperbelt | 0.51 | 3 | Copperbelt | 0.79 | 3 | Lusaka | 0.25 | 3 |
| Central | −0.02 | 4 | Southern | 0.24 | 4 | Southern | 0.20 | 4 | Central | 0.20 | 4 |
| National | −0.10 | 5 | Central | 0.20 | 5 | Central | 0.17 | 5 | National | 0.00 | 5 |
| Southern | −0.15 | 6 | National | 0.16 | 6 | National | 0.14 | 6 | Northern | −0.01 | 6 |
| Northern | −0.16 | 7 | Eastern | −0.29 | 7 | Eastern | −0.32 | 7 | Luapula | −0.11 | 7 |
| North Western | −0.21 | 8 | North Western | −0.43 | 8 | North Western | −0.41 | 8 | Southern | −0.16 | 8 |
| Luapula | −0.24 | 9 | Northern | −0.51 | 9 | Northern | −0.50 | 9 | North Western | −0.19 | 9 |
| Eastern | −0.30 | 10 | Western | −0.53 | 10 | Western | −0.55 | 10 | Eastern | −0.28 | 10 |
| Rural | −0.48 | 11 | Rural | −0.57 | 11 | Rural | −0.55 | 11 | Rural | −0.37 | 11 |
| Western | −0.59 | 12 | Luapula | −0.57 | 12 | Luapula | −0.61 | 12 | Western | −0.56 | 12 |

*Note*: Rankings within shaded groups are highly sensitive to small perturbations and should be interpreted with caution.

*Source*: Authors' calculations based on the CSO 1996, 2006, and 2010 LCMS datasets

*Flush/covered latrine* and *flush* results are remarkably similar. The *flush/any latrine* and *flush/covered latrine* results are similar once potential differences due to bootstrapping variation are taken into account. In contrast, the *own* indictor produces quite different outcomes. Most notably, Lusaka has a net domination score of only 0.25 compared to scores of at least 0.76 with the other three definitions.

### 15.5.5 *Indeterminate Outcomes*

Whether a household has its own facility does not necessarily correspond to the quality of the facility. As noted, introducing a measure of shared sanitation generates patterns of deprivation quite different from those of the other sanitation indicators. These patterns of deprivation also differ substantially from the water, shelter, fuel, and education indicators and thus lead to a high degree of indeterminate outcomes. Recall that the combination (1,0,0) is indeterminate compared to (0,1,1) because no assumptions are made whether it is better to be not deprived in the first dimension or not deprived in all other dimensions.[10] Relatively high deprivation in own sanitation in Lusaka and low deprivation in all other indicators creates an analogous scenario where Lusaka fails to dominate or be dominated by most areas. Table 15.13 illustrates the extent of the resulting indeterminacy compared to the *flush/any latrine* results reported in Table 15.7. Using the original set of indicators, as would be expected, Lusaka and urban areas dominated the nation, rural areas, and Central, Copperbelt, Lupuala, Northern, and North-Western provinces with probabilities near 50 per cent or more and in most cases close to 100 per cent. Using the *own* indicator in spatial FOD comparisons, Lusaka dominates none of these areas with probabilities greater than 5 per cent. Similarly, urban areas no longer dominate Central, Copperbelt, Lupuala, and Northern provinces.

It should be noted that extensive indeterminate outcomes are certainly not always the result of indicator definitions. Indeterminacy may also result simply because areas have extremely different deprivation levels among the FOD indicators. Mahrt and Nanivaso (Chapter 11 in this volume) find a great degree of indeterminacy in FOD analysis of the provinces of the DRC. In this case, the inability to conclusively compare welfare between provinces is more likely due to erratically different welfare profiles over time and space.

---

[10] See Chapter 11 by Mahrt and Nanivazo in this volume for a more detailed discussion of indeterminate outcomes.

**Table 15.13.** 2010 Bootstrap spatial FOD comparisons (probabilities) with sanitation defined to be not deprived if the household uses its own flush toilet or any latrine

| Areas | National | Rural | Urban | Central | Copperbelt | Eastern | Luapula | Lusaka | Northern | N.- Western | Southern | Western | Avg. |
|---|---|---|---|---|---|---|---|---|---|---|---|---|---|
| National | | 0.97 | | | | | | | | 0.07 | | **0.94** | 0.18 |
| Rural | | | | | | | | | | | | 0.02 | 0.00 |
| Urban | **0.97** | **0.97** | | | | 1 | | | | **0.71** | 1 | 1 | 0.51 |
| Central | 0.06 | 1 | | | | | 0.11 | | | **0.92** | 0.01 | **0.99** | 0.28 |
| Copperbelt | 1 | 1 | | **0.88** | | **0.96** | **0.96** | | 0.2 | 1 | 0.9 | **0.99** | 0.72 |
| Eastern | | | | | | | | | | | | | 0.00 |
| Luapula | | | | | | | | | | | | | 0.00 |
| Lusaka | | 0.01 | | | | **0.89** | | | | | **0.89** | **0.99** | 0.25 |
| Northern | | | | | | | 0.12 | | | | | | 0.01 |
| N.-Western | | 0.13 | | | | | | | | | | **0.52** | 0.06 |
| Southern | | | | | | 0.28 | | | | | | **0.73** | 0.09 |
| Western | | | | | | | | | | | | | 0.00 |
| Average | 0.18 | 0.37 | 0.00 | 0.08 | 0.00 | 0.28 | 0.11 | 0.00 | 0.02 | 0.25 | 0.25 | 0.56 | 0.18 |

*Note*: Values in bold indicate domination in the static case (FOD without bootstrapping).
*Source*: Authors' calculations based on the CSO 1996, 2006, and 2010 LCMS datasets

## 15.6 Discussion

Zambia has made strides in revitalizing its economy over the last twenty years. The country rebounded from low and even negative growth in the 1980s and 1990s to a high average annual growth rate of 7 per cent in the 2000s. Despite strong growth, structural changes over the last twenty years have brought little social transformation or employment creation (Resnick and Thurlow 2014). Though agricultural productivity has risen in recent years, productivity remains low with agriculture's contribution to GDP steadily declining. Furthermore, policy attempts in the 2000s to reduce rural poverty through farm input subsidies and price supports have largely failed to reach the poorest subset of rural households, small-scale farmers (Mason et al. 2015; Mason and Tembo 2014). Ultimately, impressive economic growth did not translate to substantial monetary poverty reduction for rural agricultural households compared to rural non-agricultural and urban households.

In contrast, strong growth and government efforts to increase spending on poverty reduction programmes and the delivery of public services appear to have had an impact on multidimensional poverty. FOD results provide evidence of broad-based gains in rural welfare in Zambia between 1996 and 2010—gains driven by small-scale farm and non-agricultural rural households. FOD also suggests urban welfare gains between 2006 and 2010, driven by gains in urban low-cost housing areas. While these results are not robust to all choices of sanitation indicators, access to any sanitation facility is a general and broadly accepted goal. Despite these welfare gains, rural households, particularly small-scale farm households, continue to lag significantly behind their urban counterparts. Nevertheless, the results indicate that, in terms of the multidimensional indicators employed, some of the fruits of the improved government investments and growth performance have been translated into real progress in important development indicators on the ground.

Finally, considering the sensitivity of FOD outcomes to indicator definitions, temporal results varied considerably using alternative sanitation indicators, while spatial results were robust to the use of the *flush, flush/covered,* and *flush/any latrine* indicators. However, the *own* indicator produced quite different results, including a high degree of indeterminate outcomes, as patterns of sanitation quality and patterns of own facility usage differ significantly. When indicators follow vastly different patterns among populations over time or space, FOD comparisons are likely to result in indeterminate outcomes and provide less information regarding relative welfare.

Given the sensitivity of the results to indicator definitions, further analysis is warranted. Applying FOD analysis to the 2010 and 2013 Zambia Demographic and Health Surveys would permit the use of the more relevantly defined sanitation indicator, flush/covered, and provide a brief glimpse of access to covered latrines over time. Furthermore, considering alternative indicators measuring aspects of welfare such as health, nutrition, or access to information would better our understanding of the sensitivity of results to indicator selection as well as deepen our knowledge of the evolution of welfare in Zambia.

## References


African Development Bank (AFDB) (2013). 'Development Effectiveness Review 2013: Zambia'. Tunis: African Development Bank.

Arndt, C., A. Hussain, V. Salvucci, F. Tarp, and L. Østerdal (2013). 'Advancing Small Area Estimation', Working Paper 2013-051. Helsinki: UNU-WIDER.

Bonnick, G. G. (1997). *Turning an Economy Around: Zambia Country Assistance Review.* Washington, DC: World Bank.

Central Statistical Office (CSO) (1997). *Living Conditions and Monitoring Survey I, 1996.* Lusaka: CSO.

Central Statistical Office (CSO) (2005). *Living Conditions and Monitoring Survey Report, 2004.* Lusaka: CSO.

Central Statistical Office (CSO) (2010). *Living Conditions and Monitoring Survey Report, 2006 and 2010.* Lusaka: CSO.

Central Statistical Office (CSO) (2012). *Census of Population and Housing Report.* Lusaka: CSO.

Government of the Republic of Zambia (GRZ) (2006). *Vision 2030: A Prosperous Middle-Income Nation by 2030.* Lusaka: GRZ.

Government of the Republic of Zambia (GRZ) (2011a). *Fifth National Development Plan (FNDP), 2011–2015.* Lusaka: GRZ.

Government of the Republic of Zambia (GRZ) (2011b). *Sixth National Development Plan (SNDP), 2011–2015.* Lusaka: GRZ.

Mason, N. M., T. S. Jayne, and R. Mofya-Mukuka (2013). 'Zambia's Input Subsidy Programs', *Agricultural Economics*, 44: 613–28.

Mason, N. M., T. S. Jayne, and R. J. Myers (2015). 'Smallholder Supply Response to Marketing Board Activities in a Dual Channel Marketing System: The Case of Zambia', *Journal of Agricultural Economics*, 66(1): 36–65.

Mason, N. M. and S. T. Tembo (2014). 'Do Input Subsidies Reduce Poverty among Smallholder Farm Households? Evidence from Zambia'. Selected paper prepared for presentation at the Agricultural & Applied Economics Association (AAEA) Annual Meeting, Minneapolis, MN, 27–29 July 2014.

Masumbu, G. and K. Mahrt (2016). 'Assessing Progress in Welfare Improvements in Zambia: A Multidimensional Approach', in C. Arndt, A. McKay, and F. Tarp (eds), *Growth and Poverty in Sub-Saharan Africa.* Oxford: Oxford University Press, 263–89.

Mofya-Mukuka, R., S. Kabwe, A. Kuteya, and N. M. Mason (2013). 'How Can the Zambian Government Improve the Targeting of the Farmer Input Support Program?', Working Paper 53. Lusaka: Indaba Agriculture Research Institute.

Resnick, D. and J. Thurlow (2014). 'The Political Economy of Zambia's Recovery Structural Change without Transformation?', Discussion Paper 01320. Washington, DC: International Food Policy Research.

UNDP (2000). *Human Development Report 2000*. New York: UNDP.

UNDP (2013). 'Millennium Development Goals: Progress Report, Zambia 2013'. Lusaka: UNDP.

UNDP (2014). *Human Development Report 2014*. New York: UNDP.

World Bank (2013). 'Zambian's Jobs Challenge: Realities on the Ground', Zambia Economic Brief, Issue 2. Washington, DC: World Bank. Available at <http://www.worldbank.org/content/dam/Worldbank/document/Africa/Zambia/Report/zambia-economic-brief-october-2013.pdf>.

World Bank (2014). 'World Development Indicators'. Available at <data.worldbank.org>.

WHO (World Health Organization) and UNICEF (2014). 'Progress on Drinking Water and Sanitation—2104 Update'. Geneva: WHO.

Zulu, J. J. (2006). 'Zambia after the HIPC "Surgery" and the Completion Point', Policy Brief. Lusaka, Zambia: Jesuit Centre for Theological Reflection (JCTR).

# Part III
# Summing-Up and Lessons Learnt

# 16

# Synthesis

*Channing Arndt, Kristi Mahrt, and Finn Tarp*

## 16.1 Introduction

This synthesis chapter seeks to draw general lessons from the case studies presented in Part II. It does not include a review or summary of each chapter. For this, the reader is referred to the chapter abstracts. Instead, we revert to themes that emerged from Part I. Specifically, we argue that appropriately assessing living standards is challenging, and we focus on the different nature of the challenges for consumption poverty line estimation and multidimensional poverty measurement. Conclusions are provided in Chapter 18.

## 16.2 Absolute Poverty Lines

The six case studies uniformly indicate that the process of drawing appropriate absolute poverty lines is not straightforward and cannot be done mechanically. This is so principally due to five key factors: heterogeneity, volatility, vulnerability, data, and theory. The first three factors are usefully grouped together. In all of the case countries considered, poor people are heterogeneous, frequently live in environments with strikingly high levels of volatility, and are, almost by definition, vulnerable to shocks. The upshot of these combined factors is a high level of variation in living standards, particularly at lower levels of aggregation.

In Madagascar, an ongoing political crisis strongly and negatively impacted living standards in urban zones while the overall rural poverty rate stagnated at a high level (see also Stifel et al. 2016). Climate shocks powerfully affect welfare, negatively and positively, particularly in rural zones. In large countries, such as Ethiopia, Mozambique, and Tanzania, climate shocks can be geographically concentrated with some domains experiencing positive shocks while other domains experience negative ones. The Mozambique case illustrates that the combination of abnormally high global food and fuel prices with local negative weather shocks can be particularly powerful. This underlying variability of living standards (across space, through time, by household characteristics, by nature of the shocks experienced, etc.) complicates essentially all aspects of the analytical task from sample design to the process of analysis.

The next challenge relates to data. Household consumption information is far too expensive to collect for every household in a population. Hence, all countries rely on randomly selected samples. Samples inherently limit the scope for specificity (as emphasized in Chapter 4) and add sample variation to the fundamental variation in welfare outcomes discussed in the preceding paragraph. More perniciously, datasets in developing country settings almost invariably suffer from a fairly high level of non-sample error. While problems with units are particularly common (e.g. Malawi), they are by no means the only problem encountered. Unfortunately, there is no substitute for knowing the data well, cross-checking with other sources, and making careful deliberate choices.

Finally, while consumer theory provides an elegant grounding for welfare analysis, it provides little firm guidance across a vast array of practical choices. The consistency versus specificity debate discussed in Chapter 2 is just one salient example. There is no substitute for careful consideration of the circumstances. For this reason, the case country applications almost invariably modify the PLEASe code in order to handle local specificities. And, because country circumstances vary greatly, the modifications imposed vary substantially across the country cases as well.

With these challenges recognized and with the allocation of an appropriate level of effort, the results of the studies presented here can be highly informative. For example, in the case of Ethiopia, discussed in Chapter 5, official results, which depict substantial declines in poverty, are largely confirmed. For Madagascar, Chapter 6 finds that rural poverty rates were likely more stable than official estimates, which showed an aggravation of rural poverty. In Malawi, the authors of Chapter 7 argue that poverty rates likely fell by more than the official estimates indicate between 2004/5 and 2010/11. In Chapter 8, official estimates of poverty trends through time in Mozambique are confirmed and sensitivity of the regional poverty profile to methodological choices is discussed. The analysis of Pakistan in Chapter 9 provides the greatest divergence between official and revised estimates. The chapter shows that consumption poverty has likely been increasing through time rather than declining as official estimates suggest. Chapter 10 argues that, in Uganda, an updated bundle is required, resulting in an altered regional poverty profile and generally higher poverty levels corresponding to revised basic-needs baskets.

We argue that these are all exceedingly useful insights derived with due consideration to country circumstances and available data. As emphasized in Chapter 1, these insights refer to private consumption possibilities with a particular focus on households living 'near' the reference welfare level targeted by absolute poverty lines. We argue as well that private consumption results are, on their own, not sufficient to make fully general statements about the evolution of wellbeing. In addition, as emphasized in the companion volume to this book (Arndt, McKay, and Tarp 2016), a broader analysis can help to develop a coherent narrative. Ideally, this narrative both helps to explain why living conditions are evolving in the ways observed and enhances confidence in overall conclusions as observations across multiple datasets and multiple facets of welfare become mutually reinforcing. Accordingly, the reader is referred to Arndt, McKay, and Tarp (2016) where narratives for five of the six countries with PLEASe applications (Pakistan is the exception) are developed.

In developing these narratives, multidimensional measures can be usefully employed. Furthermore, it is sometimes the case that the data for poverty measurement of private consumption possibilities are inadequate or would require enormous efforts to get into shape for rigorous analysis. In other instances, a focus on multidimensional analysis appears to be a more promising path for advancing knowledge and the state of debate. These observations lead us to our cases where first-order dominance (FOD), operationalized by EFOD, was in focus.

## 16.3 First-Order Dominance

Multidimensional methods, such as the first-order dominance approach in focus here, are also complementary to the drawing of absolute poverty lines in terms of methods. In many ways, the practical implementation of many multidimensional methods is substantially more straightforward than the evaluation of private consumption. This divergence begins with data. Frequently, the indicators employed for multidimensional analysis are much easier to observe than household consumption patterns and, as a consequence, very plausibly less subject to non-sample error. For example, important indicators of asset quality, such as the type of roof on a house, are typically quite easy to observe. In contrast, consumption poverty requires information on consumption values, quantities, and estimated prices at detailed product levels. Furthermore, in many households, consumption expenditures are diffused across multiple members. In some cases, one or more household members do not wish to disclose categories of expenditure to other household members, substantially complicating the task of the enumerator.

It is not the case that all possible multidimensional measures are easy to observe. For example, one could employ the household's consumption poverty status as an indicator in an FOD analysis. Obviously, then all of the difficulties associated with estimating absolute poverty lines also apply to the multidimensional analysis. Nevertheless, the five case countries considered develop a series of reasonably robust and informative indicators even in relatively data-poor environments, such as the Democratic Republic of the Congo and Nigeria.

In addition, once the series of indicators has been selected and appropriate cut points between deprived and non-deprived populations have been determined, the implementation process that follows tends to be much more routine. This feature of FOD analysis helpfully puts the accent on the choice of indicators and choices for cut points within indicators. For example, suppose that, as in Ghana and Tanzania, we would like to use anthropometric data to develop one of a number of indicators for considering the welfare of children aged zero to 60 months. If we are to employ only one anthropometric indicator, then the standard measures associated with stunting, wasting, and underweight must be combined. We might define a child as deprived if it is considered one or more of stunted, wasted, or underweight, using standard definitions.

While certain technical considerations do enter the appropriate choice of indicators and cut points (see section 4.3.1 in Chapter 4), it is imminently possible to engage in a broad debate across stakeholders with respect to the choice of appropriate indicators and cut points. There is no general rule that necessarily prioritizes one particular indicator over another, and cut points that define one subgroup as deprived and not deprived for particular indicators are clearly open for discussion in the right contexts and circumstances. This has the salutary effect of opening the potential for a reasonably inclusive analytical process. In contrast, the potential for an inclusive process is much more circumscribed with respect to consumption poverty. The efforts of this book to lower the barriers to entry to poverty analysis notwithstanding, the technical choices involved in poverty line estimation will remain exactly that, technical choices, with more limited scope to benefit from broad-based inputs.

While data collection for multidimensional analysis, such as FOD, and its subsequent analytical implementation are frequently more straightforward than poverty line estimation, the interpretation of results can be somewhat less direct. The idea that a poverty line can divide households into poor and non-poor groups on the basis of total private consumption is fairly easy to grasp and has been around for a long time.[1] The concepts driving FOD results, while

---

[1] While the poverty headcount (e.g. the share of the population living below the poverty line) is straightforward to grasp, the concepts behind the poverty gap and squared poverty gap are less intuitive and less well understood across the broad community that uses/consumes poverty analysis.

reasonably intuitive, are not nearly as clear-cut. Work must be done to explain what is meant by first-order dominance and by 'net probability of domination'.

There is also a need to build up a corpus of experience in order to properly interpret results. For example, is a 50 per cent probability of advance in five key indicators at the national level over a five-year period a good or a bad performance? Based on the results for the five cases presented here, a 50 per cent probability of advance would appear to be a reasonably favourable result. This is so due to the stringency of the FOD criteria, which require advance across all indicators that is broadly shared across the full population.

Finally, particularly with respect to spatial comparisons, mainly indeterminate outcomes (A does not net-dominate B, nor does B net-dominate A) require some further analysis in order to determine the root of the indeterminacy. Welfare comparisons between two regions may yield indeterminate outcomes because the two regions are very similar. It could also be because they are very different with one region lagging in one indicator and the other region lagging in a different indicator. It is normally not difficult to ascertain the nature of an indeterminate outcome—a look at the mean values of the indicators by spatial domain is often (but not always) sufficient; but this analytical work needs to be done and then explained.

Overall, we find that the cases illustrate that FOD analysis, as implemented by EFOD, represents a powerful addition to the analytical toolkit. Similar to many other multidimensional approaches, FOD shares the desirable properties that data challenges are frequently relatively mild and implementation is straightforward. These two features allow for a focus on choice of indicators and cut points. With some technical guidance, a relatively open and inclusive process involving key stakeholders in choices of indicators and cut points is imminently possible. At the same time, effort is required to adequately interpret and explain FOD results. This is especially true at this point in time when experience with multidimensional measures in general and FOD in particular is relatively limited.

## References


Arndt, C., A. McKay, and F. Tarp (eds) (2016). *Growth and Poverty in Sub-Saharan Africa*. Oxford: Oxford University Press.

Stifel, D., T. Razafimanantena, and F. Rakotomanana (2016). 'Utility-Consistent Poverty in Madagascar, 2001–10: Snapshots in the Presence of Multiple Economy-Wide Shocks', in C. Arndt, A. McKay, and F. Tarp (eds), *Growth and Poverty in Sub-Saharan Africa*. Oxford: Oxford University Press, 370–92.

# 17

## Keep It Real

## Measuring Real Inequality Using Survey Data from Developing Countries

*Ulrik Beck*

### 17.1 Introduction

Measures of inequality are often used to direct and evaluate policy. In developing countries, inequality estimates are typically based on a consumption module included in nationally representative surveys. Based on this, a consumption aggregate is constructed. This aggregate is a measure of the value of consumption by a household. There are some technicalities involved with estimating the consumption aggregate: housing costs are often imputed, the cost of durable goods must be spread out over multiple years, etc. (Grosh and Deaton 2000; Deaton and Zaidi 2002). Nevertheless, at its heart, the value of consumption is reached by multiplying current prices with quantities. As such, the standard consumption aggregate is a nominal concept. Inequality indices derived from nominal consumption aggregates are therefore also nominal in their nature.

There are at least two reasons why basing inequality estimates on a real consumption aggregate—and thereby estimating what I will refer to as real inequality—is relevant. First, the poorest households tend to dedicate a higher share of their spending towards basic food items, the prices of which have been rising faster than other prices in recent years. I refer to this as the composition effect. Second, if there is a systematic difference in the prices faced by households over the income distribution, nominal inequality will differ from real inequality. Specifically, this can arise when the poor tend to purchase items in smaller quantities which can lead to higher prices. I refer to this as the quantity discounting effect. This chapter aims to empirically estimate deflators of these two effects, proceed to estimate real consumption aggregates, and use these to compute estimates of real inequality. Many types of deflation can lead to different types of real consumption aggregates on which real inequality can be estimated. For example, nominal consumption is often both temporally and spatially deflated to arrive at a real consumption measure with implications for inequality. In this chapter, I use the term 'real' to denote nominal consumption deflated to account for the composition effect and the quantity discounting effect. This conversion from a nominal to a real value is described in detail in section 17.2.

I overcome the substantial data requirements for this task by building on the set of country-specific databases which were constructed as part of the Growth and Poverty Project (GAPP) conducted under the auspices of UNU-WIDER. Using fifteen surveys from six different countries (Ethiopia, Madagascar, Malawi, Mozambique, Pakistan, and Tanzania), collected in the period 1999 to 2011, and covering over 220,000 households, I construct household-specific indices of the composition and the quantity discounting effects.

The chapter proceeds by investigating how real inequality estimates affect poverty figures when estimated using a method developed in series of papers by Sala-i-Martin and Pinkovskiy. This method finds poverty rates by fitting two-parameter consumption distributions using inequality estimates obtained from survey data and national accounts information on income per capita (Pinkovskiy and Sala-i-Martin 2009, 2014; Sala-i-Martin 2006; Sala-i-Martin and Pinkovskiy 2010). I refer to this approach as the SiMP methodology. Using this approach, the authors find that poverty is falling much faster than what is observed by other methods of poverty estimation. Pinkovskiy and Sala-i-Martin (2014) state that the discrepancy is mainly caused by differences in the growth rates of mean per capita consumption observed in the surveys and the mean per capita GDP observed from the national accounts. These differentials are not disputed; however, this chapter shows that using the proper inequality estimates also matters.

The strength of the two estimated effects differs substantially across countries. In some countries, the poorest households were subject to a double penalty which is the result of a combination of high food inflation rates for the consumption bundle of the poor, and of the poor buying in smaller quantities. In continuation of this, the decline in poverty using the SiMP methodology may be overestimated, and level of poverty underestimated. This chapter therefore explains part of the gap between the very optimistic results of Pinkovskiy and Sala-i-Martin (2014) and other, more mixed findings.

## 17.2 Empirical Framework

This section explains how the two effects described briefly in section 17.1 arise and how they are estimated.

### 17.2.1 *The Composition Effect*

The composition effect occurs when the relatively poor spend a larger part of their income on basic food items and there are disproportionate increases in the prices of these items. This effect has been studied in some detail for developed countries (see, for instance, Muellbauer 1974; Cage, Garner, and Ruiz-Castillo 2002; Leicester, O'Dea, and Oldfield 2008). A higher consumption share of food items by the poor has also been found in developing countries, even though the impact on inequality has not been the focus of the majority of this body of work (Pritchett, Suryahadi, Sumarto, and Suharso 2000; Deaton 2003; Günther and Grimm 2007; Aksoy and Isik-Dikmelik 2008).

The hike in food price inflation after 2000, culminating in the price spike of the food price crisis of 2007–9, provides a rationale for estimating the magnitude of such effects (Mitchell 2008; Wiggins, Keats, and Compton 2010). A few recent papers have explored the link between the composition effect and inequality in developing countries more directly (Goñi, López, and Servén 2006; Mohsin and Zaman 2012). The work most closely related to this chapter in its approach to estimating the composition effect is Arndt et al. (2015). The authors find that the structure of consumption bundles varies across the income distribution. Due to more rapid inflation in the prices of basic goods, nominal inequality was found to underestimate real inequality by several Gini points for Mozambique in 2008.

In this chapter, I follow the method proposed by Arndt et al. (2015).[1] Consumption items are divided into three groups: core food items, non-core food items, and non-food items. A household-specific Paasche price index which takes into account differential inflation rates of these three groups of items is then given by:

$$CPI_{COMP}^{i,t} = \left( \frac{p_c^1}{p_c^t} s_c^{i,t} + \frac{p_{nc}^1}{p_{nc}^t} s_{nc}^{i,t} + \frac{p_{nf}^1}{p_{nf}^t} s_{nf}^{i,t} \right)^{-1} \tag{17.1}$$

$p_a^t$ is the index price in year $t$ of group $a$ products, where $a$ can be either core $(c)$, non-core $(nc)$, or non-food $(nf)$. $s_a^{i,t}$ is the share of consumption used for group $a$ products purchased by household $i$ in year $t$.[2]

---

[1] Arndt et al. (2015) also consider spatial differences in price levels. If poorer households are overrepresented in spatial domains with lower price levels, failing to correct for this will overestimate inequality. I do not consider spatial differences in prices in the estimation of the composition effect; instead, a spatial price index is applied throughout where available. Thus, the 'nominal' inequality estimates of this study contain spatial price corrections.

[2] Arndt et al. (2015) do not use a Paasche index. This study uses a true Paasche index as its properties are well known. Specifically, if there is substitution towards goods that become relatively cheaper, a Paasche index will underestimate the rate of inflation. This means that inflation estimates reported here are a lower bound on the true inflation rates in the presence of substitution. The Paasche index is written in share expenditure form to ease estimation.

There are two principal challenges associated with implementing this approach consistently across countries. The first is how to choose which food items should be included in the core and the non-core food groups, respectively. This choice should be country-specific since food consumption patterns vary substantially between countries. It should also be general since cross-country results can only be meaningfully compared if the decision rule is consistent across countries. An option which fits both of these criteria is to define the core food items as those included in the food poverty lines estimated by the Growth and Poverty Project in year $t$ of each country. The poverty food basket is chosen consistently across countries, and across surveys within countries, in order to represent the most important food items for the poor. This makes this group of products an ideal candidate for the core food group. I do not use the inflation rates of the food poverty line as an estimate of the temporal change in $p_c^t$, since items are allowed to move in and out of the food poverty bundle over time, and since the prices used to estimate the poverty lines are often estimated specifically for the poor. Instead, I re-estimate weights and price increases for the food items in the food poverty bundle directly from the survey data. Since the poverty lines vary at the subnational level, and since this chapter is concerned with estimating food inflation at the national level, a procedure to reconcile this difference is needed. I choose to keep only items which are present in the poverty lines of two or more spatial domains of year $t$, and also present in the first survey ($t = 1$), though not necessarily part of the poverty basket in the first survey. In order to increase precision of the estimated unit prices, I further restrict the group of food items to those items where each survey has at least 200 recorded purchases.

The second challenge is to estimate price changes of core foods, non-core foods, and non-food items separately. It is not feasible to estimate all price changes from survey information alone due to missing prices and few purchases of some goods. Furthermore, detailed CPI information at the product level is not always available, especially for rural areas. For the core food items, the surveys contain sufficient information to calculate price changes directly from the survey. However, this is not the case for the non-core food items and the non-food items. The non-core food items are not observed as frequently in the data, and using the survey prices is not an option. The non-food items are typically only reported as (nominal) values, not as prices and quantities. Instead of using the survey data, I use external sources of CPI information which is available separately for food and non-food items. For the non-food group of items, the non-food CPI series can be directly used.

For the non-core food items, I proxy the non-core food inflation by the total food CPI series. One can think of the total food CPI series as a weighted average of core food and non-core food CPI series. Therefore, estimation of the core food inflation from the household data means that the direction of the bias of the non-food inflation index is known. As will become clear, the bias will tend to attenuate the magnitude of the composition effect; the estimates presented here can therefore be seen as a lower bound on the true effect sizes.

### 17.2.2 *The Quantity Discounting Effect*

The quantity discounting effect arises when the poor purchase smaller amounts at a time, thereby missing out on quantity discounts. There are several potential explanations for why the poor would do so: the poor consume less and lack capacity to securely store perishable foods; the poor may be credit-constrained and the poor may lack transport options to transport larger amounts.

The quantity discounting effect has been studied using unit prices, i.e. prices calculated from quantities and values reported by households. The main pitfall with this approach is that the quality of the consumed items is variable and unobserved. A specific item code in the consumption module of a questionnaire must by necessity cover a variety of qualities but higher-quality items will have higher unit prices. This is difficult to separate from a potential quantity discounting effect when high- and low-quality items share the same survey code. The problem of separating quality issues from true price variation has been referred to as the unit value problem (Deaton 1988; Crawford, Laisney, and Preston 2003; Chung, Dong, Schmit, Kaiser, and Gould 2005; Beatty 2010; McKelvey 2011).

One way of reducing the confounding of quality effects and quantity discounting effects is to use a survey instrument specifically tuned to separate different qualities of the same product into different questionnaire items (Rao 2000; Aguiar and Hurst 2007). However, such specialized datasets are often not available, especially in developing countries. Alternatively, one could limit the study to reasonably homogenous items (Attanasio and Frayne 2006). However, when the topic of interest is national inequality, it is necessary to use a method which works with all items of consumption and in addition to use the nationally representative surveys which exist.

In the following, I develop such a method which exploits information about the size of the purchases. By exploiting this information, one can non-parametrically estimate a household-specific price index which at least partially controls for quality differences. As the point of departure, I take the expensiveness index of Aguiar and Hurst (2007). The authors construct a household-specific expensiveness index in order to compare how expensively households bought their specific basket of goods. The index is given by:

$$p^i_{AH} = \frac{\sum_m [p^i_m * q^i_m]}{\sum_m [\bar{p}^i_m * q^i_m]} \tag{17.2}$$

Here, $p^i_m$ is the price paid for product $m$ by household $i$, $\bar{p}^i_m$ is the average price paid for product $m$ in a geographical area where $i$ resides, and $q^i_m$ is the quantity household $i$ bought of product $m$. This measure compares actual expenditures of household $i$ with the cost of this bundle of food items, priced at the average prices. If the index is larger than one, the household is paying more for its bundle than the average household would have done. Next, I introduce product-specific quantity bins. Using these bins, a more specific version of the index can be calculated, where $u$ denotes the quantity bin of each purchase:

$$p^i_{AH-u} = \frac{\sum_m \sum_u [p^i_{m,u} * q^i_{m,u}]}{\sum_m \sum_u [\bar{p}^i_{m,u} * q^i_m]} \tag{17.3}$$

This version of the index only compares products which were in the same quantity bin. Both (17.2) and (17.3) are affected by quality in the same way. The quantity discounting effect can now be isolated by taking the ratio of the two indices and exploiting that the numerator in both (17.2) and (17.3) is total household expenditure. This gives the final household-specific quantity discounting price index:[3]

$$CPI^i_{QUANT} = \frac{p^i_{AH}}{p^i_{AH-u}} = \frac{\sum_m \sum_u [\bar{p}^i_{m,u} * q^i_{m,u}]}{\sum_m [\bar{p}^i_m * q^i_m]} \tag{17.4}$$

The necessary assumption for the quantity discounting index to exactly isolate the quantity discounting effect is that the quantity of purchase is uncorrelated with quality. If there is a correlation between quality and quantity of purchase it will continue to affect (17.4). Since one can expect richer households to buy higher-quality items, this effect will bias results in the opposite direction of quantity discounting. Therefore, if it is found that the poor pay more for their food, the estimated effect can be seen as a lower bound on the true effect size. I construct four bins separated at the twenty-fifth, fiftieth, and seventy-fifth percentile of the product-specific unit price distribution.

The index of (17.4) makes use of all variation in prices in the survey. However, if there is real price variation between geographical areas (Deaton 1988), the performance of the quantity-adjusting index can be improved by estimating average prices at a smaller geographical area than the national level. This will matter if the poor are disproportionately likely to live in either high- or low-price areas. The final index is shown in equation (17.5). Here, $\bar{p}^g_{m,u}$ denotes the average price of unit-size $u$ of item $m$ in geographical area $g$ which

---

[3] The index is subsequently normalized to have a mean of one.

household $i$ lives in. In this version, the household-specific deflator of household $i$ is based only on variation within the geographical area of household $i$.

$$CPI^i_{QUANT} = \frac{\sum_m \sum_u [\bar{P}^g_{m,u} {}^* q^i_{m,u}]}{\sum_m [\bar{P}^g_m {}^* q^i_m]}$$

(17.5)

The geographical area employed in the remainder of the chapter is the survey stratum. This means that any differences in prices between strata do not affect the quantity discounting effect. The number of strata is survey-specific; the surveys used in this chapter have between eight and thirty-one strata.

### 17.2.3 Estimating Inequality

The deflated consumption aggregate for household $i$ in year $t$ is estimated as:

$$Y^{i,t}_{real} = \frac{(y^{i,t}_c + y^{i,t}_{nc})/CPI^{i,t}_{QUANT} + y^{i,t}_{nf}}{CPI^{i,t}_{COMP}}$$

(17.6)

Where $y_a$ denotes nominal consumption aggregates of core, non-core, and non-food consumption, respectively and $Y^{i,t}_{real}$ is real consumption. All other notation is the same as above. Using population weights, nationally representative real Gini coefficients are estimated.

### 17.2.4 Estimating Poverty

The poverty rate is the share of people who consume less than a given poverty line. A standard approach to estimating national poverty lines is to use information on consumption from nationally representative surveys and a caloric requirement in order to estimate the cost of consuming the caloric requirement, given the actual consumption structure of the poor. Subsequently, non-food requirements are estimated. The sum of the food and non-food requirements equals the total poverty line. This is the so-called cost of basic needs (CBN) approach (Ravallion and Bidani 1994; Tarp, Simler, Matusse, Heltberg, and Dava 2002). The CBN methodology can be made robust to both the composition and the quantity discounting effects. The composition effect is implicitly handled since the poverty line is by definition the cost of a certain amount of the consumption bundle consumed by the poor. It is therefore price changes of the poor which influence the intertemporal change in the poverty line. The quantity discounting effect can be handled by pricing the consumption bundle using the prices paid by the poor, which is frequently done in practice. Another common approach is to impose an exogenously defined poverty line. The leading example of such a poverty line is 1.25 PPP-adjusted US$ in 2005 prices, proposed by Ravallion, Chen, and Sangraula (2009).

Recently, Sala-i-Martin and Pinkovskiy (SiMP) have proposed a third approach (Pinkovskiy and Sala-i-Martin 2009, 2014; Sala-i-Martin and Pinkovskiy 2010). This approach uses inequality estimates and national accounts information on GDP to fit a two-parameter consumption distribution for each country. For most developing countries (and all countries considered in this chapter), the inequality information is based on the same consumption surveys used to estimate poverty. Using the fitted distribution and the US$1.25-a-day poverty line, Pinkovskiy and Sala-i-Martin (2014) estimate poverty using the cumulative distribution function. The US$1.25-a-day poverty line is measured in real 2005 international (PPP-adjusted) prices. For this reason, Pinkovskiy and Sala-i-Martin (2014) use a real measure of GDP to anchor the income distribution. If all households face the same prices, it is unnecessary to deflate inequality estimates, because the Gini coefficient is unaffected by scalar multiplications. However, the deflator need not be constant over the income distribution. Therefore, if one wants to take seriously the notion of estimating poverty using a fitted distribution, the use of a real inequality estimate is necessary.

In section 17.4.3 we therefore investigate the impact of using real inequality poverty rates when following the baseline methodology of Pinkovskiy and Sala-i-Martin (2014), i.e. by fitting a log-normal distribution using mean GDP per capita from the World Bank World Development Indicators and estimates of inequality.[4]

In addition to those we have discussed, there are several other differences between the CBN and the SiMP methodologies (see Guénard and Mesplé-Somps 2010; Arndt, Tarp, and McKay 2016; as well as the working paper version of the current chapter). Comparing the two directly is like comparing apples and oranges and I refrain from doing so in this chapter. Instead, I compare SiMP measures of poverty using nominal and real consumption aggregates.

## 17.3 Data

The various data sources used for this chapter, as well as some descriptive statistics, are detailed in Table 17.1. As mentioned previously, the results build upon work done in relation to the GAPP project. Building on this body of work, I have compiled a standardized database of consumption information which allows real inequality measures to be computed at the household level

---

[4] Pinkovskiy and Sala-i-Martin (2014) adjust estimates of consumption inequality to make them comparable with other surveys based on income. For the sake of simplicity, and since only consumption-based surveys are used in this study, I do not make an adjustment here.

**Table 17.1.** Data sources and descriptive statistics

| Country and survey years | Household survey reference | CPI reference | No. of households | No. of EAs | No. of strata | 2005 PPP USD | | | |
| --- | --- | --- | --- | --- | --- | --- | --- | --- | --- |
| | | | | | | Survey mean (consumption) | GDP per capita (nat. accounts) | 10th percentile/ mean cons. | 90th percentile/ mean cons. | National poverty rate |
| Ethiopia | Stifel and Woldehanna | NBE (2014); | | | | | | | | |
| - HICES (1999/ 2000) | (2016) | CSA (2015) | 17,332 | 1264 | 20 | 1.40 | 1.44 | 0.48 | 1.60 | 46.8 |
| - HICES (2004/5) | | | 21,595 | 1548 | 18 | 1.69 | 1.74 | 0.46 | 1.58 | 46 |
| - HICES (2010/11) | | | 27,830 | 1966 | 20 | 2.07 | 2.56 | 0.42 | 1.64 | 23.8 |
| Madagascar | Stifel, Razafimanantena, | instat.mg | | | | | | | | |
| - EPM (2001) | and Rakotomanana | (2015) | 5080 | 303 | 12 | 0.91 | 2.54 | 0.27 | 2.06 | 57.8 |
| - EPM (2005) | (2016) | | 11,781 | 561 | 12 | 0.83 | 2.38 | 0.31 | 1.83 | 59.1 |
| Malawi | Pauw, Beck, and Mussa | NSO (2015) | | | | | | | | |
| - IHS2 (2004/5) | (2016) | | 11,280 | 564 | 30 | 1.33 | 1.77 | 0.35 | 1.72 | 47 |
| - IHS3 (2010/11) | | | 12,271 | 768 | 31 | 1.89 | 2.17 | 0.29 | 1.78 | 38.8 |
| Mozambique | Arndt, Jones, and Tarp | INE (2015) | | | | | | | | |
| - IHS2 (2004/5) | (2016) | | 8700 | 857 | 11 | 1.29 | 1.60 | 0.31 | 1.78 | 54.1 |
| - IHS3 (2010/11) | | | 10,832 | 1060 | 11 | 1.51 | 2.12 | 0.31 | 1.75 | 54.7 |
| Pakistan | Nazli et al. (2015) | MoF (2015) | | | | | | | | |
| - HIES (2001/2) | | | 14,649 | 1050 | 8 | 1.74 | 5.05 | 0.51 | 1.60 | 21.4 |
| - HIES (2005/6) | | | 15,374 | 1109 | 8 | 2.21 | 5.87 | 0.51 | 1.61 | 23.0 |
| - HIES (2007/8) | | | 15,441 | 1113 | 8 | 2.54 | 6.36 | 0.51 | 1.65 | 26.0 |
| - HIES (2010/11) | | | 16,295 | 1180 | 8 | 2.52 | 6.60 | 0.53 | 1.57 | 27.0 |
| Tanzania | Arndt, Hussain, Leyaro, | CountrySTAT | | | | | | | | |
| - HBS (2000) | Jones, and Tarp | (2015) | 22,176 | 1158 | 20 | 0.83 | 2.37 | 0.38 | 1.79 | 35.7 |
| - HBS (2007) | (2013) | | 10,407 | 447 | 20 | 1.13 | 3.15 | 0.37 | 1.79 | 33.6 |

*Source*: Author's compilation based on the following consumption surveys: HICES is the Ethiopia Household Income, Consumption, and Expenditure Survey (HICES, multiple years). EPM is the Enquête Périodique auprès des Ménages (INSTAT 2002, 2006). IHS is the Integrated Household Survey (NSO (National Statistics Office Malawi) 2005, 2012). IAF is the Inquérito aos Agregados Familiares (MPF et al. 2004). IOF is the Inquérito ao Orçamento Familiar (MPF et al. 2010). HIES is the Household Integrated Economic Survey (FBS 2003, 2007, 2009, 2013) and estimates exclude Azad Jammu and Kashmir, Federally Administered Tribal Areas, and Northern Areas (PBS 2006, 2007, 2009, 2013). HBS is the Household Budget Survey (NBS 2002, 2011), and covers only mainland Tanzania (excludes Zanzibar). The poverty rates are from the sources listed above, except for Tanzania, where the estimates are from Arndt, Demery, McKay, and Tarp (2016). PPP conversion factors and national accounts information are from World Bank (2012).

for the more than 220,000 household observations in the database. In particular, the consumption aggregates used to calculate poverty rates are used to calculate the Gini coefficient. Nationally representative consumption questionnaires are often collected over an extended period of time, typically an entire year. Since prices change within this time frame, all prices and consumption aggregates presented are deflated using a temporal (within-survey) price index. Such an index is available for each of the GAPP country studies.[5] Since prices also vary spatially, I also deflate consumption aggregates by the spatial indices.

The countries cover a range of different experiences. Consider the survey mean consumption, converted to constant 2005 US$ using the PPP-adjusted exchange rate. The mean per capita consumption of Pakistan in 2007/8 was more than double that of Tanzania (in 2007) and three times that of Madagascar (in 2005). Trends also differ. At one end of the spectrum is Madagascar where the mean per capita consumption in 2001 was US$0.91 dollars a day; this fell slightly to US$0.83 in 2005. At the other end of the spectrum are Ethiopia and Pakistan where mean per capita consumption increased annually by 4 per cent from the first to the last survey (from US$1.4 to US$2.07 in Madagascar; from US$1.74 to US$2.52 in Pakistan). The picture in terms of trends is generally consistent if one instead looks at GDP per capita; however, the level is generally substantially higher. This difference in levels is consistent with the existing literature (Pinkovskiy and Sala-i-Martin 2014).

The level of inequality also varies across countries: Madagascar and Malawi are the most unequal; here, the tenth percentile of the population consumes between 0.27 and 0.35 of mean income, whereas the ninetieth percentile consumes between 1.72 and 2.06 of mean income. There are differences in inequality trends as well: while the consumption spread has decreased in Madagascar, it has increased in Malawi. Pakistan is the least unequal of the countries: the tenth and ninetieth percentile consumed respectively 0.50 and 1.65 of mean consumption in the latest survey round.

Information on nominal inequality in the form of Gini coefficients can be readily obtained from the WIDER World Income Inequality Database, or WIID (UNU-WIDER 2014). However, I use nominal Gini coefficients estimated directly from the household-level consumption aggregates of the database. This is necessary since only by using the micro-level datasets can the household-specific deflators be applied. For the estimation of poverty using the SiMP methodology, I obtain time series of PPP-adjusted GDP per capita in constant 2005 dollars from the 2012 version of the World Bank's World

---

[5] The Madagascar surveys and Ethiopia in 2000 and 2005 are exceptions where no such indices are used since those surveys were collected over a relatively short period of time, i.e. over a couple of months.

Development Indicators (World Bank 2012). The same data sources were used by Pinkovskiy and Sala-i-Martin (2014). Therefore, the inequality estimates are the only source of difference.

## 17.4 Results

### 17.4.1 *The Composition Effect*

Table 17.2 shows the CPI indices used for the price changes of core food, non-core food, and non-food inflation. Taking the first survey in each year as the baseline, the core food items are rising in price faster than the non-core food (proxied by the food CPI) items in all countries except Ethiopia and Madagascar. Since total food inflation is a weighted average of core and non-core food inflation rates, in the four (two) countries where core inflation is higher (lower) than total food inflation, the use of total food inflation as a proxy measure of non-core food inflation overestimates (underestimates) the true rate of non-core inflation.

Why do core food prices in Ethiopia and Madagascar behave differently? Between 2000 and 2005, Ethiopia experienced several good harvests which put downward pressure on food prices (Durevall, Loening, and Ayalew Birru

**Table 17.2.** Food and non-food CPIs

| Country and year | Core food | Non-core Food | Non-food | Ratio (CF/NCF) | Ratio (CF/NF) |
|---|---|---|---|---|---|
| Ethiopia | | | | | |
| - 1999/2000 | 100.0 | 100.0 | 100.0 | 1.00 | 1.00 |
| - 2004/5 | 98.9 | 145.7 | 112.8 | 0.68 | 0.88 |
| - 2010/11 | 249.0 | 315.8 | 254.7 | 0.79 | 0.98 |
| Madagascar | | | | | |
| - 2001 | 100.0 | 100.0 | 100.0 | 1.00 | 1.00 |
| - 2005 | 152.4 | 176.3 | 149.9 | 0.86 | 1.02 |
| Malawi | | | | | |
| - 2004/5 | 100.0 | 100.0 | 100.0 | 1.00 | 1.00 |
| - 2010/11 | 248.5 | 177.6 | 188.2 | 1.40 | 1.32 |
| Mozambique | | | | | |
| - 2002 | 100.0 | 100.0 | 100.0 | 1.00 | 1.00 |
| - 2008 | 228.2 | 200.4 | 139.8 | 1.14 | 1.63 |
| Pakistan | | | | | |
| - 2001/2 | 100.0 | 100.0 | 100.0 | 1.00 | 1.00 |
| - 2005/6 | 132.0 | 131.1 | 124.4 | 1.01 | 1.06 |
| - 2007/8 | 182.8 | 144.6 | 131.9 | 1.26 | 1.39 |
| - 2010/11 | 290.3 | 279.2 | 207.1 | 1.04 | 1.40 |
| Tanzania | | | | | |
| - 2000 | 100.0 | 100.0 | 100.0 | 1.00 | 1.00 |
| - 2007 | 199.1 | 158.8 | 131.4 | 1.25 | 1.52 |

*Note*: Non-core and non-food inflation are calculated by the author based on the sources listed in Table 17.1. All CPIs are normalized to 100 in the first survey year.

*Source*: Core CPIs are calculated by the author based on survey data

2013). In particular, prices of domestically produced foods, which constitute the majority of core food items, were subjected to downward pressure. From 2004/5 to 2010/11, core food prices rose faster than non-core food prices. A partial explanation in the Malagasy case could be that in 2004, due to a partially failed harvest of rice, the main staple of Madagascar, the Malagasy government intervened in the rice market by slashing import tariffs and by importing state-bought rice (Dorosh and Minten 2006). This, combined with a better domestic rice harvest in 2005, contributed to downward pressure on rice prices near the end of 2005, which is when the second Malagasy survey was conducted.

In all countries except for Ethiopia, the prices of core foods outpace those of non-food, compared to the first survey of each country. The magnitude of the price differentials varies between countries. For instance, core prices in Mozambique rose 63 per cent faster than non-food prices from 2002 to 2008. However, in Madagascar, the difference was only 2 per cent from 2001 to 2005. To conclude, the data presented here shows that in many, but not all, of the included countries, food price inflation has been higher than non-food inflation in the period considered.

Figure 17.1 shows the mean consumption shares of the three groups of items for each percentile of the consumption distribution, across countries and surveys. The percentile-specific means are calculated for ease of illustration; deflators are household-specific as indicated by equation (17.1). A consistent picture, which matches what Arndt et al. (2015) found for Mozambique, emerges: as one moves up through the income distribution, the share of consumption expenditures allocated to core foods declines. Instead, the non-food share and in many cases also the non-core food share increases. The core food consumption profiles of Madagascar and Mozambique have somewhat more u-shaped curves, where the very poorest spend less on food and more on non-food than those who consume a little more.

In all countries except Ethiopia, the non-core food share increases along the income distribution. This empirical regularity, combined with the use of the general food inflation index as the non-core food index which overestimates non-core inflation for all countries except Ethiopia and Madagascar, means the increase in inequality due to the composition effect is underestimated in all countries except Madagascar, where the composition effect may be overestimated.

Figure 17.2 shows the composition CPIs for each percentile of the consumption distribution. Results are as expected, given the inflation rates and the consumption shares reported above: in all countries except Ethiopia and Madagascar, the composition CPI index is highest for the lower part of the distribution. This indicates that the consumption structure of the poor combined with the observed price changes have resulted in higher price increases for the poor. The magnitudes of the effects are country-specific. For instance,

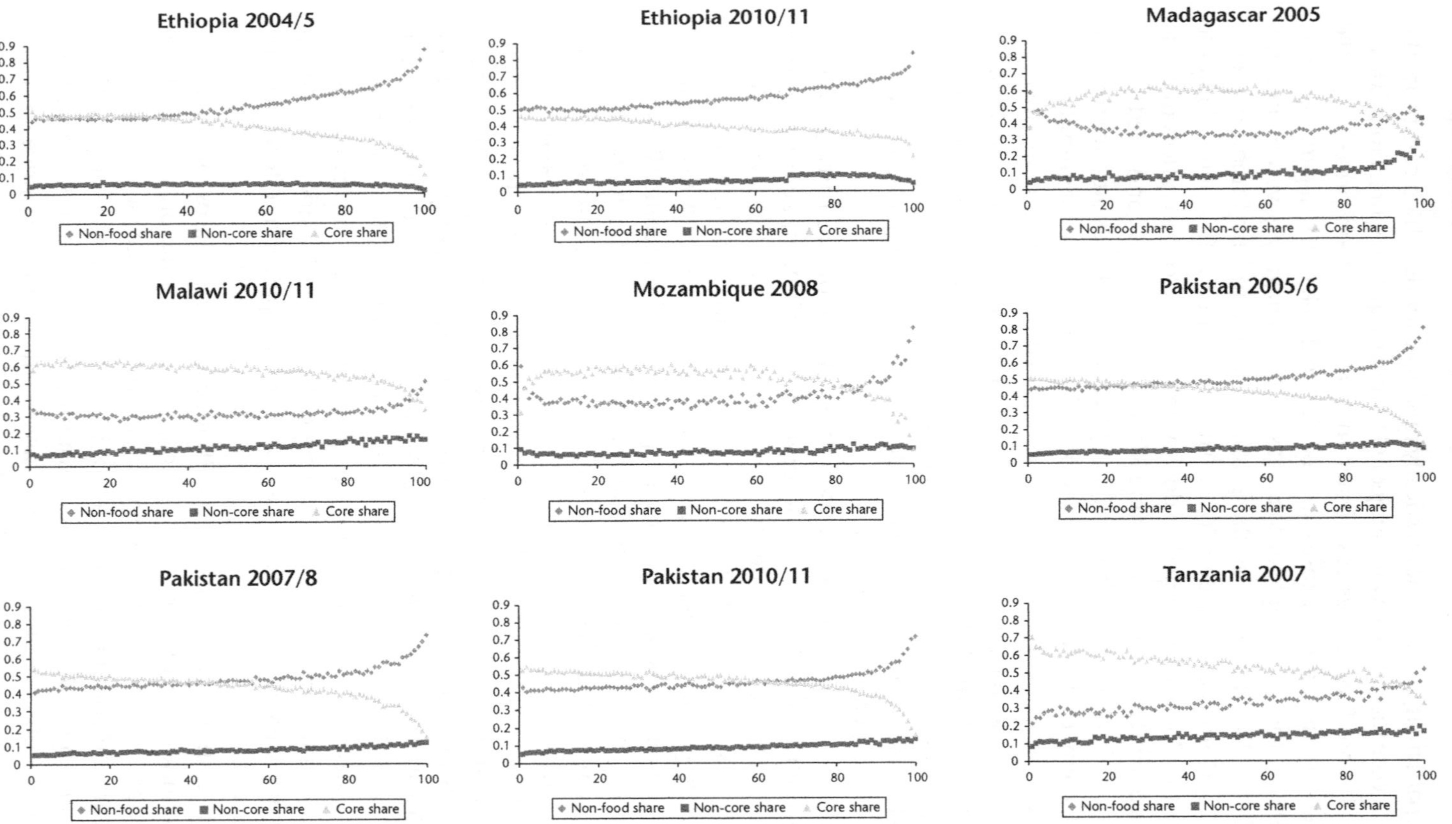



**Figure 17.1.** Consumption shares by consumption percentiles

*Note*: Each dot represents a percentile of the consumption distribution.

*Source*: Author's calculations

there is only a slight slope over the consumption distribution in Malawi. In Pakistan for the 2005/6 survey, only the top percentiles are notably different.

### 17.4.2 *The Quantity Discounting Effect*

Figure 17.3 shows the estimated quantity discounting CPIs by percentiles. In Mozambique, Tanzania, and Malawi, the estimated deflator is downward-sloping over the consumption distribution. In these countries, it appears that the quantity discounting effect is indeed at work in the sense that the poorest are paying higher unit prices solely due to the size of their purchase. On the other hand, Ethiopia, Pakistan, and Madagascar show no sign of a quantity discounting effect.[6]

### 17.4.3 *Inequality and Poverty*

Table 17.3 shows the real Gini coefficients estimated by applying the household-specific deflators presented in section 17.4.1 and 17.4.2. The first thing to note is that even the nominal Ginis of the WIID and the nominal Ginis from the GAPP database differ. In some cases, such as Malawi, this is partly caused by the re-estimation of the consumption aggregate by Pauw et al. (2016). Another source of variation is the temporal and spatial deflation of the nominal consumption aggregates. However, these differences are not driving the results in the following—the effects on the Gini coefficients would have been qualitatively similar if the household-specific deflators had been applied to consumption aggregates which exactly reproduce the WIID Ginis.

The composition effect means that real inequality is higher than nominal in all countries except Ethiopia and Malawi where the effect is slightly negative. For example, while one would draw the conclusion from the nominal Ginis that inequality in Mozambique was unchanged (or decreasing, using the WIID information), the real Gini show an increase of 44.3−41.5=2.8 Gini points. This is qualitatively consistent with the conclusion drawn by Arndt et al. (2015). In Tanzania, the nominal (GAPP) inequality measure increases by 1.1 Gini points from 2000 to 2007. However, applying the composition deflator increases this to 2.5 Gini points (36.7−34.2).

The annualized change in the composition-adjusted Gini coefficient, compared to the annualized change in the nominal (GAPP) Ginis, varies from 0.06 (for Pakistan from 2007/8 to 2010/11) over 0.47 (for Mozambique from 2002 to 2008) to 1.08 (for Pakistan from 2005/6 to 2007/8). To give an idea about magnitudes, these figures can be compared to the average annual absolute

---

[6] For additional discussion of this finding, see the working paper version of this chapter.

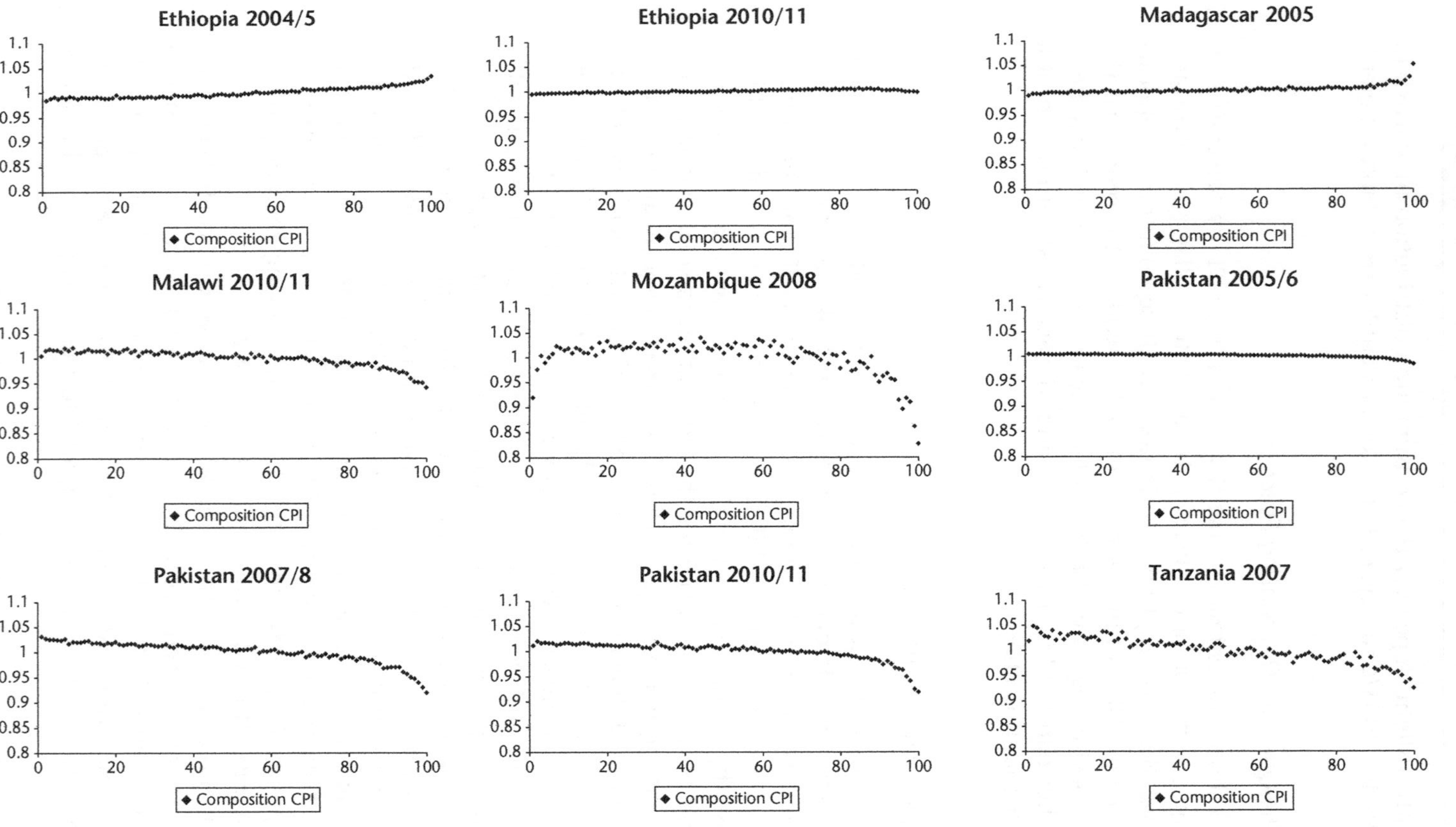

**Figure 17.2.** Composition CPIs by country

*Note:* Each dot represents a percentile of the consumption distribution. A few percentile dots are outside the graph areas. The year of first survey for each country against which the effects are calculated are as follows: Ethiopia: 1999/2000; Madagascar: 2001; Malawi: 2004/5; Mozambique: 2002; Pakistan: 2001/2; Tanzania: 2000.

*Source:* Author's calculations

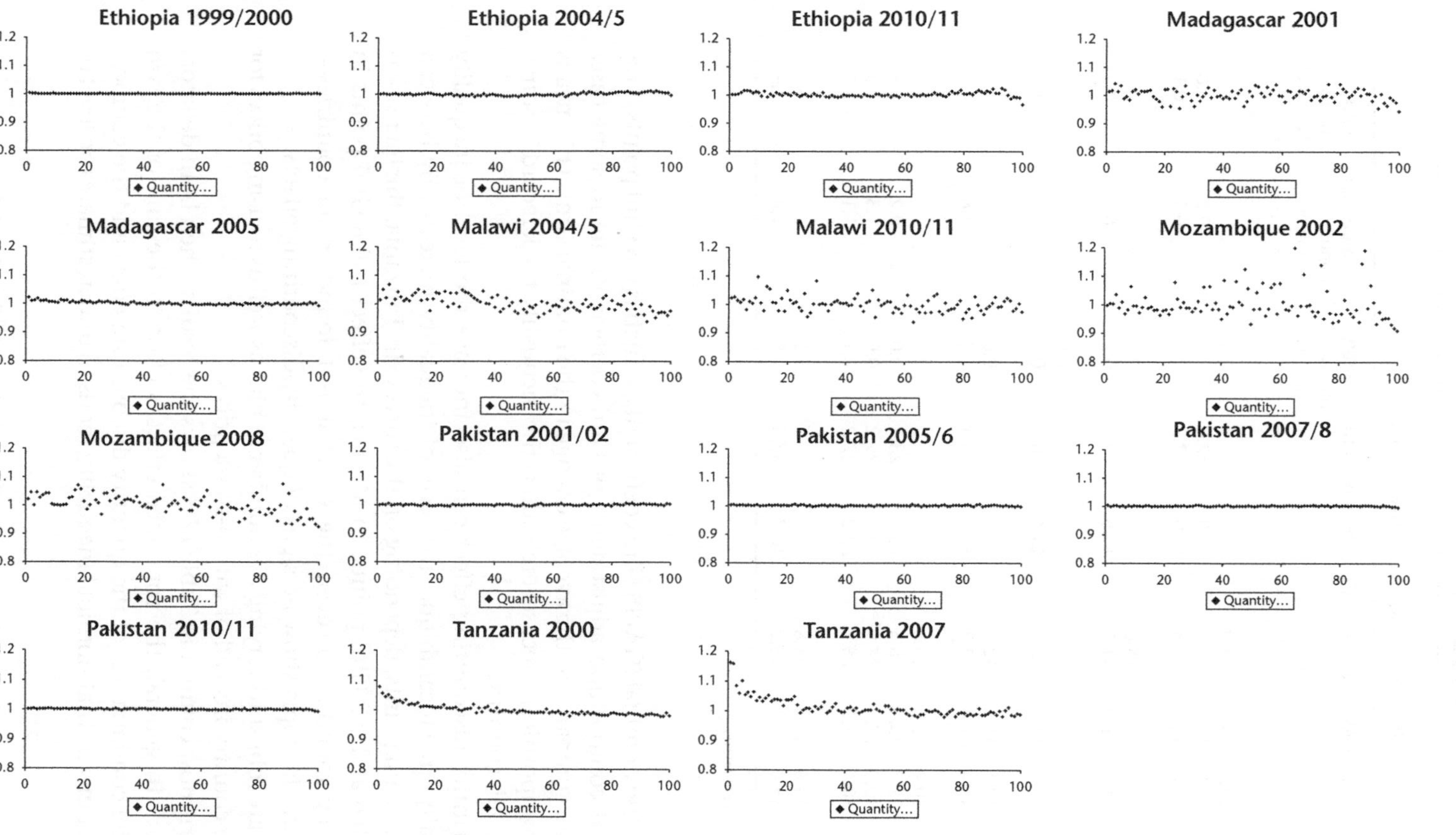


**Figure 17.3.** Quantity CPIs by country and survey

*Note*: Each dot represents a percentile of the consumption distribution. A few percentile dots are outside the graph area.

*Source*: Author's calculations

**Table 17.3.** Gini coefficients using alternative deflators

| | WIID | GAPP | Quantity | Composition | Both | Quantity minus Nominal | Composition minus Nominal | Both minus Nominal |
|---|---|---|---|---|---|---|---|---|
| Ethiopia | | | | | | | | |
| - 1999/2000 | 30.0 | 28.9 | 28.9 | | | 0.0 | | |
| - 2004/5 | 29.8 | 32.6 | 32.6 | 32.0 | 32.0 | 0.0 | −0.6 | −0.6 |
| - 2010/11 | 29.8 | 32.1 | 32.3 | 32.0 | 32.2 | 0.0 | −0.1 | 0.1 |
| Madagascar | | | | | | | | |
| - 2001 | 45.3 | 45.4 | 45.6 | | | 0.2 | | |
| - 2005 | 41.0 | 41.0 | 41.1 | 40.6 | 40.8 | 0.2 | −0.4 | −0.2 |
| Malawi | | | | | | | | |
| - 2004/5 | 41.0 | 41.9 | 42.7 | | | 0.8 | | |
| - 2010/11 | 39.3 | 44.5 | 45.3 | 45.4 | 46.2 | 0.8 | 1.0 | 1.7 |
| Mozambique | | | | | | | | |
| - 2002 | 47.1 | 41.5 | 42.1 | | | 0.6 | | |
| - 2008 | 41.4 | 41.4 | 42.7 | 44.3 | 45.4 | 1.3 | 2.8 | 4.0 |
| Pakistan | | | | | | | | |
| - 2001/2 | 30.4 | 26.8 | 26.8 | | | 0.0 | | |
| - 2005/6 | 32.7 | 28.5 | 28.5 | 28.7 | 28.7 | 0.0 | 0.2 | 0.3 |
| - 2007/8 | 30.0 | 27.9 | 27.9 | 29.2 | 29.2 | 0.0 | 1.3 | 1.3 |
| - 2010/11 | 30.6 | 26.0 | 26.1 | 27.2 | 27.2 | 0.1 | 1.1 | 1.2 |
| Tanzania | | | | | | | | |
| - 2000 | 34.6 | 34.2 | 34.8 | | | 0.6 | | |
| - 2007 | 35.0 | 35.3 | 36.2 | 36.7 | 37.6 | 0.9 | 1.4 | 2.3 |

*Source*: Author's calculations

change in the nominal (GAPP) Gini coefficients, which is 0.5 Gini points. This means that composition adjustments of Gini coefficients are in some cases substantial, compared to the average change in the nominal Gini. This means that the composition effect severely alters the inequality track record in some, but not in all, countries.

The quantity discounting effect can also increase the level of inequality substantially. In Mozambique, the level of inequality increases by between 0.6 and 1.3 Gini points, depending on the survey. In Tanzania, the increase is between 0.6 and 0.9 Gini points. In Malawi, the effect is 0.8 Gini points in both survey rounds. However, the effect is not found in all countries— Pakistan and Ethiopia show no signs of quantity discounting effects.

Results are robust to varying the number of bins as well as to using prices for the entire country instead of within-strata prices.[7]

The rightmost column in Table 17.3 shows the results when both deflators are applied. In general, the combined effect is close to the sum of the two effects. The combination of the quantity discounting effect and the composition effect means that nominal inequality tends to underestimate the level of

---

[7] See the working paper version of this chapter for detailed results.

**Table 17.4.** Poverty rates and changes using different inequality measures

| | WIID | GAPP | Quantity | Composition | Both | Quantity minus Nominal | Composition minus Nominal | Both minus Nominal |
|---|---|---|---|---|---|---|---|---|
| Ethiopia | | | | | | | | |
| - 1999/2000 | 50.3 | 49.5 | 49.5 | | | 0.0 | | |
| - 2004/5 | 36.6 | 39.8 | 39.8 | 39.1 | 39.1 | 0.0 | −0.6 | −0.7 |
| - 2010/11 | 14.6 | 17.6 | 17.8 | 17.5 | 17.7 | 0.2 | −0.1 | 0.1 |
| Madagascar | | | | | | | | |
| - 2001 | 34.2 | 34.3 | 34.5 | | | 0.2 | | |
| - 2005 | 32.2 | 32.1 | 32.3 | 31.7 | 31.9 | 0.2 | −0.5 | −0.3 |
| Malawi | | | | | | | | |
| - 2004/5 | 45.2 | 47.8 | 48.6 | | | 0.7 | | |
| - 2010/11 | 41.2 | 40.4 | 41.3 | 41.4 | 42.2 | 0.8 | 1.0 | 1.8 |
| Mozambique | | | | | | | | |
| - 2002 | 56.7 | 52.7 | 53.1 | | | 0.5 | | |
| - 2008 | 38.1 | 38.1 | 39.5 | 41.1 | 42.4 | 1.4 | 3.0 | 4.2 |
| Pakistan | | | | | | | | |
| - 2001/2 | 1.2 | 0.4 | 0.4 | | | 0.0 | | |
| - 2005/6 | 1.1 | 0.3 | 0.3 | 0.3 | 0.3 | 0.0 | 0.0 | 0.0 |
| - 2007/8 | 0.3 | 0.1 | 0.1 | 0.3 | 0.3 | 0.0 | 0.1 | 0.1 |
| - 2010/11 | 0.3 | 0.0 | 0.0 | 0.1 | 0.1 | 0.0 | 0.0 | 0.0 |
| Tanzania | | | | | | | | |
| - 2000 | 24.4 | 23.9 | 24.7 | | | 0.8 | | |
| - 2007 | 13.1 | 13.5 | 14.6 | 15.2 | 16.2 | 1.1 | 1.7 | 2.7 |

*Note*: Poverty rates are reported in %.

*Source*: Author's calculations

inequality and overestimate reductions in inequality. Since country growth performance and policy effectiveness are often evaluated in the context of such changes, it is important to consider the possibility that nominal inequality measures may be severely downwards biased.

Table 17.4 shows the poverty rates calculated using the national accounts means and the Gini coefficients of Table 17.3. For the countries such as Mozambique and Tanzania where substantial differences in inequality were found, sizable differences in poverty are also found. For instance, the combination of the quantity discounting and composition effect raises the poverty rate by 4.2 percentage points in Mozambique in 2008, by 2.7 percentage points in Tanzania in 2007, and by 1.8 percentage points in Malawi in 2010/11. In Ethiopia and Madagascar, the estimated effect is smaller and sometimes even slightly negative, as expected from inspection of Figures 17.2 and 17.3. Since the composition effect builds up over time, the discrepancy in poverty estimates is bigger in later surveys. The composition effect alone raises the poverty estimate by 3.0 percentage points in the 2008 Mozambique survey and by 1.7 percentage points in the 2007 Tanzania survey. On this background, the optimistic picture of very fast poverty reduction in sub-Saharan African countries of Pinkovskiy and Sala-i-Martin (2014) should be interpreted with caution: while the technique still shows substantial poverty reductions when real inequality estimates are used, the level is higher and the pace of reduction is slower overall.

## 17.5 Conclusion

This chapter shows how two different effects can drive wedges between estimates of nominal and of real inequality. The first effect works through the combination of differential consumption structures across the consumption distribution and differential price increases of different product groups. The second effect works through quantity discounting: the poor may pay more for their food consumption since they buy smaller quantities. Household-specific deflators are calculated for fifteen surveys from six different countries which cover a range of varying experiences in terms of consumption levels and trends over time. A key advantage of this method is that it relies only on information which is available in existing nationally representative surveys of developing countries.

A composition effect was found in Malawi, Mozambique, Pakistan, and Tanzania but not in Ethiopia and Madagascar. Non-negligible quantity discounting effects were found in Mozambique and Tanzania; a smaller effect was found in Malawi; and no effects were found in Pakistan, Madagascar, and Ethiopia.

In most cases, the estimated effects are lower bounds on the true effect sizes. Nonetheless, the impacts on inequality and on the derived poverty estimates are in some cases substantial. Estimated real Gini coefficients are between $-0.6$ and 4.0 Gini points higher than nominal Gini coefficients. In some countries (Malawi, Mozambique, Pakistan, Tanzania), real inequality is higher than nominal inequality. Using real inequality indices can also affect inference on the speed of inequality reduction (Malawi, Pakistan, Tanzania). In the most extreme cases, it can change the direction of inequality change so that a decrease in nominal inequality conceals an increase in real inequality (Mozambique). However, in some countries (Ethiopia, Madagascar), real inequality does not appear to be different from nominal.

Finally, the inequality estimates matter for estimating poverty based on national accounts means and an estimate of inequality. In countries where the composition and quantity discounting effects affect the Gini coefficients, the poverty rates are also affected. While the quantity discounting effect potentially affects inequality indices in every year, the composition effect builds up over time as prices diverge. This means that in the countries where later surveys are more heavily influenced by the composition effect, the use of nominal inequality indices does not only introduce a source of bias in the *level* of poverty but may also overestimate the *rate* of poverty reduction.

The effects are highly country-specific. Why do effect sizes differ from country to country? For the composition effect, this is caused by differences in consumption structures and differences in inflation rates. Inflation rates are affected by a complex interaction of domestic conditions, such as harvests and government policies, as well as international changes in world market prices. Especially for the surveys conducted in the years of the food price crisis of 2007–9, world market prices of basic food items were very high. As new survey rounds become available it will be interesting to see if the composition effect shrinks, or if it is a longer-lasting phenomenon. For the quantity discounting effect, the cross-country differences are likely caused by a mix of real differences in the magnitude of quantity discounting present, and of differences due to varying survey instruments and methodologies.

Since the estimation of the composition and the quantity discounting effects requires only data which is generally available, and since the two effects are easily estimated, I suggest doing so for other countries, and whenever a new survey becomes available, in order to check whether keeping inequality in real terms matters in the country- and time-specific context.

## References

Aguiar, M. and E. Hurst (2007). 'Life-Cycle Prices and Production', *The American Economic Review*, 97(5): 1533–59.

Aksoy, M. A. and A. Isik-Dikmelik (2008). 'Are Low Food Prices Pro-Poor? Net Food Buyers and Sellers in Low-Income Countries', World Bank, Policy Research Paper No. 4642. Washington, DC: World Bank.

Arndt, C., L. Demery, A. McKay, and F. Tarp (2016). 'Growth and Poverty Reduction in Tanzania', in C. Arndt, A. McKay, and F. Tarp (eds), *Growth and Poverty in Sub-Saharan Africa*. Oxford: Oxford University Press, 238–62.

Arndt, C., M. A. Hussain, V. Leyaro, S. E. Jones, and F. Tarp (2013). 'Poverty and Growth in Tanzania'. Paper presented at the conference 'Inclusive Growth in Africa: Measurement, Causes and Consequences', 20–1 September, Helsinki.

Arndt, C., S. E. Jones, and V. Salvucci (2015). When Do Relative Prices Matter for Measuring Income Inequality? The Case of Food Prices in Mozambique', *The Journal of Economic Inequality*, 13(3): 449–64.

Arndt, C., S. E. Jones, and F. Tarp (2016). 'Mozambique: Off-Track or Temporarily Sidelined?', in C. Arndt, A. McKay, and F. Tarp (eds), *Growth and Poverty in Sub-Saharan Africa*. Oxford: Oxford University Press, 190–217.

Arndt, C., F. Tarp, and A. McKay (2016). 'Two Cheers for the African Growth Renaissance (but not Three)', in C. Arndt, A. McKay, and F. Tarp (eds), *Growth and Poverty in Sub-Saharan Africa*. Oxford: Oxford University Press, 11–39.

Attanasio, O. and C. Frayne (2006). 'Do the Poor Pay More?'. Mimeo.

Beatty, T. (2010). 'Do the Poor Pay More for Food? Evidence from the United Kingdom', *American Journal of Agricultural Economics*, 92(3): 608–21.

Cage, R. A., T. I. Garner, and J. Ruiz-Castillo (2002). 'Constructing Household Specific Consumer Price Indexes: An Analysis of Different Techniques and Methods', Bureau of Labor Statistics Working Paper No. 354. Washington, DC: US Department of Labor.

Chung, C., D. Dong, T. M. Schmit, H. M. Kaiser, and B. W. Gould (2005). 'Estimation of Price Elasticities from Cross-Sectional Data', *Agribusiness*, 21(4): 565–84.

CountrySTAT (2015). Available at <http://countrystat.org/>, accessed 22 March 2015.

Crawford, I., F. Laisney, and I. Preston (2003). 'Estimation of Household Demand Systems with Theoretically Compatible Engel Curves and Unit Value Specifications', *Journal of Econometrics*, 114(2): 221–41.

CSA (Central Statistical Agency) (2015). *Country and Regional Level Consumer Price Indices*. Information No. 23. Addis Ababa: Central Statistical Agency.

Deaton, A. (1988). 'Quality, Quantity, and Spatial Variation of Price', *The American Economic Review*, 78(3): 418–30.

Deaton, A. (2003). 'Prices and Poverty in India, 1987–2000', *Economic and Political Weekly*, 38(4): 362–8.

Deaton, A. and S. Zaidi (2002). *Guidelines for Constructing Consumption Aggregates for Welfare Analysis*. Washington, DC: World Bank.

Dorosh, P. A. and B. Minten (2006). 'Rice Price Stabilization in Madagascar: Price and Welfare Implications of Variable Tariffs', Paper No. 25478, International Association of Agricultural Economists Annual Meeting, 12–18 August, Queensland, Australia.

Durevall, D., J. L. Loening, and Y. Ayalew Birru (2013). 'Inflation Dynamics and Food Prices in Ethiopia', *Journal of Development Economics*, 104: 89–106.

FBS (2003). 'Household Integrated Economic Survey, Round 4: 2001–02', Technical Report, Federal Bureau of Statistics Pakistan, Islamabad, Pakistan.

FBS (2007). 'Household Integrated Economic Survey, 2005–06', Technical Report, Federal Bureau of Statistics Pakistan, Islamabad, Pakistan.

FBS (2009). 'Household Integrated Economic Survey, 2007–08', Technical Report, Federal Bureau of Statistics Pakistan, Islamabad, Pakistan.

FBS (2013). 'Household Integrated Economic Survey, 2011–12', Technical Report, Federal Bureau of Statistics Pakistan, Islamabad, Pakistan.

Goñi, E., H. López, and L. Servén (2006). 'Getting Real about Inequality: Evidence from Brazil, Colombia, Mexico, and Peru', World Bank Policy Research Working Paper 3815.

Grosh, M. and A. Deaton (2000). 'Consumption', in P. Glewwe, A. Deaton, and M. Grosh (eds), *Designing Household Survey Questionnaires for Developing Countries: Lessons from Ten Years of LSMS Experience*. Washington, DC: World Bank, 91–133.

Guénard, C. and S. Mesplé-Somps (2010). 'Measuring Inequalities: Do Household Surveys Paint a Realistic Picture?', *Review of Income and Wealth*, 56(3): 519–38.

Günther, I. and M. Grimm (2007). 'Measuring Pro-Poor Growth When Relative Prices Shift', *Journal of Development Economics*, 82(1): 245–56.

HICES (multiple years). 'Household Income, Consumption and Expenditure Survey'. Dataset 2000, 2005, and 2011. Available at <http://microdata.worldbank.org/index. php/catalog/1068>.

INSTAT (Institut national de la statistique) (2002). *Enquete aupres des menages 2001—rapport principal*.

INSTAT (Institut national de la statistique) (2006). *Enquete aupres des menages 2005—rapport principal*.

instat.mg (Institut national de la statistique de Madagascar) (2015). Available at <http://instat.mg/>, accessed 22 March 2015. Antananarivo: Institut national de la statistique de Madagascar.

Leicester, A., C. O'Dea, and Z. Oldfield (2008). 'The Inflation Experience of Older Households', IFS Commentary No. 106. London: Institute for Fiscal Studies.

McKelvey, C. (2011). 'Price, Unit Value, and Quality Demanded', *Journal of Development Economics*, 95(2): 157–69.

Mitchell, D. (2008). 'A Note on Rising Food Prices', SSRN Scholarly Paper No. ID 1233058. Rochester, NY: Social Science Research Network.

MoF (Ministry of Finance Pakistan) (2015). *Pakistan Economic Survey*. Islamabad: Ministry of Finance Pakistan.

Mohsin, A. and K. Zaman (2012). 'Distributional Effects of Rising Food Prices in Pakistan: Evidence from HIES 2001–02 and 2005–06 Survey', *Economic Modelling*, 29 (5): 1986–95.

MPF (Ministry of Planning and Finance), International Food Policy Research Institute, and Purdue University (2004). *Poverty and Well-Being in Mozambique: The Second National Assessment*. Maputo: Ministry of Planning and Finance.

MPF (Ministry of Planning and Finance) and National Directorate of Studies and Policy Analysis (2010). *Poverty and Well-Being in Mozambique: Third National Assessment*. Maputo: Ministry of Planning and Finance.

Muellbauer, J. (1974). 'Prices and Inequality: The United Kingdom Experience', *The Economic Journal*, 84(333): 32–55.

National Institute of Statistics Mozambique (INE) (2015). 'Índices de preços no Consumidor Moçambique'. Data obtained as supplementary material from the National Directorate for Studies and Policy Analysis (DNEAP) in Mozambique. Maputo: National Institute of Statistics Mozambique.

Nazli, H., E. Whitney, and K. Mahrt (2015). 'Poverty Trends in Pakistan', WIDER Working Paper No. 2015/136. Helsinki: UNU-WIDER.

NBE (National Bank of Ethiopia) (2014). *Annual Report: National Bank Annual Report 2013–2014*. Addis Ababa: National Bank of Ethiopia.

NBS (National Bureau of Statistics Tanzania) (2002). *Household Budget Survey 2000/01*. Dar es Salaam: National Bureau of Statistics Tanzania.

NBS (National Bureau of Statistics Tanzania) (2011). *National Household Budget Survey 2007*. Dar es Salaam: National Bureau of Statistics Tanzania.

NSO (National Statistical Office Malawi) (2005). *Integrated Household Survey 2004–2005, Volume I: Household Socio-Economic Characteristics*. Zomba: NSO.

NSO (National Statistical Office Malawi) (2012). *Integrated Household Survey 2010–2011: Household Socio-Economic Characteristics Report*. Zomba: NSO.

NSO (National Statistical Office Malawi) (2015). Available at <http://www.nsomalawi.mw/>, accessed 22 March 2015.

Pauw, K., U. Beck, and R. Mussa (2016). 'Did Rapid Smallholder-Led Agricultural Growth Fail to Reduce Rural Poverty? Making Sense of Malawi's Poverty Puzzle', in C. Arndt, A. McKay, and F. Tarp (eds), *Growth and Poverty in Sub-Saharan Africa*. Oxford: Oxford University Press, 89–111.

PBS (Pakistan Bureau of Statistics) (2006). *Household Integrated Economic Survey, 2004–05*. Islamabad: Pakistan Bureau of Statistics.

PBS (Pakistan Bureau of Statistics) (2007). *Household Integrated Economic Survey, 2005–06*. Islamabad: Pakistan Bureau of Statistics.

PBS (Pakistan Bureau of Statistics) (2009). *Household Integrated Economic Survey, 2007–08*. Islamabad: Pakistan Bureau of Statistics.

PBS (Pakistan Bureau of Statistics) (2013). *Household Integrated Economic Survey, 2011–12*. Islamabad: Pakistan Bureau of Statistics.

Pinkovskiy, M. and X. Sala-i-Martin (2009). 'Parametric Estimations of the World Distribution of Income', NBER Working Paper No. 15433, National Bureau of Economic Research.

Pinkovskiy, M. and X. Sala-i-Martin (2014). 'Africa Is on Time', *Journal of Economic Growth*, 19(3): 311–38.

Pritchett, L., A. Suryahadi, S. Sumarto, and Y. Suharso (2000). 'The Evolution of Poverty during the Crisis in Indonesia, 1996–99', Policy Research Working Paper No. 2435. Washington, DC: World Bank.

Rao, V. (2000). 'Price Heterogeneity and "Real" Inequality: A Case Study of Prices and Poverty in Rural South India', *Review of Income and Wealth*, 46(2): 201–11.

Ravallion, M. and B. Bidani (1994). 'How Robust Is a Poverty Profile?', *The World Bank Economic Review*, 8(1): 75–102.

Ravallion, M., S. Chen, and P. Sangraula (2009). 'Dollar a Day Revisited', *The World Bank Economic Review*, 23(2): 163–84.

Sala-i-Martin, X. (2006). 'The World Distribution of Income: Falling Poverty and . . . Convergence, Period', *The Quarterly Journal of Economics*, 121(2): 351–97.

Sala-i-Martin, X. and M. Pinkovskiy (2010). 'African Poverty is Falling . . . Much Faster than You Think!', Working Paper No. 15775, National Bureau of Economic Research.

Stifel, D., T. Razafimanantena, and F. Rakotomanana (2016). 'Utility-Consistent Poverty in Madagascar, 2001–10: Snapshots in the Presence of Multiple Economy-Wide Shocks', in C. Arndt, F. Tarp, and A. McKay (eds), *Growth and Poverty in Sub-Saharan Africa*. Oxford: Oxford University Press, 370–92.

Stifel, D. and T. Woldehanna (2016). 'Poverty in Ethiopia, 2000–11: Welfare Improvements in a Changing Economic Landscape', in C. Arndt, A. McKay, and F. Tarp (eds), *Growth and Poverty in Sub-Saharan Africa*. Oxford: Oxford University Press, 48–63.

Tarp, F., K. Simler, C. Matusse, R. Heltberg, and G. Dava (2002). 'The Robustness of Poverty Profiles Reconsidered', *Economic Development and Cultural Change*, 51(1), 77–108.

UNU-WIDER (2014). *World Income Inequality Database (WIID3.0b)*.

Wiggins, S., S. Keats, and J. Compton (2010). *What Caused the Food Price Spike of 2007/08? Lessons for World Cereals Markets*. Food Prices Project Report. London: Overseas Development Institute.

World Bank (2012). 'World Development Indicators 2012', May 2012 edition. Accessed October 2015.

# 18

# Conclusions and Looking Forward

*Channing Arndt and Finn Tarp*

## 18.1 Introduction

This volume has sought to contribute to improving the practice of measuring poverty and wellbeing in developing country contexts. The contributions include: two sets of software code designed to provide an advanced yet flexible basis for consumption (PLEASe) and multidimensional (EFOD) poverty analysis; a review of the theoretical foundations underlying the methods expressed in the code; discussion of practical issues encountered in the analysis of poverty and wellbeing both in general terms (Chapter 4) and in the eleven country cases included here; a synthesis of general lessons emerging from the case studies as a group (Chapter 16); and an extension to the analysis of inequality (Chapter 17). The hope is that this combined package will facilitate the conduct of rigorous analysis of poverty and wellbeing and enhance transparency and reproducibility.

The volume was not designed to suggest an exact cookbook approach to conducting analysis or to permit analyses to be produced more quickly. Rather, the analytical packages are meant to permit the analyst to spend more time thinking, cross-checking, and judging and less time on mechanical tasks. As emphasized, the default code sets, particularly for the estimation of consumption poverty (PLEASe), are unlikely to correspond to country circumstances. Analysts are near certain to be obliged to modify the PLEASe code to account for specific country circumstances. For both PLEASe and EFOD, careful checking that peculiarities of the circumstances/data are not generating erroneous results is required.

As noted in Chapter 1, many countries remain strongly dependent on external assistance for the conduct of their own assessments of poverty and wellbeing. This is, in no small measure, a reflection of the complexity of the task. While it is hoped that the materials contained in this book will help developing country analysts to grapple with this complexity, many of the challenges posed in rigorously measuring poverty and wellbeing are essentially irreducible. As a consequence, the attainment of one of the overarching goals of the volume, to facilitate locally produced analysis of poverty and wellbeing, will only be achieved via the development of a community of skilled analysts in developing countries.

## 18.2 Building Capabilities for Rigorous Measurement: Looking Forward

Training of individuals in the theory and practice of the measurement of welfare, as in this volume, is clearly necessary. However, it is not likely to be sufficient. The shape of the overall programme for monitoring and evaluating wellbeing is likely to strongly influence the rate of growth of local capabilities. Our experience, combined with the experiences presented in the case chapters, points to a series of design choices for programmes of measurement of wellbeing that can improve the quality of analysis and prospects for capacity-building often without a significant increment to the financial resources allocated to the task. We consider four choices—or maybe better areas of concern—in sections 18.2.1 to 18.2.4.

### 18.2.1 *Increased Frequency of Consumption Surveys*

The frequency of consumption-based surveys and data is often insufficient. Conduct of a consumption survey once every five or six years, as is frequently the case in Africa, allows too much time to elapse between surveys. This is true purely for analytical reasons. As discussed in Chapter 16, nearly all the evidence for poor regions of developing countries indicates that the determinants of welfare are frequently volatile. Hence, measured welfare can be expected to shift fairly dramatically as a consequence of shocks. A smaller number of measurement points increases the difficulty of differentiating between long-term trends and short-term shocks. Is a decline in measured consumption poverty the result of a negative shock to welfare in the initial period and a positive shock to welfare in the subsequent period or the result of real gains registered as part of an ongoing development process? This separation of shocks and trends is more difficult with fewer data points.

Capacity-building considerations provide further impetus for more frequent periodicity of consumption surveys. If consumption surveys occur only once every five or six years, then the development of a functional community of analysts becomes very difficult. As emphasized, the task of consumption poverty measurement is challenging. In developing countries, demand for individuals with the talents to undertake this analysis is invariably high. Once the analysis of a survey is complete, these individuals will be pulled into other areas in the absence of a coherent and relatively continuous programme of welfare monitoring. After four or five years have passed, reassembling the core team members that conducted the previous analysis is practically impossible. As a result, the analysis of each survey is often undertaken with a brand new team and an associated need for external assistance.[1]

Hence, both for the information provided and for capacity-building, countries should plan to conduct a household consumption survey approximately once every two to three years and explicitly consider the modes for the development of the necessary community of analysts. Moreover, the degree of complexity of the more frequent surveys proposed here needs careful reflection and must in practice be established in light of the specific financial and human resources available in concrete country contexts.

### 18.2.2 *Avoid Excessive Complexity*

For the large majority of national statistical agencies in developing countries, obtaining an accurate picture of consumption for a household is challenging. Complicating the task with a series of additional objectives, such as sources of income (including a detailed look at agricultural production), migration dynamics, time use, and (occasionally) all of the above and more in a panel dataset, risks undermining the attainment of all of the targeted objectives due to proliferation of non-sample error.

The utility of data that permits comprehensive and cross-referenced analysis of household behaviour broadly defined is not in doubt. And answering many important questions requires adequate panel data. These advantages of more complicated data collection efforts are well established. At the same time, it is also perfectly clear that statistics agencies in developing countries frequently struggle with the challenge of adequately capturing consumption. Adding tasks may detract from attaining this basic objective.

A greater degree of collaboration between national statistical services and universities and/or other research/training-oriented organizations likely offers the most promising path forward. While national statistical services are in the process of developing and consolidating capacity to generate the fundamental statistics necessary to manage a country, including welfare statistics, advanced efforts to collect broader arrays of data, whether in panel or not, should be located in universities or other non-government organizations

---

[1] A similar set of arguments pertain with respect to the process of data collection as discussed in section 18.2.2.

(NGOs).[2] Properly organized, these data collection and analysis efforts, housed outside of the national statistics agency, should also serve as human resource development centres for the statistics agency.

### 18.2.3 *Come to Grips with the Nominal and the Real and Ensure Transparency in Methodological Choices*

A basic challenge in undertaking meaningful consumption-based poverty analysis is the critical importance of prices, i.e. of coming to grips with how nominal consumption aggregates are converted into measures of real consumption over time and space as well as among different population groups. It is well established that aggregate inflation measures may not capture the rate of change in the prices actually faced by poorer households. Several of the case studies in this volume and the companion volume by Arndt, McKay, and Tarp (2016) illustrate this conundrum. A similar challenge exists in relation to ensuring methodological comparability over time in more general terms.

For example, Chapter 14 noted that in Tanzania, price inflation as measured by the household budget survey differs drastically from inflation rates derived from the published consumer price index (CPI) and the GDP deflator. It also made the observation that to complicate matters further the World Bank (2015) assessment of consumption poverty trends over the most recent period (2007–11/12) includes changes in the data collection methods employed in 2011/12 compared with all earlier surveys. The Bank assessment also took the opportunity to apply a series of methodological changes to the computation of the nominal consumption aggregate and the poverty lines. These differentials in effect render the analyses of the 2011/12 non-comparable with published analyses from 2007 and earlier; and in order to account for these differences, a series of steps were taken to revise 2007 data and calculations.

The revisions to the 2007 data are considerable. World Bank (2015: 2) reports as noted in Chapter 14 that 'consumption per adult rose by almost one-third'. The poverty line was also adjusted upward substantially, leaving the measured poverty rate at the national level essentially at the same value as reported in previously published assessments. Nevertheless, the issue of achieving comparability and transparency in data and methods applied clearly dominates any analysis of consumption poverty trends over the 2007 to 2011/12 period.

---

[2] A period of consolidation is almost perennially forsaken in environments characterized by a high level of donor engagement. Aid bureaucrats get little kudos for aiming to accomplish what had been accomplished before, even though periods of consolidation are likely to be an essential part of the process of building individual and institutional capability.

Chapter 17 provides another illustration of comparability issues when estimating inequality. First, poorer people allocate much more of their budget to food, particularly basic foods. If the price of basic foods rises relative to other prices, the poor will be disproportionately affected. Second, poor people may tend to purchase goods in smaller quantities at higher unit prices than those who are better off. These specific effects, which have implications for inequality, are held in focus in Chapter 17.

On this background, household-specific deflators are estimated in Chapter 17 using fifteen surveys collected in six countries in the period 1999–2011 and analysed as an integral part of the UNU-WIDER Growth and Poverty Project. In some countries (Mozambique, Tanzania, Malawi, and Pakistan), measured inequality is higher when these two additional factors are considered. In other countries (Ethiopia and Madagascar), no differences are found. The analysis suggests that poverty estimation based on national accounts consumption means and estimates of inequality from consumption surveys should account for these two effects. Had Pinkovskiy and Sala-i-Martin (2014) accounted for these effects, the adjustments would, by and large, increase their estimated levels of poverty and reduce the rate of decline in poverty over time. The magnitude of the adjustment is—as noted in Chapter 17—country- and year-specific, stressing the need for better data and understanding of this area of poverty and inequality inquiry.

### 18.2.4 *Emphasize a Variety of Measures*

The desirability of a multiplicity of poverty measures, reflecting the numerous facets of wellbeing, is by now well established (Ravallion 2016; Alkire et al. 2015). Successful survey programmes, such as the demographic and health surveys that are regularly conducted across the developing world, provide a wealth of non-monetary indicators that furnish critical insights into any broad-based assessment of wellbeing. The first-order dominance methods (FOD) held in focus in Chapters 11–15 provide one useful means for deriving general conclusions across a series of indicators. As discussed in Chapter 3, the FOD approach identifies welfare differentials between populations using multiple binary welfare indicators without imposing weighting schemes or making assumptions about preferences for each indicator. Other techniques, such as those elaborated in Alkire et al. (2015), provide a series of alternatives. As revealed in the Tanzania case (Chapter 14), application of multiple techniques can enhance insight (in this case about the multidimensional welfare of two subgroups of children) even if the same set of indicators are employed.

When a variety of methods are employed, the result is a dashboard of basic welfare indicators that should provide reasonably detailed insight into a series of important dimensions of welfare (Stiglitz et al. 2009). This dashboard has been proposed as a substitute for 'mashup' indices that collapse a series of non-monetary indicators into a single number analogous to the consumption poverty headcount (Ravallion 2010). However, we see no reason why 'mashup' indices, such as the Alkire–Foster (AF) multidimensional index, should not form a part of a comprehensive dashboard of quantitative indicators, particularly if the limitations of each indicator in the dashboard are clearly elucidated.

It is perhaps useful to note that Ravallion (2010) defines a 'mashup' index as one that is not 'informed by theory or practice'. The FOD, given its basis in theories of dominance, would not qualify as a 'mashup' index.

## 18.3 Final Observations

These elements—a regular household consumption survey, coming to grips with price trends and differentials, concerted efforts to monitor non-monetary indicators such as those in focus in demographic and health surveys, and a series of more advanced and pointed surveys including panel elements, likely conducted from a university base—provide ample raw material for the emergence of a healthy and active community of quantitative analysts.

The cost of collecting this information is not likely to be substantially different from the amounts currently allocated. While increasing the frequency of consumption surveys clearly increases costs, the associated call for reduced complexity reduces costs. In addition, the capacity-building gains associated with greater frequency apply equally well to data collection as to data analysis capabilities, opening the door to more cost-efficient as well as higher-quality data collection.[3]

If the quantitative information both informs and is informed by a similarly active qualitative research programme, many of the desiderata of an idealized welfare monitoring programme will have been fulfilled. Indeed, there exists a reasonably large international community of analysts who work largely within these confines.

There are, however, good reasons to extend this scope of activity. Welfare outcomes, such as the consumption poverty rate, are macroeconomic variables similar to gross domestic product (GDP). Triangulation of welfare

---

[3] One would also have to fund the more complicated, but smaller-sample, university-based surveys. The dynamics that are frequently in place are a large number of small, independently funded surveys. These ad hoc series of small surveys are often a reaction to inadequacy in national monitoring programmes. Mobilizing even a share of these resources into a coherent national programme that articulates with a complementary university-based effort offers the prospect of generating more information at lower overall cost.

outcomes from the surveys with national accounts, price data, trade data, weather outcomes and more provides at least two distinct benefits. First, if indicators derived from within the survey are broadly confirmed by indicators external to the survey, confidence in both indicators is enhanced. Second, recourse to a broader array of data can help to generate a much better understanding of the reasons for movement (or lack thereof) in welfare indicators, thus helping to distinguish, for example, between transitory shocks to welfare and more permanent shifts.

Drawing conclusions based on this triangulation across multiple sources is the focus of the companion volume to this book (Arndt, McKay, and Tarp 2016). As the techniques in focus in the present volume for country-focused poverty analysis become internalized, readers are referred to the companion volume for broader-based welfare assessment and triangulation.

# References


Alkire, S., J. Foster, S. Seth, M. E. Santos, J. M. Roche, and P. Ballon (2015). *Multidimensional Poverty Measurement and Analysis*. Oxford: Oxford University Press.

Arndt, C., A. McKay, and F. Tarp (eds) (2016). *Growth and Poverty in Sub-Saharan Africa*. Oxford: Oxford University Press.

Pinkovskiy, M. and X. Sala-i-Martin (2014). 'Africa Is On Time', *Journal of Economic Growth*, 19(3): 311–38.

Ravallion, M. (2010). 'Your New Composite Index Has Arrived: Please Handle with Care', VOX, <http://www.voxeu.org/article/your-new-composite-index-has-arrived-please-handle-care>.

Ravallion, M. (2016). *The Economics of Poverty: History, Measurement, and Policy*. Oxford: Oxford University Press.

Stiglitz, J., A. Sen, and J. P. Fitoussi (2009). *Report by the Commission on the Measurement of Economic Performance and Social Progress*, <http://www.insee.fr/fr/publications-et-services/dossiers_web/stiglitz/doc-commission/RAPPORT_anglais.pdf>.

World Bank (2015). *Tanzania Poverty Assessment*. Washington, DC: World Bank.

# User Guide to Poverty Line Estimation Analytical Software—PLEASe

*Channing Arndt, Ulrik Beck, M. Azhar Hussain, Kristi Mahrt,*
*Kenneth Simler, and Finn Tarp*

## A.1 Introduction

This technical guide presents the Poverty Line Estimation Analytical Software (PLEASe). PLEASe comprises a flexible set of Stata and GAMS codes designed to estimate regional poverty lines using household budget survey data. In this approach, the estimation of absolute poverty lines is rooted in the cost of basic needs method, which forms the core PLEASe code stream. Specifically, poverty lines are based on the typical consumption patterns (food bundles and prices) of the reference population (relatively poor households). The cost of food bundles, which attain minimum caloric needs, at prices paid by relatively poor households, yields a food poverty line. The total poverty line is determined by the sum of the food poverty line and the cost of non-food items for households with total consumption levels close to the food poverty line.

Some key aspects of the default PLEASe approach merit mentioning. First, the typical consumption pattern of the reference population, poor households, is estimated using an iterative procedure to identify which households are deemed poor. Second, the approach recognizes the value of accounting for differences in regional and temporal consumption patterns. Thus, the approach allows poverty lines to be estimated in multiple spatial domains based on flexible consumption bundles that vary over time and space. Third, revealed preference tests are evaluated to determine whether regional and temporal consumption bundles represent a consistent level of utility. Finally, if these revealed preference conditions fail, a minimum cross-entropy methodology is employed to adjust consumption bundles to satisfy constraints. The reader is referred to Chapters 2 and 4 for a more detailed discussion.

This guide aims to provide the information needed to apply PLEASe to poverty line estimations in a multitude of country settings. The goal is not to give the user prepackaged software, but to provide a launching point such that, with relevant modifications to data, parameters, or the code stream, the software can be appropriately adapted to accommodate country-specific circumstances. With slight modifications, it is straight-forward to implement a large array of approaches. For example, while the PLEASe code stream was designed to estimate poverty lines based on flexible utility-consistent regional consumption baskets, the code can be modified to accommodate alternative approaches, including but not limited to regional baskets fixed over time, a single national consumption basket priced at national prices, or a single national basket priced at regional levels. In addition, revealed preference constraints can be imposed on flexible baskets spatially, spatially and temporally, or not at all.

This appendix focuses on specific details of understanding and implementing the PLEASe code stream. After presenting data and software requirements in section A.2, section A.3 presents the code stream step by step, including required inputs. Section A.4 provides guidelines to assembling necessary datasets. Lastly, section A.5 provides some final thoughts.

## A.2 Requirements

### A.2.1 *Software*

The PLEASe package is executed in Stata and GAMS. High skill levels in Stata are a distinct advantage. Only a basic understanding of GAMS is needed. The Stata code was produced using Stata version 12; however, the code will run in Stata 11.[1] The GAMS code will run on versions 22.7 and later.

### A.2.2 *Data*

Estimating poverty lines using the PLEASe software requires disaggregated household budget survey data—specifically, consumption expenditures for food at the household and product level and non-food expenditures at the household level. For food items, quantities are also necessary for estimating food prices (unit costs). If consumption quantities are not reported, local prices must be obtained from an alternative source, such as community price surveys. Additional required data include household-level survey data (survey periods, regions, household size, and household weights), individual data (age, sex, and the presence of a child's mother in the household), fertility rates by age and urban/rural area, and calories per gram of food items. Greater detail on compiling datasets is provided in section A.4.

## A.3 Description of the Code Stream

This section presents the specifics of the code stream and inputs necessary to adapt the software to individual country cases. While more substantial changes to the code may be desired to adapt the software to specific conditions in each country, this section focuses on basic requirements. The beginning of each subsection lists the relevant code files as well as an overview of required modifications.

---

[1] Versions prior to Stata 11 will require modifications such as reverting to old merge syntax.

### A.3.1 *Directory Structure*

The PLEASe directory consists of a master directory containing a subdirectory of the code files as well as subdirectories for each survey year. The provided PLEASe code contains the code subdirectory named *new*. The user must create subdirectories containing the input data for each survey year. Survey directories can be named as desired. Within each survey directory all input data will be provided by the user in the subdirectory *in*. The initial structure is as follows:

*PLEASe*
> *new*
> *year1*
>> *in*
> *year2*
>> *in*

The PLEASe code will create several subdirectories as needed. After the initial execution the directory structure will appear as follows:

*PLEASe*
> *new*
> *year1*
>> *in*
>> *work*
>> *out*
>>> *t_plus1*
>> *rep*
> *year2*
>> *in*
>> *work*
>> *out*
>>> *t_plus1*
>> *rep*

Where *work* contains working datasets, *out* contains final results, and *rep* contains logs from each Stata do-file. The subdirectory *out/t_plus1* contains data necessary for revealed preference tests in the subsequent time period.

### A.3.2 *Initialization*

*000_boom.do, 010_initial_$year.do, 060_in_2_work.*

- *In 000_boom.do, three global macros must be specified: the file path to the PLEASe directory, the name of the subdirectory of the survey year being analysed, and if applicable, the subdirectory of the prior survey year.*
- *In 010_initial_$year.do, global macros used throughout the code stream are defined.*

The Stata do-file, *000_boom.do*, is the master file from which the entire code stream can be executed. This file, therefore, also functions as a table of contents of all Stata and GAMS code files. The code stream relies on a number of global macros that are set in

*000_boom.do* and *010_initial_$year.do*. These globals allow customization of the specific aspects of the code without the need to directly modify individual Stata do-files. Every global should be reviewed and set accordingly. See Table A1 for more detailed descriptions of the globals.

**Table A1.** Global macros

| Global Macro | Use | Description | Values |
|---|---|---|---|
| path | general | file path to PLEASe | file path |
| year | general | name of the directory containing files for the year of analysis | directory name |
| prevyear | general | name of the directory containing files for the previous year of analysis. If only one year or the first of a series of years is being analysed, this global is left blank. | directory name |
| food_cat | general | code that will determine how food products will be selected in the code stream | e.g. food_cat = 1 |
| spdom_n | general | number of spatial domains | 1, 2, 3 … |
| tpi_bottom | TPI | percentile that defines the relatively poor for the TPI | percentile |
| product_tpi_switch | TPI | specifies how food products in the TPI will be chosen | 0, top food items<br>1, specified set of food items. |
| product_tpi_n | TPI | if product_tpi_switch = 0, specifies the number of food items in the TPI basket | number of food items |
| product_tpi | TPI | if product_tpi_switch = 1, specifies code that will select the set of products | code |
| tpi_reg_n | TPI | number of TPI regions | 1, 2, 3, 4 … |
| survtemp | TPI | time unit for TPI adjustments | survquar/survmon |
| temp_n | TPI | number of TPI periods | 1, 2, 3, 4 … |
| bottom | iterations | initial percentile for determining the relatively poor | percentile |
| it_n | iterations | number of iterations | 1, 2, 3 … |
| cut_reg | iterations | controls whether the relatively poor are determined by regional or national bottom percentiles | 0, spatial domain<br>1, nation |
| pass | iterations | denotes the round of iterations (automatically set within *100_iterate.do*) | 1, 2, … *$it_n* |
| no_temp_rev | revealed pref. | specifies whether temporal revealed preference constraints will be checked | * no temporal<br>" " temporal |
| revpref | revealed pref. | GAMS revealed preference file | spatial only: *250_spat_consistent.bat*<br>spatial and temporal: *255_spat_temp_consistent.bat* |

*Source:* See text

### A.3.3 *Consumption Aggregates*

Assembling and fine-tuning consumption data to conform to the PLEASe format is time-consuming and requires care. It is certainly an important task in implementing PLEASe. However, the steps needed to prepare the data are specific to each survey and therefore cannot be standardized. The do-files used to compile consumption data from Mozambique household surveys are provided for reference purposes only and are not incorporated into the code stream. Rather, for each survey a new set of do-files must be created.

### A.3.4 *Working Datasets*
*060_in_2_work.do.*

File *060_in_2_work* preserves original user-provided datasets by creating a set of working datasets that are saved in the *work* directory. This file also merges the consumption dataset, *cons_nom_in.dta*, with household data and produces two convenient datasets for later use, *cons_nom.dta* and *cons_nom_trans.dta*. The differences between these two datasets hinges on the availability of transaction-level data. Some surveys report food consumption at the transaction level, i.e. consumption values and quantities are reported separately each time a household acquires a particular food item. Other surveys only report the total value and quantity of each product consumed during the recall period. If consumption values are available at the transaction level, *cons_nom.dta* is collapsed to a single observation per product, per household. The dataset *cons_nom_trans.dta* retains transaction-level data for food product pricing. These datasets are essentially the same if food consumption is not available at the transaction level, though *cons_nom_trans.dta* keeps only food products while *cons_nom.dta* keeps food and non-food products. After the temporal price index is created, consumption in *cons_nom_trans.dta* is temporally adjusted for price calculations.

### A.3.5 *Caloric Needs and Content*
*070_calpp.do.*

This file calculates the average per person daily caloric requirements in each spatial domain. Using individual-level data contained in *indata.dta*, caloric needs are set according to sex and age, with adjustments for the probability of breastfeeding and pregnancy. We employ age and urban/rural-dependent fertility rates from other statistical sources to estimate caloric needs for women. Individual caloric requirements contained in the do-file, *070_calpp.do*, are based on international standards for moderately active individuals and are applicable to all countries (WHO 1985). However, fertility rates are country-specific and must be provided by the user in *fert_rate.dta*.

To account for pregnancy, we assume that pregnant women need 285 additional calories in the last trimester of pregnancy. Since one trimester is three months, or one fourth of a year, the probability that a given woman is in the third trimester of pregnancy is the relevant fertility rate divided by four. Applying the probability of pregnancy to all women is appropriate as food poverty line calculations are based on average caloric needs in a spatial domain rather than individual needs. The resulting caloric requirement for women is thus a standard requirement of 2100 plus 285 times the probability of being in the third trimester of pregnancy.

Caloric needs are also adjusted to account for the additional 500 calories per day required by breastfeeding mothers. The assumption that all children under six months of age whose mothers live in the household are breastfed allows the breastfeeding caloric requirement to be added to the caloric requirements of all children under one. Assuming that 60 per cent of children under one are less than six months old, we add 300 calories to the daily requirements of all children under one whose mothers reside in the household. As with fertility rates, these assumptions are appropriate as average caloric requirements by spatial domain are used in food poverty line calculations. If information on the presence of the mother in the household is not available, one approach is to assume that all children under six months are breastfed and set the variable *motherhh* to one for all children.

### A.3.6 *Per Capita Consumption*
*080_conpc.do.*

For convenience, the dataset *conpc.dta* is created which contains per capita nominal food, non-food, and total household consumption. This file also creates the share of food consumption of total expenditures and per capita calorie consumption. In the next step, the intra-survey temporal price index is used to generate temporally adjusted per capita consumption variables in *conpc.dta*.

### A.3.7 *The Temporal Price Index*
*090_temp_index.do.*

The intra-survey temporal price index (TPI) allows temporal adjustment of consumption values to account for seasonality of prices and associated variations in purchasing power. TPI calculations involve four key steps. The first step identifies households with per capita nominal household consumption in the bottom X percentile as specified by the global *tpi_bottom*. Consumption at this percentile is used as a cut-off to define the relatively poor throughout the TPI calculations.

Second, a TPI food basket is identified that contains the most important food items in each TPI region. This step can be accomplished in one of two ways, which the user specifies with the global *product_tpi_switch*. By default, food items with the highest weighted expenditure shares among the relatively poor are selected. The number of items in the food basket is determined by the global *product_tpi_n*. Alternatively, the user may specify the global *product_tpi* to include particular food products.

Third, unit value prices for TPI food basket items are calculated. Before computing unit prices, we toss out the top and bottom 5 per cent of household-level prices for each region and product combination, eliminating the influence of these potential outliers. Then, using sample and quantity weighting, household-level consumption quantities and expenditures for each product, region, and time period are aggregated. From these regional aggregates, unit prices are calculated.

Finally, we determine the consumption share of each item in the food basket of relatively poor households. Because the TPI basket comprises a subset of all food consumption, average regional product shares of food basket items are scaled so that shares sum to one in each region. Using these shares as weights, we calculate a price index of food basket prices by region and quarter. Then for each region we normalize the index by dividing each quarterly index value by the value of an arbitrary quarter.

The last step in this do-file temporally adjusts food expenditures in the data files *conpc.dta* and *cons_nom_trans.dta*. Note that only food expenditures are deflated with the TPI. Total real consumption is therefore the sum of TPI-adjusted food consumption and nominal non-food consumption. At this point, all temporal deflation is complete.

### A.3.8 *Consumption Statistics*
*095_descriptives.do.*

This file provides initial descriptive statistics of the consumption aggregate that may be useful both in understanding the consumption aggregate and in troubleshooting poverty line estimation. Among the values reported is per capita calorie consumption based on reported food consumption, which can help identify calorie under-reporting. Calorie under-reporting may be an issue for a variety of reasons such as a more diverse array of food consumed than the survey food recall lists account for or a failure to report food consumed outside the home. Calorie totals may also fall short of actual calorie consumption due to inaccurate mapping from reported consumption to actual calories consumed. A mismatch between per capita consumption and per capita calorie consumption may signal a problem with the consumption aggregate or the reported calories per gram, or it may identify an underlying shortfall in the survey data. See DNEAP (2010) for a detailed discussion of calorie under-reporting in Mozambique.

### A.3.9 *Estimating Poverty Lines with an Iterative Procedure*
*100_iterations.do.*

Food prices, baskets, and the resulting poverty lines are calculated for relatively poor households using an iterative procedure to ensure that poverty lines are based on the consumption patterns of poor households. In a preliminary iteration, relatively poor households are identified as those with temporally adjusted per capita consumption in the bottom X per cent, where the macro global *bottom* specifies a national cut-off X. The consumption patterns of these households yield food prices, food baskets, and poverty lines for each spatial domain. As regional poverty lines reflect regional variations in the cost of attaining the same standard of living, it is possible to calculate a spatial price index with which (already temporally deflated) per capita household consumption is spatially deflated. Spatially adjusted poverty lines applied to real consumption yield poverty headcount rates. These poverty headcount rates provide updated spacial-domain-specific cut-off percentiles, and together with real per capita consumption, form the basis for identifying relatively poor households in the subsequent iteration. With an updated set of relatively poor households, food baskets, and food prices, a new set of poverty lines and poverty headcounts are calculated. This process continues until the poverty rates converge. Convergence generally occurs within five iterations. The number of iterations is set with the global *it_n*.

The do-file, *100_iterations.do*, runs the iterative process by first selecting relatively poor households in each iteration and then executing four subsequent do-files that calculate food prices (*110_price_unit.do*), food bundles (*120_food_basket_flex.do*), poverty lines (*130_povline_flex.do*), and the spatial price index and Foster–Greer–Thorbecke

(FGT) class of poverty measures (*140_povmeas_flex.do*) (Foster et al. 1984). The process is executed for a preliminary iteration (called iteration 0) and the subsequent 1 through *it_n* iterations.

### A.3.9.1 FOOD PRICES
*110_price_unit.do.*

This do-file generates unit food prices by spatial domain based on the consumption of relatively poor households. After tossing out the top and bottom 5 per cent of household-level prices, several methods are employed to calculate the price of each product in each spatial domain. By default, PLEASe uses the value share weighted mean price per gram; however, alternative price specifications are possible and are calculated in this do-file. Prices are recalculated, in each iteration, using the updated set of relatively poor households.

### A.3.9.2 FLEXIBLE FOOD BUNDLE
*120_food_basket_flex.do.*

Spatial-domain-specific flexible food baskets include the bundle of most commonly consumed food products by the relatively poor. The dataset is restricted to relatively poor households and food products with quantities, calorie information, and prices based on at least ten observations.[2] Food expenditures on items such as restaurant meals are often reported without quantities or lack calorie data and in these instances are not used in poverty line calculations. By spatial domain, each product's weighted share of total food expenditures among relatively poor households is determined. The food basket contains those products comprising the top 90 per cent of food expenditures. The rationale for restricting analysis to the top 90 per cent is that the bottom 10 per cent tends to contain a great number of food items typically consumed by relatively few households. It is appealing to exclude such items and limit the consumption bundle to items consumed by a larger share of poor households. The process of calculating food bundles is repeated in each iteration using the reselected group of relatively poor households.

### A.3.9.3 FLEXIBLE POVERTY LINES AND POVERTY MEASURES
*130_povline_flex.do, 140_povmeas.do.*

For each spatial domain, the food poverty line represents the cost of meeting regional daily per person calorie requirements with each food basket item contributing according to its regional share of total consumption. The food basket represents 90 per cent of expenditures, which is assumed to meet 95 per cent of calorie requirements. Once the food poverty line is derived, it is scaled to reflect 100 per cent of food expenditures and therefore the cost of meeting 100 per cent of the regional calorie requirement.

The non-food poverty line is the weighted average of non-food expenditures for households with total per capita expenditures within 20 per cent of the food poverty

---

[2] The *food_basket_missing* data files identify those items with sufficient expenditure levels to fall in the top 90 per cent of consumption but excluded from the food basket for lack of calorie or price data.

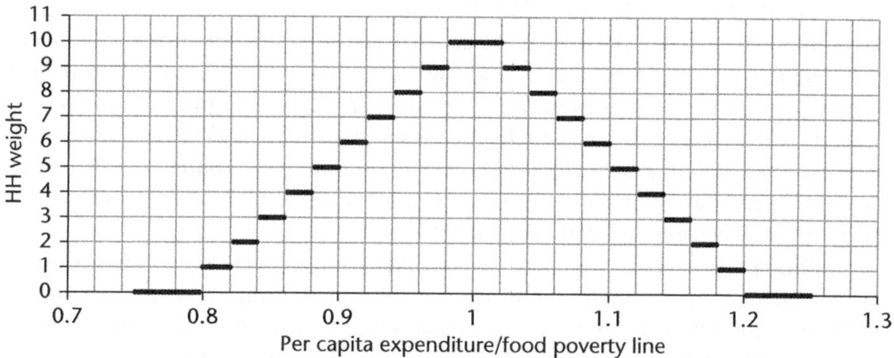

**Figure A1.** Extra household weights used to estimate non-food expenditure

line. A triangular weighting scheme is used to give greater weight to those with expenditures closest to the food poverty line (Figure A1). The total poverty line is simply the sum of the food and non-food poverty lines.

Finally, this do-file executes *140_povmeas.do* to calculate the spatial price index and FGT poverty measures. The poverty headcount defines the next round's bottom percentile for determining the relatively poor. Though poverty lines are calculated for specific spatial domains, the FGT poverty measures can be calculated for any area by finding the average number of households in that area with real per capita consumption falling below the relevant spatial domain's poverty line. This file outputs poverty rates for the nation, rural/urban, TPI regions, spatial domains, strata, and a regional variable, *news*.

The do-file, *140_povmeas.do*, is also executed later in the code stream to calculate the fixed (based on the previous time period's entropy-adjusted food basket and current period prices) and flexible entropy-adjusted spatial price indices and poverty measures.

### A.3.10 *Preparing Data for Revealed Preference Conditions*
*200_rev_pref_spat_1.do, 210_rev_pref_temp_1.do, 220_rev_pref_temp_2.do.*

Files *200* to *220* prepare datasets containing prices, quantities, poverty lines, regional caloric requirements, and calories per gram from the current survey period and the previous period, when applicable, for use in revealed preference tests. Refer to Chapters 2 and 4 for discussions of revealed preference tests and the entropy adjustment procedure. Recall that revealed preference conditions are expressed in the following three constraints, where $i$ indexes food products; $r$ and its alias, $s$, represent the set of spatial domains; and $p_1, p_2, q_1, q_2$ represent prices and quantities in the first and second time period.

$$\sum_i p_{2ir} * q_{2is} \geq \sum_i p_{2ir} * q_{2ir} \qquad \forall r, s \quad r \neq s \qquad (A.1)$$

$$\sum_i p_{2ir} * q_{1ir} \geq \sum_i p_{2ir} * q_{2ir} \qquad \forall r \qquad (A.2)$$

$$\sum_i p_{1ir} * q_{2ir} \geq \sum_i p_{1ir} * q_{1ir} \qquad \forall r \qquad (A.3)$$

### A.3.10.1 SPATIAL REVEALED PREFERENCES

The do-file *200_rev_pref_spat.do* exports product codes, prices, quantities, calories per gram, regional caloric requirements, and the food poverty line from the last iteration for spatial revealed preference tests and entropy corrections in GAMS. This do-file also conducts initial spatial revealed preference tests (constraint A.1). These tests simply provide an initial look at spatial revealed preference outcomes. Spatial revealed preference tests used in analysis and entropy adjustments are conducted in the GAMS files *250_spat_consistent.gms* and *250_spat_consistent.bat*.

In testing spatial revealed preference conditions, we can effectively compare the food poverty line in region *r* to a food poverty line calculated using the region *r* prices and the region *s* food basket. To ensure comparability, the poverty lines must reflect the same calorie target. Product codes, prices, quantities, calories per gram, regional calorie requirements, and food poverty lines are exported for analysis in GAMS.

### A.3.10.2 TEMPORAL REVEALED PREFERENCES

The do-files *210_rev_pref_temp_1.do* and *220_rev_pref_temp_2.do* prepare data from the previous survey period and the current survey period to test the temporal revealed preference constraints (constraints A.2 and A.3). These do-files are only executed when conducting intertemporal comparisons as determined by the global, *no_temp_rev*. Both files use *match_t1_t2.dta* to harmonize product codes between the two surveys, enabling prices and quantities to be matched between surveys.

The do-file, *210_rev_pref_temp_1.do*, addresses constraint A.2. The right-hand side of the equation is simply the current survey food poverty line. To calculate the left side, we calculate a fixed poverty line using previous period quantities and current period prices. However, several adjustments are required. First, because quantities in each period are scaled to meet regional calorie requirements, it is necessary to account for the fact that regional calorie requirements are likely to be different between survey periods. Specifically, we scale previous period quantities to reflect current period caloric requirements. Second, because not all items in the previous food basket were consumed in the current period, we account for missing products when scaling the poverty line to meet 100 per cent of expenditures. This fixed poverty line is exported for use in GAMS.

The do-file, *220_rev_pref_temp_2.do*, prepares data to evaluate revealed preference constraint A.3. The right-hand side of constraint A.3 is the previous period poverty line. Previous period prices, after harmonizing product codes, and poverty lines are exported for use in GAMS.

### A.3.11 *Fixed Poverty Lines and Poverty Measures*
*230_ povline_fix.do, 140_povmeas.do.*

Do-file *230_povline_fix.do* calculates total poverty lines from the fixed food poverty lines. The fixed poverty lines were derived in *210_rev_pref_temp_1.do* and reflect previous period consumption bundles evaluated at current period prices. This file is only executed when conducting intertemporal comparisons as determined by the global, *no_temp_rev*. The total poverty line in the fixed case is calculated differently than in the flexible cases (e.g. in *130_povline_flex.do* and *270_povline_flex_ent.do*). As previous period non-food consumption evaluated at current period prices is not available, the previous period food poverty line to total poverty line ratio is used to derive the total poverty line. Finally, *140_povmeas.do* is executed to calculate spatial price indices and FGT poverty measures.

### A.3.12 *Revealed Preference Tests and Entropy Adjustments*

*250_spat_consistent.gms,     250_spat_consistent.bat     255_spat_temp_consistent.gms, 255_spat_temp_consistent.bat.*

- *250_spat_consistent.bat (spatial revealed preferences only) or 250_spat_temp_consistent. bat (spatial and temporal revealed preference constraints) must be adapted such that the first line points to the directory containing the GAMS software. This allows Stata to initiate the GAMS files as GAMS is on the DOS path.*

The GAMS file *250_spat_consistent.gms* tests spatial revealed preference constraints while *255_spat_temp_consistent.gms* tests spatial and temporal revealed preference constraints. Both files perform entropy adjustments to resolve any utility inconsistency among food bundles, thereby producing utility-consistent consumption bundles and food poverty lines. These files may be run directly in GAMS or may be shelled from Stata via *250_spat_consistent.bat* or *255_spat_temp_consistent.bat*. As noted, in order for the *bat* files to work, the first line must be modified to point to the directory that contains the GAMS software so that GAMS is on the DOS path.

Poverty lines are calculated to meet specific calorie requirements that vary by time and space. To ensure comparability in revealed preferences, poverty lines must reflect the same calorie target. This is accomplished in two ways. First, poverty lines based on the previous period's quantities ($\sum_i p_{1ir} * q_{1ir}$, and $\sum_i p_{2ir} * q_{1ir}$) are scaled to reflect a calorie target of 2150. Second, poverty lines based on the current period's quantities, which are endogenous to the model, are not scaled. Rather, in entropy maximization, $q_{2ir}$ and $q_{2is}$ are constrained to satisfy revealed preferences while attaining a calorie target of 2150. Once entropy adjustments have been made, current period quantities and food poverty lines are scaled to satisfy each spatial domain's caloric requirements.

The output file *povline_rp_inout.csv* merits a brief explanation. This file contains two matrices in which rows represent row spatial-domain-specific food bundles (quantities) and columns represent column spatial-domain-specific prices. The values in the matrix identify the row spatial domain's food bundle evaluated at each column spatial domain's prices. The diagonal values are the row/column spatial domain's food poverty lines. The top matrix presents pre-entropy values. Reading down a column, any value less than that spatial domain's poverty line (the diagonal value) violates revealed preferences. If the bundles represent the same level of utility, a rational consumer would choose the least-cost basket. Pairs are mutually consistent when revealed preferences are satisfied for region A as compared to region B and vice versa. The bottom matrix presents post-entropy quantities evaluated at each region's prices. All values satisfy revealed preferences and all pairs are mutually consistent.

### A.3.13 *Flexible Entropy-Adjusted Poverty Lines and Poverty Measures*
*260_povline_ent_flex.do, 140_povmeas.do.*

Do-file *260_povline_ent_flex.do* closely follows *130_povline_flex.do* to obtain entropy-corrected, utility-consistent food poverty lines and the associated non-food poverty and total poverty lines. It executes *140_povmeas.do* to calculate spatial price indices and FGT poverty measures.

### A.3.14 *Preparing for the Next Survey*
*290_future_revealed_preferences.do.*

This do-file saves data for intertemporal comparisons in subsequent surveys. Previous period data is required for temporal revealed preference tests and for calculating fixed food bundles and poverty lines. Files needed for revealed preference tests in the next survey are saved in the folder *out/t_plus1*. In the last iteration of price calculations, all prices are saved to *out/t_plus1/price_unit_t1.dta*. This do-file saves quantities, prices, calories per person, product-level food expenditure shares, food poverty line ratios, and the food poverty line to *out/t_plus1/food_pov_t1.dta*.

### A.3.15 *Output*
All summary statistics produced during the execution of PLEASe can be accessed in do-file logs in the *rep* folder. Intermediate working datasets are saved in *work*. Descriptive statistics, food baskets, the FGT poverty measures and poverty lines derived from the final-iteration flexible bundles, the entropy-adjusted utility-consistent flexible bundles, and the fixed bundles are saved in *out*. Files in *out* are saved as comma-separated text files and can be opened in Excel.

### A.3.16 *Executing PLEASe*
The entire code stream, including the GAMS code, can be run from *000_boom.do*. Once the initialization file is executed, most do-files may also be run individually. The iterative process, do-files *100* to *140*, is run through *100_iterate.do*. After the iterative process is run once, do-files *110* to *140* may be run individually. Note the postscript on many file and variable names refers to the iteration. Specifically, the global macro *pass* indicates the iterative pass where 0 indicates the initial iteration.

## A.4 Compiling Data

This section provides general descriptions of the required data as well as guidelines to compiling data. As each survey differs both in terms of data provided and the structure of raw datasets, these are merely guidelines and the analyst must be knowledgeable about the household survey and other supplemental data. Tables A2–A6 provide specific information about the structure of each user-provided dataset.

### A.4.1 *Household Data*
The dataset *hhdata.dta* contains household characteristics and survey information, including regions, survey periods, sample strata, household size, and household weights. Required variables are described in Table A2.

**Table A2.** Household characteristics and interview details

**Variable names:**

| | |
|---|---|
| psu | primary sampling unit |
| bswt | bootstrap weights: set = 1 for all households |
| survquar | interview survey quarter—must be sequential |
| survmon | interview survey month—must be sequential |
| hhweight | household sample weight |
| hhid | household ID |
| hhsize | household size |
| strata | geographical stratification variable used in the survey sample design |
| rural | 0,1: 1 if rural, 0 if urban |
| reg_tpi | regions used for temporal price index calculations (1,2,3 . . .) |
| spdomain | poverty lines are constructed for each spatial domain (1,2,3 . . .) |
| news | geographical regions such as north, east, central, west, south (set = 1 for all areas if not relevant) |

**Dataset name:**
hhdata.dta

**Record:**
One record per household

**Comments:**
Both *survmon and survquar* may be included in the dataset. It is also possible to include one or the other.

When selecting regions for TPI calculations, consider that the TPI is calculated by region and survey quarter/month using the consumption patterns of the relatively poor. If the TPI region is too small, it is possible for an area to have no relatively poor households in a given time period.

If no TPI calculations are necessary set *reg_tpi, survquar,* and/or *survmon* equal to one for all observations.

*Source*: See text

Regions for defining poverty lines (*spdomain*) should be chosen based on statistically representative areas, with an aim to preserve urban and rural areas, to preserve homogenous regions in terms of prices and preference, and to maintain a minimum number of households per region (DNEAP 2004). Because poverty lines are based on the consumption patterns of the poor, each spatial domain should include no fewer than 200 households and ideally spatial domains should include significantly more poor households.

The intra-survey temporal price index is calculated by region (*reg_tpi*) and by survey quarter (*survquar*) or month (*survmon*). Therefore, TPI regions are likely to need to be more aggregated than those used for defining poverty lines in order to maintain a minimum sample size. If the TPI region is too small, it is possible for an area to have few relatively poor households in a given time period. Furthermore, because sampling is not necessarily representative by survey period, care must be taken to ensure that a sufficient number of relatively poor households are present within each region, in each period. If a survey is conducted in a single quarter, it is possible to avoid the intra-survey TPI adjustments by setting all TPI regions and all survey periods to one. The resulting TPI equals one and thus no temporal adjustments are made.

### A.4.2 *Individual Data*

The dataset *indata.dta* contains the demographics of individual household members needed to calculate spatial-domain-specific caloric requirements. Specifically, three

**Table A3.** Individual demographics

**Variable names:**

| | |
|---|---|
| hhid | household ID |
| sex | 1,2: 1 = male, 2 = female |
| age | age |
| motherhh | 0,1: 1 if a child's mother lives in the household |
| | If this variable is not available, set the value to **1** for all children. |

**Dataset name:**
indata.dta

**Record:**
One observation for each member of each surveyed household

**Comment:**
If data on the presence of mothers in households is not available, set *motherhh* to 1 for all children.

*Source:* See text

**Table A4.** Fertility rates

**Variable names:**

| | |
|---|---|
| sex | 2 = female |
| rural | 0,1: 0 = urban, 1 = rural |
| age | age |
| fert_rate | birth rates |

**Dataset name:**
fert_rate.dta

**Record:**
One observation for every relevant age by urban and rural areas.

*Source:* See text

variables are defined for each household member: sex, age, and an indicator identifying whether a child's mother lives in the household (*motherhh*). The information from this dataset is used to estimate average per person caloric requirements in each spatial domain. If information on the presence of a child's mother in the household is not available, set *motherhh* to one for all children. See Table A3 for details on variable names and formatting.

### A.4.3 *Fertility Rates*
Data on birth rates are used to adjust average regional caloric needs. The standard code requires the dataset *fert_rate.dta*, containing fertility rates by urban/rural area, and age. The user must provide this data. See Table A4 for dataset format details.

### A.4.4 *Food Calories*
The dataset *calperg.dta* provides the caloric content of commonly consumed food items. These data are needed for items in each region's food consumption bundle. Ideally, no item should be dropped from analysis due to missing caloric data and attempts should be

**Table A5.** Caloric content of food items (calories per gram)

**Variable names:**

| | |
|---|---|
| product | food product code (consistent with cons_nom_in.dta) |
| descript | product description (consistent with cons_nom_in.dta) |
| calperg | caloric content of food product: calories per gram |
| source | source of calorie information, e.g. FAO, web page, etc. (optional) |

**Dataset name:**
calperg.dta

**Record:**
One observation for each food product.

**Comment:**
Make sure the food product code is correct for each survey year.

*Source:* See text

made to update the data as necessary.[3] The unit of measurement is calories per gram of a given food item. See MPF/UEM/IFPRI (1998) for information on compiling food calorie data. In addition to national departments of health or agriculture, possible sources include West et al. (1987, 1988), the US Department of Agriculture (1998), and the US Department of Health, Education, and Welfare (1968). See Table A5 for dataset format details.

### A.4.5 *Product Codes*
The dataset *match_t1_t2.dta* contains product codes for the current survey and the previous survey. It is necessary to match product codes in order to match product prices and quantities across surveys. Due to different product code aggregations across surveys, a single product code in one survey may correspond to multiple product codes in the other survey. The code stream is equipped to handle this possibility. The dataset should have one line for each item in the most disaggregated survey. For example, if the current survey only records consumption for the category grains but the previous survey is disaggregated with categories maize, millet, sorghum, the product code for grain should be entered three times under the variable *product* with the corresponding product codes for maize, millet, and sorghum in *product_t1*. See Table A6 for variable and format details.

### A.4.6 *Consumption*
The dataset *cons_nom_in.dta* provides consumption values for all food and non-food items and quantity data for food items, by household and product (see Table A7 for dataset format). Not all surveys collect quantities of food consumed. In such cases, prices must be obtained from other sources, such as community surveys, in order to calculate quantities.[4] If available, transaction-level data should be reported for each

---

[3] The output file *food_basket_missing_$it_n.csv* reports food items that should be included in the food basket but are dropped due to missing calories.

[4] Prices should be supplied at the most local level possible. At a bare minimum, prices should be supplied for each region in which poverty lines are constructed.

**Table A6.** Product code matching

**Variable names:**

| product | product code in the current survey, t2 |
|---|---|
| product_t1 | product code in the previous survey, t1 |

**Dataset name:**
match_t1_t2.dta

**Record:**
One observation for each product, product_t1 combination.

**Comment:**
The dataset should contain one line for each item in the most disaggregated survey.

*Source*: See text


**Table A7.** Total value and quantity of consumed products (food and non-food)

**Variable names:**

| hhid | household ID |
|---|---|
| product | product code |
| descript | product description |
| food_cat | 0, 1: 0 = non-food, 1 = food |
| prod_cat | product categories: 1,2,...,12, e.g. COICOP codes |
| quantity | quantity of food product consumed, daily values in kilograms |
| cons_nom | total household expenditure on given product (food and non-food), daily values |

**Dataset name:**

cons_nom_in.dta

**Record:**
One observation per household per product per transaction (if possible) for food products.
One observation per household per food product is also acceptable when transaction-level data is not available.
One observation per product per household for non-food products.

**Comments:**
All consumption values are nominal.

Convert all food quantities measured in non-kilogram units to kilograms. This includes food items not measured in weight units, such as litres. Retain documentation of the conversion factors.

Include food consumption for food items even when quantities are not available. Though items without quantity data cannot be included in poverty line calculations, they should be included in total consumption.

*Source*: See text

food item. Specifically, a separate observation should be entered each time the household acquires a food item. Many surveys do not provide transaction-level food expenditures and quantities. While transaction-level data is not required, it is useful in price calculations. Both quantity and expenditures should be converted to daily values. The quantity of food items consumed must be converted to kilograms.

Potentially the most important and messiest aspect of assembling data is carefully checking consumption data for errors and outliers. Unit errors can have surprisingly large impacts on poverty lines. Errors can occur both in the reported unit and in the conversion to standard units (e.g. kilograms or grams). Consumption values and quantities should be scrutinized and cleaned to eliminate the undue influence of outliers.

This section provides an overview of general guidelines for assembling consumption data; see Deaton and Zaidi (2002) for a thorough discussion of consumption aggregates. In addition, the PLEASe code provides the do-files employed to transform raw Mozambique survey data to *cons_nom_in.dta*. These files are provided for reference only, since survey formats vary significantly from country to country and sometimes within a country over time. Nonetheless, the actual code as well as the documentation within each file may be informative.

While ideally all household consumption would be included in the household consumption aggregate, practically some categories of consumption are purposely excluded. Imputing consumption values of home-produced services and public goods and services is impractical and these categories of consumption are excluded. Notably the value of free public education is excluded (see Chapter 2).

## A.4.6.1 FOOD CONSUMPTION

Food consumption includes all food consumed by all members of the household, including food consumed away from home. Sources of food consumption include purchased food and meals, home-produced food, and food gifts, subsidies, remittances, and in-kind payments.

Not all surveys report values for in-kind and home-produced food consumption. When self-reported prices are not available, prices must be obtained from an additional source, such as community surveys. If possible, the distinction between farm-gate prices and market prices should be considered (Deaton and Zaidi 2002).

## A.4.6.2 NON-DURABLE AND SEMI-DURABLE NON-FOOD CONSUMPTION

Non-food consumption incorporates the consumption of non-durable, semi-durable, and durable goods, and rent. This section addresses non-durable and semi-durable goods, which are goods purchased and consumed over a relatively short period of time. This is a broad category and includes everything from laundry soap and fuel, to clothing and housewares, to internet services, health insurance, and private education. Values of non-food items may be collected for a number of recall periods and must be converted to daily values. Quantities consumed are generally not collected and are not used in the PLEASe analysis.

Care must be taken to distinguish between household consumption and income. The purchase of financial assets, interest payments, rents received, and debt payments are not included in consumption. However, the purchase of financial *services* is included. Likewise, taxes, fees, levies, and fines are deductions from income and are not included in household consumption.

In-kind gifts could be excluded from giving households' consumption to avoid double counting (Deaton and Zaidi 2002). In-kind gifts and subsidies (e.g. housing, transportation to work, and education) are included in the receiving households' consumption. Remittances are considered income and are not included in either the giving or receiving households' consumption.

Households are treated separately from home businesses and farms, and thus business expenses and assets are excluded from consumption. While consumption of home-produced goods is included, consumption of home-produced services is excluded due to the difficulty of valuing such services.

### A.4.6.3 DURABLE GOODS

Durable goods require special treatment because their consumption value is not reflected in the purchase transaction but in the value of their use over many years. The approach adopted here is to include the use value of the durable good determined by the value of investing the durable expenditure in the market. It is necessary to specify a relevant interest rate and, for each durable good, a depreciation rate. Depreciation rates can be estimated based on the expected life of each durable good. Durable goods bought more than one year ago, 'old' durables, are, by default, valued at half the buying price. The sample do-file, *033_durables.do*, provides an example of how to impute use values. In this file, the following formula is specified:

$$use\_value = (val\_old + val\_new) * \left( \frac{r + dep\_rt}{1 - dep\_rt} \right)$$

where *val_old* is the value of durables purchased more than a year ago, *val_new* is the value of durables purchased in the last twelve months, *r* is the interest rate, and *dep_rt* is the product-specific depreciation rate (Deaton and Zaidi 2002).

### A.4.6.4 HOUSING RENT

When households pay rent, the actual paid rent is the household's consumption expenditure for housing. For others, the housing consumption expenditure may need to be imputed. Hedonic regression analysis is applied to estimate rental values for households without either an actual paid rent or a self-imputed rent. Separate regressions should be carried out for rural and urban households. Right-hand-side variables are selected in part by data availability. Generally, household size, house ownership, and dummies for strata can be included. Other variables include dwelling characteristics, e.g. roof material, solidity of walls, sanitation standard, water source, and the type of energy used in the kitchen and for lighting. The sample do-file *034_rent.do* provides an example of one method of specifying the hedonic regression.

### A.4.7 *Previous Survey Output*

Finally, when more than one survey round is being compared, data from the previous round is required for temporal revealed preference constraints. This data is automatically produced in the code stream and automatically retrieved from the previous periods directory, *out/t_plus1/*.

## A.5 Final Thoughts

This appendix is designed to orient the user within the code stream. It is not possible or desirable to provide discussion of every detail within the code. Users are encouraged to carefully look through each file. When running with data, users are encouraged to insert pause or stop commands (typing stop just produces an error) in order to examine the datasets in memory and to better understand what has happened with each step. While this is a time-consuming process, it is certainly more rapid than writing the code.

Users should also expect a long iterative process of interrogating the data, identifying errors, and adapting the code stream to country circumstances. In our experience, this process is never simple or easy. Errors are common, with unit errors in data being particular ubiquitous but certainly not the only error that is likely to be encountered. Nonsensical results are a good sign that something is wrong. With experience, users will develop search methods for locating errors. Once the error is located and understood, fixing it is normally relatively straightforward.

The most pernicious errors are those that only mildly influence results or only influence results under special circumstances. While substantial efforts have been expended to produce clean code, the potential presence of errors is not excluded. Users employ PLEASe at their own risk.

Finally, it is our hope that neither the PLEASe code nor the associated manuals will remain static. Experience is an excellent, if stern, teacher. The PLEASe code and associated manual are offered in the spirit of allowing future analysts to stand on the shoulders of current analysts. There is no doubt that the existing package can be improved. Our hope is that the package enhances the quality of future analysis and that, in the process, the package itself is improved.

## References


Deaton, A. and S. Zaidi (2002). 'Guidelines for Constructing Consumption Aggregates for Welfare Analysis', Living Standards Measurement Study Working Paper No. 135. Washington, DC: World Bank.

DNEAP (2004). *Poverty and Well-Being in Mozambique: The Second National Assessment.* Maputo: National Directorate for Studies and Policy Analysis, Ministry of Planning and Development (DNEAP/MPD).

DNEAP (2010). *Poverty and Well-Being in Mozambique: The Third National Assessment.* Maputo: National Directorate for Studies and Policy Analysis, Ministry of Planning and Development (DNEAP/MPD).

Foster, J., J. Greer, and E. Thorbecke (1984). 'A Class of Decomposable Poverty Measures', *Econometrica*, 3(52): 761–6.

MPF-UEM-IFPRI (Ministry of Planning and Finance, Eduardo Mondlane University, International Food Policy Research Institute) (1998). *Understanding Poverty and*

*Well-Being in Mozambique: The First National Assessment (1996–97)*. Maputo: Ministry of Planning and Finance and Eduardo Mondlane University and Washington, DC: International Food Policy Research Institute.

USDA (United States Department of Agriculture) (1998). 'Composition of Foods Commonly Eaten'. Data files. Washington, DC: USDA.

USHEW (United States Department of Health, Education, and Welfare) (1968). 'Nutrient Content of Foods Commonly Eaten in Africa'. Washington, DC: USHEW.

West, C. E., F. Pepping, I. Scholte, W. Jansen, and H. F. F. Albers (1987). 'Food Composition Table for Energy and Eight Important Nutrients in Foods Commonly Eaten in East Africa'. Technical Center for Agriculture and Rural Cooperation of the ACP/ECP Convention of Lomé, and the Food and Nutrition Cooperation Department of Human Nutrition. Wageningen: Wageningen Agricultural University.

West, C. E., F. Pepping, and C. R. Temalilwa (eds) (1988). *The Composition of Foods Commonly Eaten in East Africa*. Wageningen: Wageningen Agricultural University.

WHO (World Health Organization) (1985). 'Energy and Protein Requirements', Technical Report Series No. 724. Geneva: WHO.

# User Guide to Estimating First-Order Dominance Software (EFOD)

*Channing Arndt and Kristi Mahrt*

## B.1 Introduction

This user guide presents the Estimating First-Order Dominance (EFOD) software developed to implement the first-order dominance (FOD) approach presented in Arndt et al. (2012). The FOD approach is a straightforward method of conducting multidimensional welfare comparisons between population groups based on a set of binary welfare indicators where individuals or households are either deprived or not deprived in each welfare dimension. The approach imposes no restrictions on the nature of the social welfare function or on the relative importance of each indicator. Rather, it relies simply on the idea that it is better to be deprived than not deprived in any indicator. FOD is well suited for comparing welfare performance across time and space. Binary FOD indicators can be defined directly from the non-monetary welfare modules of censuses or household surveys by specifying thresholds that distinguish between outcomes that are considered deprivations and those that are not. Thus, the method is highly relevant as FOD indicators and indicator thresholds can be chosen to correspond to specific public policy goals.

EFOD comprises a series of Stata and GAMS code files that perform four key steps: dataset preparation and software initialization, bootstrap sampling, FOD comparisons, and processing results. The code maintains a high degree of flexibility in that it allows FOD to be implemented for up to seven binary welfare indicators across multiple time periods, levels of area aggregations, and population groups. The EFOD software provides a flexible format for conducting FOD comparisons where populations are specified in terms of areas and time periods. Areas may be specified for multiple aggregate levels such as the nation, urban/rural areas, provinces, or regions. The data can be classified into multiple population groups, referred to as categories. Categories might include groupings such as households, children, or women.

This chapter outlines the technical aspects of implementing the EFOD software. Refer to Chapter 3 for a presentation of the FOD methodology and Chapter 4 for a discussion of applying the FOD methodology in practice. Section B.2 outlines data and software requirements. Section B.3 presents a step-by-step overview of the code stream, including required inputs. Finally, section B.4 discusses possibilities of extending FOD comparisons beyond areas within a single country.


## B.2 Requirements

### B.2.1 *Software*
The EFOD package is implemented in both Stata and GAMS. While an intermediate skill level in Stata is necessary, only a basic understanding of GAMS is needed. The Stata code was produced using Stata 12; however, the code will run in Stata 11 or higher.[1] The GAMS code will run on versions 22.7 and later.[2]


### B.2.2 *Data*
The EFOD code begins with the Stata dataset *FOD_input.dta*, which contains the FOD indicators and other variables described in Table B1. The dataset must be structured with one observation per unit of analysis (household and/or individual).


**Table B1.** Incoming data

| Variable | Description | Notes |
| --- | --- | --- |
| ID (optional) | Household or individual ID | Not required |
| Time period | Survey or census year (numeric) | When analysing only one survey year, the time period variable can be created within EFOD. |
| Category | Population groups (numeric) | When analysing one population group, the category variable can be created within EFOD. |
| Indicators | Welfare indicators coded such that<br>0 = deprived<br>1 = not deprived | Up to seven indicators may be defined for each category. |
| Area aggregates | A separate variable must be included for each area aggregate, e.g. urban/rural, states, zones, etc. Area values should be a numerical but do not need to be consecutive. | The national aggregate variable can be created within EFOD. |
| Weights | Appropriate weights for each category | For example, in a survey:<br>household weight = hhsize * sample weight<br>individual weight = sample weight<br>If the data contains both household and individual categories, the weight should be appropriately specified for each category. |
| Gender (optional) | Gender of the household head or gender of the individual (numeric) | The gender variable is used to produce descriptive statistics and is not used in FOD comparisons. |

*Source:* See text


[1] Versions prior to Stata 11 will require modifications such as reverting to the old merge syntax.
[2] Note, EFOD cannot run with the free GAMS licence; a licence must be obtained.

No observation can have a missing value in any of the FOD indicators. See Chapter 14 for a discussion of how this requirement can influence indicator choices. If multiple survey years are included, the years are stacked with the time period variable distinguishing the years. Similarly, if multiple population categories are included, categories are stacked with a category variable distinguishing each population.

When choosing area aggregates and population categories, it is useful to consider how EFOD makes welfare comparisons. Spatial FOD comparisons are made between all areas for each time period, population category, and bootstrap iteration. Temporal FOD comparisons are conducted between time periods for a given area, population category, and bootstrap iteration. FOD comparisons are never made between population categories; rather, the software is capable of making spatial and temporal comparisons independently for different categories in a single execution of EFOD.

Consideration of sample sizes is crucial in choosing areas of aggregation, population categories, and the number of FOD indicators. The smallest area evaluated must be no smaller than the area for which the survey is designed to be statistically representative. Following the survey structure most likely will ensure adequate sample sizes for households, but not necessarily for population groups. Samples in each area, for each category, in each year should be no smaller than approximately 400 households or individuals. Furthermore, samples are divided into subsamples of households or individuals falling into each combination of welfare outcomes, thus the number of FOD indicators must also be balanced with sample size.

### B.2.3 *Directories*

The code stream requires a specific directory structure. The subdirectories of EFOD and their functions are described in Table B2. The subdirectory *new* contains the EFOD code stream. The user must create and transfer the input dataset *FOD_input.dta* to the *work* subdirectory.[3] The code stream creates *rep* and *out* as necessary.

**Table B2.** EFOD folders

| Subfolders | Initial contents | EFOD created files |
| --- | --- | --- |
| new | all Stata do-files and GAMS code files | |
| work | *FOD_input.dta* | intermediate datasets |
| out | initially empty | output tables |
| rep | initially empty | logs from each code file |
| in (optional) | raw data | |

*Source*: See text

[3] Note, Stata creates and deletes a temporary folder called *temp*.

## B.3 EFOD Code Stream

EFOD is comprised of four parts. The files are numbered in the order they are called in the code stream. The first set of Stata do-files prepares the data, defines global macros that allow the remaining do-files to run without modification, and produces descriptive tables (*000_master.do* to *018_Table_descriptive2.do*). The second set of do-files conducts the bootstrap sampling and transforms the data into shares of the population falling into each combination of welfare indicator outcomes (*020_boot_control.do* to *024_Table_shares.do*). The third set of files contains batch files and the GAMS code that conducts the FOD linear program (*030_FOD_base.bat* to *038_temporal.inc*). The final set of do-files processes the FOD outcomes to produce a collection of spatial, temporal, and ranking tables (*040_FOD_data.do* to *046_Table_Rank.do*).

This remainder of this section discusses the code stream file by file. For ease of reference, each subsection begins with a list of relevant Stata and GAMS files as well as an overview of required modifications. The code is structured such that the user must make very few modifications within the main code stream. All required modifications occur in the first three do-files (*000_master.do*, *010_data.do*, *012_initialization.do*) and in the GAMS control files (*030_FOD_base.gms*, *030_FOD_base.bat*). The entire code stream, including the GAMS code, can be run from *000_master.do*. Once the initial set of do-files is executed, most do-files may be run individually.

### B.3.1 *Initialization*
*000_master.do, 010_data.do, 012_initialization.do, 013_global_reset.do, 014_globals.do, 016_Table_descriptive1.do, 018_Table_descriptive2.do.*

- Modify *000_master.do* to define the global macros *path* and *cty*.
- Modify *010_data.do* to define variables described in Table B3.
- Modify *012_initialization.do* to define global macros described in Table B4.

#### B.3.1.1 MASTER STATA DO-FILE
Once all required modifications are complete, the entire code stream, including GAMS files, can be executed from the master do-file, *000_master.do*. As this file lists each Stata and GAMS file in the order they are executed, *000_master.do* also serves as a table of contents of all do-files and their functions. To get started, the global *path* must be defined to point to the EFOD directory. The global *cty* is used to identify the country or survey and can be set as desired. This master file provides the option to pause the code stream three times to verify that global names and indicators are specified correctly. In the first execution of EFOD with new data or new initialization values, this feature is recommended and the line 'pause on' should be activated. In subsequent runs, this feature may not be useful and could be changed to 'pause off'.

#### B.3.1.2 INPUT DATASETS
The do-file, *010_data.do*, transforms the incoming dataset, *FOD_input.dta*, to conform to variable formats used in the code stream and saves a new dataset, *FOD_data_$cty.dta*. The file should be modified as needed to ensure that *FOD_data_$cty.dta* has the proper format.

328

**Table B3.** Variables created in *010_data.do*

| Description | Variable | Examples | Values | Notes |
|---|---|---|---|---|
| Time periods | t | years | 1, 2, 3, … Must use consecutive values starting with 1. | Denotes the survey or census year. |
| Population categories | c | households, women, children | 1, 2, 3, … Must use consecutive values starting with 1. | Denotes subgroups in the population to be analysed independently. |
| Welfare indicators | d1, d2, d3, … d7 | water, sanitation, housing, education, health | 0 = deprived 1 = not deprived | Welfare indicators may vary by category. |
| Survey strata | strata1, strata2, … | urban/rural, regions, provinces | Numeric—no need to be consecutive | Define the survey strata variable(s). |
| Survey cluster | cluster | primary sampling unit | Numeric—no need to be consecutive | Define the survey cluster variable. This variable is not used with census data. |
| Aggregate areas | area1, area2, area3 … | nation, urban/rural, region, provinces | Numeric—no need to be consecutive. 1 = urban 2 = rural | Define the aggregate areas to be analysed in the FOD comparisons. |
| Sample weights | weight | weight * hhsize, weight | Numeric | Weights may vary with household (weight * hhsize) and individual categories (weight). In a full census the individual weight is 1 and the household weight is hhsize. |
| Gender (optional) | gender | gender of hh head, gender of individual | 0 = male 1 = female | Used in descriptive statistics but not in FOD comparisons. |

*Source*: See text

Refer to Table B3 for a description of possible modifications. The extent to which this do-file must be modified depends on the state of *FOD_input.dta*. It is useful to note that it is possible to define a different set of indicators for each population category. Population categories may include groups of households or individuals and therefore it may be necessary to define weights differently by category. For example, when working with survey data, the appropriate weight for individuals is the sample weight, whereas the sample weight multiplied by household size may be preferred for households.

### B.3.1.3 GLOBAL MACROS

The initialization file, *012_initialization.do*, defines global macros used throughout the code stream. The user must carefully specify global macros to allow the remaining do-files to run without further modification. Global macros are described in Table B4.

**Table B4.** Globals specified in *012_initialization.do*

| Description | Global | Purpose | Values |
|---|---|---|---|
| Bootstrap iterations | its | Set the number of bootstrap iterations. The default value is 100. | numeric |
| Naming variables in the tables | yearlist | Specify how years will be called in the tables. Because years are numbered, this global gives the years a name for tables. The years must be listed in the order of the year variable, t. | e.g. 1998, 2000, 2010 … |
| | catlist | Specify how categories will be called in the tables. Because categories are numbered, this global gives the categories a name for tables. The category names must be listed in the order of the category variable, c. | e.g. households, women, children |
| | deplist1, deplist2, … | Specify how indicators will be called in the tables. Because indicators are numbered, this global gives the indicators a name for tables. A different deplist must be specified for each category even if the indicators are the same for every category. The indicator names must be listed in the order the indicator variables d1, …, d7. | e.g. water, housing, education |
| | areaname1, areaname2, areaname3 … | Corresponding to the area aggregation variables, specify how each area will be called in the tables. For example, if the aggregation is the nation, this global will list Nation. If the aggregation is province, the global will list all province names. The order of area names must correspond to the numeric sequence of areas within area variables. | Nation, Urban Rural, Western, Northern, Central … |
| Areas to be included in each FOD table | rankkeeplist | List the area aggregates by their globals to indicate which levels will be included in the FOD rank table. | $area1, $area2, $area3 … |
| | shkeeplist | List the area aggregates by their globals to indicate which levels will be included in the shares of welfare combinations tables. | $area1, $area2, $area3 … |
| | spatkeeplist | List the area aggregates by their globals to indicate which levels will be included in the spatial FOD tables. | $area1, $area2, $area3 … |
| | tempkeeplist | List the area aggregates by their globals to indicate which levels will be included in the temporal FOD tables. | $area1, $area2, $area3 … |
| Descriptive 1 table | urban | Specify the area variable that defines urban/rural. | area2, area3 … |
| | gender_switch | Specify if conducting gender analysis | 0 = no gender<br>1 = gender |
| Survey/census structure | datatype | For bootstrapping, specify whether the data is from a survey or a census. | 1 = survey<br>2 = census |
| | stratalist1, stratalist2 … | For each year, 1, 2, …, list the survey strata specified by the variables strata1, strata2, …. Multiple strata may be listed for each year. This variable is used with | strata1, strata2 … |

| | | | |
|---|---|---|---|
| | | census data to guide bootstrap sampling and is determined by the user. | |
| | minstrata | If using census data, a minimum sample size can be set to force bootstrap samples of each stratum to be the same size. This global is optional. | no greater than the population of the smallest stratum |
| GAMS processors | GAMS | Specify the number of processors that will be used running FOD in GAMS. | 1–4 |

*Source*: See text

The global macros used to define area names, categories, years, and deprivations must be set with care. It is particularly important for the names to be listed in sequential order exactly corresponding to the numeric order of the relevant variable values.[4] For instance, suppose there are three population categories with the category variables valued 1, 2, 3, where 1 refers to households, 2 refers to children, and 3 refers to women. Then the category global must be specified in the corresponding order:

global catlist households children women

The do-file *014_globals.do* automatically generates additional globals. This file does not need to be modified. In addition, this file saves a log that lists variable values with the corresponding names specified in the globals *yearlist, catlist, areaname1, areaname2, . . .*, and *deplist*. It is advisable to view these lists in the results window, if *'pause on'* is activated, or in the log file, *rep/014_globals.log*, to verify that the naming globals are properly specified.

### B.3.2 *Descriptive Statistics*
*016_Table_descriptive1.do and 018_Table_descriptive2.do.*

Descriptive statistics do-files generate sample sizes and weighted means of the welfare indicators. A comma-separated text file is created for each population category. Indicator means are interpreted as the share of the population not deprived in each indicator. The first set of tables generates means and sample sizes for the nation, urban and rural areas, and if specified, gender. The second set of tables generates means and sample sizes for every area included in the analysis, with the areas organized by area aggregates.

Weighted means are produced early in the code stream, allowing analysts to scrutinize the data before moving forward with bootstrapping and FOD comparisons. When 'pause on' is activated, Stata pauses at the end of *016_Table_descriptive1.do* and *018_Table_descriptive2.do*, allowing the user to examine means in the results window or text files before proceeding.

---

[4] If the area variables have value labels, it is easy to find the relationship between area names and area numbers using the Stata commands *tabulate* or *label list lblname*, where *lblname* is the variable's value label. The command *describe* is useful to determine the name of the value label.

### B.3.3 *Bootstrapping and Compiling Shares*
*020_boot_control.do, 022_shares.do, 024_Table_shares.do.*

The do-files *020_boot_control.do* and *022_shares.do* work together to conduct bootstrap sampling and generate shares of an area's population that fall into each combination of welfare indicators for every category, year, and iteration. *022_shares.do* is executed from *020_boot_control.do* and cannot be run independently. The do-file *020_boot_control.do* cycles through several loops and sub-loops. The exterior loop cycles through the bootstrap iterations where the number of iterations is defined by the global *its*. It begins with the zero iteration, which contains the actual survey data, and then continues by drawing bootstrap samples in iteration one through the final iteration.[5]

Within the given iteration, *022_shares.do* loops through years and population categories with a sub-loop through all areas to calculate the proportion of a given area's population attaining each possible combination of welfare outcomes. For a given area, time period, and category, the shares across all combinations of indicators sum to one. When the time and category loops are complete in a given iteration, Stata returns to *020_boot_control.do,* where that iteration's share data is appended to the data file *work/ boot_final_$cty.dta*. This process continues through all iterations until *work/boot_final_ $cty.dta* contains shares for all areas in each time period and category, for every iteration. This file is also saved as a text file, *work/data_bs_100.csv*, that will be imported into GAMS for FOD comparisons.

Before proceeding to FOD, the do-file *024_Table_shares.do* creates tables by category containing shares of the population by combinations of welfare indicators and by number of deprivations in the static sample. The combinations of welfare indicator tables are only generated for areas specified by the global *shkeeplist.* Table B5 is a sample table, which displays the combinations of welfare indicators at the national level. Number of deprivations measures the total number of deprivations faced by a household or an individual. The share of the population with a given number of deprivations is equal to the sum of the shares of all welfare combinations with that number of deprivations. For example, supposing five indicators are in focus, the share of the population with one deprivation is equal to the sum of the shares of the population with welfare combinations (1 0 0 0 0), (0 1 0 0 0), (0 0 1 0 0), (0 0 0 1 0), and (0 0 0 0 1). The total shares across all numbers of deprivations for a given area (in a specific year and category) sums to one. The deprivations tables are presented in a long and a short form. Table B6 provides an example of a number of deprivations table. The long form includes all areas while the short form includes only areas specified by the global *shkeeplist.*

---

[5] Note, bootstrap samples are drawn randomly, and without intervention each execution of EFOD could produce a different set of bootstrap samples. However, the capacity to replicate results is desirable and is possible by specifying a 'seed'. On a given machine and with a given set of input data, the seed forces the same bootstrap samples to be drawn, allowing results to be reproduced.

**Table B5.** Combination of welfare indicators, *table_shares_1.csv*

| Water | Sanit | House | Educ | Info | National 2004 | National 2010 | National_change |
|---|---|---|---|---|---|---|---|
| 0 | 0 | 0 | 0 | 0 | 6.8726 | 6.8797 | −13.2620 |
| 0 | 0 | 0 | 0 | 1 | 6.1608 | 5.7849 | 0.8490 |
| 0 | 0 | 0 | 1 | 0 | 3.6046 | 4.2612 | −0.0889 |
| 0 | 0 | 0 | 1 | 1 | 5.6834 | 6.5246 | 3.4989 |
| 0 | 0 | 1 | 0 | 0 | 0.2131 | 0.1921 | −0.1853 |
| 0 | 0 | 1 | 0 | 1 | 0.6247 | 0.8597 | −0.1757 |
| 0 | 0 | 1 | 1 | 0 | 0.3519 | 0.3719 | 0.1551 |
| 0 | 0 | 1 | 1 | 1 | 2.0807 | 2.4545 | 1.3803 |
| 0 | 1 | 0 | 0 | 0 | 0.0000 | 0.0167 | −0.0521 |
| 0 | 1 | 0 | 0 | 1 | 0.0862 | 0.0513 | 0.0141 |
| 0 | 1 | 0 | 1 | 0 | 0.0000 | 0.0318 | 0.0199 |
| 0 | 1 | 0 | 1 | 1 | 0.0034 | 0.0366 | 0.0194 |
| 0 | 1 | 1 | 0 | 0 | 0.0452 | 0.0023 | −0.0078 |
| 0 | 1 | 1 | 0 | 1 | 0.0526 | 0.0762 | 0.0599 |
| 0 | 1 | 1 | 1 | 0 | 0.0032 | 0.0682 | 0.0292 |
| 0 | 1 | 1 | 1 | 1 | 0.5169 | 1.1511 | 0.9863 |
| 1 | 0 | 0 | 0 | 0 | 15.1621 | 12.2475 | −14.6200 |
| 1 | 0 | 0 | 0 | 1 | 14.9753 | 12.1967 | 3.9844 |
| 1 | 0 | 0 | 1 | 0 | 8.3381 | 7.6366 | −0.1913 |
| 1 | 0 | 0 | 1 | 1 | 13.1270 | 12.8563 | 7.3944 |
| 1 | 0 | 1 | 0 | 0 | 1.0865 | 1.2374 | −0.2660 |
| 1 | 0 | 1 | 0 | 1 | 3.4522 | 2.8978 | −1.2036 |
| 1 | 0 | 1 | 1 | 0 | 1.4996 | 1.6262 | 0.1844 |
| 1 | 0 | 1 | 1 | 1 | 10.1295 | 10.2820 | 3.7224 |
| 1 | 1 | 0 | 0 | 0 | 0.0353 | 0.1238 | −0.1554 |
| 1 | 1 | 0 | 0 | 1 | 0.2773 | 0.1765 | 0.0974 |
| 1 | 1 | 0 | 1 | 0 | 0.0353 | 0.1065 | 0.0924 |
| 1 | 1 | 0 | 1 | 1 | 0.1165 | 0.5966 | 0.5338 |
| 1 | 1 | 1 | 0 | 0 | 0.1068 | 0.2910 | 0.2122 |
| 1 | 1 | 1 | 0 | 1 | 0.6369 | 0.8045 | 0.3230 |
| 1 | 1 | 1 | 1 | 0 | 0.3204 | 0.5954 | 0.4939 |
| 1 | 1 | 1 | 1 | 1 | 4.4019 | 7.5626 | 6.1580 |

*Source*: Based on calculations in Arndt et al. (2014) using the 2004/5, 2010 TDHS (National Bureau of Statistics and Macro 2005, 2011)

**Table B6.** Number of deprivations, *table_shares_1_num.csv*

| num_dep | National 2004 | National 2010 | National_change | Rural 2004 | Rural 2010 | Rural_change | Urban 2004 | Urban 2010 | Urban_change |
|---|---|---|---|---|---|---|---|---|---|
| 0 | 4.4019 | 7.5626 | 6.1580 | 0.8586 | 1.3157 | 1.0155 | 15.6553 | 28.3526 | 23.1706 |
| 1 | 11.7202 | 13.4295 | 6.0592 | 4.9436 | 7.3434 | 4.7315 | 33.2425 | 33.6845 | 10.0390 |
| 2 | 20.6382 | 20.5898 | 8.2659 | 19.1846 | 21.3244 | 12.9707 | 25.2549 | 18.1451 | −7.7582 |
| 3 | 31.2266 | 29.0360 | 6.8762 | 35.5143 | 34.2169 | 11.5780 | 17.6090 | 11.7936 | −8.7273 |
| 4 | 25.1405 | 22.5024 | −14.0973 | 30.7850 | 27.2588 | −13.8055 | 7.2138 | 6.6730 | −14.6567 |
| 5 | 6.8726 | 6.8797 | −13.2620 | 8.7139 | 8.5409 | −16.4902 | 1.0246 | 1.3512 | −2.0673 |

*Source*: Based on calculations in Arndt et al. (2014) using the 2004/5, 2010 TDHS (National Bureau of Statistics and Macro 2005, 2011)

### B.3.4 *FOD*

*030_FOD_base.bat, 030_FOD_base.gms, 031_process1.bat, 031_process1.gms, 032_process2.bat, 032_process2.gms, 033_process3.bat, 033_process3.gms, 034_process4.bat, 034_process4.gms, 036_spatial.inc, 038_temporal.inc.*

- Modify *030_FOD_base.bat and 030_FOD_base.gms*

FOD comparisons are conducted entirely in a linear program executed by GAMS. The file *030_FOD_base.gms* uses the dataset *data_bs_100.csv* and several include files to create required variables, equations, and parameters and save them to a base file. A file for each processor, *031_process1.gms* to *034_ process4.gms*, then executes *036_spatial.inc* and *038_temp.inc* to conduct the FOD comparisons using the base file.

The user can execute the GAMS code in three ways. First, FOD can be shelled directly from *000_master.do* in Stata. Second, the user can manually execute FOD in GAMS IDE. Third, the user can execute FOD from a command window. FOD involves a large number of comparisons that increases with the number of areas, survey years, population categories, and bootstrap iterations. In order to reduce processing time, the FOD comparisons are divided by bootstrap iteration and executed using up to four processors. It is possible to assign iterations to fewer processors depending on hardware capabilities. The process time can be lengthy, even when taking advantage of four processors, and can vary from minutes to several hours.

### B.3.5 *FOD Tables*

*040_FOD_data, 042_Table_FODspat.do, 044_Table_FODtemp.do, 046_Table_Rank.do.*

Depending on the number of processors utilized, GAMS saves up to four spatial (*res_spat1.csv*...) and four temporal (*res_temp1.csv*...) text files to the *work* directory. The Stata do-file *040_FOD_data.do* appends these files and creates two datasets (*work/ res_spat.dta* and *work/res_temp.dta*). From these datasets, three collections of tables are created that present temporal results, spatial results, and area rankings.

### B.3.5.1 SPATIAL FOD TABLES

The do-file *042_Table_FODspat.do* creates spatial FOD tables for static and bootstrapped samples by area, category, and period. FOD results are averaged across bootstrap iterations and are interpreted as the probability of domination. A table is produced for static (Table B7) and bootstrap results (Table B8). Within each table, a blank cell indicates an indeterminate outcome between the row and column area. In static tables, a '1' indicates the row (column) area dominates (is dominated by) the column (row) area. In bootstrap tables, values indicate the estimated probability that the row (column) area dominates (is dominated by) the column (row) area (probability is defined as total number of iterations where a domination outcome occurs divided by the total number of bootstrap iterations). The row (column) average yields the average number of times or the average probability that the row (column) area dominates (is dominated by) all other areas for the static and bootstrap cases, respectively.

Bootstrap sampling introduces variation to the results and therefore small values should be interpreted with caution. For instance, Table B8 indicates that the nation

**Table B7.** Spatial FOD results (static), *FOD_spat_1_1_static.csv*

| Area | National | Rural | Urban | Central | Eastern | Lake | Northern | S_Highlands | Southern | Western | Zanzibar | Average |
|---|---|---|---|---|---|---|---|---|---|---|---|---|
| National | | 1 | | | | | | | | | | 0.1 |
| Rural | | | | | | | | | | | | 0 |
| Urban | 1 | 1 | | 1 | 1 | 1 | 1 | 1 | 1 | 1 | | 0.9 |
| Central | | | | | | | | | | | | 0 |
| Eastern | 1 | 1 | | 1 | | 1 | | 1 | 1 | 1 | | 0.7 |
| Lake | | | | | | | | | | | | 0 |
| Northern | | 1 | | | | 1 | | | | 1 | | 0.3 |
| S_Highlands | | | | | | | | | | | | 0 |
| Southern | | | | | | | | | | | | 0 |
| Western | | | | | | | | | | | | 0 |
| Zanzibar | 1 | 1 | | 1 | | 1 | | 1 | 1 | 1 | | 0.7 |
| Average | 0.3 | 0.5 | 0 | 0.3 | 0.1 | 0.4 | 0.1 | 0.3 | 0.3 | 0.4 | 0 | 0.2455 |

*Source*: Based on calculations in Arndt et al. (2014) using the 2004/5, 2010 TDHS (National Bureau of Statistics and Macro 2005, 2011)

**Table B8.** Spatial FOD results (bootstrap), *FOD_spat_1_1_boot.csv*

| Area | National | Rural | Urban | Central | Eastern | Lake | Northern | S_Highlands | Southern | Western | Zanzibar | Average |
|---|---|---|---|---|---|---|---|---|---|---|---|---|
| National | | 1 | | 0.05 | | 0.41 | | 0.26 | 0.04 | 0.33 | | 0.209 |
| Rural | | | | 0.01 | | 0.01 | | | | | | 0.002 |
| Urban | 1 | 1 | | 0.96 | 0.74 | 1 | 0.95 | 1 | 1 | 0.99 | 0.16 | 0.88 |
| Central | | 0.17 | | | | 0.09 | | 0.04 | 0.25 | 0.1 | | 0.065 |
| Eastern | 0.79 | 0.97 | | 0.56 | | 0.79 | 0.22 | 0.86 | 0.91 | 0.69 | 0.01 | 0.58 |
| Lake | | 0.04 | | | | | | 0.01 | 0.01 | | | 0.006 |
| Northern | 0.13 | 0.57 | | 0.06 | | 0.47 | | 0.3 | 0.07 | 0.35 | | 0.195 |
| S_Highlands | | 0.18 | | 0.02 | | 0.05 | | | 0.03 | 0.03 | | 0.031 |
| Southern | | | | | | | | | | | | 0 |
| Western | | 0.03 | | 0.03 | | 0.02 | | 0.01 | | | | 0.009 |
| Zanzibar | 0.3 | 0.77 | | 0.42 | 0.06 | 0.42 | 0.06 | 0.38 | 0.83 | 0.4 | | 0.364 |
| Average | 0.222 | 0.473 | 0 | 0.211 | 0.08 | 0.326 | 0.123 | 0.286 | 0.314 | 0.289 | 0.017 | 0.2128 |

*Source*: Based on calculations in Arndt et al. (2014) using the 2004/5, 2010 TDHS (National Bureau of Statistics and Macro 2005, 2011)

dominates Central with a probability of 0.05, which is likely too small to conclude that the nation outperforms Central.

### B.3.5.2 TEMPORAL FOD TABLES

The do-file *044_Table_FODtemp.do* creates temporal and net temporal FOD tables for each category. Temporal tables present static and bootstrap results for all year combinations for each area. As in spatial analysis, bootstrapped FOD results are averaged across iterations and are interpreted as the probability of domination. Temporal results are presented in two ways. First, *FOD_temp_$cat.csv* presents static and bootstrap temporal outcomes for both later years dominating earlier years and earlier years dominating later years (Table B9). Second, *FOD_net_temp_$cat.csv*, presents net temporal domination, which measures the difference in the probabilities of later years dominating earlier years and earlier years dominating later years (Table B10). In the case of no welfare regression, net results are equivalent to the results for later years dominating earlier years.

In static temporal columns, a '1' indicates that a given year dominated the other year, while a blank cell indicates the given year did not dominate the other year. When both years have a blank entry, FOD was indeterminate. In the net temporal table, '1' indicates the later year dominated the earlier year; a blank cell indicates FOD was indeterminate; and, '−1' indicates the earlier year dominated the later year. There is no difference in the amount of information in the static temporal and the static net temporal tables, rather the difference lies in the presentation.

In the bootstrap temporal columns, entries indicate the probability that a given year dominates the other year. A blank indicates the year did not dominate in any iteration and '1' indicates that year dominated in every iteration. When both years have a blank entry, FOD was indeterminate in all cases. In the net temporal table, positive probabilities indicate that the later year dominated in more iterations than the earlier year, and negative probabilities indicate that the earlier year dominated in more iterations than the later year. A net result of 0.2 could mean that the later year dominated in 20 per cent of iterations, the earlier year never dominated, and 80 per cent of the iterations were indeterminate. Or, for example, it could mean that the later year dominated in 60 per cent of the iterations, and the earlier year dominated in 40 per cent of the iterations. The exact scenario should be determined by the user. Similarly, a blank cell could indicate that the outcome was indeterminate in every iteration or that each year dominated with the same frequency. Thus, in cases with frequent backsliding, the full temporal table provides a more complete story than the net temporal table.

For example in Table B9, both 1996 dominates 1992 and 1992 dominates 1996 with positive probabilities in Northern and Southern Highlands. In Table B10, with the exception of Northern and Southern Highlands, static and bootstrap net domination results are the same as those in Table B9. Net domination is different in the case of Northern and Southern Highlands because there are small probabilities of 1992 dominating 1996.

### B.3.5.3 AREA RANKINGS

Area ranking tables use spatial bootstrap FOD results to compare areas based on the net probability of domination, which measures the average probability that an area

**Table B9.** Temporal FOD results, *FOD_temp_1.csv*

| Area | stat_ 1992 1996 | stat_ 1992 2004 | stat_ 1996 1992 | stat_ 1996 2004 | stat_ 2004 1992 | stat_ 2004 1996 | boot_ 1992 1996 | boot_ 1992 2004 | boot_ 1996 1992 | boot_ 1996 2004 | boot_ 2004 1992 | boot_ 2004 1996 |
|---|---|---|---|---|---|---|---|---|---|---|---|---|
| National | | | 1 | | 1 | 1 | | | 0.3 | | 0.99 | 0.95 |
| Rural | | | 1 | | 1 | | | | 0.28 | | 0.71 | 0.45 |
| Urban | | | 1 | | | | | | 0.22 | | 0.11 | 0.03 |
| Central | | | | | | | | | 0.14 | | 0.14 | 0.13 |
| Eastern | | | 1 | | | | | | 0.35 | | 0.42 | 0.18 |
| Lake | | | | | 1 | | | | | | 0.62 | 0.17 |
| Northern | | | | | 1 | 1 | 0.05 | | 0.02 | | 0.68 | 0.85 |
| S_Highlands | | | | | 1 | 1 | 0.01 | | 0.13 | | 0.67 | 0.46 |
| Southern | | | | | 1 | 1 | | | 0.06 | | 0.55 | 0.69 |
| Western | | | 1 | | | | | | 0.27 | | 0.23 | 0.12 |
| Zanzibar | | | 1 | | 1 | 1 | | | 0.22 | | 0.99 | 0.86 |

*Source*: Based on calculations in Arndt et al. (2014) using the 2004/5, 2010 TDHS (National Bureau of Statistics and Macro 2005, 2011)

**Table B10.** Net temporal FOD results, *FOD_net_temp_1.csv*

| Area | stat_ 1996 1992 | stat_ 2004 1992 | stat_ 2004 1996 | boot_ 1996 1992 | boot_ 2004 1992 | boot_ 2004 1996 |
|---|---|---|---|---|---|---|
| National | 1 | 1 | 1 | 0.3 | 0.99 | 0.95 |
| Rural | 1 | 1 | | 0.28 | 0.71 | 0.45 |
| Urban | 1 | | | 0.22 | 0.11 | 0.03 |
| Central | | | | 0.14 | 0.14 | 0.13 |
| Eastern | 1 | | | 0.35 | 0.42 | 0.18 |
| Lake | | 1 | | | 0.62 | 0.17 |
| Northern | | 1 | 1 | −0.03 | 0.68 | 0.85 |
| S_Highlands | | 1 | 1 | 0.12 | 0.67 | 0.46 |
| Southern | | 1 | 1 | 0.06 | 0.55 | 0.69 |
| Western | 1 | | | 0.27 | 0.23 | 0.12 |
| Zanzibar | 1 | 1 | 1 | 0.22 | 0.99 | 0.86 |

*Source*: Based on calculations in Arndt et al. (2014) using the 2004/5, 2010 TDHS (National Bureau of Statistics and Macro 2005, 2011)

**Table B11.** FOD rankings, *table_rank_1.csv*

| Area | Net Domination 2004 | PNet Domination 2004 | Rank 2004 | Net Domination 2010 | PNet Domination 2010 | Rank 2010 | Change |
|---|---|---|---|---|---|---|---|
| Eastern | 518 | 0.74 | 1 | 504 | 0.72 | 1 | 0 |
| Zanzibar | 208 | 0.2971429 | 2 | 144 | 0.2057143 | 2 | 0 |
| S_Highlands | −154 | −0.22 | 6 | −17 | −0.0242857 | 3 | −2 |
| Northern | 38 | 0.0542857 | 3 | −54 | −0.0771429 | 4 | 1 |
| Lake | −97 | −0.1385714 | 5 | −80 | −0.1142857 | 5 | −2 |
| Southern | −62 | −0.0885714 | 4 | −83 | −0.1185714 | 6 | −2 |
| Western | −191 | −0.2728571 | 7 | −143 | −0.2042857 | 7 | 1 |
| Central | −260 | −0.3714286 | 8 | −271 | −0.3871429 | 8 | 4 |

*Source*: Based on calculations in Arndt et al. (2014) using the 2004/5, 2010 TDHS (National Bureau of Statistics and Macro 2005, 2011)

dominates all other areas minus the average probability of the same area being dominated by all other areas. If the same areas are presented in the spatial and rank tables, the probability of net domination is equivalent to the spatial ranking row average minus the column average. The do-file *046_Table_Rank.do* produces separate tables for each category. See Table B11 for an example of ranking outcomes.

Ranking results should be interpreted carefully. Because bootstrapping results may vary from one execution of FOD to the next, rankings may be sensitive to small perturbations. The difference in net domination scores is often insufficiently large to distinguish between differences in welfare outcomes and variability introduced through random bootstrapping. For example, in Table B11, the difference in net domination between Lake and Southern in 2010 is extremely small. However, even the difference between Northern and Lake may not be robust to bootstrap variation.

## B.4 Alternative Specifications

Thus far, the language in this description of the EFOD software has been geared towards welfare analysis of areas over time. However, EFOD is flexible and can be applied to alternative specifications. This section provides three examples of possible variations.[6]

- To this point, the discussion has focused on analysis within a single country. Alternatively, welfare comparisons can be made internationally. With comparable indicators, areas could be specified as individual countries yielding spatial FOD comparisons between countries and temporal FOD comparisons for each country.

- Thus far, population groups have been discussed independently of each other. However, FOD comparisons can be made between populations if the analyst defines the area parameters to specify population groups instead of areas. See Chapter 14 where Mahrt and Masumbu specify FOD comparisons in Zambia by rural economic activity and urban housing cost areas. One area variable would now classify the different population groups, similar to the category variable in the standard format. If areas are still of interest, additional area variables can also be used to compare the population groups to aggregate areas such as urban/rural.

- In analysis focused on a single population group, say households, the category variable could be used to specify different sets of indicators. In this context, the category variable would serve merely to signal each set of indicators rather than defining different populations. For example, category one could include a set of health indicators, category two could contain a set of shelter indicators, and category three could contain a set of education indicators. For a given set of indicators, spatial FOD comparisons would be made across areas and temporal analysis over time for each area. FOD analysis within each indicator category would be conducted independently, thus highlighting the relative performance of areas for each set of indicators.

## References

Arndt C., R. Distante, M. A. Hussain, L. P. Østerdal, P. Huong, and M. Ibraimo (2012). 'Ordinal Welfare Comparisons with Multiple Discrete Indicators: A First-Order

---

[6] Note that the FOD code stream requires area 1 to specify the entire population, and must continue to do so.

Dominance Approach and Application to Child Poverty', *World Development*, 40(11): 2290–301.

Arndt, C., V. Leyaro, and K. Mahrt (2014). 'Multi-dimensional Poverty Analysis for Tanzania: First-Order Dominance Approach with Discrete Indicators', WIDER Working Paper 2014/146. Helsinki: UNU-WIDER.

National Bureau of Statistics (NBS) (Tanzania) and ICF Macro (2011). *Tanzania Demographic and Health Survey 2010*. Dar es Salaam: NBS and ICF Macro.

National Bureau of Statistics (NBS) (Tanzania) and ORC Macro (2005). *Tanzania Demographic and Health Survey 2004–05*. Dar es Salaam: NBS and ORC Macro.

# Index

Note 1: Tables, figures and boxes are indicated by an italic *t*, *f*, or *b* following the page number.

Note 2: As most chapters pertain to a particular country, the sub-headings for each country have not been double-entered as main entries, so the reader is advised to locate main entries of interest under the country headings.

Note 3: The following abbreviations have been used in sub-headings:

FOD: first-order dominance

PLEASe: Poverty Line Estimation Analytical Software